NATIONAL SECURITY LAW AND THE POWER OF THE PURSE

NATIONAL SECURITY LAW
AND THE
POWER OF THE PURSE

William C. Banks
Peter Raven-Hansen

New York Oxford
OXFORD UNIVERSITY PRESS
1994

Oxford University Press

Oxford New York Toronto
Delhi Bombay Calcutta Madras Karachi
Kuala Lumpur Singapore Hong Kong Tokyo
Nairobi Dar es Salaam Cape Town
Melbourne Auckland Madrid

and associated companies in
Berlin Ibadan

Published by Oxford University Press, Inc.
200 Madison Avenue, New York, New York 10016

Library of Congress Cataloging-in-Publication Data
Banks, William C.
National security law and the power of the purse /
William C. Banks & Peter Raven-Hansen.
p. cm. Includes index.
ISBN 0-19-508538-8
1. United States—Foreign relations—Law and legislation.
2. National security—Law and legislation—United States.
3. Legislative power—United States. 4. United States. Congress—Powers and duties. 5. Budget—Law and legislation—United States.
I. Raven-Hansen, Peter, 1946– II. Title.
KF4651.B36 1994
342.73'0412—dc20
[347.302412] 93-25326

2 4 6 8 9 7 5 3 1

Printed in the United States of America
on acid-free paper

To my parents
William C. Banks

To Winnie, Erik, and Anna
Peter Raven-Hansen

Acknowledgments

We are doubly indebted to Dr. Louis Fisher of the Congressional Research Service. First, his scholarship defined the field. Even a quick skimming of the endnotes for this book will attest to his impact on our work. Second, he, along with our friend and coauthor Stephen Dycus and colleagues Hal Bruff and Phil Hamburger, offered valuable comments on an early draft of the manuscript.

We appreciate the institutional support afforded our research by Syracuse University College of Law and the National Law Center of George Washington University. We would also like to thank Syracuse University law students Christina Zampas, Michael Johnson, and Charles Fox, and George Washington University law students Daniel Goldfried, Andrew G. Mergen, Anne M. McCormick, Todd Sinkin, Corby Sturges, and Amy Weiser for their research and editorial assistance, and Lynn Oatman, Mary Ann McClanahan, and Ross Isaacs for their word processing assistance.

Syracuse, New York W. C. B.
Washington, D.C. P. R.-H.
October 1993

Contents

II. THE MECHANICS OF NATIONAL SECURITY APPROPRIATIONS AND SPENDING

III. CONSTITUTIONAL LIMITS ON THE MAKING OF NATIONAL SECURITY APPROPRIATIONS

IV. THE SUBSTANTIVE SCOPE OF THE POWER OF THE PURSE IN NATIONAL SECURITY

NATIONAL SECURITY LAW AND THE POWER OF THE PURSE

Introduction

Looking back on the work of the Constitutional Convention, Thomas Jefferson wrote James Madison in 1789 that "we have already given . . . one effectual check to the Dog of War by transferring the power of letting him loose from the Executive to the Legislative body, from those who are to spend to those who are to pay."[1] He was referring not only to the power to declare war, vested in Congress by the Declaration Clause,[2] but also to the power of appropriating money for exercises of war power, vested in Congress by the Spending,[3] Army and Navy,[4] and the Necessary and Proper[5] Clauses. The Appropriations Clause[6] reinforces this power of the purse by prohibiting the spending of public revenues without appropriation. The Statement and Account Clause,[7] in turn, complements the Appropriations Clause by requiring periodic accounts of how public money is spent.

Jefferson had cause for satisfaction about the Constitution's arrangement of the powers of sword and purse. The power of the purse supplemented the Declaration-of-War Clause by allowing Congress to control war powers by specifying spending objectives or otherwise restricting spending *ex ante.* It also compensated for the possible failure of antecedent controls by giving Congress the *ex post* power of what the framers called "supply"—appropriations for raising and supporting military forces—to determine how long U.S. participation in war could continue.

The technological transformation of modern warfare and the increase of global risks to our national security have reinforced the importance of the power of the purse in military and foreign affairs, or what we term collectively national security affairs.[8] Unable to anticipate precisely and in detail the occasions for the exercise of military force,[9] Congress has increasingly ceded the initiative to the president or impliedly delegated national security authority to him by general national security appropriations, then used its power of the purse after the fact to ratify impliedly or to restrict expressly the presidential initiative. The power of the purse has become, by necessity and preference, a key congressional tool for participating in national security decision making, a congressional counterweight to presidential initiative.[10]

But it has also therefore inevitably become an issue in the struggle between Congress and the president for control of national security decisions. When national security appropriations are invoked by the president as implied statutory authority for controversial national security decisions, opponents argue either that they were not so intended or that they could not, consistently with the Constitution, delegate such authority to the president. When appropriation restrictions are used to limit presidential national security power, proponents of presidential authority mount similar challenges to the statutory and constitutional scope of the restrictive appropriations.

Believing that a more historical and analytic and less political assessment of the power of the purse is long overdue, we attempt in this book to analyze and correlate the history, mechanics, procedural scope, and substantive scope of that power in national security. We have tried not only to suggest some original analytic solutions to legal issues, but also to collect under one roof the often excellent analysis of others, into what we immodestly hope will be a primer on the power of the purse in national security.

Legal analysis has been called the art of thinking about how one thing relates to another without thinking about the other.[11] We have tried here to describe how the power of the purse relates to war and other national security powers without trying to analyze the latter in comparable detail. By adopting this singular and artificial focus, we run the risk that we will produce a distorted picture of the comparative authority of Congress and the president in national security. But we also hope thereby to compensate for the undue emphasis on war powers in the literature of national security law, an emphasis that has often resulted in cursory consideration of the power of the purse. Applied to issues of national security, our analysis cannot stand alone, but we hope that it will supply a heretofore neglected piece of the puzzle.

Two postwar national security crises frame the legal issues raised by the power of the purse in national security and serve as case studies for our analysis.

The Vietnam War

The Vietnam War was an undeclared war partly authorized, partly controlled, and ultimately ended by congressional exercises of the power of the purse. All three uses of the power raised still unresolved legal questions.

In the initial domestic legal challenges to the war, some courts found that Congress had authorized the war by appropriating funds for its conduct.[12] Others declined to draw this inference on the theory that Congress really had no practical political choice but to support U.S. troops in the field.[13] These decisions raised the question whether and when prior authorization for national security actions or subsequent ratification could be inferred from appropriations. The Supreme Court had in several cases adopted a restrictive clear statement rule of authorization when the challenged actions affect sensitive individual rights,[14] but has since seemingly departed from its own rule, citing the inherent constitutional authority of the president in foreign affairs.[15] The 1973 Congress declared its own clear statement rule in the War Powers Resolution,[16] but this rule has not yet been enforced by Congress or the courts.

Midway through the Vietnam War, Congress attempted to use its power of the purse to restrict the scope of the war. Reflecting the national aversion to the bombing and "incursion" into Cambodia, Congress cut off funds for the introduction of U.S. ground combat troops or advisers in Cambodia.[17] It also amended the Defense Appropriations Act of 1970 to prohibit funding of U.S. ground combat troops in Laos or Thailand.[18] These area restrictions raised the issue whether Congress, by exercise of its power of the purse, unconstitutionally interfered with the inherent authority of the president as commander in chief to conduct the Vietnam War.[19]

President Nixon's apparent circumvention of these restrictions also raised questions regarding the statutory scope of national security appropriation restrictions in light of executive practice. He reprogrammed previously appropriated funds (that is, he spent appropriated funds for somewhat different purposes than those originally authorized by Congress) and used contingency and emergency accounts and statutory spending discretion under the feed and forage act[20] to finance combat in Laos and Cambodia. This financing raised the question of the extent to which congressional acquiescence in a long-continued executive national security spending practice has established a statutory, if not constitutional gloss on national security appropriations. Has Congress undercut the effectiveness of its own appropriation restrictions by leaving generic spending delegations to the president in the United States Code?[21]

Finally, Congress attempted to end the war by cutting off funding.[22] Its efforts raised questions about the political practicality of "pulling the plug" on the president's exercise of war power, as well as questions of the effectiveness and construction of funding cutoffs in light of executive spending practices.

The Iran-Contra Affair

More recently, the Iran-Contra affair raised many of these same questions and several new ones. The executive branch secretly financed military aid to the Contras in Nicaragua with funds appropriated for other uses, diverted from arms sales to Iran, or donated by third countries after executive solicitations, in apparent contravention of the Boland amendments—a series of appropriation restrictions on aid to the Contras.[23]

The enactment of no fewer than thirteen such restrictions raised anew the question of the proper construction of appropriation restrictions, and their constitutional scope vis-à-vis the president in national security. The restrictions also highlighted the interpretative and durational limits of national security appropriations and defense authorization bills.

President Reagan's creative financing of Contra aid, despite these restrictions and the Appropriations Clause,[24] also raised questions anew concerning the statutory gloss on the spending power delegated to the president by national security appropriations. In addition, his reliance on third-country donations presented the new issue whether such donations were controlled by the Boland amendments[25] or by the Appropriations Clause itself.

After the administration's apparent violation of one or more of the Boland amendments was made public, supporters of the president raised the question whether the amendments were constitutional. Often proceeding from the unexamined presumption that "mere appropriations" are somehow inferior to ordinary legislation,[26] some argued generally that the Boland amendments unconstitutionally interfered with the president's plenary foreign affairs power.[27] Others claimed more narrowly that the amendments impaired his inherent constitutional information-sharing and diplomatic communication powers.[28] Commentators and courts alike are agreed that Congress may not use its power of the purse to accomplish indirectly what it cannot legislate directly,[29] but are confused or ignorant about whether the power of the purse has unique constitutional scope in light of its history and structural role.

Structure of the Analysis

To understand and analyze the foregoing issues, we begin in Part I by tracing the early history of the power of the purse in national security affairs. We examine its origins and use in England from the sixteenth through the eighteenth centuries, its use in colonial America, the experience of the Continental Congress in the revolutionary war, the framing and ratification of the appropriation provisions in the Constitution, and the experience of the first congresses and presidents. We show that appropriations for national security—"bills of supply"—have historically played a special substantive role in controlling executive uses of the war power and responding to creative executive financing of war. This history may justify giving expansive scope to many exercises of the power of the purse in our own system of checks and balances.

Part II analyzes the mechanics of the national security appropriation process and defense spending. We show that the textbook model of appropriation broke down early for national security appropriations, as the line between authorizations and appropriations blurred, "black budgets" were authorized for the intelligence community, Congress came to rely heavily on continuing resolutions and restrictive appropriation riders, and the executive branch practiced creative national security spending with contingency, reprogrammed, and transferred funds. We use the funding of the Contras from 1981 to 1986 to demonstrate some of these developments and to suggest that congressional acquiescence and generic spending legislation have conferred a limited discretion on the president to spend for national security purposes outside specific appropriations. Finally, we show that informal spending controls that Congress employs in support of its power of the purse do not violate the Constitution.

Part III then analyzes procedural limitations imposed by the Constitution on the making of national security appropriations. We show that nothing in the Constitution or the pre-constitutional history prohibits the use of "veto-proof" appropriation riders or continuing resolutions. We also show that black budgeting for the intelligence community arguably does not violate the Statement and Account Clause, but that this clause vests plenary power in Congress to exact any reporting and accounting requirement it considers appropriate from the executive branch.

Part IV analyzes the substantive scope of the power of the purse. We show that despite their sometimes "indeterminate" legislative histories and short duration, "mere" appropriations have the force and effect of law and, indeed, may carry special force as evidence of congressional acquiescence in the making of what we call customary national security law. Applying this analysis, we argue that *legitimating appropriations*—appropriations from which the executive infers national security authority—can both authorize and ratify executive actions.

On the other hand, *restrictive appropriations*—appropriation riders or defense authorizations that restrict national security initiatives by the president—must usually be construed narrowly and may not be used to impose restrictions on the president that Congress could not constitutionally impose more directly. The proper constitutional scope of such restrictions should be determined by balancing the extent of their intrusion on executive power against their legislative purposes. That balancing, we argue, will usually support their validity because of their historically substantive role in controlling executive exercise of national security powers. We also show that if Congress has impermissibly limited the president or failed to appropriate constitutionally required funds, statutory and customary law often gives him a comfortable spending cushion that avoids the thorny question whether he may cure the omission by spending without appropriation.

In conclusion, we find that both proponents and opponents of presidential national security authority have misgauged the scope of the congressional power of the purse by ignoring or misconstruing its history, its mechanics, and its structural role in our constitutional system. Properly understood and analyzed, the power of the purse in national security is sweeping, though not plenary. Using the power of the purse, Congress can both leash and unleash the Dog of War, subject only to constitutional limits that it has not yet transgressed.

I

THE EARLY ORIGINS OF THE POWER OF THE PURSE IN NATIONAL SECURITY

In this part, we examine the history of the power of the purse in national security affairs from thirteenth-century England to the first Congresses.

In chapter 1, we trace the English history of the power of the purse in national security affairs from the thirteenth to the eighteenth century. We show that the power to grant bills of military supply was critical to the evolution of parliamentary government in England. To the exercise of this power of the purse, we can trace the origins of the practice of appropriation, statements of account, parliamentary oversight of spending, and, in part, term limits on standing armies.

In chapter 2, we turn to the preconstitutional American experience with the power of the purse. We show that the lower houses of the colonial legislatures took up where the English Parliament left off and used their power of the purse to acquire unprecedented control over military affairs. Their experience taught them that the power of the purse in national security affairs was both an instrument of control and a bulwark against executive abuse of military power. The disappointing experience with early congressional committee conduct of the revolutionary war also taught them the limits of control. But the primary lesson of the revolutionary war was that the central government had to be provided the means to finance war in order to conduct it successfully. Nothing in the revolutionary war experience counselled against a strong legislative power of the purse in national security affairs, as long as it was not used to assert legislative control over the tactical conduct of military operations.

In chapter 3, we consider the framing and ratification of the pertinent constitutional provisions. We show that the framers codified the full-blown power of the purse in national security affairs and saw it as a bulwark against the misuse of a standing army. Borrowing from English history and the state constitutions, they also cemented the power of the purse by enacting a prohibition on creative executive spending in the Appropriations Clause.

Finally, in chapter 4 we trace the national security appropriation practice of the early congresses and presidents. We show that the early practice established the customs of lump sum appropriation, executive transfers between national security accounts, and ex post facto appropriation for national security exigencies. We also show that there was an early consensus that presidential spending without appropriation for national security emergencies was sometimes necessary, but unlawful, unless Congress ratified it after the fact.

1

The English Power of the Purse

The framers of the Constitution did not, of course, invent the power of the purse. Parliamentary use of that power in England dates back to the thirteenth century. But before we trace it that far, we must address several hazards of generalizing from English history to interpret the Constitution.[1]

The first hazard stems from the fact that the rise of parliamentary democracy in England did not follow a steady path. The powers of Parliament and king ebbed and flowed.[2] Generalizing from one period of that history is often unreliable; selecting a different period may yield a quite different generalization. This problem, however, is perhaps less acute in generalizing about the power of the purse than in generalizing about the allocation of power among the branches of British government generally. As we shall show, the historical trend toward parliamentary control of the army by the power of the purse is unmistakable, and, after the Glorious Revolution of 1688, relatively steady, despite some fluctuations.

A second hazard of generalization is that the framers may not have had accurate understandings of English history.[3] Even when they had, they rejected much of it in forming our government.[4] Here again, it may be easier to gauge the influence of English history on the power of the purse than on the allocation of powers generally in our government. Repeated references in colonial debates, in the Constitutional Convention (in which the framers cited English history some twenty times in just the first three weeks),[5] the ratification debates,[6] and early congressional debates[7] are evidence that many of the participants possessed a good general knowledge of the role that the power of the purse played in English constitutional history. These sources also show that while the framers squarely rejected many of the prerogative powers of the king and devised uniquely American checks on the legislature, they endorsed the parliamentary power of the purse in military affairs and borrowed heavily from it in framing the national security appropriation power.

Bearing these hazards in mind, we examine in chronological order, the power of the purse in England during the thirteenth and fourteenth centuries, the Stuart period, the Restoration, and after the Glorious Revolution of 1688.

The Thirteenth and Early Fourteenth Centuries

From at least as early as the thirteenth century, parliamentary government, the power of the purse, and royal military power were bound together in English history.

> Such Parliaments as existed in France, Castile, Aragon and other countries voted taxes enabling their Kings to keep a standing army, and in doing so signed their own death-warrants. By possessing a standing army in time of peace the rulers were in a position to obtain everything they wanted without having to appeal to their Parliaments. The Kings in such countries had to possess stronger powers to tax their peoples in order to be able to finance their standing armies. Conversely, the existence of these armies had made it more difficult for the people to resist extortionate taxes. In the absence of strong permanent armed forces—apart from the Navy which was unsuitable for enforcing despotic rule at home—the Kings of England largely depended on the willingness of their subjects to consent to pay taxes.[8]

The principle of consent was written into the Magna Carta in 1215,[9] and reaffirmed in the Confirmation of the Charters in 1297, in which Edward I pledged, "We shall take such manner of aids, tasks, nor prises, but by common consent of the realm, and for the common profit thereof, saving the ancient aids and prises due and accustomed."[10] That consent, in turn, was obtained by summoning a body which became, in time, the Commons.[11]

Edward's pledge, however, excepted "ancient aids and prises due and accustomed"—"ordinary revenue" customarily due the king from sources not requiring consent.[12] As long as the king could "live on his own"—finance the expenses of the royal household and the government from ordinary revenue[13]—he did not need to summon the Commons. "Only the outbreak of war, or chronic maladministration," Keir concludes, "could disturb this position and make it necessary to have recourse to extraordinary resources of revenue, such as supplementary grants by parliament, borrowing, the levy of gifts from the subject under the name of benevolences and the exaction of forced loans."[14]

If war was the occasion for revenue-raising through the Parliament, it also served as the occasion for its first appropriations: bills specifying the uses to which the revenues could be put. The first clear instance of parliamentary appropriation was a bill of extraordinary supply in 1340 providing that all proceeds "shall be put and spent upon the Maintenance and Safeguard of our said Realm of England, and on Wars in Scotland, France and Gascoign, and in no places elsewhere during the said Wars."[15] Three years later, the Parliament authorized the king to levy a tax on wool to be used for the war efforts.[16] By the middle of the fourteenth century, such appropriations of extraordinary supply for specific purposes—usually war expenditures—were firmly established, accompanied invariably by the stipulation that they not be otherwise spent.[17]

By that time, too, Parliament had begun to take advantage of the king's national security–driven need for extraordinary supply by insisting on redress of its grievances before it voted any grants of supply.[18] Sometimes it would implicitly condition a grant of supply on removal of unpopular officials.[19] In 1378, the Commons also asked the king to account for the expenditure of grants. He complied on the understanding that the accounting was strictly voluntary. The Commons then accepted all of his accounts except certain defense expenditures outside the realm.[20] Soon Parliament began threatening to withhold supply unless it received an accounting.[21] Although the extravagance of the king's household was sometimes the target of this early insistence on accounting, often the focus narrowed to misappropriation of defense grants.

Parliament thus gradually became a necessary instrument for royal offensive war-making. But Parliament and king were still struggling for control of the purse in this early period, and Parliament still met only when the need for extraordinary supply forced the king's hand. At the same time, "there may have been at least some legal authority for the proposition that for a defensive as distinct from an offensive war, the subject was bound, even without his own consent, to aid the king not merely with his person but with his goods."[22]

Stuart England

The struggle for control of the purse came to a climax in the reign of the Stuart kings from 1603 to 1649. By the start of the seventeenth century, it was no longer possible for the king to live of his own; royal expenditures regularly exceeded ordinary income.[23] But Parliament was increasingly insistent on redress of grievances before voting supply and grudging and quarrelsome in voting it. When foreign wars and crises forced James I to ask for extraordinary supply between 1618 and 1625, Parliament seized the occasion to dictate the purposes for which the money was to be spent and to wrest policy from the king. In connection with a grant of extraordinary supply in 1621, it even tried to dictate whom the king's son should marry and to direct that the king declare war on France, even though royal marriages and foreign policy "lay within the King's undoubted prerogative."[24]

Just when the king's foreign ventures had led to war with both France and Spain, Parliament prepared a petition of grievances, which one historian has likened to "drafting a report on civil defence while the bombs were still falling."[25] The 1628 Petition of Right

> declared and enacted, that from thenceforth no person shall be compelled to make any loans to the king against his will, ... [Y]our subjects have inherited this freedom that they should not be compelled to contribute any tax, tallage, aid, or other like charge, not set by common consent in Parliament.[26]

To obtain subsidies for military action supporting the Huguenots against the French, Charles I assented.[27] The next year, however, he dissolved Parliament, not to reconvene it for eleven years.[28]

During this interlude, Charles reigned without Parliament. But without

Parliament, he found himself without "the means to wage war."[29] Financial desperation propelled a royal search for other sources of revenue, typically under the plea of national defense.[30] The king looked to tonnage and poundage (later called "customs" because it was the custom of the crown to levy them),[31] fees from compulsory knighthoods, sales of forest rights, royal domains, patents and monopolies, prises (the compulsory requisition of goods for the royal household), purveyances (purchase of goods at below-market prices fixed by the crown), ransoms of prisoners, and payments by foreign governments as tributes or bribes.[32] The king also extended "ship money" obligations (originally primarily levies from seaports for the construction of naval vessels) throughout the realm on the theory that they were justified for defense against invasion. In *Hampden's Case*,[33] Hampden challenged this theory, but the Court of Exchequer backed the crown, refusing to draw a distinction between an "immediate" danger which required the king to act without Parliament and an "apprehended" danger which obliged him to act through Parliament.[34] Finally, the king raised money by borrowing and by forced loans, although creditors began to insist on parliamentary grants as security.[35]

But the royal need for supply for war persisted. Charles therefore summoned the Parliament to raise an army for national defense in 1640. When the Commons resolved that "till the liberties of the House and the King were cleared, they knew not whether they had anything to give or no,"[36] however, the "Short Parliament" was dissolved less than three weeks after it began.[37] Invasion by the Scottish army compelled Charles to call a new Parliament in 1641.[38] The "Long Parliament" forced Charles I to repudiate the reasoning of *Hampden's Case* as a condition of still another grant of extraordinary supply for foreign ventures. They also passed a bill granting tonnage and poundage but declaring that it was and had been the right of subjects that no custom be imposed or charged without common consent in Parliament.[39] In short, capitalizing on national security–driven demands for revenue, Parliament forced Charles to sell prerogative rights in exchange for money grants.[40]

This was ultimately a stratagem "pregnant with trouble."[41] Each "sale" only fed the Parliament's appetite for controlling the purse, and with it, policy. Yet each time the crown responded with "creative financing" of war without Parliament, it hardened parliamentary determination to ensure against unconstitutional taxation by future Kings. Historian David Keir has described the resulting standoff as follows:

> Admitting that the King might impose financial burdens by Prerogative in order to regulate trade or provide for defense, it none the less did not follow that he might use this power in order to avoid recourse to Parliament for extraordinary supply. Yet he did so. Admitting that Parliament alone could grant that supply, it did not follow that this power might be used to deprive the King of control over the executive, yet this was what Parliament attempted.[42]

The continuing dispute over the purse, coupled with other events, degenerated into outright civil war in 1642 and contributed five years later to the execution of Charles I.[43]

The Protectorate and the Restoration

A military dictatorship followed the execution of Charles I. Parliament was forced to grant the lord protector, Oliver Cromwell, substantial annual grants for defense and for civil government through 1659, leaving the methods of raising this revenue to him and his council.[44] War expenses were met by additional votes in Parliament when it was sitting, and by decision of the protector and his council when it was not. "Parliament thus conceded to Cromwell more far-reaching powers in matters of taxation than even the most despotic Monarchs ever possessed in Britain."[45]

Cromwell's death in 1658 left a void that was not satisfactorily filled until restoration of the monarchy in 1660. Among the first acts of the new Parliament was a statute in 1661 that declared "the sole supreme government of the militia and of all forces by sea and land is, and by the laws of England ever was, the undoubted right of the king and his predecessors, and that neither house of parliament could pretend the same."[46] At the same time, Parliament voted a generous annual subsidy for Charles II.[47]

Nevertheless, it was ultimately a constitutional, not a despotic monarchy that was restored. The acts of the Long Parliament under Charles I continued in effect, and "[u]nparliamentary taxation, such as ship money and forced loans, stood condemned."[48] Keeping a standing army without supply from Parliament was impossible. When the Dutch War of 1665 to 1667 went badly and Charles II had to go to Parliament for extraordinary supply, it insisted on appropriation and accounting.[49] In 1678, the parliamentary grant of supply was so niggling that the king was forced to disband part of his army for lack of funds.[50] In the same year, Parliament resolved that

> all aids and supplies and aids to His Majesty in Parliament are the sole gift of the Commons; and all Bills for the granting of any such aids and supplies ought to begin with the Commons; and that it is the undoubted and sole right of the Commons to direct, limit and appoint in such Bills the ends, purposes, considerations, conditions, limitations and qualifications of such grants; which ought not to be changed or altered by the Lords.[51]

Parliament thus progressively consolidated its hold on the purse.

The Glorious Revolution of 1688

This consolidation continued after the Glorious Revolution brought William and Mary to the throne and gained a new impetus with the Declaration of Rights (enacted as the Bill of Rights) in 1688. The declaration declared illegal the raising or keeping of a standing army during peace, and the levy of money by "pretense of prerogative," without consent of Parliament.[52] Parliament repeated this declaration in the First Mutiny Act,[53] intended to provide for court-martial of mutineers among troops bound for the Low Countries. The Mutiny Act also provided that it would be in effect only half a year. It thus for the first time effectively tied parliamentary approval of a peacetime standing army to a short, renewable term. From this time forward, Parliament renewed mutiny acts for a year or two at a time.[54] Kings who wanted a standing army were left no choice thereafter but to allow Parliament to sit every year, lest the authority of the latest mutiny act run out.[55]

"The combined effect of the Bill of Rights and the Mutiny Act made it impossible for the Crown to maintain in time of peace a standing army unauthorized by parliament. Its existence, number, pay, and discipline all were subjected to statutes."[56] Enactment of such statutes provoked numerous debates about the standing army and led to some conditions on the army itself. For example, an increase of the standing army from 1697 to 1698 was approved only on condition that no troops would be placed in the naval establishment. Another statute required the king to send his Dutch guards home.[57]

Some conditions were arguably remotely related or even unrelated to the bills to which they were attached. This so vexed the House of Lords that in 1702 it resolved that attaching nongermane conditions to bills of supply "is unparliamentary, and tends to the destruction of the contribution of this government."[58] But this was a statement of principle, not of prohibition. Charles Cooper notes that "the practice of combining unrelated matters in a single bill, however objectionable, was widely known."[59]

Parliament also pressed for "closer financial control over the fighting services in general and over the army in particular."[60] In the Bill of Aid for 1688, it included an appropriation clause that stated that the sum appropriated "may not be diverted or applyed to any other Purpose," a generic formula repeated thereafter in all acts of supply.[61] From 1689 to 1697, it exacted the price of appropriation and audit for the annual grants of supply required by the war with France.[62] Loopholes for unauthorized expenditures were gradually closed, and, after 1691, a Commission of Public Accounts was established to oversee all public accounts but the Privy Purse and Secret Service.[63] The commission's members became actively involved in policy-making and generated information that "bolstered the Commons' determination to secure fiscal responsibility."[64] For the first time, military departments—especially the army—were pressed to produce spending estimates.[65] Parliament also took a stand against *virement*, the transfer of funds appropriated for one department (often the navy) for use by another (often the army).[66]

Parliament was not completely unrelenting in pressing the power of the purse in national security affairs. Power carries with it, after all, responsibility, and few in Parliament wished to be blamed for the harm to national security that would result from denying supply altogether.[67] Moreover, despite the severely worded appropriation clauses in acts of supply for the military, the parliamentary practice was also to ignore minor spending deviations by the Crown. Looking back on this practice in 1796, William Pitt noted that such deviations occurred most often when the nation was engaged in war and when it was impossible to foresee the amount of military expenses.[68] He suggested that the test of legality which emerged was "whether [the deviation] was new and unprecedented or whether it was founded on ancient practice; whether it was clandestine and done with intent to deceive the House, or under its notice and sanctioned by its decision."[69] In times of war, Parliament also explicitly relaxed its control by passing Votes of Credit, giving the king power to spend up to set ceilings for unspecified military purposes,[70] over the objection that "every Vote of Credit we give to the Crown is a temporary suspension of our power."[71] Finally, the king helped assure favorable parliamentary votes by buying "influence" with bribery and patronage.[72] Secret Service funds—for which the Crown did not account to Parliament—were an important source of bribes.[73]

These relaxations of control were the exception, however, not the rule. The rule was consolidated parliamentary control over the military using the power of the purse. Moreover, control was focused on the military; in contrast, Parliament "gave the monarch a remarkably free hand in the sphere of *civil* expenditure."[74] It was the requirement for *military* supply that forced kings to go to Parliament. The power of the purse thus played a distinctive role in national security affairs, especially after the Glorious Revolution.[75] Sir James Mackintosh has aptly summarized the result: "The Revolution bent the neck of military power under the yoke of Law, and rendered armies the creatures of Parliament, made and destroyed by its breath."[76] Or as James Madison summarized the period more prosaically, "The sword is in the hands of the British King. The purse is in the hands of Parliament."[77]

2

The Power of the Purse in Pre-Constitutional America

The power of the purse in national security affairs traced a distinctly American course in the colonies and was influenced by the apparent failure of legislative conduct of the Revolutionary War. After describing the colonial model of government, we examine how the lower houses of the colonial legislatures used the power of the purse against the colonial governors and the status of that power on the eve of the Revolution. We then examine the power of the purse in the states during the Revolution and the evolution of legislative conduct of the Revolutionary War, before drawing lessons from the war.

The Colonial Model

Colonial America[1] lived under two governments: the English or home government and the colonial government, which managed internal police and taxed for local purposes.[2] Colonial government was modeled on the English system, with a charter proprietor or royal governor, a governor's council functioning as an upper house, and a popularly elected lower house initially created by the grace of the king.[3] The two governments intersected over legislation, because the signature of the governor, as the king's agent, was necessary to put acts of the legislatures into effect, and because laws could be suspended until they had been approved by the home government in England.[4]

By modeling colonial governments on their own system, however, the English sowed the seeds of revolution.[5] As inhabitants of English colonies, the colonists insisted on "the rights of Englishmen," including the right to be represented. Since it was inconvenient to be represented in a distant English Parliament, the colonists looked to their own assemblies for representation. "The logical corollary to this argument was that the lower houses were equivalents of the House of Commons and must per force in their limited spheres be entitled to all the privileges possessed by that body in Great Britain."[6] The Crown unintentionally encouraged this analogy by forbidding the assemblies from exercising "any power not allowed by us to the House of Commons . . . in Great Britain."[7] Royal governors completed the analogy by invoking royal prerogatives as defined by usage and modified by the development of parliamentary controls. The royal governors and the colonial assemblies alike therefore typically appealed to English parliamentary practice in arguing their political disputes,[8] as well as to local usage in which the home government was said to have acquiesced.[9]

The central English parliamentary privilege asserted by the colonists was inevitably control of the purse.[10] English colonial policy, which required the colonies to finance their own defense against local enemies and often to advance funds for defense even against foreign enemies,[11] thus strengthened the power of the purse in the hands of the lower houses.

Wielding the Power of the Purse against Colonial Governors

From the start, the lower houses insisted on control of the power to tax and resisted sharing it with the governors' councils. They successfully took advantage of military exigencies, by withholding military supply until their rights to tax and, gradually, to appropriate, were acknowledged, and by imposing riders on military supply bills. Increasingly, they insisting on making detailed appropriations for military purposes. Inevitably, they also insisted on overseeing the use of such funds according to their specifications by demanding accounts and even designating treasurers for spending.

Citing English parliamentary practice, the lower house in South Carolina was typical in its early insistence on its sole right to frame tax bills and to prevent their amendment by the governor's council.[12] It enacted a resolution ending even the practice of sending accounts to the council for its inspection. The council twice refused to accede to this legislation, but finally agreed to a money bill containing the offending resolution because the bill was needed to raise money to aid Virginia in fighting the French and Indian wars.[13] When this sequence was repeated, the governor intervened on the side of the commons against the council, citing urgent military needs for defense against the Cherokee.[14] In 1756, he again backed the commons in this dispute because he needed a tax bill in anticipation of impending war with France.[15] The lower house thus opportunistically used the colony's military emergencies to, in effect, blackmail the governor and, derivatively, the home government in England, into acknowledging its fiscal powers.

In other colonies, too, the lower houses used their control of military supply to wrest power from the upper houses or councils and their governors. In Virginia, the House of Burgesses claimed the power to tax as early as 1624 and insisted in the latter part of the seventeenth century that its right was exclusive. In 1711, it flexed its fiscal muscle by denying military supply to a popular royal governor.[16] In 1715, it conditioned military supply for defenses against Indian invasion on repeal of an unpopular tobacco act.[17] In New York, the lower house threatened to withhold military supply bills unless the governor accepted temporary (one-year) instead of longer-term bills, thus tightening its fiscal leash on him.[18] The Massachusetts lower house insisted that the governor accept its nominee as speaker in order to obtain supply for Queen Anne's War.[19] It also required him to send down his military orders and instructions. When he balked, the lower house disingenuously replied that it was "very Solicitous, that the Affairs of the War be carried on with great dispatch but . . . wholly at a loss what may be requisite to effect the same, till the Papers sent for . . . be laid before them."[20] The governor took the hint and complied. On another occasion, the house was even more blunt; it simply told the governor to dismiss two military officers, or it would withdraw part of the forces that it funded.[21] The North Carolina lower house declared that it had the sole right to tax, then used this power, coupled with the power to pass bills of military supply, to compel the governor and the upper house to assent even to bills that were contrary to royal instructions.[22]

From such manipulation of military supply bills, it was but a small step to the assumption of substantial control over military operations by detailed appropriations. The assemblies asserted that it was "their right and duty to provide all necessary safeguards for a proper application of the money to the purposes for which it was intended,"[23] and they frequently added provisions such as the Massachusetts proviso that such money was "for no other Ends and Uses whatsoever."[24] Evarts Greene concluded that

> The urgent need of supplies for military purposes occasioned by these [the French and Indian] wars enabled the assembly, in making its grants of money, to impose the most arduous conditions. This power it used in three general ways. In the first place, in granting military supplies it prescribed in detail the purposes for which they were to be expended, dictating the course of military operations and the disposition of troops. Secondly, it left in the hands of committees of the assembly, or of commissioners appointed by act of assembly, the disposition of these funds, often too with a very considerable control of the conduct of military enterprises. Finally, through the appointment and removal of officers, it went so far as to interfere with the discipline of troops.[25]

Examples of such manipulative uses of military appropriations abound. In South Carolina, the commons refused funds for James Oglethorpe's expedition against St. Augustine until it was allowed to participate in deciding the number of soldiers involved, their pay rates, and the total sum required.[26] In Virginia, the House of Burgesses "not only prescribed in detail the purposes for which military supplies were to be used, but put the disposition of these funds in the hands of committees, dictated the course of military operations, and practically, through the appointment and removal of officers, really exercised much power over the troops."[27] During the French and Indian wars, the governor objected to this interference with his derivative royal military prerogative, but finally accepted the burgesses' terms because of his urgent need for military supply.[28] In Pennsylvania, the assembly specified by appropriation how soldiers should be distributed between garrison and ranging and scouting parties.[29] In Massachusetts, the General Court (lower house) specified where soldiers should be posted on the frontier. The governor assented under protest, declaring that he did so only because of pressing military needs.[30] In New York, Governor Clinton complained that military supply appropriations were so specific that even "[p]rovisions for the Army are not subject to the Orders of the General."[31]

In addition to specific appropriations, "[t]he assemblies soon learned to make the most of these [the governors' military supply] difficulties and to increase them by . . . the practice, pursued in direct defiance of the royal instructions, of inserting items entirely foreign to the main body of the bill, of attaching legislative riders to bills appropriating money. . . ."[32] For example, the Virginia House of Burgesses added to a military supply bill a rider for payment of their special agent in London.[33] North Carolina's lower house tried the same gambit.[34] When the governor vetoed the bill because of the nongermane rider, the home government complained that although the lower house acted contrary to custom in imposing such a rider on a supply bill, this breach of custom was too trivial a reason to veto the bill.[35]

The assemblies also took advantage of executive military necessity to exact accounts of funds and audits by legislatively appointed commissioners or treasurers. In North Carolina, for example, the governor objected to the legislatively appointed treasurer's refusal to allow some military expenses. In response, the house resolved that the accounting requirement was consistent with "uninterrupted usage," then refused to grant further military supplies until the governor submitted accounts of funds previously granted to him.[36] It also used its power of the purse to conduct inquiries into executive affairs, including an examination of Oglethorpe's abortive military expedition against St. Augustine, during which it required the general to testify before its committee.[37] In New York, too, the lower house demanded explanations of expenditures by Governor Clinton and threatened to withhold further supply unless he policed expenditures more closely.[38]

The Power of the Purse on the Eve of the Revolution

By the mid-eighteenth century, the colonial assemblies had acquired a stronger power of the purse than the English House of Commons then enjoyed.[39] Nowhere was this more true than in military affairs; in the area of the civil list (nonmilitary payroll), the assemblies' aims and gains were more limited.[40]

> In using their power over money to encroach upon governors' military prerogative, American lower houses were pursuing a well marked path which the English House of Commons had traversed in the late 17th century. . . . But the English House of Commons never interfered in military matters so extensively as did the American lower houses during the 18th century. Nor did it attempt to nominate military officers or to assume the actual direction of the war through Parliamentary committee.[41]

The colonial assemblies effectively usurped the governors' military powers by specifying the purposes for which military appropriations could be spent, including the number, distribution, organization, pay, place and period of service, and supply of the officers and men to be raised.[42] Although the assemblies afforded the governors some leeway in the use of funds for military purposes in times of emergency, even then they insisted that the funds be spent consistently with the purposes of the appropriation and that the governor render an account.[43] "The tendency was rather to tie up the appropriations so closely as to limit his freedom of action as far as possible."[44] Despite his nominal royal prerogatives derived from the Crown, "the governor's military authority was virtually non-existent . . . without support from the colonial legislatures."[45] One historian has remarked with only slight exaggeration that, as a result, in the French and Indian wars "the king's representative acted merely as the correspondent of his ministers. The war was conducted by committees of assembly."[46]

The power of the purse thus played a central role in the political development of colonial America and in the exercise of war powers in the colonies. The power of the purse was, of course, the people's chief safeguard against military adventure and control on military initiatives. But to eighteenth-century Americans—including the politicians who eventually framed the United States government—it was more. It was "the determinant of sovereignty, and upon its location and extent depended the power of government, the existence of civil rights, and the integrity of representative institutions."[47] In short, control of provincial funds—chief among them those needed for military supply—"became the principal means to obtain nearly all political desiderata."[48]

The Power of the Purse in the States

After the Revolution began, most of the states constitutionalized the subordination of the executive to the legislation. Of the eight states that adopted constitutions during the first two years of the Revolution, all but New York "included almost every conceivable provision for reducing the executive to a position of complete subordination."[49] Respecting appropriations, most provided for the origination of money bills in the lower house and several limited the power of the upper house or council to amend such bills.[50] Massachusetts and South Carolina also adopted provisions prohibiting expenditures from the public treasury unless authorized by appropriation or warrant.[51] "On the whole," Gerhard Casper concludes, "the fiscal provisions of the state constitutions confirm our understanding that during the founding period money matters were primarily thought of as a legislative prerogative."[52]

Maryland alone constitutionally forbade the attachment to an appropriation of "any matter, clause, or thing, not immediately related to . . . the taxes or supplies to be raised for the support of the government.[53] As Casper notes, "[t]his germaneness requirement displays a high degree of sophistication concerning opportunities for manipulation of the legislative process."[54] It also underscores the significance of the omission of a comparable requirement in the other state constitutions, especially in view of the fact that only New York and Massachusetts recognized an overrideable veto.[55]

State legislatures picked up where colonial legislatures left off, interfering repeatedly with the executive.[56] Catering to popular causes and competing with the commerce of other states by parochial legislation, they gave life to a concern for what Thomas Jefferson called "an elective despotism," legislative tyranny.[57] In response during the late 1780s and early 1790s reformers in several states successfully urged direct election of their executives, longer terms, and other reforms that strengthened the executive.[58]

The Evolution of Congressional Control of the War

After the overthrow of royal government in the colonies, the Continental Congress itself succeeded to the military powers of the Crown[59] and the royal governors. These it exercised by committee, managing the Revolutionary War. The conventional view is that the Congress badly bungled the job and that the subsequent decision of the framers to vest exclusive military command in the president as commander in chief under the Constitution was "a reaction against the effort of the Continental Congress to conduct the Revolutionary War by committee."[60] A closer look at the supply problems of the Continental army and the chronology of the congressional efforts to meet them, however, suggests that this assessment, though not wrong, is incomplete and misleading.

After the Continental Congress agreed to adopt the ragtag army surrounding Boston in 1775 and appointed Washington commander in chief, it initially attempted to control the army and conduct the war in ad hoc committees and the committee of the whole. Responding to problems as they arose, the Congress soon established committees on everything from cannon procurement, musket manufacturing, prisoners of war, saltpeter, spies, hospitals, medical matters, health and discipline of the army, clothing, beef, salt, cavalry, militia training, and recruiting, to supply for Canadian operations—not to mention committees treating naval affairs.[61] The Congress involved itself in everything from logistics to troop movements and strategy,[62] although it did authorize General Washington to act according to his best judgment in all cases not covered by its instructions.[63] In military affairs, the Continental Congress was not just a deliberative lawmaking body, but "a deliberating executive assembly"[64] compensating for the lack of a Confederation executive.

This mix of functions proved more than the Congress could effectively manage. The Continental Congress was in equal parts inexperienced, desultory, and overburdened in its committee management of the Revolutionary War.[65] The initial defeats of the Continental army can be attributed at least in part to poor planning and organization by Continental Congress committees. Even after the ad hoc committees gave way to standing committees, congressional efficiency in conducting the war showed little improvement.[66] Its failure was captured by the image of a poorly clothed and unfed army at Valley Forge.

But the Continental army's initial military failures and inadequate supply were not solely or even primarily attributable to congressional mismanagement. An imposing array of causes beyond congressional control also contributed. One was the scale and unexpected length of the war.[67] The colonial military experience was simply not sufficient to the task of war with one of the world's greatest military powers over one of the largest battlefronts in history, no matter how that war was organized and commanded.[68] Another contributing cause was the inadequacy of short-term enlistments and the militia to fight that war,[69] a problem that continued to fetter the revolutionary effort throughout. The states' competition for supplies and their general provincialism in the military effort also dogged Continental army logistics from the start.[70] All of these factors only aggravated the supply problem that stemmed from the Congress's lack of authority to raise money.

Congress recognized its own inefficiency; it could hardly help doing so, given the workload. "Our business has run away with us," despaired Silas Deane.[71] Samuel Chase wrote that "the Congress are not a fit Body to act as a Council of war. They are too large, too slow, and their Resolutions can never be kept secret. . . . Pray divide your business into different Departments: a War Office, a Treasury Board, etc."[72] Beginning about 1777, Congress took this advice and started replacing its committees with boards composed in part of persons outside Congress.[73] Gradually it left congressmen off some of these boards. This opened the door to more experienced board members and encouraged the emergence of some professional staff. By 1780, the boards gave way to departments of war, foreign affairs, finance and naval affairs under the direction of single directors or secretaries.[74] Over the same interval, active congressional supervision of the conduct of campaigns declined, particularly after Washington's preeminence in command was firmly established.[75] In contrast, Congress continued to manage foreign affairs almost alone, insisting on direct information from ministers abroad.[76]

If committee management of the war effort was principally to blame for its failures, these reforms should have made a significant difference. But the abandonment of the committee system had little discernible payoff in improved military operations and performance.[77] Improved administration could accomplish little without military supply. Lacking the power to tax, the Continental Congress was unable to assure adequate supply. Its issue of paper currency was a rapidly declining resource, as the paper lost value. By 1779 Congress stopped issuing new notes, effectively declaring bankruptcy.[78]

The national bankruptcy forced Congress to turn back to the states.[79] But the states had proved no more prescient than the Continental Congress at predicting the length and scope of the war and were unwilling (and arguably politically unable) to tax for its support.[80] Moreover, they were as slow and inefficient as the Continental Congress at coming to the aid of the Continental army.[81] These defects were magnified by their provincialism: their reluctance to even attempt support for troops not their own, regardless of military necessities. With the resulting decentralization of supply responsibilities to the states, the administrative reforms essayed by Congress made little difference to the effective conduct of the war.[82] The army survived in part by requisitioning[83] and by using supplies purchased with French loans.

The next administrative reform, however, seems at first glance to have made a difference. The appointment of Robert Morris as superintendent of finance in

1781 was followed within the year by the surrender of General Cornwallis at Yorktown. Morris helped direct the army's logistical operations during his first months in office, instituting a contract procurement system to feed the army, and arranging French loans to fund it, and his centralized planning and direction deserve a significant part of the credit for the victory at Yorktown.[84] But the system did not avail the southern or northern armies, which continued to suffer terrible shortages.[85] Nor did the adoption of the Articles of Confederation, which took effect in 1781, significantly alleviate the problem of supplying a national army. Congress was vested with the authority to appropriate money out of the treasury for defraying public expenses and "to build and equip a navy—to agree upon the number of land forces," subject to the agreement of at least nine states.[86] But it still lacked the power to put money in; all charges of war were to be defrayed out of a common treasury to which the states were to contribute in proportion to the value of their land, but no article provided for enforcement of this provision.[87]

When the logistical problems of the whole army finally receded, it was "mainly as a result of the ensuing peace that brought stability and regularity to administrative affairs," increased foreign bankers' willingness to lend money to the Confederation, and, of course, decreased the emergency needs of the battlefield.[88] It does not diminish Robert Morris's remarkable accomplishments to note that the bankers benefited as much from the ending of the war as they contributed to it. When the war finally did formally end in 1783, the Continental army effectively disbanded for the duration of the Confederation,[89] and "Congress . . . sank into a state of impotency . . . ."[90]

To conclude that the main lesson of the Revolutionary War was the inefficiency of close legislative control of military operations is a distortion of the history. The root cause of most Continental army failures was not legislative micromanagement, but legislative want of authority to raise revenue and provide military supply. George Washington correctly concluded that to the

> want of Powers in Congress, may justly be ascribed the prolongation of the War, and consequently the expenses occasioned by it. More than half the perplexities I have experienced in the course of my command, and almost the whole of the difficulties and distress of the Army, have their origin here . . . .[91]

The expense of the Revolutionary War was unprecedented in the colonial experience. But the centralized power and legal authority required to meet this expense—by raising revenues and coercing the financial and military cooperation of the states—did not exist and would not have been tolerated.[92] The Continental Congress could provide at best only "representation without taxation."[93]

The consequence was that "[u]ntil the end of the fighting, supply and procurement remained a hurried improvisation in the face of emergency,"[94] a consequence of the relationship between the Continental Congress and the states, not of the relationship between the Continental Congress and the army. The first lesson of the Revolutionary War was therefore that effective war-making—and national defense—required a reallocation of power between the national government and the states.

The war also taught that, in Gouverneur Morris's words, "a body such as the Congress is inadequate to the Purposes of execution."[95] A multimember legislative body is not constituted to make the real-time, day-to-day decisions required for the tactical direction of military forces. This is equally true whether the legislature sits in committee to make such decisions or expresses them in specific defense appropriations and riders. Military necessity dictates a commonsense allocation of national security authority based on competency at this level of decision making.

But this lesson should not be overdrawn for purposes of construing the later work of the framers. Nothing in the Revolutionary War experience counseled a wholesale departure from the colonial model of close legislative control of national security decisions by appropriation. Any intelligent observer of the conduct of the Revolutionary War would have concluded that day-to-day command and supply decisions were beyond the competency of the Continental Congress. But there was little reason to conclude from the war that the legislature should give up other controls over the military, notably the tools of specific appropriations treating a range of military matters.

3

The Framing and Ratification of the Power of the Purse in National Security Affairs

Nowhere does our focus on the power of the purse in national security affairs run a greater risk of rendering an incomplete picture than when we trace the framing and ratification of this power in the Constitution. Contemporary discussion of the power was sparse. Except insofar as it authorized creation of a standing army, the power appeared relatively uncontroversial. The war powers provisions of the Constitution add little to the picture, because these provisions also received relatively little discussion.[1] What does emerge quite clearly from the constitutional history is the widely shared assumption that the people could risk vesting war powers and the command of a standing army in the president because Congress retained control of the means of war, an assumption consistent with a broad-scoped power of the purse.

Framing

The Federal Convention of 1787 began with a mandate only to amend the Articles of Confederation in order to address the problems that ten years' experience had brought to light. The introduction of the nationalist Virginia plan early in the Convention, however, gave evidence that many of the delegates were prepared and eager to go further, to replace the articles with a constitution granting broad new powers to the national government. Not surprisingly, in light of the experience of the Continental Congress during the Revolution, Virginia Governor Edmund Randolph opened deliberations by observing that the "first" defect of the Confederation was that it "produced no security agai[nst] foreign invasion; congress not being permitted to prevent a war nor to support it by th[eir] own authority."[2]

The obvious cure was to vest a power to tax and spend for the national defense in the national legislature. The major controversy that arose in the evolution of the Tax Clause concerned whether the national government should assume the war debts of the states. After this controversy was resolved, the

Convention approved a clause which borrowed from the Articles of Confederation to state the objects of the tax power: "The Congress shall have Power To lay and collect Taxes, . . . to pay the Debts, and provide for the common Defence and general Welfare of the United States . . . ."[3]

More controversy attended the framing of the Origination Clause, providing that revenue bills shall originate in the House, but it focused almost entirely on the proper role for the Senate in the appropriation process. Early drafts copied the origination clauses and restrictions on amendments by the upper house that had been imported from England,[4] evolved in the colonial legislatures, and had been incorporated in some state charters. Some delegates objected that restrictions on the Senate's ability to amend might encourage the House in "the practice of tacking foreign matter to money bills."[5] James Wilson agreed that the House would "insert other things in money bills" and added that the proposed restriction of money bills to the House would be "a source of perpetual contentions."[6] In the ensuing debates, Madison also noted that any proposal that left the houses in unequal positions regarding money bills would only breed disputes, and James McHenry made specific reference to the House's power of "appropriating money" as well as of "raising money" in the same vein.[7]

Wilson also spoke against any restrictions on Senate amendments of money bills because of the centrality of such bills to government: "War, Commerce, & Revenue were the great objects of the Genl. Government. All of them are connected with money. The restriction in favor of the H. of Represts. would exclude the Senate from originating any important bills whatever."[8] If Wilson's objection suggested his appreciation of the power of the purse, Randolph's rebuttal underscored its special importance in military affairs. "The means of war," he responded, "ought to remain in the less corruptible House."[9]

Eventually, the various proposals were sent to the Committee on Unfinished Portions, which reported out a compromise giving the House the power to originate money bills and the Senate the power to amend.[10] The compromise provision gave the Senate a share of the power of the purse in national security. Thus, in subsequent debate about exempting treaties of peace from the requirement for approval by two-thirds of the Senate, Gouverneur Morris argued that "if a Majority of the Senate be for peace, and are not allowed to make it, they will be apt to effect their purpose in the more disagreeable mode, of negativing the supplies for war."[11] The compromise also gave the Senate the power of self-defense against House-originated riders; it could now amend such legislation. But no one during the debates suggesting prohibiting such riders.[12]

The compromise reported by the Committee of Unfinished Portions also added that "[n]o money shall be drawn from the treasury but in consequence of appropriations made by law."[13] Alexander Hamilton later explained that

> the design of the Constitution in this provision was, as I conceive, to secure these important ends,—that the *purpose*, the *limit*, and the *fund* of every expenditure should be ascertained by previous law. The public security is complete in this particular, if no money can be expended, but for an *object*, to an *extent*, and *out of a fund*, which the laws have prescribed.[14]

There is no record of any debate about the Appropriation Clause, which, as we have seen, was a commonplace of state and colonial legislation and which traced its origins to seventeenth-century England.

The first version of the Army, or Raise and Support, Clause was prepared by Governor Randolph for the Committee of Detail.[15] With several minor revisions, the committee reported out the provision that "the Legislature of the United States shall have the right and power to raise armies; to build and equip fleets."[16] The Convention quickly approved the addition of "to support" to the army provision and the change of the navy provision to its present form.[17]

As it stood, however, the clause placed no check on the creation of a standing army. Elbridge Gerry proposed a numerical limit on the size of such an army, which was rejected on the grounds that it might hamper defense against invasion.[18] A proposal for limiting appropriations for land forces to one year at a time, however, was referred to the Committee on Unfinished Portions. It subsequently reported out substantially the present language, increasing the maximum term of such appropriations to two years, and the Convention approved this proposal. George Mason, Elbridge Gerry, and Luther Martin remained implacable, the latter decrying the provision for giving "an express and constitutional sanction" to "a standing army, that engine of arbitrary power."[19]

Convention discussions by which the president was designated the commander in chief of this army and of the militia when called into active service of the United States, and by which Congress's power to "make war" was changed to the power to "declare war," have been fully recounted elsewhere.[20] They suggest that the framers' intent was to allow the president to defend the United States against attack and to conduct authorized military operations.[21] Equally important, they yielded no express constitutional restraints on legislative delegations of national security authority to the president or on congressional acquiescence in executive assumptions of such authority.[22] Otherwise, war powers were discussed and conferred on the executive on the assumption that "the means of carrying on the war would not be in the hands of the President, but of the Legislature."[23] As Abraham Sofaer concludes, "[n]othing in the Convention proceedings is inconsistent with the Constitution's apparent grants to Congress of overwhelming authority to control all military decisions other than tactical."[24] Nor was anything said during the Convention that is inconsistent with the historical assumption that such authority would most effectively be exercised by the power of the purse.

Ratification

Although the ratifiers, like the framers, were more concerned with the relations between the national and state governments than with those between the political branches, the ratification debates[25] highlighted the foregoing assumptions on the few occasions when they turned to the national security provisions of the Constitution. While the Tax Clause occasioned substantial debate,[26] the Raise and Support, Commander-in-Chief, and Militia Clauses clearly aroused popular fears of standing armies and military dictatorship. The core of the Antifederalists' arguments against these provisions of the proposed constitution was that a government that "has all power and both purse and Sword has the absolute Gov't of all other Bodies and they must exist at the will and pleasure of the Superior."[27] Time and again, supporters of the Constitution rebutted this argument by stressing the vesting and limits of the power of the purse in the Congress.

The first line of defense to the sword-and-purse argument was that sword and purse were sharply divided between the executive and Congress in the proposed constitution. The Antifederalists had their maxim wrong, Madison argued in the Virginia Convention:

> Does it mean that the sword and purse ought not to be trusted in the hands of the same government? This cannot be the meaning; for there never was, and I can say there never will be, an efficient government, in which both are not vested. The only rational meaning is, that the sword and purse are not to be given to the same member. Apply it to the British government . . . . The sword is in the hands of the British king; the purse in the hands of the Parliament. It is so in America, as far as any analogy can exist. . . . The purse is in the hands of the representatives of the people. They have appropriation of all moneys.[28]

The correct maxim, Hamilton told the New York Convention, is that the purse and the sword shall not be placed in either the legislature or executive "singly," not that they cannot be divided between separate branches of a single government.[29]

The Antifederalists' recital of the British prohibition against standing armies was equally mistaken. The prohibition (as incorporated in the British Bill of Rights) was against "the raising or keeping of a standing army within the kingdom in time of peace, *unless with the consent of Parliament.*"[30] The concern of the British prohibition was that the king might raise a standing army on his own, not that a popularly elected legislature might raise one for command by the executive.[31] The Antifederalists' analogy was flawed by overextension. As Hamilton observed, "[t]he principles which had taught us to be jealous of the power of an hereditary monarch were by an injudicious excess extended to the representatives of the people in their popular assemblies."[32]

But what was to prevent the executive from misusing the sword, once a standing army had been created with legislative consent? Even as strong an advocate of presidential power as Hamilton acknowledged that "[i]t is of the nature of war to increase the executive at the expense of the legislative authority."[33] The answer, Madison said, lay in the power of the purse, "the most complete and effectual weapon with which any constitution can arm the immediate representatives of the people, for obtaining every redress of every grievance, and for carrying into effect every just and salutary measure."[34] With even less comparative power than the Congress, the British Commons had successfully deployed this device to curb the dictatorial tendencies of their monarchs, as Wilson Nicholas told the Virginia Convention, in a passage worth quoting at length for its detailed reliance on British history:

> This superiority resulted from their having the power of withholding or granting supplies. What will put this in a still clearer point of view, is, that the House of Commons were not originally possessed of these powers. The history of the English Parliament will show that the great degree of power which they now possess was acquired from beginnings so small, that nothing but the innate weight of the power of the people, when lodged with their representatives, could have effected it. In the reign of Edward I., in the year 1295, the House was first called by legal authority; they were then confined to giving their assent barely to supplies to the crown. In the reign of Edward II., they first annexed petitions to the bills by which they granted subsidies. Under Edward III., they declared they would not in future acknowledge any law to which they had not consented . . . . Under Henry IV., they refused supplies until an answer had been given to their petition; and have increased their powers, in succeeding reigns, to such a degree, that they entirely control the operation of the government, even in those cases where the king's prerogative gave him, nominally, the sole direction. . . . The House of Commons have succeeded . . . by withholding supplies; they can, by this power, put a stop to the operations of government, which they have been able to direct as they pleased. This power has enabled them to triumph over all obstacles; it is so important that it will in the end swallow up all others.[35]

If the House of Commons, with less power than the Congress, could so resist the Crown, then surely so could Congress resist a president intent on abusing his powers.

Command of the military was given to the president, but, said a delegate in the North Carolina Convention debates, Congress "could certainly prevent any abuse of that authority in the President—[for] they alone had the means of supporting armies."[36] Therein lay a major difference also between the British monarch and the American president, in theory at least; the former's power "extends to the *declaring* of war and the *raising* and *regulating* fleets and armies—all which, by the Constitution under consideration, would appertain to the legislature," Hamilton noted.[37] In this chorus of voices stressing the legislative power of the purse, George Mason's rebuttal during the New York Convention was drowned out: "[I]n time of war, [Congress] must and ought to raise an army, which will be numerous, or otherwise, according to the nature of the war, and then the President is to command without any control."[38]

Yet the power of the purse was no answer to the apprehension of a *legislatively* approved military dictatorship. Congress alone has the means of supporting armies, but by what means can Congress be controlled? Here, Hamilton stressed the two-year limit on appropriations for the army.[39]

> The legislature of the United States will be *obliged* by this provision, once at least every two years, to deliberate upon the propriety of keeping a military force on foot; to come to a new resolution on the point; and to declare their sense of the matter by a formal vote in the face of their constituents. They are not *at liberty* to vest in the executive department permanent funds for the support of an army, if they were even incautious enough to be willing to repose in it so improper a confidence. As the spirit of party in different degrees must be expected to infect all political bodies, there will be, no doubt, persons in the

> national legislature willing enough to arraign the measures and criminate the views of the majority. The provision for the support of a military force will always be a favorable topic for declamation. As often as the question comes forward, the public attention will be roused and attracted to the subject by the party in opposition . . . .[40]

Both the electorate and the states could thus be aroused to arm themselves against the threat. Since "[s]chemes to subvert liberties of a great community *require time* to mature for their execution," Hamilton added, the alarm will be timely.[41]

These arguments did not allay the Antifederalists' fears. They proposed numerous amendments to the military sections of the proposed constitution,[42] most of which aimed at limiting Congress rather than the executive, especially in relation to standing peacetime armies and control of the militia.[43] But the predominance of amendments aimed at congressional power is itself evidence of the contemporary perceptions of the relative war powers of president and Congress in the Constitution; "[t]he Ratifiers' stingy concept of the executive as commander in chief was . . . reflected in the concern that Congress, not the President, was the potential military despot."[44] In the end, the states only approved what became the Second and Third Amendments, and the power of the purse in national security affairs was ratified without change.

4

The Early Practice: From 1789 to 1809

The framing of the Constitution was a great theoretical enterprise. But the first congresses and presidents still had to make a real government. Their practice, and the construction they placed on the constitution they had framed, is entitled to great weight in interpreting the Constitution.[1]

Fortunately, unlike some of the appropriation history we surveyed in the first three chapters, the appropriation and spending practice of the first Congresses and presidents has been thoroughly explored elsewhere.[2] Drawing on that work, we here focus briefly on those aspects of that early practice of most significance for the power of the purse in national security. We find that the early practice established a template for lump-sum national security appropriations, discretionary executive transfers between national security accounts, and *ex post facto* appropriation for national security exigencies. The practice also produced a consensus that presidential spending without appropriation for national security emergencies was sometimes necessary, but it was also unlawful unless Congress ratified it after the fact.

Appropriations in Gross and Mingled

Although the fiscal Constitution left no doubt of the primacy of the Congress, the House in the first Congress found itself unable to estimate expenditures without the help of the executive. It therefore directed Secretary of the Treasury Alexander Hamilton, to report "an estimate of the sums requisite to be appropriated during the present session of Congress."[3] He quickly reported as ordered, and the first appropriations act adopted his estimates and enacted his four aggregate categories into a single section:

> That there be appropriated for the service of the present year, . . . the following sums, viz. A sum not exceeding two hundred and sixteen thousand dollars for defraying the expenses of the civil list, under the late and present government; a sum not exceeding one hundred and thirty-seven thousand dollars for defraying the expenses of the department of war; a sum not exceeding one hundred and ninety thousand dollars for discharging warrants issued by the late board of treasury, and remaining unsatisfied; and a sum not exceeding ninety-six thousand dollars for paying the pensions to invalids.[4]

Congress thus chose to make a lump-sum appropriation—or appropriation "in gross"—for the War Department in an "omnibus" bill, a bill that combined appropriations for divergent purposes. It followed suit in the next two annual appropriations.[5]

No one objected to the constitutionality of lump-sum appropriation, but the 1790 bill did draw an objection to the process. Senator Maclay complained that "[t]he appropriations were all in gross," that he could not get a copy of the bill, and that it was enacted in an unseemly hurry.[6] His principal criticism, however, was that such lump-sum appropriations gave the executive unwarranted spending discretion. In fact, however, that discretion was not unlimited; it was understood that the funds would be spent in accordance with the executive's estimates and pursuant to separate authorizations, as well as to general laws governing officers and their rates of pay.[7]

Nevertheless, Maclay's critique struck a sympathetic chord. The next appropriation, by incorporating the executive's estimates into the statutory text and dividing the military appropriation under twelve heads, was more specific.[8] When the House offered an equally or more specific bill for 1793, the Senate initially balked, amending it in favor of a single lump sum and a smaller sum for unspecified contingencies. An unidentified participant in the ensuing debate argued that such appropriation in gross would vest too much discretion in the secretary of war and, by keeping expenditures out of public view, make it difficult to require a public accounting.[9] The Senate gave in, and the more specific House bill was enacted.[10]

A national security crisis prompted the next stage of this emerging debate. In 1793, the Whiskey Rebellion broke out in western Pennsylvania against the excise tax. Acting pursuant to statutory authorization,[11] President Washington called out the militia to suppress the rebellion. Because Congress had not appropriated funds to this end, the call-up was provisionally funded out of the general appropriation for the War Department. Congress eventually appropriated specific funds for the operation after the fact,[12] implicitly ratifying the prior "mingling" or transfer of funds from the general appropriation.

It was left to Hamilton's successor as secretary of treasury, Oliver Wolcott, Jr., to articulate the rationale for this transfer of appropriated funds to unspecified uses:

> By far the greatest part of the expenditures for military purposes are . . . unsusceptible of such a minute distribution, as are appropriations for other objects. . . . It has been my opinion, that the appropriations for mere military purposes, ought to be general grants of such sums, as are from time to time deemed requisite for the public service, to be issued according to exigencies, and applied and accounted for according to law . . . .[13]

As Republican Albert Gallatin disapprovingly put it, sums that had been specifically appropriated under various heads for the military were "considered as making but one general appropriation for [the support of the army and the navy] . . . , and . . . the sums, thus appropriated, were indiscriminately applicable to every distinct object of the expenditure embraced under those two general heads."[14]

Defenders of the practice of mingling or transferring funds laid special stress on the need for flexibility in national security. "Would it not be absurd to confine the appropriation so strictly to the article itself," a Federalist member of Congress asked, "that if the provisions or tents of the Army should be destroyed by flood or fire, they could not be replaced, but the Army must remain without any covering, even though there should be a sufficient surplus or saving from other articles?"[15] Another member distinguished "the Military Establishment," with its emergencies, from "the Civil List Establishment," where many expenses "could be ascertained to a certainty."[16] Alexander Hamilton later sounded the same note as "Lucius Crassus," defending the Federalist practices from an implied attack in Thomas Jefferson's first annual message to Congress.[17]

Gallatin objected vigorously. If Washington needed appropriations for the militia during the Whiskey Rebellion, he should have convened Congress to that end.

> It might be a defect in the law, authorizing the expense, not to have provided the means; but that defect should have been remedied by the only competent authority, by convening Congress. The necessity of the measure may in the mind of the Executive have superseded every other consideration. The popularity of the transaction may have thrown a veil over its illegality. But it should by no means be drawn hereafter as a precedent.[18]

Gallatin also cut straight to the heart of the problem of transfers. If the executive could transfer funds freely without regard to specific appropriation heads, "there was no check to the expenditure, except the aggregate amount of all the moneys appropriated for the Military Establishment . . . ."[19] Unrestricted transfer, in other words, directly threatened congressional control of military adventures by the executive.[20]

Gallatin was not alone in his views. As early as 1793, Representative William B. Giles had offered a resolution "[t]hat it is essential to the due administration of the Government of the United States, that laws making specific appropriations of money should be strictly observed by the administrator of the finances thereof."[21] After the Whiskey Rebellion, Gallatin succeeded in putting through a resolution requiring an accounting of the spending on the militia.[22] In the 1797 military appropriation bill, Congress tightened the appropriation formula, specifying individual items of appropriation and adding the stricture "which sums shall be solely applied to the objects for which they are respectively appropriated."[23] These successes prompted Wolcott to complain to his predecessor, Hamilton, that "[t]he management of the Treasury becomes more and more difficult. The Legislature will not pass laws in gross. Their appropriations are minute; Gallatin, to whom they yield, is evidently intending to break down this department, by charging it with an impracticable detail."[24] Wolcott's plaint may well have been the grandfather of modern charges of "congressional micromanagement."

But, as Casper concludes, though Gallatin may have won some battles, he lost the war.[25] The War Department continued to transfer funds, and Congress declined to take action against the secretary of war.[26] After the House again placed the restrictive appropriation formula in the military appropriation bill for 1798, the Senate amended it in favor of a lump sum and struck the "solely applied" language. This time the Senate prevailed, and Congress thus effectively acquiesced in the transfer policy.[27] The appropriations in 1800 and 1801 also avoided the more restrictive language.[28] By the time Jefferson took office in 1801, the transfer of appropriations was "settled custom,"[29] an extrastatutory practice in which Congress had acquiesced.

Nor was the custom abandoned by Jefferson, despite his attack on the previous administration's misapplication of public funds and his rhetorical commitment to the principle of specific appropriations in his first annual message to Congress.[30] Not only did his administration continue the practice of transfers, but it also engaged in some spending "in anticipation of appropriation"—deficiency spending—especially for national security purposes.[31] By 1804, Jefferson wrote Gallatin, now secretary of the treasury, approving of Congress's practice of appropriating "in gross . . . [and] binding up the Executive discretion only by the sum, and the object generalized to a certain degree."[32]

Jefferson's defenders in Congress explained that his rhetorical commitment to specific appropriations was never intended to apply to national security spending. "[I]n military affairs, it was impossible to calculate with precision," Representative Nelson explained.[33] "Ten thousand things might arise which could not be anticipated by any human wisdom. It followed that, although an adherence to specific appropriations was highly desirable in all cases where it was practicable, as in meeting civil expenses, . . . for military purposes, they must necessarily go in the old way," that is, by lump sum.[34]

The perception that Jefferson and the Republicans held to their rhetoric about appropriations is sometimes fueled by the act of March 3, 1809, that they left behind. One provision of this act codified the specific appropriation doctrine that "the sums appropriated by law for each branch of expenditure in the several departments shall be solely applied to the objects for which they are respectively appropriated and to no other."[35] Less well known, however, was another provision of the same act that expressly authorized the president to transfer funds between accounts in the same department during congressional recesses, on the condition that he thereafter report the transfer to Congress.[36] The act thus embraced a principle of specific appropriations that was diluted in practice by appropriations for lump sums and contingency accounts in national security, at the same time that it raised to the level of statutory authority a transfer policy that had been customary. Far from reining in the executive, the act, in Lucius Wilmerding's words, "ushered in a period of laxity in the control of government spending during which the Executive discovered so many legal or quasi-legal means of varying the appropriation of public money that it almost never found itself compelled to resort to an admittedly illegal means."[37]

Emergency National Security Spending Power and Authority

When Washington called up the militia to suppress the Whiskey Rebellion, he was able to transfer funds appropriated from other accounts to pay for the call-up. When he authorized Governor St. Clair to raise militia to fight the Wabash Indians, he acted on statutory authority and Congress appropriated the necessary funds after the fact.[38] But suppose that military necessity required immediate action for which there was neither prior congressional authority nor appropriation? The early debates about specific appropriations also touched on this question and, despite differences in nuance, yielded a consensus answer.

Opposing Republican Giles's specific appropriation resolution in the 1793 debates, Federalist William Smith insisted

> that there may be cases of sufficient urgency to justify a departure from it, and to make it the duty of the Legislature to indemnify an officer; as if an adherence would in particular cases, and under particular circumstances, prove ruinous to the public credit, or prevent the taking of measures essential to the public safety, against invasion or insurrection. In cases of that nature, and which cannot be foreseen by the Legislature nor guarded against, a discretionary authority must be deemed to reside in the President, or some other Executive officer, to be exercised by the public good . . . .[39]

The Republicans did not disagree, despite the bitter debate about the application of the specific appropriation principle in less dire circumstances. Congressman William Findley, a strong proponent of the principle, conceded that "an Executive officer, pressed by some urgent and unexpected necessity, may be induced to depart from the unauthorized path of duty, and have great merit in so doing."[40] Giles himself reluctantly admitted subsequently that "imperious circumstances . . . which compelled a violation of appropriation . . . might sometimes exist . . . ."[41] Finally, even Gallatin tempered his 1798 attack on the secretary of war's spending in excess of appropriation by excepting the "case of necessity."[42]

That necessity for national security might give the president the power to spend without appropriation, however, did not mean that he had the constitutional authority or what Wilmerding in one place mischaracterizes as "the *right* . . . to transcend the laws of appropriation."[43] After all, Smith first asserted his theory in the context of a duty in the legislature to "indemnify an officer," suggesting a need for subsequent legislative action. No less a proponent of executive power than Alexander Hamilton also stressed that "provisory measures will often be unavoidable, and *confidence must sometimes be reposed in an after legislative sanction and provision.*"[44] The president, in other words, has the power, and perhaps the moral and political obligation, to respond to national security emergencies even before he has authorization or appropriation from Congress, but he must respond at his own risk, subject to subsequent "legislative sanction and provision." If Congress does not ratify his act and appropriate the necessary funds, the act stands outside the law and the actor subject to disgrace, personal liability, or impeachment.

It follows that the president whose hand is forced by necessity must report to Congress and seek ratification as soon as possible. Thus, Republican Congressman Findley remarked "in such emergency, the officer so acting will embrace the earliest opportunity to explain the matter and obtain a justification. . . ."[45] Congressman Giles also asserted that when the executive spends without specific appropriation, "the causes of it ought to be truly imperious, and ought to be stated immediately to Congress, who was the only judge of the propriety of the measure, and not the man who had usurped their decision."[46]

The attack by the British warship *Leopard* on the American frigate *Chesapeake* in 1807 presented such a case, in Jefferson's judgment. With war seemingly imminent and Congress in recess, Jefferson ordered the purchase of timber for one hundred gunboats, although none had been authorized by Congress, and the purchase on credit of ingredients for gunpowder "on the presumption that Congress will sanction it."[47] Unlike the military initiative against the Wabash Indians, these preparations were unauthorized; unlike the suppression of the Whiskey Rebellion, this spending was wholly without appropriation.

When Congress convened three months later, Jefferson made no claim of "previous sanction by law" for his initiatives.

> The moment our peace was threatened, I deemed it indispensable to secure a greater provision of those articles of military stores with which our magazines were not sufficiently furnished. To have awaited a previous and special sanction by law would have lost occasions which might not be retrieved. . . . I trust that the Legislature, feeling the same anxiety for the safety of our country, so materially advanced by this precaution, will approve, when done, what they would have seen so important to be done, if then assembled.[48]

Thus, although he had not called Congress back into session as soon as he might, he reported the action to them when they reassembled and sought their sanction to make it lawful, which he subsequently received in an *ex post facto* appropriation.[49]

If an emergency thus might sometimes necessitate national security spending without either authorization or appropriation, the resulting power of the executive was nevertheless narrowly drawn. First, of course, there had to be a true emergency, threatening war, invasion, or insurrection. Second, the executive acted at his own risk, subject to subsequent approval or disapproval by Congress. Third, he was obliged to seek that approval at the earliest opportunity.

This law of necessity thus placed a heavy burden on the executive. "The line of discrimination between cases may be difficult," Jefferson wrote after he left office, "but the good officer is bound to draw it at his own peril, and throw himself on the justice of his country and the rectitude of his motives."[50]

On the other hand, our previous survey of the actual appropriation and spending practice of the first congresses and presidents shows that in most cases, national security exigencies could be met adequately by stretching, rather than breaking statutory and customary appropriation law.[51] And when the president did break it, the emergency itself would prove the "rectitude of his motives" and probably rally the country, and the Congress, behind him, as the *Chesapeake* case shows.[52]

II

THE MECHANICS OF NATIONAL SECURITY APPROPRIATIONS AND SPENDING

This part of the book describes and assesses a labyrinth of mechanisms through which Congress "provide[s] for the common defense."

We begin in chapter 5 with a brief step-by-step description of the textbook model of the national security appropriation process. We show that this model, if it ever was the reality, has broken down over time. Our review of the evolution of the national security appropriation process traces the collapse of the customary bifurcation of the legislative process into authorization and appropriation stages with discrete policymaking and fiscal responsibilities. Although that collapse is not unique to national security, or to contemporary times,[1] it has generated a great deal of controversy and has contributed to the confusion concerning the legal effect of national security appropriations. After this historical review, we describe a subspecies of the national security appropriation process—the highly secretive process for funding the nation's intelligence community.

The national security appropriation process has become a regular forum for the short-term resolution of significant national security policy disputes, sometimes at the cost of careful deliberation of the underlying policy issues. In the main, the short-term solutions have been to control national security activities by restricting the use of funds. Often the restrictions take the form of floor- or conference-generated amendments to an appropriation. These amendments are frequently attached to continuing resolutions, catchall spending provisions that take the place of regular appropriations for all or part of a fiscal year.

In chapter 6 we assess national security appropriation restrictions generally and as they were employed in deciding the Contra funding issue. Appropriation restrictions and continuing resolutions offer advantages over the traditional process by circumventing authorizing committees and a host of parliamentary restrictions and by avoiding presidential vetoes when a funding restriction is attached to legislation that the president needs.

Chapter 7 completes our treatment of the preenactment national security appropriation process by describing how nonstatutory controls—reporting requirements, opportunities for committee consultation or veto, and other devices—influence the formal process and national security spending. We also consider and ultimately dismiss constitutional objections to nonstatutory controls.

The maze of national security appropriation processes does not by any means end when Congress enacts an appropriation. If anything, the arcane processes and complex legal maneuvering only increase when the spending side of national security appropriations is examined. Chapter 8 describes the lump-sum appropriation and other special devices, including impoundment, reprogramming, and budget transfers, by which Congress confers broad discretion on the national security agencies to spend outside specific appropriations. We show that Congress has itself by statute and custom relaxed the purse strings by vesting broad discretion in the executive for national security spending outside of specific appropriations.

5

The Evolution of the National Security Appropriation Process

The Textbook Model

Congress exercises what we call the "appropriation power" by a range of actions providing funds for national security purposes.[1] According to budget theory, the appropriation process follows a fixed chronological sequence. First the executive requests funds. Next, after deliberation, Congress authorizes the programs and activities for which the funds are sought. Typically, an *authorization* "sets up or continues the legal operation of a Federal program or agency either indefinitely or for a specific period of time or sanctions a particular type of obligation or expenditure within a program."[2] An *appropriation authorization* "authorizes the appropriation of funds to implement organic [enabling] legislation,"[3] even though an appropriation may be enacted without or in excess of a limit imposed by an authorization.[4]

Congress then enacts a separate *appropriation,* legislation "that permits Federal agencies to incur obligations or to make payments out of the Treasury for specified purposes,"[5] usually though not always after enacting the authorization.

Theoretically, the process ends when the executive spends the funds appropriated, often with considerable discretion. However, an appropriation may "earmark" the appropriated funds by restricting "the maximum or minimum amount that may be obligated or expended for specific purposes."[6] When a restriction applies only to funds appropriated by the legislation in which the restriction appears, the *appropriation limitation* is permitted as inherent in the appropriation power, recognized as such in the House rules.[7] When a restriction applies to other spending as well, however, it may be subject to procedural objection in one or both houses of Congress.[8] Whether a restriction runs afoul of congressional rules or is merely an unobjectionable appropriation limitation is frequently a difficult question.[9]

An appropriation restriction may appear in an authorization or in an appropriation as a general provision or proviso.[10] It may also be added to an appropriation by amendment, or *rider.*[11] Some scholars use *limitations rider* to refer to any restrictive amendment to an appropriation, whether or not it is subject to procedural objection in one or both houses.[12] We will use *limitation* more narrowly to be consistent with the usage in the House rules, and use *appropriation restriction* to speak generically of any restriction on the use of funds wherever it appears.

Like the overall budget process, the national security appropriation process has a textbook model.[13] The executive branch formulates requests for funds through its national security and foreign assistance agencies, mainly the Department of Defense (DOD), the Department of Energy, the State Department, and the intelligence community.[14] The president forwards the proposals along with the rest of his annual budget to the Congress. He then prepares and submits to Congress recommended authorization and appropriation bills. The committees with national security responsibility in the House and Senate must recommend and secure passage of authorizations. They include the House and Senate Armed Services Committees, the House Foreign Affairs and Senate Foreign Relations Committees, and the House and Senate Intelligence Committees. The authorizations may be for one or more years and may recommend funding levels for the requested activities.

Thereafter Congress must enact separate appropriation bills before any money can be spent. The House and Senate Appropriations Committees and their relevant subcommittees are principally responsible for this task, although the Joint Economic Committee and the House and Senate Budget Committees may also become involved.

Upon enactment of an appropriation bill, the defense agencies in the executive branch complete the traditional portrait of the national security appropriation process by spending the funds in accordance with the prescriptions contained in the authorization and appropriation. The authorizing committees would have recommended the policies which shape the national security activities, which would then be funded or not on the basis of fiscal concerns considered by the appropriations committees. Through their annual fiscal year appropriations, the national defense agencies are thus granted budget authority to commit the treasury to pay for their obligations.[15]

The early appropriation process for military affairs, described in the next section, approximated the textbook model. Deviations did occur and riders occasionally imposed conditions on spending before 1865, but the process remained essentially intact. However, as we show in the following section, the customary process gradually devolved, as political turf wars and interbranch wrangling contributed to a growing use of riders in the late nineteenth and early twentieth centuries. We then describe how significant statutory reform in 1921, aimed at restoring the customary two-step authorization-appropriation process, had little impact on the devolving custom. Programmatic legislation and permanent authorizations relegated the traditional appropriation process to a minor role. We next evaluate ongoing efforts at statutory reform of budgeting, beginning in 1974, as attempts to reinvigorate congressional primacy in fiscal affairs only complicated an already bewildering appropriation process. By the 1980s, the traditional bifurcated process was barely functioning as continuing resolutions, a species of omnibus spending legislation, dominated the process for funding the nation's national security activities. The size, complexity, and urgency of continuing resolutions have only further burdened efforts to bring careful deliberation to the national security appropriation process. We conclude the chapter by describing the special appropriation process for the intelligence community.

The Pre–Civil War Period

Judging by the text of the Constitution, all authorization and appropriation measures are simply "legislation," not distinct from one another.[16] Nonetheless the custom of subdividing the legislative process into sequential steps dates from the first appropriation enacted in 1789.[17] Although no House or Senate rules prescribed any distinction between authorization and appropriation bills for almost half a century,[18] the first appropriation, quoted in chapter 4, indicated that appropriations were understood to have a specific content and purpose.[19] It also contained the elements still common in appropriation legislation today: a fixed time for spending the funds, a definite sum of money, and specification of the object of the appropriation.[20] Of equal importance is what was *not* included in the appropriation: authorization for activities or programs, or limits on the uses to which the appropriated funds could be put.

From the beginning, the custom was for appropriations to fund activities already authorized by statute. The first Congress established the Department of War by statute, and specified its organization and duties before separately acting to appropriate funds for the department.[21] Thus, if limitations on the use of funds were desired by Congress, the limiting instructions were placed in the authorization.[22] The idea was based on efficiency; separating authorizations and appropriations helped Congress get its work done and assured that disputes over policy (the work of authorizing committees) would not interfere with providing the funds essential for the operations of government. Nor would the need to fund the government contribute to the enactment of unnecessary or unwise legislation.[23]

In the early years of the nation, the ongoing process of shaping the structures and processes of appropriating money for national security needs produced various short-term "victories" for executive and congressional prerogatives, respectively. Principle and politics influenced these developments, as the tendency to rely upon specificity of appropriations as a means of congressional control over executive branch discretion ebbed and flowed.[24] Although occasional efforts were made early on to add appropriation restrictions,[25] the only major deviation from the divided legislative process took place when Congress passed a special appropriation without a prior authorization, for a single object, such as the construction of specified warships in 1816.[26] Because these special appropriations were so clearly understood as distinct from general supply bills, their ongoing enactment did not upset the overall custom.

During the 1820s and 1830s, early signs appeared that the divided process would collapse. At first, appropriations contained boilerplate limitation language, such as an 1825 military service appropriation that said: "no money appropriated by the act shall be paid to any person for his compensation who is in arrears to the United States, until such person shall have accounted for, and paid into the treasury, all sums for which he may be liable."[27] These limitations were distinguished from "legislation" and, by implication, from policy-making riders, since the power to appropriate by its nature included the power to refuse appropriations or to condition the grant of funds. While "legislation" made new law, "limitations" merely restricted the use of appropriations. So long as the rider was a limitation, Congress had not crossed its own customary line and legislated in an appropriation act.

Legislation in appropriations apparently grew with the government. New agencies and offices sometimes acted without explicit authorization, and Congress occasionally limited or expanded agency authority in their appropriations.[28] Not surprisingly, the practice generated its own momentum, and members came to recognize the tactical advantages of attaching conditions to essential appropriations. As the divided process was increasingly tested and ignored, first the House and then the Senate adopted rules prohibiting certain types of unauthorized appropriations—riders attached to an appropriation for expenses not previously authorized.[29] The House and Senate rules were not self-enforcing and were sometimes ignored.[30] Nor did they purport otherwise to limit setting policy in appropriation bills. Only riders that themselves provided for expenditures not previously authorized were affected.[31] Thus, for example, the rules were not violated when the slavery issue was addressed in an 1856 army appropriation bill that prohibited the deployment of federal troops to enforce territorial law in Kansas.[32]

From the Civil War Through World War I

Throughout the nation's first half century, the integrity of the customary separation of authorization and appropriation was reinforced by the assignment of the two functions to different committees. Authorizations were the responsibility of various functional committees, including the separate committees for naval and army affairs. Appropriations were fashioned by the House Ways and Means and Senate Finance Committees. The magnitude of financing required by the Civil War led Congress to create separate appropriations committees in the House in 1865 and in the Senate in 1867.[33]

These new committees began to usurp the jurisdiction of the substantive committees and often appended restrictions to their regular appropriation bills. They were aided by a House change in its 1837 rule against unauthorized appropriations. In 1876, the "Holman rule" excepted from the general prohibition any "germane" rider which "shall retrench expenditures."[34] Among the most controversial restrictions passed under the guise of retrenchment was one that sought to undercut the Reconstruction laws by barring the use of the army to enforce the civil rights voting laws on election day.[35] The reaction to such measures in Congress was to transfer much of the appropriation jurisdiction to the substantive committees. While this had the desired effect of curtailing the power of the appropriations committees, it also served to weaken the authorization-appropriation distinction, and the number of appropriation restrictions increased significantly.[36]

Moreover, once the appropriation power was assigned to the substantive committees, appropriations dominated the agenda of Congress. The enactment of programmatic legislation became rarer, as Congress began to make national policy simply by appropriating money for federal departments. Detail in the appropriations determined what the departments could do. For example, during the late nineteenth and early twentieth centuries, the army and navy appropriations earmarked funds for the armed forces after the House stripped its Appropriations Committee of its authority over the army and navy budgets and transferred power to the authorization committees.[37] Congress thus began to view its major policy issues as fiscal issues. The World War I experience only confirmed this trend.

From Budget Reform to Budget Reform, 1921–1974

In the wake of World War I, Congress sought to arrest the centralization of power in the authorization committees by enacting the Budget and Accounting Act of 1921.[38] By restoring the power of the appropriations committees, the 1921 act gave new life to the two-step authorization-appropriation process. At the same time, rules changes were made—in the House to further discourage special appropriations reported by authorizing committees,[39] and in the Senate to prohibit its Appropriations Committee from reporting "new or general legislation" in an appropriation bill.[40] Finally, the act centralized executive branch budget submission by authorizing the president, through the newly established Bureau of the Budget (now Office of Management and Budget [OMB]), to submit a national budget each year.[41] Congress also sought to enhance its control over fiscal matters by establishing the General Accounting Office.[42]

As government expanded in the 1920s and then sought to cope with the Great Depression and World War II, important changes occurred, which permanently altered the appropriation process. First, the authorizing committees began to insert "authorized to be appropriated" language in authorizations, thus making explicit what had been implicit—that the creation of a program or activity in authorization legislation sufficed to legitimate a subsequent appropriation. Second, increasingly the authorizations were programmatic, while appropriations were for lump sums to be spent for broad categories of activities or whole programs. These statutes, common during the New Deal and after World War II, delegated massive powers to the implementing agencies to spend "sums as may be necessary." While such statutes typically prescribed how the funds were to be spent, their permanent authorizations were the product of massive delegations of legislative power to executive agencies for programs and activities viewed as important and permanent obligations of the federal government. Separate annual appropriations were required, but there was no need for periodic reauthorization.[43]

Beginning in the 1950s, fears of overly broad delegations in authorizing legislation and ineffective congressional oversight of agency activities led Congress to attempt to enhance control over agencies by relying on temporary, often annual, authorizations.[44] These authorizations are, like those now in effect for national security activities, permanent legislation to which a one-year "authorization of appropriations" is attached.[45] This species of authorization is not "sunset" legislation, since the permanent provisions enacted outside the annual authorization (legislation creating the agency, for example) would survive a failure to renew the authorization. Thus, Congress may simply renew the authorization clause annually without affecting the remainder of the statute, or it may—and often does—use the reauthorization as a means of changing other parts of the authorization. As a means of oversight, annual authorizations permit the substantive committees to influence agency behavior, again at the cost of weakening the integrity of the customary two-step process. Annual appropriations are made, but the authorization often recommends a fixed amount for the appropriation. The real debate is the authorization debate, though it is often a fiscal debate. The appropriation stage, often delayed pending the outcome of the authorization debate, then involves only tinkering.[46]

1974 to the Present

With enactment of the Congressional Budget and Impoundment Control Act in 1974,[47] Congress inserted a third layer, congressional budgeting, into the authorization-appropriation process. The 1974 act, as amended by the Balanced Budget and Emergency Deficit Reduction Act of 1985[48] and the Budget Enforcement Act of 1990,[49] served to further complicate an already bewildering process, while it strengthened the overall fiscal role of Congress.

Budgeting was added to the authorization and appropriation process without reforming the traditional process in light of the new requirements or prescribing the relationship between the processes. The 1974 act created the House and Senate Budget Committees[50] and the Congressional Budget Office (CBO).[51] The CBO serves as Congress's primary resource for information and analysis of fiscal matters, while the new committees prepare aggregate budget resolutions, review the impact of legislation on expenditures, monitor the Congress's fiscal actions, and oversee the CBO.[52]

Under the 1974 act, as amended, the president's proposed budget, which must be submitted on or before the first Monday in February each year,[53] is considered at the same time that Congress is fashioning its own spending goals in a report submitted by the CBO to the House and Senate Budget Committees.[54] Based on the president's budget and Budget Committee recommendations, a nonbinding concurrent budget resolution must be passed by April 15 each year.[55] The budget resolution contains one section dealing with aggregate numbers (total spending, total revenue, total public debt) instead of establishing programs or setting funding levels for activities, and another that subdivides spending goals into twenty-one functional categories (distinct from appropriation categories so as not to threaten the prerogatives of the appropriations committees), including one for national defense.[56]

The Senate and House Budget Committees now assemble the single April 15 budget resolution from February 25 reports from the relevant standing committees detailing each panel's fiscal needs for programs within its purview, the president's budget, informal discussions with members and staff, CBO analyses, and the committees' own assessments.[57] The House and Senate proposals are considered under special fast track rules prescribed by the 1974 act.[58] Once approved, the resolution has appended to it a report that distributes the total spending among functional categories developed by OMB.[59]

This blueprint is intended to guide the authorization, appropriations, and taxing committees in their annual preparation of bills. Because the functional categories employed by the 1974 act do not match up exactly with the subject matter responsibility of the House and Senate committees, a "crosswalk" procedure was developed to permit the budget resolution's figures to be allocated to the proper subcommittees within the appropriations committees.[60]

As the House and Senate Budget Committees examine program details in order to determine spending limits and establish priorities in preparation of their concurrent budget resolutions, efforts are duplicated with the authorization and appropriations committees and turf battles escalate.[61] Authorization and appropriation decisions are still made in the same way, but they are made in the context of a larger blueprint—the congressional budget. Because the deadlines are rarely met and the committees struggle to retain their independent roles in the national security appropriation process, the new budget overlay has not improved the process.[62]

More significant changes were made in the appropriation process with enactment of the Balanced Budget and Emergency Deficit Control Act of 1985.[63] Dubbed "Gramm-Rudman-Hollings" after its principal sponsors, the act itself was the product of a truncated legislative process—it was introduced on the Senate floor without prior committee hearings or floor debate and was attached to a "must pass" bill raising the national debt ceiling.[64] As amended in 1987,[65] the act's deficit reduction goal was to be met through drastic deficit reduction targets, which were in turn to be attained by across-the-board spending cuts. In 1990, the process was amended again by the Budget Enforcement Act of 1990 (BEA), enacted as part of the Omnibus Budget Reconciliation Act of 1990 (OBRA).[66]

The deficit reduction procedures prescribed by the BEA substantially revised Gramm-Rudman-Hollings and the 1974 act by altering the congressional budget process and establishing guidelines for measuring compliance with BEA requirements. BEA first divides the budget into discretionary programs and direct spending and receipts, mutually exclusive categories or "fire walls." For 1991 to 1995, spending must be at least "deficit-neutral" and deficit targets or "caps" must be met, through sequesters—automatic, across-the-board reductions—if necessary.[67] As one of the categories of discretionary programs, defense, like international and domestic spending, has an independent budget ceiling for three years—savings made in defense may not be used to increase domestic or international spending.[68] A breach of the defense limit would prompt a defense sequester, and so on. However, an exemption from sequester for military personnel expenses[69] effectively means that only about 40 percent of defense discretionary outlays are sequestrable.

In theory, then, the national security appropriation process is restored to its customary status by the BEA. Budget decisions will be made within strict spending limits prescribed by statute, but the appropriators will actually determine spending levels. In fact, the traditional model continues to be the exception rather than the rule. The House and Senate Appropriations Defense Subcommittees have increasingly found their role limited by the actions of the House and Senate Armed Services Committees.

Since the early 1980s, the armed services committees' authorization bills have set ceilings on the amount that could be appropriated for every major component of the defense budget except personnel. The high-profile defense spending issue for 1992—the B-2 stealth bomber—reflected this trend. Although the appropriations subcommittees supported the president's request for $3.2 billion to build four additional B-2s, the final appropriation reflects the armed services committees' preference—$1.8 billion to maintain production of previously authorized bombers, but no new production. The stipulations in the armed services committee reports are not part of the finished legislation—the authorization speaks of lump sums for broad categories—and thus have no binding legal effect. However, the *in terrorem* effect of the committee reports usually serves to determine executive branch behavior. Although the appropriations subcommittees occasionally debate broad policy issues and may even insert a limitation or rider to control spending, the committees' normal role is to audit defense expenditures.[70] The budget committees, along with the BEA, which locked in many budget decisions, have contributed to a situation where appropriations committees' spending decisions vary only slightly from the spring budget resolutions approved by the House and Senate.[71] The fiscal year 1992 defense budget was approved at essentially the level set by the spring agreement.[72]

Initially, it was thought that the BEA would enhance the influence of the appropriations committees. Instead, the president's Office of Management and Budget has gained power as the final arbiter of whether Congress is staying within the spending caps.[73] In the past the appropriations committees and their subcommittees could wield authority merely by dangling favorite projects before members of Congress to obtain desired results. Now, OMB may—and often has—involved itself in details of the spending decisions. Ironically, one result of BEA spending caps and the ban on transfers between budget categories has been to produce House agreement on spending bills earlier in the fiscal calendar than in recent years.[74]

In the end, the statutory reforms have not caused Congress and the president to curb the deficit, nor to come to terms with fiscal decisions in accord with fiscal year deadlines. Once again, fiscal year 1992 began with no budget. Three continuing resolutions were passed to buy time to finish the appropriations.[75]

The Emergence of Continuing Resolutions

Between 1876, when the first continuing resolution was passed,[76] and 1981, continuing resolutions were short-term funding measures, providing funding at last year's or some similar agreed-upon levels until the regular appropriation bill could be finished.[77] Since then, the use of continuing resolutions has expanded rapidly. The reliance on continuing resolutions in the 1980s and 1990s is a unique development, whereby the largest spending bills in our history authorize *and* appropriate for much of the government, including national security.[78] The emergence of continuing resolutions is attributable to many of the same problems which explain the general devolution of the two-step legislative process—the preoccupation in Congress with debt and other fiscal issues, bicameral and legislative-executive conflicts over policy and priorities, an inability to comply with budgeting deadlines imposed by the 1974 act and its progeny[79] and, in light of the harsh sequestration imposed by the BEA, reticence in bringing regular appropriations to the floor for fear of cuts.

Continuing resolutions facilitate appropriation restrictions in part because they are not "general appropriation bills" and are thus not subject to the House rule limiting riders.[80] In addition, because continuing resolutions are considered and approved under considerable time pressure, they offer an attractive vehicle for amendments that would otherwise have a difficult path to enactment.

Finally, resort to continuing resolutions substantially enhances the power of the appropriations committees.[81] The appropriations committees work with the rules committees to draft the resolution, encumbering it with whatever legislation the members favor, then restricting floor debate and amendment through rules established by the rules committee. However, floor action can and at times has defeated these tight rules. For example, in 1985 the House inserted the two-hundred-page Comprehensive Crime Control Act of 1984 into the resolution and the Senate accepted 125 of 158 amendments offered to it.[82]

Black Budgets: The Appropriation Process for the Intelligence Community

The process of funding the National Foreign Intelligence Program (NFIP) contrasts significantly with the general defense appropriation process.[83] Pursuant to the Central Intelligence Agency Act of 1949,[84] the intelligence community does not seek or obtain regular appropriation from Congress. Instead, funds are secretly transferred to it from the appropriation accounts of other agencies.[85]

In the formulation of the president's budget, the requests of the intelligence agencies are first coordinated by representatives of sponsoring agencies before being submitted to OMB for careful review of justifications and further coordination within the intelligence community.[86] Once the president's budget is submitted to Congress, the portion for the intelligence agencies is segregated from the rest and discussed by members of the House and Senate Intelligence Committees and the relevant defense appropriations subcommittees meeting in executive session.[87] The committees hold closed hearings at which agency staff answer questions and supply additional detail for the written budget justifications.

Once an NFIP budget is approved by the intelligence and defense appropriation committees, a classified schedule of the authorizations and an explanation of the budget issues considered by the intelligence committees is made available to the executive branch and to the appropriations and armed services committees. This classified schedule lists the recommended allocation for all intelligence programs. When floor debate on the larger appropriation bills begins, the NFIP budget is hidden within the recommended appropriations for other agencies, recently DOD. These appropriation accounts are inflated to reflect the pending budget transfers, but the members of Congress who are debating the budget and voting on appropriations do not know which figures are inflated or by how much. Congress is thus only mechanically involved in approving the budget for the intelligence community, and its action in approving the remainder of the budget is clouded with the shell game of hiding the intelligence figures within other accounts.

After a budget is approved by Congress and the president, OMB receives instructions from the chair of the House Appropriations Committee as to the amounts and sources of budget transfers to be made to the intelligence agencies.[88] OMB then carries out the transfers through its own highly secretive process.

Because of a dispute over post–Iran-Contra reforms,[89] the fiscal 1991 intelligence authorization bill[90] was vetoed by President Bush.[91] While the fiscal 1991 NFIP budget was included mainly within DOD accounts as usual, the result of the veto was that there was no authorization for intelligence spending. The intelligence community nevertheless continued to function, while lawyers for the CIA, Justice Department, and Intelligence Committees argued about whether a 1985 amendment to the Defense Act was satisfied by the DOD authorization. That amendment stated that "appropriated funds available to an intelligence agency may be obligated or expended to an intelligence activity only if those funds were specifically authorized by the Congress for use for such activities."[92]

The legal issue, whether the DOD authorization's classified annex, which aggregates intelligence programs under line items without defining the programs, constitutes the specific authorization required by the 1985 law, was not resolved. In the ten months before a new authorization agreement was reached, the NFIP units were simply instructed to spend in accord with the 1991 bill limits.[93]

In the fiscal 1992 intelligence authorization cycle, Congress took tentative steps toward more openness in the NFIP budget. Until conferees compromised in the face of a veto threat, the 1992 authorization would have required that the administration publicly reveal the overall NFIP budget figure.[94] The 1992 and 1993 acts recommend publication of that figure.[95]

6

The Uses and Abuses of Riders and Continuing Resolutions in National Security

Congress has been familiar with the employment of restrictions in the national security appropriation process since the early years of the nation.[1] Although riders were occasionally employed to thwart constitutional exercises of the president's power in the nineteenth century, especially during the turbulent presidency of Andrew Johnson, they were not used regularly to control the president's engagement of the military abroad until President Nixon's secret bombing of Cambodia in 1970. Since then, appropriation restrictions to control the president—and its attendant controversy—have become almost routine. Although Congress has supplied various internal correctives along the way to curb the use of riders, these devices have been largely ineffectual.

A Historical Review

While pre–Civil War riders generally reflect attempts by one House of Congress to coerce the other,[2] later riders were widely employed to coerce the president. There were reportedly 387 riders attached to appropriation bills between 1862 and 1875.[3] Although many earlier restrictions were introduced and defeated, their objectives were often obtained. Thus, it is clear that Congress has long been familiar with the device and its potential utility.[4]

In the midst of battles between congressional Republicans and President Andrew Johnson over Reconstruction, for example, Secretary of War Stanton and General of the Army Ulysses S. Grant collaborated with Republican leaders to add restrictions to the 1867 army appropriations bill designed to curb Johnson's use of the military to rescue the South and sabotage the congressional Reconstruction program.[5] The restrictions specified that Grant as commanding general of the army could not be unwillingly assigned to duty outside of Washington without the Senate's consent, that all orders to the army from the president or secretary of war must pass through Grant, and that the Southern state militias be disbanded.[6] Johnson believed that the restrictions were unconstitutional, and he wanted to veto the bill. At a cabinet meeting everyone except

Stanton and Secretary of State Seward, agreed that the bill should be vetoed. They argued that to deprive the army of funds in order to enforce the restrictions would be demoralizing to the army. Johnson reluctantly signed the bill and prepared a written protest.[7] The 1878 provision forbidding the deployment of army personnel to enforce the Reconstruction laws at the polls on election day is another example.[8]

On occasion, Congress boldly challenged presidential power by enacting riders. In 1913, Congress amended a deficiency appropriation bill to forbid the president from participating in any international conference without specific statutory authorization[9] even though this act may have interfered with the president's Article II power.[10] Congress continued to appropriate funds and thus consented to the practice anyway.

World War I saw an increase in the use of appropriation restrictions related to war activities. In 1916, before the United States entered the war, Congress amended a navy appropriation act to state that the policy of the United States was "to adjust and settle its international disputes through mediation or arbitration, to the end that war may be honorably avoided."[11] The rider also requested the president to call an international conference for the purpose of establishing a dispute settlement mechanism and to discuss disarmament.[12] Although funds were appropriated for this purpose, the amendment was ignored by the president and its provisions never had any effect.[13]

Navy appropriation act restrictions in 1921 and 1924 similarly charged the president with convening an international conference to pursue an agreement for a reduction in naval forces. The 1921 act apparently influenced President Harding's decision to call the Conference on Limitation of Armament.[14] Similar actions were taken by Congress during and after World War II and the Korean War, particularly in bills concerning foreign aid and United States participation in international organizations.[15]

Before the Vietnam War, no enacted national security appropriation restriction sought directly to control the president's use of military force abroad. However, when President Nixon's secret bombing of Cambodia in 1970 was reported in the press, Congress acted to curb the president through the appropriation process, first in 1971, with the Cooper-Church amendment to the Foreign Military Sales Act,[16] and then in 1973 and 1974, by enacting provisions in the Foreign Assistance Act of 1973,[17] the DOD authorization and appropriation acts for 1974 and 1975,[18] the State Department Authorization Act of 1973,[19] a fiscal year 1974 continuing resolution,[20] a supplemental appropriation act in 1973[21] and the Hughes-Ryan amendment of 1974.[22]

Each of these provisions except Hughes-Ryan was directed at prohibiting the expenditure of appropriated funds for United States military action in Vietnam, Cambodia, or Laos. Hughes-Ryan responded to CIA involvement in the Cambodian operations by imposing reporting requirements on the CIA before it could expend appropriated funds. Some of these were limitation riders, curbing only the use of funds within the appropriation itself, while others were unrelated restrictions ("no funds appropriated under this or any other law. . . ."). Some were the products of the traditional appropriation process, while others were introduced as floor amendments during consideration of a regular or supplemental appropriation or continuing resolution.[23]

In 1976, after it was learned that the intelligence community was secretly aiding guerilla forces in Angola, in apparent violation of the Hughes-Ryan amendment, Congress amended the Arms Export Control Act to prohibit the use of appropriated funds in support of groups engaged in paramilitary operations in Angola.[24] This Clark-Tunney amendment apparently achieved its intended objective until it was repealed in 1985.[25] No additional riders limiting combat activities appeared until the Boland amendments, a series of restrictions on funding the Nicaraguan Contras in the early 1980s.

The Role of the House and Senate Rules

In response to the collapse of the traditional appropriation process, Congress has adopted various largely ineffective internal corrective devices while it has accommodated reality. The accommodation is reflected in rules of the House and Senate which require reports describing appropriation provisions that change the application of existing law.[26] Among the correctives currently in effect are rules of the House that prohibit authorizations that contain appropriations.[27] Yet while authorizing committees may, and often do, include spending ceilings and minimums in their authorization bills,[28] the appropriations committees have the power "to make an appropriation in excess of a cost limitation contained in the original authorization act . . . incident to the power of Congress to appropriate."[29] The House rules also continue to provide that "[n]o appropriation shall be reported in any general appropriation bill, or be in order as an amendment thereto, for any expenditure not previously authorized by law."[30] In addition, a 1983 amendment to the House rules proscribes most riders during floor debate.[31]

The Senate rules also prohibit amendments proposing general legislation and those that are not germane to a general appropriation bill.[32] But it provides for exceptions when the rider is moved by a standing or select committee (including the appropriations committees) or is "in pursuance of an estimate submitted in accordance with law."[33]

The germaneness rule in the Senate was the battleground for a well-known rider, which was intended to restrict military activities in Southeast Asia in 1973. The rules provide that if a senator raises a question of germaneness concerning Senate Appropriations Committee substitute language in a general appropriation bill passed by the House, the germaneness question takes precedence over a point of order, and the germaneness must be determined by the Senate without debate.[34] However, if the amendment is determined to be germane, no subsequent point of order will lie to question whether the amendment is or is not legislation. Lack of germaneness will not bar a legislative rider to an appropriation in the Senate if the House first includes a legislative rider in a general appropriation bill.[35]

In 1973, the House voted to end U.S. combat activity in Cambodia and Laos through a rider to a supplemental appropriation bill.[36] After it became known that Senator Eagleton would seek to replicate the House tactic in the Senate, Senator Roman Hruska, a Nixon administration supporter, raised a point of order and claimed that Eagleton's language violated the rule against legislating in an appropriation bill.[37] Some senators and the Senate parliamentarian concluded that the House amendment was merely a limitation, because it restricted funds only in the bill in which it was included, but that Eagleton's amendment was legislation because it would cover funds made available in other appropriation bills as well. In response, Eagleton raised the question of germaneness, knowing that if he won on that vote he would circumvent a vote on the point of order. Eagleton won—the Senate declared the Eagleton amendment germane to the House language.[38]

Overall, the House and Senate rules have had relatively little effect upon the national security appropriation process. According to Louis Fisher, only "[r]arely does an appropriation bill pass that does not contain some form of 'legislation,'"[39] in the form of a limitation in the original appropriation or an unrelated restriction added during committee action or floor debate, or an amendment to continuing resolutions.[40] There are several reasons for this result. First, the rules are not self-enforcing; a point of order must be raised on the floor to strike a rider. Members may not wish to risk disfavor with their colleagues by making a parliamentary gambit.[41] Second, the Holman rule in the House continues to permit riders that cut authorized expenditures.[42] Thus, a rider to decrease funding for an approved weapons system is not a forbidden rider. Third, many restrictions are "limitations" and are thus not subject to the rules' prohibitions, so long as the provision is not made applicable to money appropriated in other acts and does not prescribe new duties or obligations.[43] Fourth, the rules may be waived.[44] Fifth, the Senate may, as mentioned above and consistent with its rules, substantively amend an appropriation if the House has acted first to add such a restriction.[45] Sixth, the House rule against legislating in an appropriation does not apply to committee-approved restrictions, to action taken in conference, to single-agency appropriations, or to continuing resolutions, which together have constituted the major segment of national security appropriations in recent years.[46]

While the number of regular appropriation restrictions has decreased in recent years,[47] the practice of making policy through the appropriation process has merely shifted from regular appropriation bills to special bills and continuing resolutions.[48] The continued popularity of broad, programmatic authorizing legislation and the proliferation of continuing resolutions only invites the floor amendments that bypass committee review and prohibiting rules.[49]

Funding the Contras

Nearly all the developments described in this chapter were played out at one time or another during the 1980s as the Reagan and Bush administrations sought support for the Nicaraguan Contras and Congress tried to limit funding through the Boland amendments. Early on, the policy question—should the nation support the Contras—became a fiscal issue, which was resolved through short-term accommodations in the appropriation process. Once Congress began to control support for the Contras through funding mechanisms, an array of appropriation process problems took over: deadlines were missed, deliberations were curtailed by insufficient time or conference committee maneuvers, continuing resolutions become the vehicle for resolving the funding issue, and substantive amendments to appropriations proliferated. The Contra funding case study illustrates that appropriation restrictions and continuing resolutions reflect the policy environment in which they operate. When policy disputes are as seemingly intractable as Contra funding was, appropriation riders and continuing resolutions may emerge when the traditional process fails. Their use at least facilitates getting something decided.

After the Somoza government of Nicaragua was overthrown in 1979 and replaced by Sandinista leftists, the Carter administration first explored reconciliation with the new government. Emergency food aid was sent immediately following the Sandinista takeover, and Congress appropriated an additional $75 million in emergency economic assistance in 1980.[50] During the same period, however, President Carter signed an intelligence finding authorizing covert support for opposition groups in Nicaragua, based on concern about the effects of the Sandinista victory on democratic institutions.[51] While the Sandinistas publicly expressed a desire for improved relations with the United States, there were reports that they were serving as a conduit for Cuban weapons and equipment bound for rebels fighting the United States–backed government in El Salvador.

In light of these reports and increasing Nicaraguan ties to Cuba and the Soviet Union, President Carter suspended aid to Nicaragua in January 1981. That April, President Reagan announced that the remaining $15 million in unspent appropriated aid would be withheld and that no further aid would be requested until democracy was in place in Nicaragua and assistance to the Salvadoran rebels was stopped. By the end of 1981, the Contras—the organized resistance to the Sandinistas—looked to and found support from the United States. In December, President Reagan authorized a CIA covert program to assist the Contras, from a CIA contingency fund (probably about $19 million).[52]

When the media began reporting about the not-so-covert program in early 1982, it was widely believed that the Contras were not so much concerned with the mission that the Reagan administration was publicly supporting—interdicting the flow of weapons and supplies from the Sandinistas to guerrillas in neighboring El Salvador—as they were seeking to overthrow the Sandinistas. Although administration officials denied these broader intentions, there was significant clamor inside and outside government over the prospect of engaging the nation in a guerilla war in Central America. As a result, Congress fashioned a limitation rider—first proposed as a floor amendment—to condition the $19 million in Contra support approved for use by the CIA and DOD in fiscal year 1983. The rider, first contained in a classified annex to the Intelligence Authorization Act[53] then repeated in the Defense Appropriation Act,[54] itself part of a continuing resolution for fiscal year 1983, prohibited DOD or CIA use of the funds provided in the act "for the purpose of overthrowing the government of Nicaragua."[55] Thus, the policy question—should the nation support a paramilitary war in Nicaragua—was transformed into a fiscal question.

In 1983, the intelligence committees took radically different approaches to the Contra aid question. By July, the House, upon the recommendation of its Intelligence Committee, had approved an amendment to the Intelligence Authorization Act which would have ended support for the Contras in favor of aiding friendly Central American governments in their efforts to stop the flow of arms to subversive groups in their countries. The Senate Intelligence Committee declined even to consider the bill, however, and proceeded to recommend and obtain approval on the Senate floor for an intelligence authorization bill that did not restrict Contra funding.[56]

As the 1983 fiscal year came to a close, the House and Senate remained far apart. While the Senate was on record as favoring the president's request for a higher level of funding for the Contras, the House had included an aid cutoff amendment in its version of the intelligence authorization bill and a provision prohibiting use of the CIA contingency fund to support the Contras in the fiscal year 1984 DOD Authorization Act.[57] As the 1984 fiscal year began, with the DOD operating under a continuing resolution, a conference committee proposed a compromise restriction, which was enacted on December 8. Identical provisions of the DOD Appropriations Act[58] and the Intelligence Authorization Act[59] limited to $24 million the funds available to "any . . . entity of the United States involved in intelligence activities . . . for the purpose or which would have the effect"[60] of supporting the Contras.

Thus, the policy issue had become even more vividly a fiscal issue. The authorization-appropriation process had failed to produce an agreement, fiscal year deadlines had come and gone, and the conferees simply split the difference between the House and Senate in monetary terms. The rider did more than set a cap, however. By not limiting its terms to "funds provided in this Act," it effectively extended the funding limit beyond CIA and DOD to other government agencies, and, as made clear in its legislative history, barred the use of other CIA funds to exceed the limit. Thus, the conferees made important policy through the appropriation process.

Part of the conference compromise also was reflected in an express invitation to the president to return to Congress to seek more support for the Contras.[61] Although he first obtained approval in the Senate for a supplemental appropriation of $21 million,[62] the House soundly defeated his bill and the Senate reversed itself after it was reported that the CIA had been involved in the mining of Nicaraguan harbors without adequate notice to the intelligence committees.[63]

Meanwhile, work was proceeding on the fiscal year 1985 defense and intelligence authorization and appropriation bills. After his request for a supplemental appropriation was defeated, President Reagan submitted a request for $28 million in new funds. By August, however, the House had passed its intelligence authorization bill with a provision banning support for the Contras. Once again, the Senate Intelligence Committee did not consider the bill, and the Senate Appropriations Committee included the $28 million in its version of a continuing resolution, which was being prepared for the likely event that the regular appropriation process would not be completed before October 1.

The House had also begun work on a continuing resolution, which was reported by its Appropriations Committee on September 14.[64] Its resolution incorporated the ban on aiding the Contras recommended previously by the Intelligence Committee. After a lengthy Rules Committee session concerning which amendments to the appropriation bills could be considered during floor action, the resolution was passed with the Contra aid prohibition on September 25. The Senate Appropriations Committee reported its version of the continuing resolution that same day. The Senate resolution contained thirty-five amendments as reported, including one deleting the House Contra aid ban in favor of a provision adding $28 million to the budget for the Contras. As late as October 3, an attempt on the Senate floor to approve a restriction equivalent to the House amendment failed. The next day, the Senate passed a continuing resolution which contained $28 million for the Contras.

Once again, the critical work was completed in conference. This time the House conferees won out. After a six-day conference, Congress approved amendments to the DOD appropriation and intelligence authorization acts for fiscal year 1985[65] prohibiting aid to the Contras. Because the rider was part of the continuing resolution which included all funds for DOD and many other government programs, the president accepted the rider and signed the continuing resolution into law on October 12.[66]

When the congressional investigators of the Iran-Contra Affair later questioned the administration's circumvention of the Boland amendments through the use of unappropriated funds to keep the Contras going, the administration argued that the appropriation did not or could not so limit the president in carrying out his constitutional powers.[67] It also insisted that the restrictions themselves were not well drafted, and that Congress had intended less than airtight controls.[68] In any event, the president used the CIA contingency fund without a specific appropriation to create the Contra army and to supplement other discretionary funding before and after the 1984 bans.[69]

Lessons from the Contra Funding

In the end, the national security appropriation process shaped and was itself affected by the Contra funding issue. The customary authorization-appropriation distinction was not honored; substantive legislation was enacted in appropriations. Rather than thoughtfully deliberating the question of Contra support in the authorizing committees, Congress made most of the important deals and decisions on the floor or in conference, where only a few members shaped the final legislative product. Instead of the traditional presentment of authorization and then appropriations bills for the president's signature or veto, the Contra aid restrictions were packaged in practically veto-proof continuing resolutions. The entire process was often redundant, as several committees took up the same issue. Given the parliamentary obstacles and political maneuvering, congressional consideration of the Contras' cause was anything but efficient.

The legislative history of the Boland amendments thus illustrates the vices of national security appropriation restrictions. They may retard or obstruct the consideration of appropriation bills, or whimsically reverse action previously approved after careful consideration by committees with special subject matter expertise.[70] Parliamentary confusion concerning what is permitted as a limitation and what is prohibited as a legislative rider[71] may cause dissension within each chamber and between the House and Senate.[72] Moreover, they may divide Congress and the president when they limit the president's discretion and are presented in bills which are politically veto-proof.

They have also been attacked as undemocratic, because only a few legislators may be involved in making the eventual policy.[73] When restrictions are tacked onto supplemental appropriations or continuing resolutions, the difficult decisions are normally made by conferees from each house assigned the task of reconciling bills. In conference on a continuing resolution, the appropriations committees divide up subject matter responsibility so that as few as four members of Congress iron out an agreement on an appropriation restriction.[74]

These attacks may be exaggerated for two reasons. First, as the Contra funding episode illustrates, the tendency for most critical policy choices to be framed as fiscal issues suggests that an orderly appropriation process may be impossible without a consensus on policies. Appropriation restrictions do not produce disorder so much as reflect it. Second, even though funding restrictions imposed by floor amendment appear to undermine the deliberative process and waste the expertise of the substantive committees,[75] the policy they advance has often been debated throughout the authorization-appropriation process.

The use of a continuing resolution to make national security appropriation policy is sometimes not only expedient but pragmatic, as the Boland controversy illustrates. When policy questions are presented to several committees in the House and Senate on multiple occasions within a short period of time, and consensus between the Houses or within one chamber fails to emerge, resolving the issue by continuing resolution may be an effective use of legislative resources. Redundancies may be minimized, and, if a funding gap is imminent, the crisis may encourage consensus. From this perspective, continuing resolutions may be a relatively efficient mechanism for the accomplishment of the congressional agenda.[76]

7

Informal Controls on National Security Spending

Records of committee and subcommittee hearings and floor debates, as well as appropriations and conference committee reports routinely accompany appropriations for national security activities, where they help to explain lump-sum appropriations for categories such as "operations and maintenance" or "salaries and expenses." This legislative history may include instructions about spending, usually though not always tracking the estimates supplied by the agencies. The executive branch must decide the extent to which these nonstatutory controls should be taken into account, how much weight to attach to commands or requests found somewhere other than in the statute itself.[1]

In this chapter, we will show that this informal set of controls may benefit appropriators and spenders. The statutory lump sums imply a degree of spending discretion that permits flexibility and rule avoidance in oversight and spending. We then explain how nonstatutory controls on national security spending are, in one sense, just one more form of legislative oversight of spending by agencies. We show, however, that the magnitude of lump sum funding for national security sometimes creates unique problems, when controversy erupts over a national security activity where the funding is subject to nonstatutory restrictions. Although the constitutionality of nonstatutory controls has been challenged, we conclude that such controls have no legal effect at all. They are simply political accommodations that may practically enhance presidential spending discretion.

Nonstatutory Controls and Flexible Defense Appropriation

In this substatutory context, each side needs the other. For the committees to influence outcomes after a lump sum is appropriated, the agencies must be willing to cooperate with the informally expressed committee wishes. For the agencies to continue having the flexibility to mold programs and activities as conditions change, the committees must concede considerable discretion. The advantages to both sides of cooperation have thus made informality the norm in national security appropriations. When the informal relationship breaks down, however, Congress may codify what had been an informal arrangement.

Nonstatutory controls also may be unavoidable components of the national security appropriation process. The formal process and resultant statutes simply cannot prescribe all the rules, predict all the uncertain contingencies, or resolve all the detailed questions about spending. Nonstatutory controls offer flexibility and negotiated outcomes, while they thwart substantive committee prerogatives by making policy in the appropriation process. In controlling the details of spending in areas such as procurement, personnel, and agency management, nonstatutory devices are essential supplements to the formal appropriations. The informal relationship between the defense agencies and congressional committees permits a greater degree of congressional control over details. At the same time, this informality avoids the consequences of the unrealistic expectation that appropriations can be frozen into appropriation statutes.[2]

In at least one respect, the nonstatutory elements of national security appropriations are typical of congressional efforts to make rules for an enormous bureaucracy. The appropriations committees and the defense appropriations subcommittees employ the appropriation process itself, apart from its formal product, to attempt to influence policy and to control executive branch discretion through oversight.[3] Understandings about spending objectives or limits may be reached during hearings or floor debate. Committee reports may include guidance for the exercise of administrative discretion. Further informal arrangements may be memorialized after an appropriation is enacted,[4] or in correspondence between the committees and executive officials at any time during the spending cycle.

National security appropriations nonetheless present special problems in assessing the efficacy of nonstatutory controls. The problems derive, in part, from the sheer magnitude of the task of defense budgeting and spending. We described in chapter 4 how the question of line-item versus lump-sum appropriating was resolved early on in the disputes between Jefferson and Hamilton (precipitated in part by the implications of an annual lump sum for the War Department). The tradition of lump-sum funding only shifts the task of controlling administrative discretion from the formal arena of the legislative enactment to the informal setting of committee interaction with the spenders. The nonstatutory controls may thus be necessary to ensure that lump-sum spending for national security is not "foot-loose and fancy-free."[5]

The budget estimates submitted by the defense agencies set forth in detail the purposes for the proposed spending. As the appropriations committees and floor and conference action amend agency requests and enact appropriations, most of this detail is lost in the final bill and its lump-sum funding. However, the detail, mostly in the form of line itemization and specific descriptions of spending objectives, is retained and employed in the ongoing relationship between Congress and the defense agencies.[6]

The nonstatutory understandings do not so much set policy as they fill in details which are not specified in lump-sum appropriations.[7] These nonstatutory controls may become controversial when committee reports or other legislative statements "instruct" or "direct" policy or "require" or "earmark" or "delete" spending for a specific purpose or activity. Informal policy-making has been less objectionable when the legislative history contains statements which "urge" or "expect" certain outcomes, such as the 1957 Senate Report on State Department Appropriations, which lamented the small amount requested for trade fairs behind the Iron Curtain and stated that it "was felt" that more funds would accomplish more good; the committee "urge[d]" that more be spent "if possible."[8]

The utility of nonstatutory controls in national security appropriations is enhanced and their popularity is explained in part by their immunity from House and Senate rules, particularly those which forbid policy-making riders.[9] For example, in 1962, the House Defense Appropriations Subcommittee expressed concern over the utility of using private rather than navy shipyards for repair, alteration, and conversion work. Its report asked DOD to study the relative merits of public and private shipyards and to report its results to the appropriations committees prior to consideration of the next year's budget.[10] The subcommittee thus retained the eventual choice of policy and relied on DOD to provide it with information. Because the House rules would have prohibited such a provision in the appropriation statute, the informal arrangement was preferable.[11]

The Good Friday Accords and Other Recent Examples

Yet another Contra funding episode illustrates the continuing vitality of the informal appropriation process.[12] With the election of President Bush, administration efforts to gain appropriations in support of the Contras took a decidedly different tack. President Reagan had, before and after the Iran-Contra scandal, always made requests for Contra aid and then counted on public support to force Congress to comply. Although President Bush had said on the day after his election that nonmilitary aid to the Contras would have a "high priority" in his administration,[13] an intervening peace accord reached by Central American presidents and firm opposition among congressional leaders prompted the president to send Secretary of State Baker to negotiate with Congress about Contra aid, out of public view.[14] In March 1989, after several secret meetings with members of Congress, Baker revealed the "Bipartisan Accord on Central America,"[15] in which Congress agreed to limited nonmilitary funding for the Contras through February 28, 1990.[16] The so-called Good Friday Accords were enacted, as always, through bicameral passage and presentment of the enrolled bill to the president for his signature.

There was more to the bipartisan accord than the formal statute, however. For many members of Congress, some interim review of the accord was essential to insure the administration's sincerity in seeking a negotiated peace settlement in Central America and elections in Nicaragua. The breakthrough in negotiations was offered by Representative David Obey. Employing Obey's proposal, the president agreed through a separate exchange of memoranda to obtain the explicit support of certain party leaders and committees before releasing the remaining money. The agreement also gave the party leaders and each of the four congressional committees an opportunity to terminate the funding after November 30, 1989, if, upon review of the changing political and military situation in Nicaragua, the party leaders or committees determined that additional support was not warranted.[17]

While interbranch disputes occasionally erupted over these nonstatutory controls before 1983,[18] the Supreme Court's decision in that year, invalidating statutory provisions for legislative vetoes[19] ironically prompted an increase in the use of nonstatutory controls to accomplish policy goals at the same time it has hardened executive branch opposition to the practice. The *Chadha* decision, in Louis Fisher's words, "drove underground a set of legislative and committee vetoes that used to operate in plain sight."[20] More than 140 legislative vetoes were adopted after *Chadha*, and many were informally honored.[21] However, as the practice of enacting vetoes continued during President Reagan's second term, those opposed to the device (or to the oversight it provided) temporarily seized the initiative.

In 1988, OMB director James Miller informed all federal agency heads that appropriations committee report language would not be regarded as legally binding. After Congress threatened to pass a statute that would purport to make committee language binding, Miller backed off and advised agencies to abide by committee instructions as a "matter of comity."[22]

In early 1990, Miller suggested that the president simply compile and issue a list of committee-generated spending instructions for which he would refuse to authorize any expenditure of funds.[23] Although President Bush apparently did not systematically refuse to abide by committee-generated spending instructions, he did flag the practice in some signing statements by stating, for example, when he signed the 1990 Department of Defense Appropriations Act, that "Congress cannot create legal obligations through report language" and that "such language has no legal force or effect."[24]

When executive branch spenders disapprove of requirements or specifications on spending in committee reports, the knowledge that the same limits could be imposed by statute is normally sufficient incentive to continue the informal relationship. When the spenders openly reject nonstatutory limits, however, as President Bush did in signing the fiscal 1990 Defense Appropriations Act, Congress may and did in the fiscal 1991 Defense Appropriations Act[25] codify what had been an informal limit on spending discretion. The change affects secret or black budget programs, described in chapter 5. To preserve the secrecy of such spending, the funds are hidden within the Pentagon budget, and a classified committee report specifies how the funds should be spent. DOD had flouted committee spending instructions on strategic communications, reconnaissance programs, certain covert operations, and the SR-71 Blackbird spy plane. After Bush signed the statement described above, Congress added a section to the 1991 act stating that the classified spending restrictions "shall have the force and effect of Law."[26] A similar provision appeared in the 1992 DOD Appropriations Act.[27]

The Political Effect of Nonstatutory Controls

As described previously, in 1989 President Bush and Congress entered into the Good Friday Accords, by which Congress agreed to enact a ten-month renewal of aid to the Contras on the informal (unenacted) condition that the president obtain committee and party leader approval to continue spending the appropriation after November 30 of that year. White House Counsel C. Boyden Gray reportedly objected to the agreement, arguing that the still-secret accord constituted an unconstitutional legislative veto.[28] A straightforward application of *Chadha,* other critics maintained, renders the Good Friday Accords unconstitutional. Because the committee review provided for in the accords "had the purpose and effect of altering the legal rights, duties, and relations of persons . . . outside the legislative branch,"[29] they "flout the reasoning" of *Chadha* and violate the presentment and bicameralism requirements of the Constitution.[30]

Other critics, such as former judge Robert Bork, took a broader swipe at the accords. He said that they were "one more example of Congress and congressional committees trying to manage the details of foreign affairs."[31] His criticism implies that the committee veto provision undermines the president's constitutional powers and/or the separation of powers.[32]

Gregory Sidak summarized the constitutional challenge to the Good Friday Accords. They "subverted the law," he said, because

> Congress cannot condition appropriations on its ability to veto subsequent Executive decisions. . . . The secret agreement violates bicameralism . . . . Of course, the Congress and President took these actions in the name of political expediency, bipartisanship, and pragmatism but those are the same genre of reasoning that the Court rejected in *Youngstown.* The net effect of the Bipartisan Accord is to erode the unitary Executive by ceding power from the President to the Congress. . . .[33]

These critics, however, make a common but mistaken threshold assumption—that the Good Friday Accords or any other similarly structured nonstatutory restriction on national security appropriations has a *legal* effect.[34] In fact, the objectionable condition was not a part of a bill that could have been bicamerally considered and was never enacted *as law.* The Article I processes for lawmaking were not violated by a side political deal that never had, nor was intended to have, legal effect. More specifically, the Congress did not condition the relevant appropriation on a legislative veto to be exercised in the future. The enacted law—the appropriation—contained no conditions. Congress reserved no opportunity in it to veto future spending. The eventual disapproval of three months of Contra aid by one of the committees or party leaders therefore would not create any legal rights or obligations, and the president was legally free to ignore it and keep spending the original appropriation.[35]

The negotiations and eventual agreement between Secretary Baker and members of Congress reflect the extralegal character of the accords. The administration was seeking an exemption from restrictions on reprogramming, which, since 1977, state that reprogramming above a certain threshold amount may not occur without the assent of the four committees—assent manifested by the failure to disapprove of the requested reprogramming within a prescribed time. The change in reprogramming processes codified in 1977 worked just as it was intended to in 1989. When the committees were approached to approve significant reprogramming, aid for the Contras at a time when a peace accord and elections were in the wind, they simply struck a deal: "We can't go along with ten months, but if you give the committees and several party leaders an informal chance to stop the flow of dollars after seven months, we will vote for the ten-month package." The 1989 deal was, unlike the 1977 arrangement, not memorialized in the resulting statute. The negotiations simply produced a set of political accommodations.

If the committee and party leader approval condition had no legal effect, what effect did it have? The Federal Circuit has suggested the answer. In *City of Alexandria v. United States*,[36] the city challenged the constitutionality of a requirement in the surplus property statute that before the General Services Administration (GSA) may convey federal property it must transmit an "explicit statement of the circumstances" of the proposed transfer to congressional committees. This requirement, typical of so-called statutory report-and-wait provisions, created the possibility that a single congressional committee could practically stall or even block a proposed sale by informally persuading the General Services Administration to abandon its effort to consummate a sale, or by informing the full Congress, so that it could act formally or informally to stop the transaction.[37] Nonetheless, the court concluded that a committee vote of disapproval would not have any *legal* effect.

It could, however, have great "moral" and political effect, the court noted.

> Officials in the executive branch have to take these committees into account and keep them informed, respond to their inquiries, and it may be, flatter and please them when necessary. Committees do not need even the type of "report and wait" provision we have here to develop enormous influence over executive branch doings. There is nothing unconstitutional about this: indeed, our separation of powers makes such informal cooperation much more necessary than it would be in a pure system of parliamentary government . . . . Disapproval . . . has great moral effect . . . .[38]

The president's agreement to the Good Friday Accords, too, may have had "great moral effect" and political effect. But the accords were not, on that account, enforceable as law. The president, like the GSA, was free to disregard them at whatever political cost that entailed, just as he is free to break his word to a powerful committee chairman or to defy the unlegislated will of the Congress. In short, in Louis Fisher's pithy phrase, informal controls like the Good Friday Accords "are not legal in effect. They are, however, in effect legal."[39]

Moreover, not only did the accords thus not violate the Article I process, they also did not undermine presidential power. The president achieved a net gain—the accords provided aid to the Contras that Congress had no obligation to provide, and which it would have denied without the informal agreement. The accords were the product of an ongoing effort by the congressional committees to be sure that reprogramming discretion is not abused. Without the committee review, Congress may choose not to permit the reprogramming.[40] Congress simply fashioned its proceedings to produce a political deal that has no legal effect.[41] The accords may have been unwise, but they were not unconstitutional.

The accords were also unusual. The more common forms of informal controls on national security are the committee report instructions and other forms of legislative oversight described earlier in this chapter. Like the accords, committee reports and other typical informal controls are constitutional. They have no legal effect. In addition, also like the accords, the typical informal control is part of deal making that enhances presidential spending discretion.

8

The Mechanics of National Security Spending

It would tell only part of the story to describe the preenactment national security appropriation process—the procedural path to a budget and the limitations or prescriptions contained in a bill. One of the most significant aspects of the national security appropriation process is much less visible. In this chapter we examine the spending discretion vested in the executive by Congress and explain how the defense agencies and Congress interact in the exercise of that discretion.[1] In particular, we examine four broad categories of congressionally conferred discretion in national security appropriations: lump-sum appropriations, reprogramming, budget transfers, and impoundment.

Spending discretion is, of course, subject to the constitutional requirement that the executive branch be authorized by Congress to spend. Likewise, the Constitution obligates Congress to exercise effective control over spending discretion.[2] This latter duty is reflected in the Anti-Deficiency Act, which makes it unlawful for a federal agency to "make or authorize an expenditure or obligation exceeding an amount available in an appropriation."[3] While we postpone a treatment of these constitutional requirements to chapter 14, we explore here instances where the Anti-Deficiency Act has been narrowly construed to permit significant spending discretion.

Lump-Sum Appropriations

A lump-sum appropriation is made for more than one specific object.[4] The very first U.S. appropriation was a lump-sum appropriation, as we saw in chapter 4, and in national security lump-sum appropriations have been common. If the first congresses and presidents found lump-sum appropriations unavoidable for the military, it would be fanciful today to contemplate line-item appropriations for a $300 billion defense budget. For example, when DOD shifts funds within a program area, such as Strategic Forces, from one project described in budget estimates to a different project, the agency has simply exercised lump-sum spending discretion.[5] We are not as concerned, however, with the general practice of lump-sum funding (for example, for a research and development account and how Congress monitors whether the lump sum is expended on the projects specified in the president's budget request) as we are with a few special categories of lump-sum appropriation that confer a high level of discretion in carrying out military activities.

In general, Congress has required more than administrative convenience to justify significant lump-sum budgeting in national security appropriations. Thus, lump sums have been employed most during times of war or other national emergency. For example, appropriations during the Civil War, Spanish American War, and World Wars I and II included expansive delegations to spend large sums "as the exigencies . . . may require,"[6] or "for the national defense . . . to be expended at the discretion of the President."[7] Although these and other lump-sum accounts have been subject to nonstatutory understandings that sums would be spent in accordance with details contained in the itemized budget requests, the delegations have at times been sweeping.[8] The following subsections describe four categories of lump-sum funding.

Contingency Funds

In national security appropriations, Congress has sought to plan for the unforeseeable and thus provides the president with separate accounts to cover contingencies. However, to recognize that national security contingencies will arise is one thing. To monitor and control the use of a blank check for contingencies is another. As was said during a 1906 debate in Congress, creating such an untethered fund "is like giving a child more money than he wants for a trip uptown and back; he will surely spend the balance of it before he gets home."[9]

While contingency funds created during times of declared war have not been controversial, abuses have occurred at other times. The Foreign Assistance Act (FAA) contingency fund, available to the president for uses "in the national interest,"[10] was particularly vulnerable to this charge. President Kennedy established the Peace Corps by executive order and financed it from the FAA contingency fund for seven months until an explicit appropriation was forthcoming.[11] Presidents Johnson and Nixon also relied upon the FAA contingency fund, in part, to pay for items as diverse as the President's Commission on Civil Disorders and the Bahamas Livestock and Research project.[12] As Congress grew more disturbed with the uses to which the FAA fund was put, it inserted restrictions prohibiting use of the fund for any activity that had been rejected by Congress, decreased the size of the fund, and, beginning in 1973, stated that it was "primarily for disaster relief purposes."[13]

Before 1974, the presidents apparently had not employed a contingency fund for an expressly prohibited purpose. Such an abuse may have occurred, however, in President Nixon's gift that year of a helicopter to President Anwar Sadat of Egypt. The president found most of the money for the gift in the Agency for International Development (AID) contingency fund, an account established for famine and disaster relief, which vested sweeping discretion in the president. Congress reacted by establishing a separate famine and disaster relief account, again reducing the amount of the contingency fund, and explicitly prohibiting its use to pay for gifts to foreign officials "made heretofore or hereafter."[14]

Perhaps the most widely reported employment of a contingency fund occurred in 1981 when President Reagan used the CIA contingency fund to support the Nicaraguan Contras. The CIA contingency fund is not the product of the traditional appropriation process and is even less subject to congressional oversight than other contingency funds. As was described in chapter 5, the CIA budget is secret, approved by the intelligence committees, and hidden within the larger budget for the Pentagon. DOD transfers approved sums to the CIA, including a contingency fund, the level and purposes of which have been set, again, by the intelligence committees.[15] Congress had thus implicitly given the president the discretion to support the Contras with the contingency fund subject to his reporting to the intelligence committees.

Use of the CIA fund permitted the president to support the Contras without coming to Congress for an explicit appropriation. At the same time, employment of the contingency fund avoided a congressional debate on the wisdom of the overall policy of supporting the Contras, officially reported as an effort to interdict Cuban weapons moving through Nicaragua to rebels in El Salvador,[16] while it allowed the administration to obscure the apparent real purpose of U.S. support: overthrowing the Sandinista government. Thus, although the president satisfied the letter of the intelligence oversight law in reporting the covert aid, and while the funds were lawfully available to the CIA for contingencies, the fund was arguably misapplied to activities the true purpose of which was neither authorized by Congress nor reported to the intelligence committees.

When it was later reported that the CIA contingency fund was being spent for purposes inconsistent with those earlier represented to Congress and in excess of the appropriation's funding limit, first the intelligence committees and then Congress acted to limit such uses of the CIA's contingency fund in Nicaragua. However, notwithstanding abuses of the fund that were uncovered during the investigations of the Iran-Contra affair,[17] Congress apparently has not acted to limit further expenditures from the fund in any way.[18]

Special Authority for Emergency Spending

Emergency funds do not provide additional budget authority. Instead, agencies divert budget authority provided in a general appropriation to fund the emergency and then ask Congress for either a supplemental appropriation or a like amount in the next year's appropriation to liquidate the obligations incurred during the emergency.[19] Of course, any such extrabudget commitments by the executive would, absent a statutory exception, violate the terms of the Anti-Deficiency Act,[20] which has explicitly proscribed deficiency spending since 1905. However, the executive's national security spending activities have regularly ignored the law,[21] while they benefited from a curious and open-ended statutory exception.

The authority for the oldest and largest emergency fund is a species of contract authority that permits officials to commit government spending in advance of appropriations. The DOD Authorization Act each year permits the president, whenever he "determines such action to be necessary in the interest of national defense,"[22] to incur obligations for various military activities, including an airborne alert or an increase in the number of military personnel on active duty above the number authorized.[23] These expenditures are thus exempt from the Anti-Deficiency Act prohibition against excessive obligations. After the presidential finding, the secretary of defense is required to "immediately advise" Congress if any action is taken under this authority.[24] After advising Congress, the secretary invokes provisions of the feed and forage law,[25] which permits army, navy, and air force contracting for "clothing, subsistence, forage, fuel, quarters, transportation, or medical and hospital supplies" without an appropriation.[26] Spending under this provision is limited only by the needs for the current year.[27] Once the obligation is made by DOD, Congress has no choice but to appropriate funds to pay for it later.

The origins of the feed and forage law suggest that it was not intended to fund today's DOD. First enacted in 1799,[28] and revised in 1820 and 1861,[29] the law was designed to allow advance funding authority for military essentials under conditions involving remote assignments and slow communications, which could prevent, say, an army encampment from learning whether an appropriation had been passed to fund their continued existence.[30]

However, the feed and forage law mechanism has been retained and was even expanded in 1959 and 1961 to permit the airborne alert and military personnel increase mentioned above.[31] During Senate Appropriations Committee hearings in 1972, Senator Proxmire described an effort in Congress to block the defense appropriation bill unless it contained an amendment to withdraw all troops from Vietnam by August 31, 1972. When Proxmire asked Defense Secretary Laird what spending power would remain for the president in such a situation, Laird named the feed and forage law as "the only legislation which would permit us to operate."[32] When Congress threatened to cut off funds for the bombing of Cambodia in 1973, Defense Secretary Richardson testified before the Senate Appropriations Committee that, if the funds were denied, "[w]e can find the money. . . . [W]e could invoke [the feed and forage law] authority. . . ."[33]

Operation Desert Shield was initially financed by DOD through the feed and forage law. For August and September of 1990, funds were reallocated from other programs to pay for the deployment. Congress responded by appropriating $2.1 billion to fund these fiscal year 1990 expenses.[34] Fiscal year 1991 spending for the deployment and Desert Storm also occurred under feed and forage law authority until Congress enacted the Operation Desert Shield/Desert Storm Supplemental Appropriations Act in April 1991 to fund the obligations.[35] Thus, the feed and forage law is still used, even though continuing resolutions sustain the department when regular appropriations are not enacted; supplemental appropriations may be and are obtained for various DOD functions that were not anticipated at the beginning of the year; and DOD possesses contingency funds, transfer and reprogramming authority, and lump-sum appropriations for personnel and operations and maintenance.

The Defense Production Act (DPA),[36] a Korean War–era law that gives the president authority to divert goods and services to military use in an emergency, is another example of a more or less permanent grant of discretionary spending authority. Ostensibly a temporary means of mobilizing the economy for the Korean War, Congress has kept in place this "sweeping delegation of power" for the president.[37] While the act has expired several times, most recently during Operations Desert Shield/Desert Storm,[38] short-term extensions of some of the acts's provisions were approved in 1991 and 1992.[39]

The act instructs the president to mobilize industrial production for defense needs, to "assure . . . domestic energy supplies" so as "to ensure national defense preparedness, which is essential to national security," and to expand "productive capacity beyond the levels needed to meet the civilian demand" so as to "reduce the time required for industrial mobilization."[40] The act empowers presidents to order industry to give priority to defense contracts over civilian contracts,[41] to "take appropriate actions to assure that critical components of critical technology items are available from reliable sources when needed" as they think national security requires,[42] and to guarantee loans for defense mobilization purposes.[43]

While the Economy Act permits presidents to thwart other appropriation limits, the Defense Production Act allows them to wield significant power over the nation's economy.[44] Nonetheless, just as the Economy Act lingers on, Congress has not acted to limit presidential discretion under the DPA in any meaningful way. Only a few of the less important provisions have reporting requirements. The legislative veto by concurrent resolution included in the act was vitiated by *Chadha*.[45] A sunset provision that has required the act's periodic renewal has only served to call attention to lapses such as the one that occurred in the Persian Gulf War buildup. The courts that have been asked to overturn executive branch action under the act have declined.[46]

Other Special Funds, Defense Drawdown, and Contra Funding

For a number of years before 1971 the foreign assistance acts gave the president large, practically untethered special funds to spend outside the requirements of the act whenever he deemed it to be "important to the security of the United States."[47] While he was generally required to report his use of the funds to members of Congress,[48] up to $50 million could be spent without further reporting when the president certified "that it is unadvisable to specify" how the funds were used.[49] These same acts permitted the president to "draw down" (to spend from a lump sum appropriation without further, more specific appropriation) up to $300 million from the DOD budget if he determined that it was "vital to the security of the United States."[50] President Nixon used this drawdown authority to support the secret war in Cambodia in the early 1970s.[51] Thereafter, Congress amended the act to require prior notice and detailed findings of the need for such funds before they are employed.[52]

To increase military aid to El Salvador in 1981 and 1982, President Reagan employed the special discretionary spending mechanisms available to DOD, including statutory drawdown authority, to spend from a special fund that had been earmarked for military emergencies.[53] Although no actual emergency existed,[54] the president followed the literal requirements of the statute and declared the existence of an "emergency" requisite to trigger release of the funds in order to avoid debate on a request for a supplemental appropriation.[55]

In Nicaragua, after the fiscal 1984 Boland amendment limited aid to the Contras to $24 million, the limit was circumvented, first, by charging some expenses, like the 1984 mining of Nicaraguan harbors, to accounts unaffected by the Boland rider; second, by building an airfield for the Contras in Honduras as part of a DOD exercise; and third, through DOD donations or transfers at reduced charges of ships, planes, and weapons to the CIA.[56] In the summer of 1983, CIA sent a list to DOD, requesting that $28 million in equipment be transferred to it "free-of-charge."[57] The list included medical supplies, aircraft, and personnel. After the Joint Chiefs of Staff proposed that the four services simply divide the cost of the transfers, the DOD general counsel opined that the nonreimbursed transfer would violate the Economy Act, a Depression-era law which permits interagency fund transfers,[58] but which requires reimbursement for agency transfers except for surplus equipment. However, before the transfers project was terminated on February 12, 1985, the CIA had obtained three surplus Cessna aircraft at no cost, as well as night vision goggles, a night vision sight, and a cannon at cost.[59]

Donated Funds and Gift Authority

The Miscellaneous Receipts statute[60] reflects the general rule that all funds received for the government must be placed in the treasury and then appropriated before they may be spent. Among the exceptions to the rule, statutory gift authority[61] had effectively conferred a subset of lump-sum spending discretion for national security activities. Especially since the New Deal, many agencies had been given statutory authority to spend without further appropriation gifts earmarked for the agency.[62]

Gift authority for national security activities was especially generous. The "gift loophole," however, has now been tightened, if not closed, for defense spending. First enacted as temporary legislation in 1942[63] and then reenacted permanently in 1954, the act authorized the secretary of the treasury to "accept or reject on behalf of the United States any gift of money or other intangible personal property made on condition that it be used for a particular national security purpose."[64] After accepting, the secretary was permitted to place the gift funds in "such of the various appropriation accounts as in his judgment will best effectuate the intent of the donors."[65] An indeterminate amount of national security spending was thus authorized without additional appropriations.

This spending discretion applied, of course, only to gifts earmarked for national security. However, if a gift was only generally limited—for example,"for the defense of the United States"—the treasury secretary could permit the gifted agency to direct the spending for activities not previously authorized. Even if the gift was more specifically earmarked—for example, "for the defense of Kuwait"—the agency still determined which objects would benefit from the spending. Whether this relatively untethered spending discretion was constitutional is an important question,[66] which we discuss in chapter 13. The problematic relationship between spending discretion conferred by the 1954 Gift Act and the solicitation of donated funds is sharply presented by the Contra funding schemes. As has been more thoroughly described elsewhere,[67] the limited appropriations available for the Contras through the Boland amendments and the looming prospect of a complete denial of congressional funds prompted Lt. Col. Oliver North to organize and conduct a secret Contra-aid operation through an "off-the-shelf" covert organization (the Enterprise). The Enterprise operated as a surrogate for the National Security Council (NSC) and was financed in part by contributions from foreign governments and private individuals, not by funds appropriated for that purpose. These solicited contributions were clearly gifts under Gift Act authority. The largest contribution, $32 million over two years, came from the government of Saudi Arabia.[68] At the criminal trial of North, evidence revealed that at least ten countries were solicited for support for the Contras, after which several received increased U.S. aid.[69]

The 1954 act would have permitted the treasury secretary to receive "any gift" for the "defense purpose" of supporting the Contras. The funds could apparently be placed in any account—including any CIA account—to "effectuate the intent of the donors." On the other hand, the strictest Boland amendments provided that "no funds available" to agencies involved in intelligence activities could be spent for the Contras. The specific prohibitions thus arguably trumped the general permission in this instance. The 1984 Boland amendment also limited support to the terms of the appropriation. The secrecy of solicitations for the Contras during the period of the strictest Boland amendment is thus understandable.

The chance that significant national security spending could occur without an appropriation, pursuant to the Gift Act, was also presented soon after Iraq invaded Kuwait in August 1990. Spending for the early stages of the Desert Shield deployment was obligated without a specific appropriation—funds were shifted from other programs to pay for the deployment.[70] While DOD was fashioning its request for a supplemental appropriation, the administration was implementing its plan to form a coalition of nations allied against Iraq. Although most of the forces for the coalition would be provided by the United States, contributions were sought from governments all over the world to help defray the cost of deployment and eventual war. Such contributions would have created what Senator Byrd called a "huge defense slush fund."[71]

It was this prospect that prompted Congress to repeal the Gift Act when it enacted the supplemental appropriation for Desert Shield.[72] In its place, Congress established the Defense Cooperation account, into which any contribution of money or proceeds from the sale of any property accepted by the secretary of defense from any "person, foreign government, or international organization" shall be credited.[73] Cash must be subsequently appropriated before it may be spent. Property may be retained and used without further authorization or appropriation in the form in which it was donated, sold, or otherwise disposed of by DOD, or converted into usable form by DOD, so long as it is not used in a way that would violate a "prohibition or limitation otherwise applicable to such program, project, or activity."[74]

The combination of the 1990 statute and the Miscellaneous Receipts statute now means that, absent other statutory gift authority, only DOD may accept gifts for use by DOD[75] and, except for gifts of tangible property, gifts may not be spent without an appropriation, whatever their source. A foreign or domestic citizen sympathetic to a covert U.S. national security activity may still support it with a gift, but the funds must enter the treasury through DOD and be subsequently appropriated. After thirty-six years, the gift loophole has been tightened, if not closed.

Reprogramming

Reprogramming procedures have been developed as one response to the frustrations of accommodating Congress's interest in accountable spending and the defense agencies' interest in retaining flexibility to modify programs and activities after they are funded. Reprogramming permits funds in an account to be used for different purposes than those contemplated when the funds were appropriated.[76] Most DOD reprogramming is used for procurement, military pay, and research and development. When a program area, such as Strategic Forces, shifts funds from one project to another, no formal reprogramming has occurred. DOD has merely exercised its discretion to spend within a lump-sum account.[77]

Statutes typically neither authorize nor prohibit reprogramming. Instead, by informal agreement between an agency and a congressional committee, the agency is permitted to reprogram any unobligated funds,[78] usually after notice to or approval by one or more committees, if the new expense is within the general purpose of the appropriation and is not otherwise prohibited by statute.[79]

The principal historical problem with reprogramming, from the congressional perspective, was that it could be used to thwart the appropriation process. An agency could ask for item A, knowing it will be funded, all the while expecting to use the funds for item B, which Congress would not support.[80] The Defense Department apparently initiated defense reprogramming through a World War II "gentlemen's agreement" that permitted shifting funds with the approval of the military appropriations subcommittees.[81]

After the war, the practice continued. Congress reacted by requiring reporting to and sometimes prior approval by committees.[82] Through a series of formal and informal changes, Congress has continued to permit DOD reprogramming but with an ever greater congressional presence. Reporting requirements have been supplemented by prescribed reprogramming thresholds, monetary amounts that trigger congressional review.[83] The thresholds do permit considerable reprogramming without committee knowledge.[84]

Reprogramming authority was employed, however, to fund Central American activities during the Reagan administration. Funds earmarked for military exercises in the Operations and Maintenance account, intended as a sort of petty cash account, were used to station combat troops in Honduras and to construct permanent bases there without authorization for military construction. These bases and arms were then made available to the Contras, providing the guerrillas with assistance beyond what Congress had explicitly authorized.[85]

In the wake of the Contra funding scandal, Congress sought to control DOD reprogramming discretion by limiting reprogramming requests to "higher priority items based on unforseen military requirements" and by prohibiting the practice "where the item for which reprogramming is requested has been denied by Congress."[86] Reprogramming between the CIA and DOD is now prohibited "for any intelligence or special activity different from that previously justified to Congress," unless the Director of Central Intelligence or the defense secretary notifies the appropriations committees of such an activity.[87] In turn, DOD now has extensive regulations detailing its reprogramming procedures.[88]

Transfers

Transfers between Accounts

In contrast to reprogramming, transfer is the shifting of funds between appropriations. Budget transfer is prohibited without statutory authority.[89] Defense and foreign assistance agencies typically are given transfer authority, with a percentage limit on the amount of an account which may be transferred or increased.[90] DOD transfer authority appears in its annual appropriation act. It currently permits the Pentagon to transfer up to $1.5 billion when the secretary determines it to be "necessary in the national interest."[91]

Notwithstanding the current general statutory prohibition[92] and the various specific defense and foreign assistance controls, transfer authority abuses are fairly common. As we saw in chapter 4, the executive "mingled" or transferred between military appropriations from the very start, to the consternation of many in Congress. But, knowing the practice, Congress often acquiesced. By 1816, John C. Calhoun spoke of the "great evil . . . which resulted to the public interest from the practice, particularly in the War Department, of permitting funds to be diverted from one object of appropriation and applied to another."[93] Although reporting requirements and other devices were inserted beginning in 1820 to place tighter controls on transfer authority,[94] commingling of funds continued through the Civil War years[95] until an 1868 statute repealed existing transfer authority and declared that "no money appropriated for one purpose shall hereinafter be used for any other purpose than that for which it is appropriated."[96]

Perhaps the best known abuse of transfer authority is still another chapter in President Nixon's Cambodian bombing campaign. Acting under the Foreign Assistance Act, the president "borrowed" from aid programs appropriated for other countries and committed the funds to bombing in Cambodia. Then, after the 1973 cease-fire agreement and the withdrawal of American troops from Vietnam seemingly eliminated the need for further military action, the president continued bombing Cambodia, this time financed in part by DOD transfer authority. At the time, transfer authority was subject to prior-approval reprogramming procedures, arrangements that were abused by tardy Pentagon reporting.

Eventually, after President Nixon requested a $500 million increase in transfer authority for DOD in March 1973, the Senate passed the Eagleton amendment to a supplemental appropriations bill (which had already decreased the transfer authority request) denying the use of *any* funds to support United States combat activities in Cambodia or Laos.[97] After House passage and a Nixon veto, Congress failed to override the veto, and a new compromise bill was passed that permitted the president forty-five more bombing days before a new Eagleton-like prohibition would take effect.[98] Ironically, the new bill did not repeat the original request for new transfer authority, causing some to conclude that the prior request had only been a guise for obtaining more bombing funds.[99] In 1974, Congress prohibited DOD transfers "where the item for which funds are requested has been denied by Congress."[100]

Nonetheless, after the fiscal 1984 Boland amendment limited aid to the Contras to $24 million, the Reagan administration relied upon DOD transfer authority, but arguably violated the transfer restrictions when it charged the expense of mining the Nicaraguan harbors to other accounts.[101]

Transfers between Agencies

The same general prohibition against transfer without statutory authority also applies to transfers between agencies.[102] In national security appropriations, the important source of authority for interagency transfers is the Economy Act,[103] which permits the president to respond to dramatic spending cuts by transferring funds from one agency to another to cushion the cuts. Pursuant to the Economy Act as originally enacted in 1932, up to 12 percent of an agency budget could be transferred as long as the effect was not to exceed an appropriation by more than 15 percent.[104] In the case of the War and Navy Departments, transfers had to be approved by the president; others could be approved by the director of the budget.[105] Objecting to the bill during debate, congressman Vinson feared that "no longer will Congress have the right to itemize the appropriations and say how each and every dollar shall be spent . . . . [T]he Navy . . . and War Department [will be able] to say how the money shall be allocated . . . ."[106] As with the feed and forage law, Congress has paid little attention to the possibility that the president may utilize discretion conferred by the Economy Act to frustrate the objectives of other legislation.

For example, in the summer of 1983, the CIA feared that Congress might decline to appropriate funds for the Contras in fiscal year 1984. The agency then bypassed the appropriation process by having the DOD secretly transfer military equipment to the CIA without charge. The agency then dispensed the equipment to the Contras, even though nothing was said in an intelligence finding[107] about a donation of DOD materiel to the Contras through the CIA. Apparently because of an Economy Act provision that requires reimbursement for transfers except for "surplus" equipment, only "surplus" airplanes were transferred without charge, although a few other items were transferred at cost.[108]

Impoundment

Viewed broadly, "impoundment occurs whenever the President spends less than Congress appropriates for a given period."[109] Impoundment may have two quite different practical functions—protecting the fisc or undermining it. The first function of impoundment arises from Congress's inability to predict economic trends with certainty and to make accurate program spending estimates. When Congress estimates on the low side, a supplemental bill may have to be passed, or the executive may be able to find the needed funds through reprogramming or transfer. When it estimates on the high side, on the other hand, and appropriates more than is required to attain the programmatic goals of the authorizing legislation, the president may impound a portion of the appropriation to achieve a savings. This "programmatic impoundment" is an exercise of presidential discretion to protect the fisc pursuant to the president's duty to faithfully execute the laws and as such is welcomed by Congress. Alternatively, however, presidents may refuse to spend appropriated funds because they disapprove of the program. This "policy-based impoundment" is contrary to Congress's instructions to spend appropriated funds.

Historically, problems have arisen when the political branches disagree on which kind of impoundment is at issue in a given instance. Once again, the extent of spending discretion intended by Congress involves construing the underlying appropriation (authorizing legislation for the program in question) or laws that contain general instructions to the executive.[110] While Congress has tried to clarify impoundment through the passage of the 1974 Congressional Budget and Impoundment Control Act,[111] the role of impoundment in national security appropriations remains subject to the vagaries of legislative drafting, statutory interpretation, and the separation of powers.

Programmatic or Routine Impoundments Prior to 1974

The earliest impoundment occurred in 1803, when President Jefferson declined to spend a $50,000 appropriation for gunboats to protect the Mississippi River.[112] Jefferson saw no need for the expenditure because the Louisiana Purchase had ended the need for the boats. Congress did not dispute Jefferson's action; the change in conditions clearly obviated the need for the expense.[113] Thus, the gunboat impoundment exemplifies the kind of discretion Congress generally intends to confer on the president—appropriated funds may remain unspent "to the extent . . . the work can be done for less."[114]

At times Congress has explicitly directed budgetary savings or the achievement of other policy goals through use of the impoundment device. After the 1929 stock market crash, Presidents Hoover and Roosevelt asked for and received authority to reorganize executive departments and to lay off and reduce the salary of employees. Executive orders followed that made sweeping policy and greatly enhanced the president's role in fiscal affairs while they effected considerable savings. Similar steps were taken after World War II. A 1950 amendment to the Anti-Deficiency Act permitted the president to establish reserves for any appropriation where savings occur because of "changes in requirements, greater efficiency of operations, or other developments."[115] In an omnibus 1950 appropriation, for example, president Truman was directed to find at least $550 million in savings in the budget, without impairing national defense.[116] Similar means were employed by Congress in 1967, 1968, 1969, and 1970, when a budget-cutting formula permitted the administration to choose the programs and activities that would suffer the cuts. Vietnam programs were excepted.[117]

Debt ceiling legislation has worked in much the same way. President Eisenhower ordered cuts and deferrals in national security programs to comply with the debt limit established by Congress. Although adherence to the debt ceiling appears to be a case of following congressional intent, presidents have sometimes felt free to give preference to administration programs at the expense of those favored by Congress.[118]

In foreign assistance, the president at times has been directed to withhold economic assistance where the recipient has purchased a sophisticated weapon system, unless the president informs Congress that withholding assistance would have a detrimental effect on national security. This unusual mandatory impoundment responds to the practice in foreign assistance of spending all available funds, sometimes including funds "borrowed" from other accounts or programs.[119]

In national security appropriations, impoundment became a significant spending device for the president in the World War II era. As with the Jefferson impoundment, however, President Roosevelt's impoundment of funds for various domestic projects to release more funds for the war effort was not controversial.[120]

Policy Impoundments Prior to 1974

On the few occasions when national security appropriations impoundments have precipitated widespread controversy, the president has argued that impoundment authority was derived from a president's inherent powers concerning national security and the national economy, other strategic needs, or the Commander-in-Chief Clause.[121] President Truman relied on all these bases for authority in 1948 when he impounded $735 million, the amount appropriated by Congress to fund air force groups beyond the number requested in the president's budget.[122] Although Truman's impoundment caused controversy, there was at first no serious clash between the political branches. Ameliorating factors included the fact that the Senate supported the president and only agreed to the House appropriation to break an impasse in the Congress at adjournment time. In addition, a new secretary of defense and the Hoover Commission concurred in the then-fashionable view that a combination of congressional profligacy and Soviet strategy were bankrupting the economy through massive defense spending. Finally, President Truman had established a record of relying on budget surpluses and debt retirement to combat inflation.[123] It therefore was not until a year after this policy impoundment that the House Appropriations Committee found the impoundment to be unjustified under the statute and to be an unconstitutional usurpation of Congress' national security appropriation powers.[124]

A similar dispute was waged over weapons system impoundment during the Kennedy administration. The B-70 bomber was initiated as a prototype program in the Eisenhower administration, although President Eisenhower eventually restricted the program because he believed that the nation's strategic forces would increasingly consist of missiles. In 1961 and 1962 Congress nonetheless supported quickened development of the B-70, and an appropriation in 1961 and a House bill in 1962 significantly expanded the funds requested by the administration for the bomber.

Defense Secretary McNamara declined to release the appropriated funds. The 1962 House Armed Services Committee then reported an authorization bill that "directed, ordered, mandated, and required" the administration to spend the authorized amount.[125] In response President Kennedy objected in a letter to the committee, arguing that "authorizing" rather than "directing" that the funds be spent would be more appropriate for an authorization bill and "more clearly in line with the spirit of the Constitution."[126] The offending language was not enacted, and the president got his way by building just two prototypes of the bomber. One crashed in 1966, while the other found its way to the Air Force Museum.[127]

As with the Eisenhower example, it would be wrong to conclude that the president won a constitutional showdown with the Congress over impoundment authority. Only the air force supported the Armed Services Committee. The other armed services branches, as well as the Appropriations Committee and House leadership, were opposed, the former to what they viewed as a wasteful project,[128] and the latter to the Armed Services Committee's attempt to "direct" spending.

A similar dispute erupted over the construction of nuclear powered frigates in 1966. Anticipating President Johnson's resistance, the authorizing statute required that "the contract for the construction of the . . . frigate . . . shall be entered into as soon as practicable unless the President fully advises the Congress that its construction is not in the national interest."[129] The first frigate was built in 1967, but when no funds were spent for long lead-time components of a second frigate the House Armed Services Committee used language similar to the 1966 authorization recommending that two more frigates be constructed. Before the full Congress could act, the president ordered construction of the new frigate to begin.[130]

Controversy over impoundment authority finally reached a critical point in the Nixon administration. After a 1947 dispute with the Post Office over deficiency spending, Congress considered ways to amend the Anti-Deficiency Act to improve its effectiveness. While recognizing that it was impossible to eliminate deficiency spending required by unforeseen conditions, Congress also knew that changed conditions could produce surpluses. Although the act was amended in 1950 to permit the buildup of reserves to pay for deficiencies in some other area,[131] a General Accounting Office/Bureau of the Budget report emphasized that the amendment should not be read to grant to the president authority to cancel programs or curtail the spending of appropriated funds.[132] The House Appropriations Committee report stated that the new authority should not be construed as "justification for the thwarting of a major policy of Congress by the impounding of funds."[133]

Notwithstanding this legislative history, beginning in 1970 the Nixon administration claimed that "other developments" justified impoundments in a variety of domestic policy settings to reduced inflationary pressure.[134] In response, Congress amended the Anti-Deficiency Act in 1974 by removing the "other developments" language, retaining the authority to create reserves "solely" to provide for contingencies or to effect savings.[135]

The contest over spending priorities between the Democratic Congress and Republican president reached a climax in 1973 when the president ignored authorization language that provided for $6 billion in water pollution control funds.[136] The Supreme Court ordered the president to release the funds,[137] although the Court's opinion relied on the plain language of the instructions in the authorization bill and did not directly comment on the constitutionality of impounding appropriated funds.[138]

Congressional Budgeting and Impoundment Control Act of 1974

After President Nixon aggressively impounded funds to further his domestic policy goals, Congress considered various bills to limit impoundment authority. However, the prospect of a Nixon veto and close votes on measures that would have strictly limited impoundment forced it to abandon these bills. Instead, it enacted a compromise in the Congressional Budgeting and Impoundment Control Act of 1974.[139] One part of the act, reviewed in chapter 5, established congressional budgeting in an effort to wrestle control over the fisc from the president. The other part sought to put an end to unilateral policy impoundments by the president. Under the act, if the president wishes to rescind programs or spend less than an appropriation requires, new legislation has to be enacted within forty-five days of the rescission request.[140] Otherwise the appropriated funds must be spent. If the president wants to "defer" spending, he or she can act unilaterally, after reporting to Congress, subject to either house passing a resolution requiring that the funds be spent.[141] The General Accounting Office is charged with evaluating proposed deferrals or rescissions and determining, based on the president's formal message or on its own initiative absent a message,[142] that the impoundment is properly characterized.[143]

The comptroller general is expressly empowered to sue if required budget authority is withheld by an executive agency beyond the provisions of the act.[144]

Notwithstanding Congress's objective of altering the structure of government spending, the impoundment portion of the act backfired on Congress in its first decade of implementation. Beginning with President Ford, presidents simply used the act to flood Congress with deferral notices, sometimes to achieve programmatic savings and sometimes to reduce a disfavored program. Unable to react in a timely fashion to these notices, Congress witnessed continuing unilateral presidential impoundment, for the first time ironically graced with explicit statutory authority by the Impoundment Control Act itself.[145]

However, in 1983 the fail-safe provision in the act for legislative veto by one-house resolution was rendered unconstitutional by the Supreme Court's reasoning in the *Chadha* decision.[146] Consequently, when local government officials challenged President Reagan's policy-based deferral of $5.6 billion in housing and urban assistance development funds for fiscal year 1985 in *City of New Haven v. United States,* the Court of Appeals struck down the president's deferral authority on the grounds that it was inseverably tainted by the now unconstitutional veto provision.[147] The court reasoned that because Congress would not have granted deferral authority without retaining an opportunity to veto its exercise, the entire deferral mechanism had to be scrapped, except when the impoundment is intended to accomplish programmatic savings that Congress has tacitly approved in the appropriations themselves.[148]

Ironically, vitiating the legislative veto restored Congress's theoretical control over impoundment. Since the decision in *City of New Haven,* the scope of impoundment authority is determined as it used to be—from the appropriations themselves.[149] Moreover, the important question remains unaffected by the act or *City of New Haven:* What constitutes a "policy" as opposed to a "programmatic" or routine impoundment? Only the appropriation or a related authorization can reveal what kind of impoundment authority was intended by Congress. As a practical matter, however, Congress is, as it was before 1974, unable to control policy-based deferrals.[150]

Although Congress reenacted the comptroller general's authority to sue for the release of funds following a policy impoundment,[151] political and perhaps separation-of-powers considerations deter such lawsuits. The only one filed since the 1974 act was dismissed.[152] Moreover, since the longest deferrals may last for one fiscal year, litigation is as likely to facilitate as to prevent policy deferrals. Partisan bickering has prevented Congress from passing a proposal to amend the deferral provision to make it operate like the rescission mechanism, requiring Congress to approve deferrals before they take effect.[153] Despite the advantages of an amendment of this sort—removing the distinction between rescission and deferral and between programmatic and policy deferrals, so that Congress can simply decide whether the impoundment should be permitted, and expressly permitting the president to propose policy deferrals, congressional action is not imminent. Although the Reagan administration sought no policy impoundments after the 1987 amendment to the deferral provision,[154] thus quieting any controversy over impoundment, President Bush impounded funds controversially, as the following example illustrates.

The dispute regarding advance procurement funds to build production representative models for the Navy V-22 Osprey tilt-rotor helicopter illustrates the ongoing uncertainty of impoundment discretion.[155] In December 1989, DOD decided to cancel the V-22 because of its high costs and the availability of lower-cost alternatives. Part of the fiscal 1989 appropriation was used for termination and other costs; $200 million remained available for other purposes.[156]

President Bush announced a deferral of the $200 million in February, 1990, due to termination of the V-22 and to avoid additional costs. The GAO determined that the deferral was effectively a policy deferral and was thus not permitted under the Impoundment Control Act.[157] The DOD fiscal 1991 budget request did not include procurement funds for the V-22. Nonetheless, the 1991 Defense Authorization Act earmarked $165 million plus the $200 million from 1989 "for advance procurement of the production representative V-22 aircraft."[158] The same act authorized $238 million for V-22 research and development, while prohibiting use of such funds on any other helicopter project.[159] The fiscal 1991 DOD appropriation includes these items in lump-sum accounts.[160]

Then the president proposed the $200 million in fiscal 1989 funds for rescission because the V-22 was not sufficiently developed to enter production. Congress effectively rejected the proposal in its Dire Emergency Supplemental Appropriation for fiscal year 1991 by mandating obligation of the $200 million for the V-22, available on a no-year basis until expended.[161] DOD then withheld the new $165 million and sought to transfer the funds to navy R&D for the V-22 by reporting to Congress and waiting for transfer approval. OMB reasoned that, because the $165 million was apportioned[162] and available for obligation, no impoundment had occurred. Thus, the president did not send a deferral message to Congress.[163]

In May 1991, the GAO determined that a deferral should have been reported because, even though technically available for obligation, the funds were being withheld pending congressional action on a transfer request. Moreover, GAO found that the deferral was unauthorized.[164] Conceding that the V-22 was experiencing developmental difficulties that could affect full-scale testing and eventual production, GAO found clear congressional intent to spend $165 million for advance procurement of the production representative V-22. The conference report accompanying the fiscal 1991 authorization recognizes the technical questions in deciding whether to build the V-22 and expresses the desire to test at production scale to "prove conclusively the promise inherent in the V-22 design."[165] In short, Congress wanted immediate advance procurement of production representative V-22s. As with the February 1990 deferral, GAO found that the DOD action "is an attempt to replace the policy decision already made by Congress with its own."[166]

Ironically, the GAO determinations are themselves precatory, because the agency's authority to compel release of impounded funds was linked to the section of the 1974 act invalidated by the *City of New Haven* court. As the comptroller general predicted shortly after *City of New Haven* was decided, the executive branch will continue to defer spending for policy reasons,[167] and the GAO will continue reporting them as such to Congress.[168]

III

CONSTITUTIONAL LIMITS ON THE MAKING OF NATIONAL SECURITY APPROPRIATIONS

Although the Constitution has not been read to impose any "due process of lawmaking"[1] requirements equivalent to due process requirements for adjudication, a few specific constitutional provisions merit our attention because they may limit the national security appropriation processes that we have analyzed in part II.

First, in chapter 9, we examine limits on appropriation riders and omnibus spending bills that may be derived from the president's veto power and requirements of bicameralism. Second, in chapter 10, we examine whether the Statement and Account Clause[2] forbids or limits black budgets for the nation's intelligence and diplomatic activities, which we described in chapter 5.

9

The Veto Clause as a Constitutional Limit on Omnibus Appropriations

Our assessment of the history and mechanics of the power of the purse in national security provides the backdrop for consideration of one possible constitutional limit on that power: the presidential veto.[1] First, we will see that a combination of curtailed impoundment authority and deficit reduction mechanisms have reduced the opportunities of presidents to defeat spending that they disfavor, at the same time that the use of omnibus spending bills and continuing resolutions has increased. We then describe Congress's tendency to bundle varied proposals for legislation in omnibus appropriation bills which seemingly threaten the president's veto power as a limit on the appropriation process. Arguments based on the text and structure of Article I assert that omnibus bills that bundle proposals for legislation are not the discrete "bills" contemplated by the Constitution and that the practice of bundling thwarts important purposes of the president's veto.

We answer that, in general, neither the text or structure of the Constitution nor separation-of-powers principles are threatened by the bundling of nongermane legislation. Instead, we conclude that the president's veto remains formidable in the preenactment wrangling over the contents of an omnibus spending bill and in rejecting even so-called must-pass spending bills. Indeed, because national security appropriations have become the most effective tools by which Congress can exercise both *ex ante* and *ex post* control over presidential military initiatives, a germaneness rule or item veto would only negate this essential check.

The Problem

Although the first appropriation bills were brief and uncomplicated by modern standards, they bundled discrete objects and categories into one bill, as we saw in chapter 4. Bundling and germaneness concerns were addressed by rules that provided a partial corrective, but uneven application illustrates that shaping the appropriation process was a uniquely legislative task, performed pursuant to Article I authority.

Riders appeared in legislation as early as 1820, when the bill for admitting Maine to the union was amended by adding a provision for the admission of Missouri.[2] As the practice of adding restrictions to appropriation legislation increased, in part as a means of coercing the president to sign bills he would not sign if individual provisions were separately presented,[3] disgruntled presidents complained.[4] The item veto was explicitly incorporated into the Constitution of the Confederacy,[5] and after the Civil War, states began to incorporate or discover item veto provisions in their constitutions.[6]

The first presidential appeal for a line-item veto was made by President Grant in 1873, in the form of a recommendation that Congress consider a constitutional amendment for an item veto that would have been subject to a two-thirds override.[7] President Hayes took a less modest tack. He successfully vetoed five appropriation bills in 1879, asserting their unconstitutionality on the grounds that they contained prescriptive riders, which, in his view, "strike[s] from the Constitution the qualified negative of the President."[8] All subsequent presidents except Taft have urged that a line-item veto be created by statute or constitutional amendment.[9]

In the appropriation process, however, complaints were less frequent and more muted because presidents exercised considerable influence in shaping spending bills and were granted postenactment spending discretion. At least as early as 1921, the president enjoyed broad discretion to choose not to spend appropriated funds by impounding them, while he often dominated the appropriation process through his control over budget preparation and the technical data and economic assumptions upon which spending decisions were based.

Presidential complaints increased after the 1974 Budget Act curtailed impoundment and asserted a new congressional role in preparing aggregate budget figures and supplying technical support for appropriators through the new budget committees and Congressional Budget Office. The president's fiscal prerogatives were restricted at a time when Congress was increasingly relying on omnibus appropriations and continuing resolutions to accomplish its annual appropriation tasks and making important policy decisions through appropriation restrictions. As a result, the president is increasingly presented with take-it-or-leave-it omnibus appropriation bills (which also often contain nongermane restrictions) that he is hard-pressed to veto.[10]

The problem may be illustrated by recalling our earlier discussion of funding the Nicaraguan Contras in chapter 6. After the first aid for the Contras was expended from the CIA contingency fund, subsequent Contra support provisions were forged in the crucible of the defense appropriation process. The fiscal year 1983 aid ($19 million that could not be used by DOD or the CIA "for the purpose of overthrowing the government of Nicaragua") was first proposed as a limitation by floor amendment and eventually enacted in the Intelligence Authorization and Defense Appropriations Acts that were part of a larger continuing resolution. Fiscal year 1984 began with DOD operating under a continuing resolution, while a conference committee completed work on the DOD Appropriations Act by agreeing to insert a restriction that essentially split the House and Senate/administration difference and limited to $24 million the support available to "any . . . entity of the United States involved in intelligence activities . . . for the purpose or which would have the effect" of supporting the Contras.

In fiscal 1985 the final product was different—an end to appropriations for the Contras—but the process was by then familiar. The appropriation for defense was not enacted by the end of the fiscal year, both the House and Senate had their own versions of continuing resolutions prepared in advance, and a conference committee worked out the final deal. This time the House conferees won out, and they inserted the funding prohibition as an amendment to a continuing resolution that included funds for DOD and many other government programs for the entire fiscal year.[11] President Reagan reluctantly signed the continuing resolution, while later expressing his dismay that Congress had failed to support the Contras.[12] He clearly would have preferred an "unbundled" measure on which to exercise his veto.

With the enactment of the Gramm-Rudman-Hollings Deficit Control Act in 1985 and its amendment in 1987, the recent tendencies of Congress to fence the president out of the appropriation process were accentuated. The budget deficit reduction goals of the act do not depend upon independent congressional or presidential initiative, but instead prescribe automatic mechanisms—the sequestration procedure—to ensure that the annual budget conforms to deficit reduction goals. The ironic effect of Gramm-Rudman-Hollings has been to encourage delay in the appropriation process, because no appropriations committee wants to bring to the floor a bill that may be subject to new cuts to meet the deficit reduction goals.[13] The second round of cuts could trim the appropriation bill to meet a budget resolution, and then subject it to automatic sequestration because another spending bill has failed to meet the budget resolution limit.

The possibility of sequestration, along with the chance that economic indicators will improve, thus discourages producing appropriation bills in a timely fashion. This in turn encourages continuing resolutions and delay until the eleventh hour, as well as nongermane amendments. When an omnibus continuing resolution funding a significant part of the government comes to the president several weeks after the fiscal year deadline, on the day an existing continuing resolution is set to expire, the president may have little choice but to sign the bill. Meanwhile, there may not be time for executive branch officials to give careful attention to the potentially varied policy decisions made in the bundled package that is presented as a bill, along with the usually massive appropriation provisions to which the restrictions are affixed. Furthermore, the president cannot exercise the veto to eliminate the harmful portions of the legislation without rejecting the entire package.

To counter bundling, a series of constitutional amendments and bills have been introduced in the Congress in recent years[14] granting a line-item veto to the president.[15] Late in 1987, the controversy reached a new level when President Reagan lambasted Congress after signing a fiscal 1988 continuing resolution funding more than $600 billion in government operations, including defense, in a 1,057-page bill accompanied by a 1,053-page conference report.

Completed in conference late on December 22, almost two months into the fiscal year for which it was appropriating funds, the bill was carried in boxes to the House and then the Senate floor, where members approved it within hours, obviously not having had time to read the provisions. The president signed the bill the next morning, again without enough time for him or his advisers to read, much less reflect, on its provisions.[16]

After President Reagan received a well-publicized letter from a New York lawyer in 1987 arguing that the president had the constitutional authority to veto separate provisions in an appropriation,[17] initial reactions among administration supporters were cautious, even skeptical.[18] But President Bush stated to the press early in his presidency that he would consider testing the line-item veto idea in court.[19] Beginning in November 1989, he began to assert a functional equivalent of the line-item veto by purporting to excise or refusing to recognize provisions in bills he signed that he viewed as unconstitutional. In signing the 1990 Defense Department appropriation, for example, President Bush pointed to language in the statute instructing DOD to follow procedures for spending outlined in a committee report. The president simply stated that "such language has no legal force or effect."[20]

The Constitutional Challenge

Proponents of the line-item veto or of a germaneness requirement for legislation make the following argument, based on the presentment clauses of the Constitution.[21] Although the word "veto" does not appear in the text of the Constitution, the presidential veto was intended to accomplish two objects: the protection of the presidency from legislative encroachment and the prevention of enactment of harmful laws. When the framers called for presentment of "bill[s]" to the president for signature or veto, they contemplated the presentation of numerous, discreet proposals for legislation not bundled with nongermane add-ons and not consolidated into omnibus continuing resolutions. The second purpose of the veto may only be served if the president has the authority to veto separate objectionable lines or sections of such bundled or omnibus legislation.

Most contemporary advocates of the line-item veto concede the uncertain constitutionality of the device, at least when in its most literal incarnation—as the power to veto any "line" in an appropriation bill.[22] It is argued that a line-item veto might nonetheless effectively be exercised in variants that are not themselves line-item vetoes and which may thus be less vulnerable to constitutional challenge. A subject veto would permit, for example, the veto of nongermane riders to defense appropriations. The nongermane item would be deemed a "bill" for presentment clause purposes, thus validating the veto.[23] Functionally, it is argued, the subject veto works just like presidential impoundment worked before the 1974 act.[24]

If neither the literal line-item nor the subject veto is constitutionally permissible, those who believe that omnibus appropriations and nongermane riders dilute the presidential veto assert that the president may have the Article II authority either to excise unconstitutional provisions from a valid bill as part of the duty "to faithfully execute the laws," or, at least, to excise those provisions that would interfere with the president's own constitutional authority.[25]

It has also been argued that the structure of Article I and various parallel constructions within its text support a narrow interpretation of the phrase "Every Bill." When the framers wanted a legislative task to be performed infrequently, the argument goes, they said so:[26] Congress shall assemble at least once in every year;[27] "from time to time" each house shall publish a journal;[28] and "a regular Statement and Account of the Receipts and Expenditures of all public Money" shall be made.[29] Thus, when the Constitution requires that "Every Bill" be presented, it contemplates "sequential, periodic, contemporaneous action being taken by Congress."[30]

The Rebuttal

Constitutional Text

It is generally agreed that the Constitutional Convention did not illuminate the contemporary debate surrounding germaneness and the item veto.[31] While the Orders Presentment Clause was apparently inserted to prevent Congress from evading the presidential veto through labeling a bill as an act or resolution,[32] neither the debates surrounding the presentment clauses nor anything else in the Convention, ratification debates, or *The Federalist* discusses disaggregating the presidential veto to portions of bills. Instead, the framers' concerns were whether the veto should be absolute or qualified; whether the veto should be exercised jointly with the courts or by the president alone; and whether the override should require two-thirds or three-fourths of the Congress.[33]

At the Convention, the veto was variously called the president's "negative," "qualified negative," "revisionary power," or "revisionary check."[34] Recent debate has focused on the meaning of these terms as they were understood at the time of the framing. Suffice it to say that, like debate about original intent in general, there is no clear answer to the question of the framers' specific intentions with respect to the president's veto. Advocates of presidential power emphasize the idea of "revision" and extrapolate a presidential authority to revise legislation.[35] Others maintain that revising something in the 1780s meant simply reviewing it.[36] While it is generally agreed that the framers conceived of the veto to protect the presidency from legislative encroachment and to prevent the enactment of harmful laws,[37] only some other textual authority or limit could extend the veto to separable parts of bills presented to the president unless each "bill" requires discrete subject matter.

It has been argued that "[t]he same constitutional silence that sanctions the bundling of bills may *also* sanction their veto on something other than an all-or-nothing basis."[38] If the framers contemplated bundling, it may be because they also thought that the president would exercise the veto when bundling became excessive. This argument not only lacks historical support,[39] it also assigns the president a premature role in the legislative process. It is Congress, not the president, that makes the rules for carrying out the legislative process through presentment. The president becomes a participant in the legislative process[40] only after presentment of legislation in the form determined by Congress.

The presidential veto implicit in the presentment clauses must, of course, be assessed in light of other provisions of the Constitution, including the bicameralism requirement and opportunity for override, as well as the grant to Congress to "determine the rules of its proceedings."[41] Without the opportunity for override following an item veto of a nongermane provision of a bill, the president could sign into law a statute that Congress would not have presented in such expurgated form for his signature.[42] The resulting law would take legal effect without ever having received bicameral approval. As the Court said in *Immigration & Naturalization Service v. Chadha,*[43] except for a few instances not relevant to the item veto,[44] *all* exercises of federal legislative authority must comport with the "single, finely wrought and exhaustively considered"[45] bicameralism and presentment requirements of Article I. The Article I bicameralism requirement thus stands squarely in the way of any form of an item veto. The president's exercise of an item veto would itself be a "legislative" act within the meaning of Article I[46] and would thus violate the bicameralism provision.[47]

The possibility that Congress may be permitted an opportunity to override items vetoed does not rectify the bicameralism problem. First, bicameralism prevents the president from taking any action on legislation that has not received majority approval in both houses of Congress.[48] Likewise the original bicameralism requirement may not be satisfied by a later override without presentment. Second, because override requires a supermajority vote,[49] an item veto that was sustained in an attempt at override would permit the president to *make* law opposed by a majority of Congress. With an ordinary veto, the president can only hope to *prevent* the making of law supported by less than a supermajority. Third, vetoes are rarely overridden.[50] An item veto would be even more difficult to override because it would divide legislators who traded votes in support of separate provisions to get an entire bill passed. In short, the purpose of the override opportunity would be undermined by the item veto.

Finally, even a statute that granted an item veto to the president with an opportunity for override by a simple majority vote would not cure the constitutional defect. Assuming that Congress could define what constitutes a "bill" in such a hypothetical statute so that an item veto could be exercised, the purported majority override fails to comply with the Article I requirement that two-thirds may override. Ironically, such a statute could be enacted, an item veto exercised, the simple majority override voted, and the president could plausibly refuse to execute the override for want of a two-thirds vote.

Nor, in any event, does the Constitution impose any rules to insure the efficacy of the legislative process, including the president's role in it in a particular case.[51] In *Field v. Clark,*[52] a section of the enacted bill was omitted from the enrolled bill signed by the president, the Speaker of the House and the president of the Senate. The procedural gaffe did not diminish the legal effect of the bill as passed. Although the Court noted that there is "no authority [to view] as a legislative act, any bill not passed by Congress,"[53] it held that the signature of the Speaker and president of the Senate constitute a "declaration" that the bill has received "the sanction of the legislative branch of the government."[54] Presumptively, then, the Article I, section 7 requirement that bills be bicamerally passed and presented to the president may be satisfied through any prior legislative process accepted by the Congress. Thus, House and Senate rules on germaneness and riders, limitations on debate, and the like are all within Congress's discretion to "determine the rules of the proceedings" and are not called into question by the presentment clauses.

As the Supreme Court has said, the words of the presentment clauses must be understood "in their natural and obvious sense, and are to be given the meaning they have in common use unless there are very strong reasons to the contrary."[55] One potential limit on the size and scope of a "bill" is the ten-day presentment period. In *Edwards v. United States*,[56] the Court affirmed that the "fundamental purpose" of the ten-day presentment period is "to provide appropriate opportunity for the President to consider the bills presented to him."[57] This limitation is more hypothetical than real, however. None of the megabills presented to the president has been so massive that it could not be thoroughly examined in ten days. The more practical problem is that continuing resolutions are sometimes presented on or close to the date upon which an existing continuing resolution and the spending authority conferred therein are to expire. The solution to this form of coercion is political—the president can and has vetoed resolutions which condition the continuation of basic government spending authority on the acceptance of omnibus appropriations laden with restrictive amendments.

Practice

The argument that the Article I "bill" is "a legislative instrument setting forth one or more propositions of law, all related, however, to a single subject matter"[58] is based on speculation about the framers' intent, including speculation that they did not foresee bundled legislation on today's scale.[59] As noted, critics of omnibus legislation must speculate about the original understanding because neither the Constitution, the debates at the Constitutional Convention, nor *The Federalist* discusses, much less defines, what is meant by "bill." At the same time, there is evidence that the framers knew of and approved the bundling of appropriations and nongermane legislation by the Congress, because this was a common practice in colonial legislation.[60]

Patterned on the English Constitution, the colonial charters granted the governor an absolute veto over legislation. Some of the governors or the Crown, acting through the Board of Trade, also possessed the item veto.[61] Chapter 2 shows that as the colonial assemblies found that they could effectively deny the royal governors some measure of control over the affairs of the colonies by limiting their ability to initiate or amend appropriation bills;[62] they also learned to employ restrictions in necessary appropriations as a means of evading the governors' veto.[63] It was, indeed, fairly common for colonial legislatures to bundle legislation and add restrictive amendments in attempts to coerce a governor's signature.[64] The disdain for the royal governors increasingly led to assembly-dominated governments, particularly in the area of controlling provincial funds, especially those needed for military supply.[65]

The colonial experience thus establishes that the framers were aware of the practices of bundling legislation and affixing nongermane restrictions to bills. In the years after the Declaration of Independence, most state governments eliminated many of the royal characteristics of the governor, including the absolute veto.[66] States typically prohibited governors from any participation in the legislative process, and none of the few governors who retained a veto power exercised it before 1787.[67]

At the same time, the postrevolutionary period saw the continuation of executive spending discretion. Although the appropriation power was solidly placed in the legislatures, the governors retained the equivalent of the modern impoundment power, spending appropriated funds or not as they saw fit.[68] This impoundment power functioned similarly to an item veto. While practice underscores the general familiarity of the framers and members of early Congresses with the executive's discretion not to spend appropriation funds, as explained in chapter 8, impoundment is legally distinct from the power to veto lines in appropriations.

The strong distaste for executive power which permitted bundling and nongermane restrictions to emerge in the colonies was considerably tempered during the 1780s under the Articles of Confederation. By the time of the 1787 Constitutional Convention, the need for a stronger national government and a strong central executive was widely felt, although the precise contours of the relationship between the elected branches in the shaping of fiscal and other policy had yet to be worked out.

We noted in chapter 4 that the first appropriations bill enacted by the first Congress in 1789[69] aggregated all expenditures into the four categories that the newly appointed treasury secretary Alexander Hamilton had employed in making the budget estimates which he submitted to Congress.[70] The single-section bill was at once omnibus[71] and relatively short—it occupied less than a single double-spaced page.[72] Nongermane restrictions were not affixed to this or to other early appropriations of the First Congress, which were longer than the first bill and still omnibus in nature, though pictures of brevity by today's standards.[73]

Nevertheless, the House adopted a rule in its first session prohibiting nongermane amendments during floor debate.[74] It is telling that the Senate did not follow suit until much later and that the rules make nongermane amendments subject only to a point of order. If nongermane riders had been thought by the framers to be unconstitutional, the members of the first Congress would have known and these rules would have been superfluous.

By 1793, the Appropriations Act consisted of just one paragraph, covering almost three pages in the Statutes at Large.[75] In chapter 4, we briefly traced some of the political battle that then erupted between the Republicans, led by Congressman (later Treasury Secretary) Albert Gallatin, and the Federalists, led by Hamilton and Wolcott, concerning the degree of spending discretion Congress should confer on the executive branch, particularly in military affairs. As we noted there, Gallatin's attempts to retain legislative supremacy over fiscal matters were more or less permanently defeated by 1798 when Congress approved lump-sum appropriations for the military by omnibus legislation and executive transfers among military accounts by acquiescence.[76] Thus, at the same time Congress was learning the art of omnibus appropriations, albeit on a small scale, the president was being given significant spending discretion by both statute and custom.

Historically, presidents have failed to assert a line-item veto power because they believed that they had no such authority. They requested greater discretion in applying the veto, but they knew that it had to come by a constitutional amendment, or, at the very least, from Congress.

Presidential impoundment has been characterized as the functional equivalent of the line-item veto.[77] Given impoundment's long history and congressional acquiescence until 1974, it is argued that it is reasonable to conclude that the custom of the line-item veto has thus been established as a gloss on the Constitution.[78]

There are two flaws with the argument, either of which is fatal. First, if the gloss existed before 1974, the chain was explicitly broken in 1974 when unilateral impoundment was effectively eliminated.[79] Second, impoundment and the line-item veto are not fungible. While the line-item veto permits disaggregated choices between signing and vetoing provisions in an appropriation, impoundment includes the far more expansive power of permitting the president to adjust spending from line to line, within accounts, or within any other combination of provisions or programs.[80] Impoundment is the greater power. The two are hardly constitutional equivalents.

In signing the Competition in Contracting Act of 1984,[81] President Reagan noted that he regarded certain provisions as unconstitutional encroachments on Article II powers and that he would instruct federal agencies not to comply with those provisions. The Ninth Circuit Court of Appeals later upheld the provisions in question[82] and said this about President Reagan's attempt at a line-item veto:

> Article I, sec. 7 does not empower a President to revise a bill, either before or after signing. It does not empower the President to employ a so-called "line-item veto" and excise or sever provisions of a bill with which he disagrees. The only constitutionally prescribed means for the President to effectuate his objections to a bill is to veto it and to state those objections upon returning the bill to Congress. The "line-item veto" does not exist in the federal Constitution, and the executive branch cannot bring a de facto "line-item veto" into existence by promulgating orders to suspend parts of statutes which the President has signed into law.[83]

President Reagan did not veto an appropriation, nor did he claim that any provision was not germane. Nonetheless, this dictum underscores that the plain meaning of the presentment and bicameralism clauses effectively answers the arguments for a constitutional germaneness rule or line-item veto.

Conclusion: An Unneeded Constitutional Solution

Consider still another chapter in the Contra aid story. The fiscal 1988 continuing resolution for defense revealed Congress at its worst: A 2,100-page bill and conference report was patched together in the shadow of an imminent shutdown of government, prompting Congress to promulgate rules to preclude debate, prevent amendment, and practically deny access to the final bill. The end product was the work of a handful of powerful legislators and their staffs.[84] In his 1988 State of the Union Address, President Reagan scathingly criticized Congress for its budget process and asserted that he would not sign "another one of these."[85]

The 1988 continuing resolution was developed under internal rules in the House that effectively limited debate in considering important policy questions to thirty minutes.[86] In the Senate, amendments piled on a wide array of provisions, most not germane to the appropriations under consideration. Burdened by an interest in the fast-approaching Christmas adjournment, the Senate considered all seventy-seven proposed amendments in one day.[87]

By the time the bill reached conference, it was already close to its final form in terms of the amount of appropriations—over $600 billion. The fiscal year deadline had come and gone. The hugeness of the appropriations and the need to keep the government from closing down had already made this one of those critical "must sign" pieces of legislation. Once again, Congress had managed to coerce a signature from a president who was trying to uphold fiscal responsibility as well as to preserve the integrity of the presidential veto.

Yet, ironically, it was the president who prevailed on most of the critical policy choices in the fiscal 1988 continuing resolution, and it was his use of the veto threat that shaped the final package. The administration was well represented at the conference, where the most important unresolved issues concerned the FCC fairness doctrine and Contra aid. After threatening to veto the continuing resolution unless it included aid for the Contras and excluded the fairness doctrine, the president held his ground and prevailed.[88] The *in terrorem* threat of the Reagan veto appears to have been roughly as coercive as the congressional tactics of bundling a massive appropriation with nongermane riders (at least one of which was only introduced during conference), made ready for presentment well into the fiscal year for which it was appropriating and a few days before the traditional holiday recess.

Omnibus bills are thus *not* veto-proof. The veto threat still moderates the contents of the bills.[89] Indeed, the political horse-trading that goes on in conference or elsewhere before presentment works something like a preenactment item veto, particularly where the president remains steadfast as Reagan did on his fiscal 1988 Contra aid. As the omnibus format has become more popular, perhaps because its broad parameters permit a more politically acceptable legislative product overall, the president's participation in the legislative process as a "recommender" has likewise grown in importance. Compromise may have become more possible.[90]

It is thus hard to muster sympathy for an executive branch with a supposedly weakened veto power. The ordinary presidential veto is rarely overridden—President Bush suffered only one override (a cable television regulation bill) in more than thirty-five attempts.[91] Bush vetoed six spending bills—five because of abortion-related provisions and the sixth to pressure Congress to make concessions during the 1990 budget talks.[92] Moreover, as we have shown elsewhere in this book, the executive has considerable national security spending discretion, notwithstanding the statutory proscription on impoundment.

Moreover, the lump-sum funding preferred by the executive branch and the Congress to enhance spending discretion is normally not directly controlled in the appropriations themselves, but in committee reports.[93] As presently structured, the appropriation bills would offer a president exercising a line-item veto little additional control over individual activities.[94] In addition, given the importance of the national security appropriation power for legislative control over the executive's use of force, a germaneness rule or item veto would only make the president less subject to an essential check on the war powers.

It is arguable that in an extreme case—most obviously if Congress bundled every bill passed during a session into one omnibus bill for presentment to the president[95]—that his veto power would be unconstitutionally diluted.[96] The test of constitutionality would be whether the resulting intrusion on the president's veto power would be justified by an overriding need to promote some constitutional objective within the constitutional authority of Congress.[97] Even in such an extreme hypothetical case, it is unclear whether presidential excision or item veto would be permissible or whether the president would have to rely alone on his considerable political powers to rally the voters and threaten Congress. Absent such a case (to which we have not even come close, in our view), there is neither a textual constitutional limitation on congressional authority to package legislation nor a presidential authority to disaggregate legislation in exercising the veto.

10

The Statement and Account Clause as a Constitutional Limit on Black Budgets

The requirement that "a regular Statement and Account of the Receipts and Expenditures of all public Money shall be published from time to time"[1] complements Congress's power to "raise and support" the army[2] and the provision that "[n]o Money shall be drawn from the Treasury, but in Consequence of Appropriations made by Law . . . ."[3] While Congress controls the fisc, and all spending must be supported by an appropriation, Congress also must publicly account for its expenditures. The public accounting requirement prods Congress to assure itself that executive agencies are not violating the object and amount limitations in their appropriations, at the same time that it keeps the people informed about how both political branches have spent tax revenues.

The reality has been very much at odds with this constitutional ideal. On many occasions when the president and Congress have shared a common defense policy objective, the political branches have conspired to permit secret spending that has escaped the Statement and Account requirement. Despite statutes that implement the requirement by mandating disclosure of public spending and General Accounting Office (GAO) audits of most federal expenditures,[4] billions of dollars in confidential and secret funds remain concealed from the public and from most members of Congress every year.

The sections below will review the original understanding of the Statement and Account Clause and the delegations of confidential and secret fund authority that have frequently appeared in national security appropriations. We then provide an assessment of the Statement and Account requirement in light of ongoing confidential and secret spending.

The Original Understanding of Statement and Account

On the one hand, the framers "deemed fiscal information essential if the electorate was to exercise any control over its representatives."[5] As Congressman Randolph remarked in an early session of Congress, "unless the House examines if the amount of appropriation is exceeded by the expenditure; or if it be misapplied, that is, if money appropriated for one object be expended for another; unless we do this, sir, our control over the public purse is a mere name—an empty shadow."[6] On the other hand, the idea that some affairs of government must be conducted in secret to protect the national security is as old as government itself. The first Americans were aware of the need for secrecy in the conduct of certain affairs by the English Crown, and, when they declared independence from Britain, they conducted the sessions and maintained the records of the Continental Congress in secret. Through congressional boards and committees, they also directed some diplomatic, military, and financial matters in secret.[7]

When they drafted a Constitution, in a convention that was itself conducted secretly, the framers specifically addressed the question of the publicity that should attend its fiscal decisions.[8] While they retained for Congress the option of exempting from publication in its journal "such Parts as may in their Judgment require Secrecy,"[9] and only required that the president "from time to time give to the Congress Information on the State of the Union,"[10] they imposed the Statement and Account requirement for "all public Money."

Although the statement and account language was not proposed until late in the Convention, the delegates uniformly endorsed the idea that government should give a public financial accounting. The debate concerned the extent and timing of the obligation.[11] The question was resolved by the unanimous adoption of Madison's motion to substitute "from time to time" for Mason's original proposal to require reports "annually."[12]

However, comments by delegates Wilson, Madison, and Mason indicate that at least some who voted for the change understood that it might permit a delay in the publication of certain expenditures that might require a veil of secrecy[13]—delay, but not permanent concealment. Mason himself later recognized that while "some matters, such as ongoing diplomatic negotiations and military operations, might require secrecy, he did not conceive that the receipts and expenditures of the public money ought ever to be concealed."[14]

Did Mason simply fail to account for the possibility that disclosing the expenses of an ongoing military operation could undermine its success? Probably not. The framers knew that secrecy was sometimes essential.[15] In *The Federalist,* former diplomat John Jay argued that "in the negotiation of treaties . . . perfect secrecy and immediate dispatch are sometimes requisite."[16] Again, however, Jay's argument appears to support merely a brief delay in publication of the costs of a diplomatic or military operation. Nothing in *The Federalist* or in any of the Convention or ratification debates, except for executive power advocate Gouverneur Morris's oblique claim that the publication requirement would be "impossible in many cases,"[17] supports an interpretation of the Statement and Account Clause that would permit permanently concealing the receipt or expenditure of public funds.

Congress's Delegation of Confidential and Secret Fund Authority

Confidential fund authority is a product of the traditional appropriations process, where "vouchers" normally record the details of spending, which is in turn then subject to a GAO audit[18] and to reporting in the Treasury Department's Combined Statement of Receipts and Expenditures.[19] Pursuant to an appropriation which authorizes confidential spending, however, the agency uses "certificates" rather than vouchers to record expenditures. Certificates generally affirm that the funds were spent for authorized confidential purposes, with each certificate "deemed a sufficient voucher for the sum or sums therein expressed to have been expended."[20] Because the certificate lacks detailed information about the expenditure, the GAO cannot perform its customary audit[21] and no description of the spending appears in the Combined Statement.[22] Furthermore, because secret funds are also not products of the open appropriation process, they thus effectively remain covert from appropriation to spending to auditing.[23]

The need for secrecy in conducting diplomatic affairs was recognized by the Congress in 1790 when $40,000 was appropriated in an account for the president "for the support of such persons as he shall commission to serve the United States in foreign parts."[24] The expenses of these appointments could be publicly accounted for or not, at the president's discretion. Although this fund was made permanent in 1793 and still exists today,[25] no other confidential funds were created until this century.

World War I precipitated a 1916 navy appropriation for unvouchered funds for "obtaining information from abroad and at home,"[26] while World War II caused Congress to confer significant additional confidential funds authority for the president's use in the nation's war and diplomatic efforts.[27] The World War II funds were more generic in nature, much larger in amount, and broadened to include the secretary of war as well as the president.[28] Although the creation and use of these wartime confidential funds were largely uncontroversial, restrictive language in the 1943 and 1944 statutes indicates that Congress was reacting to the president's use of these funds for programs that the Congress had trimmed from the president's budget.[29]

President Roosevelt also persuaded a few members of Congress to effectively authorize secret funding for development of the first atomic bomb. The Manhattan Project was initially funded out of an army Engineer Service account and the Expediting Production account. When an additional appropriation was needed, the administration prevailed upon House leaders who successfully produced a lump-sum appropriation with only a handful of members of Congress knowing anything about the project.[30]

The number of confidential funds grew after the war. In addition to confidential funds for operation and maintenance for the service branches and the defense agencies, and a contingency fund for the Defense Department, appropriations had, by 1975, created confidential funds for emergencies in the diplomatic and consular service, the Atomic Energy Commission, the National Aeronautics and Space Administration, and the FBI, among others.[31]

The largest confidential funds are within the DOD budget. Legislation in 1966 and 1967 permitted funds to support Vietnamese "and other free world forces in Vietnam [Laos and Thailand] . . . on such terms and conditions as the Secretary of Defense may determine."[32] DOD only had to report expenditures to the armed services and appropriations committees of both houses.[33] Hearings in 1969 and 1970 uncovered a Nixon administration program using this fund to confer sizeable subsidies to the Philippines, Thailand, and South Korea in return for their military or other support for the American war effort.[34] Hearings also revealed that monies appropriated for various AID assistance programs, including its Food for Peace program, had been used to support paramilitary operations in Laos and other military efforts in Southeast Asia.[35]

Prompted by revelations that confidential funds had been abused by the administration in the coverup of the Watergate scandal, Congress acted to consolidate some of the smaller funds and proceeded to enact authority for most of the existing funds in authorizing legislation after 1974.[36] Today such funds typically appropriate sums that "can be used for emergencies and extraordinary expenses" upon certification by the secretary that the funds were required for "confidential military purposes."[37]

Secret funds for the nation's intelligence community dwarf all other unvouchered defense expenditures.[38] As described in chapter 5, the Central Intelligence Agency Act of 1949 provided that CIA funds "may be expended without regard to the provisions of law and regulations relating to the expenditure of Government funds."[39] Confidential tasks undertaken by the CIA can therefore be accounted for by certificate.[40]

At first, this secret funding of the intelligence community was virtually unchecked by legislative oversight. Agency staff would report to the intelligence subcommittees of the House and Senate Appropriations Committees, but these reports were delivered infrequently and in executive session. Members of Congress generally took the attitude that they did not want to know about the details of agency operations or, sometimes, even of their existence.[41]

Not until the extensive involvement of the CIA in the war in Southeast Asia was reported did Congress begin to assert some control over CIA expenditures and budget transfer authority. When the press reported (and members of Congress first learned) that the CIA had been supporting paramilitary actions in Laos and Cambodia, Congress included a provision in the Foreign Assistance Act of 1971 limiting military assistance for Cambodia to $341 million.[42] This measure effectively denied the administration the option of enhancing its appropriated funds with CIA funds for the Cambodian operation transferred from another agency.

Further legislation emerged in 1974, in the form of the Hughes-Ryan amendment to the Foreign Assistance Act,[43] which required presidential approval and reporting to some members of Congress for any CIA spending abroad other than for intelligence gathering. Thus, while the Hughes-Ryan limit on the use of appropriated funds exempted intelligence collection and merely required reporting "in a timely fashion,"[44] at least some members of Congress would learn of most special operations. Then, in 1976, separate intelligence committees were created in the House and Senate in a further effort to enhance the quality and quantity of oversight of intelligence community expenditures.[45] Reports of CIA expenditures are now made to these committees.[46]

Although various legislative proposals for publication of the CIA budget and for audit of agency activities were made in the 1970s, the budgets of the intelligence community remain secret from the public.[47] In 1990 Congress acted to permit any member of Congress to examine the intelligence budget.[48] The General Accounting Office Act[49] permits the GAO to perform a limited audit of unvouchered expenditures, but the CIA is exempt. The president is permitted to exempt other foreign intelligence and law enforcement activities, and the audit itself is only for the purpose of determining whether the expenditure was made and whether it was authorized.[50] Given the broad delegations of confidential and secret fund authority, this reform is practically no reform.

Even Congress's best efforts have not reigned in unauthorized military spending. For example, neither Hughes-Ryan nor the 1980 GAO audit authority succeeded in controlling the Reagan administration's support of the paramilitary war in Nicaragua. In 1981, when the administration committed itself to support the Contras, it began its activities without public or congressional debate or specifically appropriated funds. Instead, as noted in chapter 8, the contingency fund of the CIA, a secret fund within a larger secret fund, was used to get the Contras' campaign going. Although the existence of the contingency fund is known to Congress, and its use in this instance was within statutory authority, the only "publication" of the costs of this support came in the form of President Reagan's report to Congress, pursuant to Hughes-Ryan, that nearly $20 million had been committed for the 1982 fiscal year to assist the Contras in interdicting arms and supplies that were reportedly being exported from the Sandinistas to rebels in neighboring El Salvador.[51]

Until Congress acted explicitly in 1983 to forbid the use of the CIA contingency fund to augment appropriated funds in support of the Contras,[52] there was no public accounting or even notice to most members of Congress of the actual investment in the Contras' cause. According to the congressional committees that later investigated the Iran-Contra affair, the administration continued to rely on the contingency fund to supplement its other unappropriated funds in support of the Contras even after the 1984 Boland amendment cut off appropriated funds.[53]

Two other Iran-Contra examples further illustrate the extent to which unvouchered funds escape the apparent limits of the Statement and Account Clause. As described previously, the DOD budget contains sums that may be spent by the Pentagon solely on the certificate of the secretary of defense. Among the items that have been funded out of this black budget are the special forces.[54] When appropriated funds for the Contras were exhausted in 1984, the administration relied on DOD to augment the military equipment assigned to the special forces, and the equipment was then diverted to the NSC and CIA personnel who were coordinating the Contra resupply effort.[55] Second, when the administration decided to transfer arms to Iran directly in early 1986, the president was advised that he could transfer the arms "outside the requirements" of the Arms Export Control Act if he used the CIA. While the arms to be transferred were the subject of an appropriation and their sale would normally be reported in the GAO annual statement, the 1932 Economy Act would, the president was advised, permit DOD to transfer the arms to the CIA, which could then carry out the transfer to Iran as a covert action. The costs would never be publicly reported.[56]

An Assessment of the Statement and Account Clause

Does the historical record comport with the letter or the spirit of the Statement and Account Clause? A definitive answer has not been and probably will not be provided by the federal courts. Although citizens and members of Congress have sued to end secret CIA spending, the suits have been dismissed as nonjusticiable.[57] Certainly it is impossible to square permanently secret accounts with the text of the Constitution. "All public Money" is a clear prescription, and "from time to time" does not excuse permanent secrecy. Confidential fund accounts, on the other hand, can perhaps be defended because the public is informed about the appropriation in bulk and may thus influence the debate about the activities which may be undertaken with the funds.[58] At least before the Central Intelligence Agency Act of 1949, Congress always made public the amount in an unvouchered fund either when the appropriation was approved or at some later time.[59]

Perhaps the strongest argument for Congress's power to delegate sweeping authority over unvouchered funds to the president is that it has the power to "arrange its appropriation processes so as to protect national security."[60] According to a Supreme Court dictum, "Congress has plenary power to exact any reporting and accounting requirement it considers appropriate," in spite of what the Constitution says.[61] Unless a political impasse develops between Congress and the president concerning the authority to make unaccounted-for expenditures, the courts are likely to continue to insist that the constitutional requirements be shaped through the political processes.[62]

However, if a change in the political winds prompts Congress to require that the CIA budget be published, it is unlikely that the president could constitutionally resist, notwithstanding President Bush's threatened veto of the fiscal 1992 Intelligence Authorization Act, which had included a publication requirement.[63] The plain meaning of the Statement and Account Clause, coupled with Congress' Necessary and Proper Clause authority implicitly recognized by the Supreme Court, solidly supports publication of the CIA budget. The Court's very recognition of Congress's "plenary" Statement and Account power suggests the constitutionality of its exercise to require such publication.

IV

THE SUBSTANTIVE SCOPE OF THE POWER OF THE PURSE IN NATIONAL SECURITY

Because appropriations have played a major role both in legitimating—authorizing or ratifying—and in restricting national security actions by the executive, debate concerning the legality of such actions has often centered on the statutory and constitutional scope of the appropriations. Can a mere appropriation legitimate a national security action by the executive? If so, is a clear statement of congressional approval required, or may such approval be inferred from an ambiguous appropriation? Conversely, can a mere appropriation, consistently with the separation of powers, restrict the executive's discretion to take a national security action? Does Congress's failure to appropriate funds impliedly restrict such discretion? If either kind of restriction is unconstitutional, can the executive avoid the restriction by spending funds without appropriation?

One common ingredient in this debate is the implication suggested by many that "mere" appropriations do not carry the same force and effect as "ordinary" or "substantive" legislation. In chapter 11, we therefore start with an examination of this proposition. We show that although appropriations in general have the same force and effect as any other kind of legislation, the process by which they are made often produces a truncated or indeterminate legislative history that can make them harder to construe than other legislation and that justifies application of several rules of narrow statutory construction. We conclude, however, that these rules must sometimes be relaxed to account for the special role of appropriations in the development of customary national security law.

The force and effect of particular national security appropriations may depend on whether they are used to legitimate executive national security actions or to restrict them. In chapter 12, we discuss the scope of what we will call *legitimating appropriations*, appropriations from which the executive infers national security authority. We argue that they can be used to legitimate national security actions before, during, or even after the actions as part of customary national security law.

In chapter 13, we discuss the scope of what we will call *restrictive appropriations*, which purport to limit the use of the appropriations for designated national security actions.[1] We show that they cannot be used to impose restrictions on the executive that Congress could not constitutionally enact as more direct legislation.

We also argue, however, that the proper scope of a restrictive national security appropriation is usually determined by balancing the extent of its intrusion on executive power against the need for the restriction to accomplish legislative purposes. In that balancing, history weighs in favor of the restriction because of the historically substantive role of such appropriations in controlling the exercise of war and related national security powers.

In chapter 14, we discuss the president's authority to avoid restrictive appropriations and cure funding omissions[2] by spending in disregard of the restrictions or without a national security appropriation. We conclude that when a restrictive appropriation is unconstitutional, the president may disregard the restriction and therefore spend the appropriation to which it attaches. When, however, the restriction arises from Congress's failure to fund a constitutionally mandated national security activity, a more difficult constitutional question is presented. We cast doubt on claims that the executive then has inherent constitutional authority to cure the omission by spending third party or unappropriated public funds, even if it has the *power* to act subject to congressional ratification by *ex post facto* appropriation. We find, however, that the thorny constitutional questions presented by spending third-party or unappropriated funds are usually avoided because of the availability of discretionary spending authority for the executive by statute or custom.

11

The General Force and Effect of National Security Appropriations

In this chapter we examine first the general force and effect of "mere" appropriations. We then consider the effect of indeterminate legislative history on the proper statutory construction of appropriations. Finally, we examine the role of national security appropriations in the development of what we call customary national security law.

The Force and Effect of "Mere" Appropriations

The first (and at this writing, only) federal court in our history to declare an appropriation rider unconstitutional for infringing on the constitutional authority of the executive noted in passing that the rider was "merely an appropriations measure by which no substantive rights or causes of action are created."[1] In denigrating "mere" appropriation measures, the court was not alone; numerous prior federal judicial opinions contrast "mere" appropriations with "substantive" legislation.[2] One implication of this language is that appropriation measures somehow carry less force and effect as law than other legislation; that appropriations are not independent exercises of the lawmaking power, but simply implemental legislation for the limited and specific purpose of funding separately authorized activities.[3] A brief exploration of the reasons offered to distinguish appropriations from other measures, however, shows conclusively that they have the same force and effect as other legislation and that there is no constitutional basis for the apparently low esteem in which they are sometimes held.

The case law reflects the traditional distinction in the Congress between authorizations and appropriations. The General Accounting Office defines an authorization as "[s]ubstantive legislation . . . that sets up or continues the legal operation of a Federal program or agency . . . or sanctions a particular type of obligation or expenditure within a program."[4] As we noted in chapter 5, authorizations generally precede appropriations; appropriations make funds available to execute previously authorized activities.[5] The Supreme Court has explained that

> [t]he distinction is maintained "to assure that program and financial matters are considered independently of one another. This division of labor is intended to enable the Appropriations Committee to concentrate on financial issues and to prevent them [the Committee] from trespassing on substantive legislation."[6]

Many courts reason from this traditional legislative distinction that "mere" appropriations do not change prior authorizing legislation, and, indeed, create no substantive rights or duties.[7]

They also cite Congress's own procedural rules in support of this conclusion.[8] As we noted in chapters 5 and 6, House rules prohibit the attachment of riders to appropriations not previously authorized by law and the inclusion in general appropriation bills of provisions or amendments "changing existing law," except provisions that reduce expenditures for matters related to the appropriation.[9] Senate rules prohibit "propos[ing] general legislation" by amendment to a general appropriation bill.[10] The existence of these rules has prompted at least one judge to deny effect to appropriation measures that allegedly "flout[ed] them,"[11] without an expressed congressional desire to the contrary.

Another scholar has driven the traditional distinctions past these moorings to argue that Congress violates the Constitution when it legislates by appropriation. When Congress restricts the use of funds to execute substantive legislation without amending such legislation, Archie Parnell asserts, it "unconstitutionally intrudes into the domain of the executive branch"[12] by preventing the president from taking care that the law be faithfully executed.

If the distinction between "mere" appropriations and substantive legislation had constitutional significance, however, one would expect it to find support in the text. On the contrary, appropriations and other laws alike originate as "bills" and, after bicameral approval and presentment to the president, become "Law."[13] The first textual reference to appropriation is the Army Clause, which is part of the itemization of Congress's substantive lawmaking powers.[14] Nothing in this itemization suggests that this appropriation power is any less substantive than any other. The other textual reference is the Appropriations Clause, which refers to "Appropriations made by Law."[15] In *Immigration & Naturalization Service v. Chadha*,[16] the Supreme Court held that laws can only be made by satisfying the requirements of bicameral approval and presentment. The flip side of *Chadha* is equally informative: those bills that satisfy the requirements carry the force and effect of law. Neither the text nor the structure of Article I lends any support to the notion that appropriations are lesser creatures of the law.

Chadha, however, also asserts that the bicameralism requirement was intended to assure that "the legislative power would be exercised only after opportunity for full study and debate in separate settings."[17] By legislating through appropriations, Congress can avoid its own division of labor to the possible detriment of "full study and debate," placing substantive issues before appropriations committees without special expertise to debate them or bypassing committee consideration altogether by amending appropriations from the floor, as we noted in chapter 6. If, however, the Constitution *encourages* full study and debate, "[n]either due process nor the First Amendment *requires* legislation to be supported by committee reports, floor debates, or even consideration, but only by a vote."[18] Neither in *Chadha* nor in any other opinion has the Supreme Court laid down

> a rigid constitutional mandate, requiring courts to make a quantitative determination whether each house has given a measure *sufficient consideration* before voting in favor of it. Such an intrusion into Congress' legislative deliberations would pose serious separation-of-power problems, and neither the language nor logic of the Constitution compels such an inquiry.[19]

Any legislative consideration that the Constitution requires has presumptively been given any bill that becomes law,[20] and the mechanics of the appropriation process therefore afford no basis for diminishing the force and effect of appropriations as law.

Far from challenging this conclusion, Congress's own rules support it. The very fact that Congress has adopted rules against changing existing law by appropriation measures is evidence that the Constitution poses no barrier, or else the rules would be unnecessary. In addition, they do not apply to many kinds of appropriation measures.[21] More important, neither house absolutely prohibits changing existing law by appropriation; the rules simply subject such appropriation measures to procedural objection. If the objection is not made, made but not sustained, waived by a special rule in the House, or disregarded for any of the other reasons discussed above,[22] the measure may be enacted in spite of the rules. Objections are often withheld or overruled,[23] and votes on the objections unsurprisingly turn less on whether members of Congress think that a particular measure satisfies the procedural rule than on whether or not they support the measure.[24] The result is that "legislative" appropriations are common.[25] Finally, both houses have also adopted rules that admit the possibility of legislating through appropriation measures by requiring any committee reports that accompany such measures to identify the provisions that change existing law.[26]

In short, Congress's rules concern institutional governance, not constitutional necessity.[27] "Rules limiting amendment [by appropriation], even if enforced, are not of constitutional significance," as a federal court has found.[28] Indeed, for a court to enforce them (by denying an appropriation measure the force and effect of law),[29] when Congress has not, would itself constitute an unconstitutional intrusion on congressional housekeeping.

Moreover, our analysis of the mechanics of appropriation in chapter 5 shows that even the traditional legislative distinction between authorization and appropriation has blurred over time. Surveying the budgetary process, Louis Fisher observed that "authorization bills contain appropriations, appropriations bills contain authorizations, and the order of their enactment is sometimes reversed."[30] The traditional linchpin of the case law deprecating "mere" appropriations has thus loosened.

Notwithstanding the appellation "mere," therefore, appropriations carry the force and effect of law and can change existing law.[31] "Congress . . . may amend substantive law in an appropriations statute, as long as it does so clearly," the Court held as recently as 1992.[32] Appropriations are, in Neal Devins's words, "the constitutional equivalent of authorizations."[33] The claim that Congress is somehow interfering with the president's duty to enforce the laws by enacting appropriation measures is fundamentally misconceived. Instead, Congress is properly changing the law that the president must enforce. The distinction between mere appropriations and substantive legislation has no bearing on the force and effect of appropriations as law, whatever its utility as political science.

The Effect of Indeterminate Legislative History

In qualifying its conclusion that "Congress . . . may amend substantive law in an appropriation" by adding "as long as it does so clearly," the Supreme Court hinted at what really lies behind the persistence of the deprecatory appellation "mere." This persistence reflects doubt not about the force and effect of appropriations, but about their intent.[34] The difficulty is not that an appropriation measure is "mere" but rather that its legislative history is often "sheer"—truncated or slight because of the process by which the measure was enacted. The difficulty is compounded by the durational limits of appropriation measures. In response, the courts have fashioned special rules of construction, as discussed later on.

We have shown that the legislative process is often truncated and pressured by time.[35] As the legislative history of the Boland amendments illustrates, appropriation measures are often introduced and debated outside the authorizing committees with expertise in the subject.[36] Indeed, they are often introduced for the purpose of bypassing the authorization committees.[37] An appropriation or conference committee may not debate the measure, may not produce a committee report, and, if it does produce a report, may not give detailed attention to the appropriation measure in it.[38] Moreover, many of the key legislative decisions are made in conference at the last minute by a handful of members of Congress.[39] Finally, if the appropriation measure takes the form of a rider to a continuing resolution, these problems are only exacerbated, as we noted in chapter 6.

Not only is the resulting legislative history for national security appropriations therefore likely to be shallow and confused, but there is usually no "legislation as a whole" to which lawyers and judges can refer in construing the typical appropriation measure because it is enacted by itself or as part of a continuing resolution and not as part of a comprehensive statutory scheme.[40]

Durational limits of appropriation measures compound the resulting problems of statutory construction. Most appropriations—and modern Department of Defense authorization acts, which may restrict appropriations—are single-year legislation.[41] When circumstances change, the appropriation measure may be changed with them, as the multiple Boland amendments perfectly demonstrate.[42] Ordinarily any substantive legislation enacted by appropriation should lapse with the appropriation. But in some cases, the legislative history may reflect Congress's intent that the change in substantive law be permanent, surviving the appropriation in which it was made.[43] Identifying those cases, however, usually requires interpretation of the truncated legislative history described previously.[44] Jacques LeBoeuf concludes that "[l]egislating through appropriations riders . . . makes it difficult for citizens to know what the law is. A person looking at a statute has no way of knowing whether it has been modified or repealed through the use of an appropriations bill."[45]

The courts have responded to these difficulties with two closely related rules of narrow construction. First, they have declared that ratification by appropriation is disfavored absent clear evidence that Congress knew of and acquiesced in a precise course of executive conduct.[46] The prevalence of lump-sum appropriations and continuing resolutions makes it difficult to infer knowing approval from the fact of appropriation alone; Congress may appropriate funds for an agency without either knowing or approving of particular uses of the funds by the agency. As a result, the Supreme Court has insisted that "the appropriation must plainly show a purpose to bestow the precise authority which is claimed,"[47] although the purpose can be reflected in legislative history, as well as on the face of the appropriation.

On the proper showing, however, the courts will find that by appropriating funds for an executive action the legislature has ratified the action.[48] The predicate for such ratification is evidence that Congress knows and intends that a specific action is part of the program for which it appropriates,[49] and that the executive has "at least an arguable legal basis for its action."[50]

The second closely related rule of narrow construction is the strong presumption against implied repeal by appropriation.[51] Although the courts have long applied a general presumption against implied repeal to all legislation,[52] the Supreme Court has held that it applies "with even *greater* force when the implied repeal rests solely on an Appropriations Act"[53] because of the often summary nature of the process by which such acts are enacted and the consequently few members of Congress who may be knowledgeable about the appropriation measures. Thus, merely by appropriating lump-sum appropriations for an action contrary to existing law, Congress is not presumed to have repealed such law.

The presumption against implied repeal by appropriation is not irrebuttable, however. It is rebutted when the intent of the legislature "is expressed in the most clear and positive terms, and where the language admits of no other reasonable interpretation."[54] If the legislative history clearly shows that Congress was aware of the prior law and intended to change it by the appropriation measure, its intent will be given effect.[55] Thus, when Congress repeatedly reappropriates funds for a project prohibited by substantive law, when the appropriations committee highlights the repealer effect of the appropriations in formal committee reports and debates it in hearings, and when the appropriations contain a prohibition on use of the funds to comply with the prior law, the courts will construe the appropriations as an implied repeal of the prior substantive legislation. "This 'repeal,' if it should be called that, . . . [is] straightforward, direct and after hearings on the subject,"[56] a federal court has concluded.

Even when an appropriation rider is more ambiguous, the presumption against implied repeal may be rebutted by a legislative history of heated floor debate about its effects, suggesting broad awareness in Congress of those effects from which an intent to repeal can be inferred. The very fact of the debate, and objections during it to substantive legislation by appropriation, show that "Congress realized it was using the unusual and frowned upon device of legislating via an appropriation measure to accomplish a substantive result."[57] In contrast, when the legislative history shows that the appropriations committee alone debated an appropriation measure and described its effect only in its committee report, without an indication that the rest of Congress knew of that effect, the presumption is not rebutted.[58]

National Security Appropriations and Customary National Security Law

The foregoing rules of narrow construction are general rules, which do not apply with equal force to all subjects.[59] They cannot be applied to national security appropriations without taking account of the special role of custom and congressional acquiescence in the evolution of national security law. As affirmative acts of Congress, appropriation measures can signal congressional acquiescence in or disapproval of executive national security practices and thus help to establish, confirm, or change customary national security law. The context of custom may sometimes affect application of both the rule of ratification by appropriation and the presumption against implied repeal.

Custom has played a special role in the development of national security law because of practical limitations on Congress's capacity to forge antecedent standards for executive national security action. The Supreme Court has recognized that in the areas of foreign affairs and national security, "Congress cannot anticipate and legislate with regard to every possible action the President may find it necessary to take or in every possible situation in which he might act."[60] The unpredictability of national security events, the flexibility and speed required for effective response, and the need for current and sometimes secret information may make it impractical for Congress to delegate specific national authority to the president in advance of the need. Consequently, the Court has found that legislation "must often accord to the President a degree of discretion and freedom from statutory restriction which would not be admissible were domestic affairs alone involved."[61] Similarly, it has held that the power to delegate authority "is especially significant in connection with constitutional war powers . . . which [require] the exercise of broad discretion."[62]

The same factors which permit broad, almost standardless delegations of national security authority sometimes require presidents to act without antecedent legislation at all. "[C]ongressional inertia, indifference or quiescence . . . [may then] enable, if not invite, measures on independent presidential responsibility," as Justice Jackson put it.[63] In such cases, presidents act subject to congressional ratification or countermand; they initiate, and Congress reacts.[64] When they act with sufficient consistency over time, and Congress knowingly acquiesces, the interaction may create customary national security law. The custom is evidence of the political branches' joint interpretation of the president's constitutional or statutory authority.

Such law has been called "quasi-constitutional custom" when the president has acted in the area of concurrent national security powers.[65] "[A] systematic, unbroken, executive practice," Justice Frankfurter noted in *Youngstown*, "long pursued to the knowledge of the Congress and never before questioned, . . . making as it were such an exercise of power part of the structure of government, may be treated as a gloss on 'executive Power' vested in the President by § 1 of Art. II."[66] Practice and acquiescence may also evolve as a gloss on a statute.[67] When the executive has consistently acted under a statute in a manner known to Congress, and Congress has acquiesced in the practice by inaction, rejection of contrary legislation, or reenactment, the statutory authority for the executive practice is implied into the statute.[68] The theory of customary law actually antedates both the constitution and American statutory law; as noted in chapter 1, it was described by William Pitt as early as 1796 in connection with earlier royal military spending.

The Supreme Court applied the theory of customary law to uphold President Carter's suspension of pending claims against Iran as part of the hostage release agreement in *Dames & Moore v. Regan*.[69] The Court first found that neither the International Emergency Economic Powers Act (IEEPA)[70] nor the Hostage Act[71] specifically authorized the suspension of claims in American courts. Emphasizing the impossibility of anticipating and legislating with respect to every action a president might have to take in a national security emergency, however, the Court endorsed the theory of customary law "[a]t least . . . where there is no contrary indication of legislative intent and when, as here, there is a history of congressional acquiescence in conduct of the sort engaged in by the President."[72] It then traced the 180-year history of executive claims settlements, noting that no fewer than eighty executive agreements to liquidate claims had been made between 1817 and 1917, at least ten of them since 1952.[73] It also found that Congress was on notice of the practice of executive claims settlement and had "implicitly approved" of it by enacting collateral legislation regarding procedures for distribution of settlement funds, by indicating in IEEPA and the Hostage Act "congressional willingness that the President have broad discretion when responding to the hostile acts of foreign sovereigns," by holding hearings on the Iranian agreement itself without acting to disapprove or modify it, and by consistently "fail[ing] to object to this longstanding practice . . . , even when it had an opportunity to do so."[74]

In short, long-continued, consistent, and publicly known executive practice, in which Congress has acquiesced both by inaction (failing to disapprove) and collateral legislative action, had created a customary authority in the president to settle foreign claims by executive agreement and to suspend pending claims in American courts accordingly.

Dames & Moore shows, however, that customary law is not created by just any "series of essentially random acts that happen to form a pattern of usage."[75] Justice Frankfurter's articulation of the theory of customary law in *Youngstown* suggests several strong predicates for its creation. First, the executive practice must be "systematic, unbroken" and long-pursued.[76] Satisfaction of the first predicate enables us to identify a custom in the practice and to articulate and delimit the authority that it establishes. By giving notice to Congress of the claim of authority by the executive, consistent practice also helps satisfy the second predicate: knowing acquiescence by Congress.[77] If Congress has had notice of the practice and the corresponding claim of authority through its customary information-gathering channels, then its failure to object when it has a practical opportunity to do so, its reenactment of general legislation, or its enactment of collateral, but consistent, legislation, may be taken as acquiescence in the practice sufficient to establish customary law. Absent notice to Congress of the practice, however, neither Congress's inaction nor general legislation—including lump-sum appropriations—can be taken as acquiescence in the practice.[78] Finally, the Supremacy Clause and the Constitution's provision for amendment suggest a third, typically unstated but universally assumed predicate of customary law: that the executive practice must not violate any constitutional provision[79] or statute.[80]

Satisfaction of the second predicate has presented the most difficult obstacle to the creation of customary national security law. The obstacle arises because national security disputes often "will not involve clear congressional affirmations and will thus require a determination of whether consent can be inferred from silence or no action."[81] But it is now commonplace to observe that such a determination is problematical;[82] legislative silence or inaction is often unfathomable. Rejecting the theory of congressional acquiescence as a tool of statutory construction, Justice Scalia has noted that legislative inaction may signify "(1) approval of the status quo, as opposed to (2) inability to agree on how to alter the status quo, (3) unawareness of the status quo, (4) indifference to the status quo, or even (5) political cowardice."[83] Another interpretivist objection is that the theory of customary law places improper weight on the inaction of subsequent congresses in interpreting the meaning of prior legislation they had no part in enacting.[84]

When a bill fails in a single house or committee, reliance on congressional inaction for the creation of customary law also encounters formalist objections. In giving the force and effect of law to the inaction of part of Congress, the theory is inconsistent with the formalist theory of constitutional lawmaking set forth in the *Chadha* decision, insisting on bicameralism and presentment as conditions for giving legal effect to congressional action.[85] Another formalist objection is that customary law violates the delegation doctrine, by finding implied delegations of authority to the president in wholly standardless inaction by Congress.[86]

National security appropriation measures, however, meet many of these objections to inferences of congressional acquiescence or disapproval from mere inaction. In the first place, as affirmative legislative acts they contain the best evidence of congressional intent: plain language. This is not to say that they avoid interpretivist objections altogether (as the courts' rules of narrow construction of appropriations demonstrate), but they are less susceptible to them than is inaction by the Congress. Nor do they pose the problem of construing the intent of a prior Congress in light of subsequent congressional inaction, since they carry independent force as affirmative law and can properly supersede, modify or even repeal prior legislation. Because appropriations are usually annual, specific appropriations may also reflect close year-to-year congressional oversight and therefore knowledge of a particular executive practice, justifying the inference that they have created customary law. By comparison, the Court has observed that even congressional silence is most significant "when the area is one of traditional year-by-year supervision."[87]

Second, appropriation measures present no "vertical" problem of ascribing to Congress the perceived intent of one of its parts, because they are the work product of the entire Congress, fully subject to bicameral approval and presentment. In the making of customary law, they carry at least the evidentiary weight of the collateral legislation relied upon by the Court in *Dames & Moore,* and of general legislation reenacted by a Congress on notice of an executive practice under it.[88]

National security appropriations also may meet the delegation objection to customary law based on inaction. Not only do they often contain quite specific standards for the exercise or restriction of executive power, but, more important, they also function in an area to which the strict delegation model does not apply with the same force that it does to domestic affairs. Scholars who have voiced this formalist objection to customary law based on congressional acquiescence have failed to distinguish between purely domestic law and foreign affairs law,[89] and have therefore ignored the Court's admonitions that delegations of foreign affairs or war powers may confer broader discretion on the president than delegations of domestic powers.

Not only do national security appropriation measures thus meet many of the objections to the making of customary national security law, but they can also be especially effective as "red lights"[90] against the making or continuation of such law. It was crucial to the finding of customary legal authority for executive claims settlement in *Dames & Moore* that Congress had not "in some way resisted the exercise of Presidential authority."[91] Restrictive appropriations can serve as the strongest evidence of such resistance to an executive national security practice; on a spectrum of devices for expressing congressional objection to an executive practice, appropriation restrictions may be the clearest.[92] They are effective, as the Senate Committee on Governmental Affairs has noted,

> precisely because . . . [they] are so direct, unambiguous, and virtually self-enforcing. While agencies are able to bend the more ambiguous language of authorizing legislation to their own purposes, the dollar figures in appropriations bills represent commands which cannot be bent or ignored except at extreme peril to agency officials.[93]

Moreover, the annual cycle of appropriations affords regular opportunities for Congress to express its disapproval of executive practice. Finally, and most important for our purposes, the history of national security appropriations, set out in part I, suggests that resistance to executive national security actions is in part their raison d'être; they were originally conceived as the ultimate check on executive national security practices.

In light of these differences between appropriations and mere congressional silence in the making of customary national security law, we can now revisit and customize the general rules of narrow construction applied to appropriations. The rule disapproving ratification by appropriation is properly relaxed in favor of a contextual analysis of a national security appropriation, which takes into account the length and consistency of an executive national security practice, collateral evidence of congressional intent, and whether the practice impinges directly on constitutionally sensitive individual rights. The rule against implied repeal by appropriation may also be relaxed when a restrictive appropriation repeals not prior statutory directives, but prior customary law, dependent for its continued vitality on congressional acquiescence. In fact, to apply this rule of narrow construction too strictly to restrictive national security appropriations is to deny them their historical role as controls on shared national security powers.

12

Legitimating Appropriations

The paradigm of what we have called legitimating appropriations—appropriation measures from which the executive infers authority for national security actions—is the succession of appropriations for military activities in Southeast Asia during the Vietnam War. In this chapter, we therefore use the Vietnam War appropriations as an example of legitimating appropriations and begin by applying the general force-and-effect analysis presented in chapter 11 to these appropriations. We then consider four general objections to the use of national security appropriations to legitimate national security actions.

The General Force and Effect of the Vietnam War Appropriations

Although U.S. military assistance to the French in Vietnam dates back to at least 1950, it was in 1961 that the American commitment was both quantitatively and qualitatively enlarged by President Kennedy's dispatch of 400 Special Forces troops and 100 other military advisers to South Vietnam.[1] By the end of 1962, there were 11,000 U.S. troops in South Vietnam, and by the end of the following year, 16,000, many of them in combat roles. In April 1965, President Johnson ordered an 18,000–20,000-man increase in the number of U.S. troops, and, for the first time, ordered the marines to go on the offensive against communist forces. By the end of 1965, the U.S. troop total reached 184,000; three years later it peaked at 540,000. By the beginning of the Nixon presidency in January 1969, more than 31,000 Americans had already died in combat in South Vietnam. Although he conducted a gradual withdrawal of U.S. troops from the region, President Nixon also approved a land "incursion" and bombing in Cambodia and continuation of combat in Laos. Many more Americans died before the last American land forces were withdrawn from South Vietnam in 1973.

Despite the duration and cost of these hostilities, Congress never formally declared war. Instead, at President Johnson's request, it overwhelmingly approved the Tonkin Gulf Resolution of 1964, a joint resolution by which Congress, noting the "campaign of aggression that the Communist regime in North Vietnam has been waging against its neighbors," authorized the president "to take all necessary action to repel any armed attack against the forces of the United States and to prevent further aggression" and declared the U.S. intent, "as the President determines, to take all necessary steps, including the use of armed force, to assist any member or protocol state of the Southeast Asia Collective Defense Treaty."[2]

The initial increase in U.S. forces a half year later was kept secret to avoid the appearance of a change in policy.[3] But in May 1965, President Johnson asked Congress to vote a $700 million supplemental appropriation "to meet mounting military requirements in Vietnam."[4] His transmittal message left no doubt of the purpose of the appropriation: "This is not a routine appropriation. For each member of Congress who supports this request is also voting to persist in our effort to halt Communist aggression in South Vietnam."[5] It also left no doubt of the U.S. military buildup in Vietnam, describing the increase in combat deployments of U.S. troops to 35,000, the increase in strike sorties against military targets in North Vietnam, and the intended use of the requested funds "to continue to provide our forces with the best and most modern supplies and equipment."[6] Moreover, the president cautioned against any hope that "this will be the last request. If our needs expand I will turn again to the Congress. For we will do whatever must be done to ensure the safety of South Vietnam from aggression."[7] The House approved the supplemental appropriation by a vote of 408 to 7, and the Senate approved it by a vote of 88 to 3.[8] As enacted, the measure permitted the release of the funds "upon determination by the President that such action is necessary in connection with military activities in southeast Asia."[9]

The May 1965 appropriation was but the first in a succession of appropriations that were no less clear about their purpose. In September 1965, for example, Congress unanimously appropriated an additional $1.7 billion for "military activities in southeast Asia."[10] This appropriation appeared as a separate title of the annual appropriation act for the Defense Department. Barely four months later, President Johnson told Congress and the nation in his State of the Union Address that "special Viet-Nam expenditures for the next fiscal year" would rise by $5.8 billion.[11]

Subsequently, he proposed a $4.8 billion supplementary military and procurement authorization bill, and the White House announced that the vote on the bill would be a test vote on the war.[12] The House approved the bill by a vote of 393 to 4.[13] After a long debate during which Senator Wayne Morse attacked the bill as "a policy bill . . . [that] greatly enlarges American foreign policy in Asia . . . [and] is pregnant with a policy that will lead to the escalation of the war in Asia,"[14] the Senate followed suit by a vote of 93 to 2.[15] It also voted 94 to 2 to reject an appropriation rider that would have limited the president's authority to send draftees to Southeast Asia[16] and 92 to 5 to table a proposal to repeal the Gulf of Tonkin Resolution.[17]

The following year, an appropriation act for military procurement, research, and construction of facilities "necessary in connection with military activities in southeast Asia" declared Congress's "firm intention to provide all necessary support for members of the Armed Forces of the United States fighting in Vietnam."[18] At the same time that Congress voted these appropriations, it also extended the draft and suspended the ceiling on active duty strength of the armed forces.[19]

The repeal of the Gulf of Tonkin Resolution in 1971[20] did not change this legislative pattern. Not only did Congress at the same time reject several bills requiring troop withdrawals, but it continued afterward to appropriate funds for military activities in Southeast Asia and to extend the draft.[21] Historian Stanley Karnow counts 113 votes by Congress from July 1966 to July 1973 on proposals related to the war.[22] Many of these were votes on appropriation measures. Yet Congress did not impose any limitation on military activities in Southeast Asia until 1969 (when it enacted an appropriation rider restricting deployments in Thailand and Laos) and did not vote to stop all bombing until August 1973.[23]

This succession of appropriations clearly satisfies the predicate for ratification by appropriation: Congress knew of and intended the military actions in Vietnam[24] for which funds were earmarked, and the executive initially had at least an arguable basis for conducting them under the Gulf of Tonkin Resolution.[25] No wonder, then, that in the first major legal challenge to the war, the Second Circuit Court of Appeals asserted that "[t]he Congress and the Executive have taken mutual and joint action in the prosecution and support of military operations," citing not just the Tonkin Gulf Resolution but also the fact that "Congress has ratified the executive's initiatives by appropriating billions of dollars to carry out military operations in Southeast Asia . . . ."[26] Rejecting the appellants' arguments that congressional authorization could not be inferred from appropriations, the court concluded that "[t]he framers' intent to vest the war power in Congress is in no way defeated by permitting an inference of authorization from legislative action furnishing the manpower and materials of war for the protracted military operations in Southeast Asia."[27]

After the Gulf of Tonkin Resolution was repealed, the same court found that there "was sufficient legislative action in extending the Selective Service Act and in appropriating billions of dollars to carry on the military and naval operations in Vietnam to ratify and approve the measures taken by the executive, even in the absence of the Gulf of Tonkin Resolution."[28] When the administration subsequently appeared to escalate the conflict by mining North Vietnamese harbors, the same court still found joint authorization between "the Executive by military action and the Congress, by not cutting off the appropriations that are the wherewithal for such action."[29]

The court's allusion to Congress's power to cut off funding, however, casts doubt on the legality of the secret bombing of Cambodia from 1969 to 1970 and teaches a further lesson about authorization by appropriation. Although knowledge of military activities is a predicate for finding ratification by appropriation, Congress need not know of every military operation supporting such activities. As a practical matter, its authorization by appropriation must extend to operations that are temporarily kept secret for proper military reasons, such as preattack surveillance missions or diversionary operations.[30] When the military (or conceivably, foreign policy) necessity for secrecy has passed, however, the operations must be disclosed in order to protect Congress's ability to check the president by cutting off appropriations, which, as we have shown in part I, was a crucial consideration in the historical development of the power of the purse in national security affairs. As Geoffrey Miller has put it, the "legislative power [to cut off funding of military operations] carries with it a corresponding congressional right to be informed of the President's actions."[31] In so concluding, he was echoing the assumption of both Federalists and Republicans in the first congresses that the president "will embrace the earliest opportunity to explain the matter and obtain a justification [from Congress]."[32]

The bombing of Cambodia from 1969 to 1970 appears to have been kept secret primarily to avoid domestic American political protest, however, and not for any proper military reason (the enemy obviously knew of it) or foreign policy reason.[33] Moreover, the duration of the secrecy was not keyed to any tactical necessity; the bombing was kept secret long after it stopped, until well into 1973, thus disabling the Congress's appropriations check.[34] Consequently, we agree with John Hart Ely that congressional appropriations for military activities in Southeast Asia prior to 1970 did not constitute authorization for the secret bombing of Cambodia from 1969 to 1970.[35] For the same reasons, we share his doubt that the secret war in Laos from 1962 to 1969 was authorized, although there the problem was not the complete absence of notice to Congress, but instead insufficiently clear notice to support the inference of authorization by appropriation.[36]

Objections to the General Analysis of the Force and Effect of the Vietnam War Appropriations

At least four major objections can be leveled at the foregoing analysis of legitimating appropriations as authorization for war. The first is that the Declaration of War Clause requires a formal declaration of war in order to assure congressional accountability, and that nothing less, including appropriations, can constitutionally authorize war. Even if the Constitution does not insist on a formal declaration of war, a second objection is that it does require at least a "superclear" statement of authorization, which cannot be supplied by acquiescence and was not supplied by the Vietnam War appropriations. The third objection advances a variant on this reasoning by citing the strong clear-statement requirement in the War Powers Resolution. Finally, even if legitimating appropriations may supply *prior* authorization for war and military activities, the fourth objection is that they cannot constitutionally ratify such activities *after* they have been commenced by the president. We discuss and ultimately reject each of these objections below except insofar as they restate or reinforce the general rule of narrow construction of legitimating appropriations.

The Formalist Objection

If the Declaration Clause requires a formal declaration of war by Congress to authorize military hostilities by U.S. troops, then clearly no appropriation of any kind, no matter how clear, will suffice as authorization. Some raised just this objection to the statutory authorities cited in support of the Vietnam War.[37] More recently, Gregory Sidak has made the same objection to the Authorization for the Use of Military Force against Iraq Resolution,[38] arguing that formal declaration is required to assure the political accountability of Congress for war decisions.[39] A fortiorari, he rejects implied authorization or ratification by appropriation:

> Congress should not be able to implicitly "authorize" the initiation of war merely by appropriating funds for war purposes. A declaration of war fulfills Congress's function because it is more immediately visible to the electorate, less susceptible to ambiguity and disagreement once it is made, and thus more conducive to effective monitoring of the performance of political actors.[40]

We will show, however, that formal declaration is not compelled by the constitutional text and is contrary both to custom and case law. Moreover, a rule of formal declaration is flawed even as a principle of constitutional governance.

Sidak's argument for formalism is straightforward and logically compelling. A rule of formal declaration imposes transaction costs on the decision to go to war that serve both to discourage it, in keeping with the intent of the framers, and to promote the accountability of Congress for affirmative decisions. The solemnity of formal declaration should promote more serious deliberation than attends routine legislation, he asserts.[41] The debate is focused by the president's formal recommendation of war, which also supplies reasons for the declaration and may state the objectives of war.[42] The declaration is typically subject to a roll call vote, which precludes anonymity in the decision for war.[43] It is rarely bundled with other legislation and therefore does not occasion logrolling.[44] Thus Sidak concludes:

> By issuing a declaration of war rather than merely appropriating money for an undeclared war, Congress obligates itself to be far more specific in stating the nation's foreign policy objectives and the reasoning by which they were derived, and far more candid in confronting the moral consequences of using military force to achieve those objectives.[45]

By contrast, the separation of authorization from appropriation, the bundling of appropriations with riders, the frequent absence of roll call votes for such legislation, and the imprecision of authorization by appropriation reduce the visibility of that authorization and with it, congressional accountability.[46] Furthermore, the ambiguity of informality not only "erodes the legitimacy and obscures the purpose of using military force,"[47] but also undermines the effectiveness of the threat of force itself. A legitimating appropriation can be finely calibrated to the level of conflict and is therefore reversible. A declaration, "relative to the fine tuning of appropriations bills[,] . . . [is] difficult to reverse," and thus poses a more credible threat to our enemies than an authorization of war by appropriation or routine legislation.[48]

Whatever the policy arguments for a rule of formality, however, nothing in the constitutional text compels it. The Declaration Clause does use "declare" in describing the power vested in Congress, but diverse historians have concluded that the framers did not use it as a term of art for "formal" declaration.[49] Charles Lofgren notes that in the convention the framers frequently used "declare" in contexts that would encompass any form of authorized war and concludes that "the delegates and their contemporaries in America did not understand the term 'declare' in a narrow, technical sense."[50] His review of the ratification debates confirms the conclusion because they show that the participants equated the power to *declare* war with the Continental Congress's power of *determining on* war under the Articles of Confederation.[51] Abraham Sofaer reaches the same conclusion from his independent review of both the convention and ratification debates: "The power to 'declare' war could not tenably be read, after examining both the Convention and the ratification processes, as limiting Congress's control to formal war-making."[52]

Furthermore, the War Clause goes on to confer on Congress the power "to grant Letters of Marque and Reprisal."[53] Contemporary writers on the law of nations were of the view that reprisals and comparable uses of force could create a state of "'imperfect,' or limited, warfare that either took the place of or led to declared war."[54] Just eight years before the Constitutional Convention, these views were adopted by the Court of Appeals in Cases of Capture.[55] Clearly, Congress could constitutionally authorize imperfect war without formal declaration by providing for the grant of letters of marque and reprisal. Indeed, by the time of the Constitutional Convention, undeclared war, or "reprisals," were the norm, and formal declarations had fallen into general disuse, a fact remarked on by Alexander Hamilton in *The Federalist.*[56] It is doubtful that the framers intended by the Declaration Clause to vest only an already obsolete war-making power in the Congress.

If the plain words of the Constitution and the framing history do not resolve the question whether formal declaration is required, subsequent practice and the resulting customary national security law are dispositive. It is a serious blow to the formality objection to legitimating appropriations that our first major war was an undeclared, but congressionally authorized naval war with France. In a series of finely calibrated statutes Congress gradually escalated the hostilities with France without ever declaring war.[57] It also authorized the use of military force without formal declaration on numerous other occasions, including the suppression of pirates,[58] various Indian wars,[59] wars with the Barbary states,[60] the invasion of Spanish Florida,[61] the defense of Formosa,[62] crisis intervention in the Middle East,[63] Vietnam, and, most recently, the Persian Gulf War. While these occasions are too varied to suggest any consistent practice, they demonstrate that neither Congress, nor the presidents who accepted these authorizations without demanding a declaration, have read the Declaration Clause as narrowly as Sidak.

The practice in the naval war with France is particularly instructive because it was so close in time to the Constitutional Convention and because it was subsequently approved by the Supreme Court. In *Bas v. Tingy*,[64] the Court was called upon to review the authorization for the naval war for purposes of deciding the applicability of prize legislation. Justice Washington acknowledged that the war was not a "perfect war . . . declared in form," but he found it nonetheless a "public" "imperfect" war between the United States and France, "authorised by the legitimate authority of the two governments."[65] To the argument that Congress had passed no act saying that we were at war, he responded, "This is true; but . . . [this was not] necessary to be done: because . . . as to America, the degree of hostility meant to be carried on, was sufficiently described without declaring war, or declaring that we were at war."[66] Justice Chase added point-blank that "Congress is empowered to declare a general war, or congress may wage a limited war . . . ."[67] Justice Patterson, author of the New Jersey plan in the Constitutional Convention, also found that "this modified warfare is authorised by the constitutional authority of our country," "in the manner prescribed by the constitutional organ of our country."[68] As the Court has often noted, "[t]he construction placed upon the Constitution . . . by the men who were contemporary with its formation, many of whom were members of the convention which framed it, is of itself entitled to very great weight, and when it is remembered that the rights thus established have not been disputed during a period of nearly a century, it is almost conclusive."[69]

Sidak attempts to distinguish *Bas* as "a case about sovereignty rather than the separation of powers," arguing that

> *Bas* merely acknowledged that there exists a lacuna of undeclared war, which might be "authorized" by Congress, but which might also be directly waged by the President as Commander in Chief without prior congressional authorization (in which case Congress's "authorization" of such warfare, either prospective or retroactive, would be no more than hortatory).[70]

This reading not only presumes that Congress unnecessarily authorized an undeclared war that the president could have waged without their authorization, and that the Court gratuitously rested its finding of the war's legality on the congressional authorization instead of the president's supposed inherent power, but also that both Congress and the Court got it wrong, since Congress cannot authorize war except by declaration. Sidak's reading[71] is also flatly inconsistent with Chief Justice Marshall's assertion in a companion prize case growing out of the war with France that "[t]he whole powers of war being, by the constitution of the United States, vested in congress, the acts of that body can *alone* be resorted to as our guides in this enquiry."[72] The chief justice's assertion cannot be dismissed as a remark about sovereignty; it is about the predominance of the legislature in deciding upon war.

It hardly needs adding that the formality objection is also wholly at odds with the Vietnam era cases upholding the legality of that war.[73] These modern cases cannot be distinguished; Sidak simply dismisses them as wrong.[74]

The case against a rule of formal declaration is so strong that it is little wonder that Sidak lets slip in several places that the rule may be "better characterized as a principle of constitutional governance rather than constitutional law."[75] Even as a principle of constitutional governance, however, it is seriously flawed. In the first place, there is no historical evidence that formal declarations are attended by more serious deliberation than less formal legislation. Quite the contrary, every U.S. declaration of war but one was passed with little or no debate and with great emotion.[76] Of course, several of these followed attacks on the United States, and all were preceded by indirect debate about the appropriate U.S. response to developing foreign crises. But the same may be said of less formal authorizations for military force.

Nor is it the case that declarations are "more specific" in stating war objectives and their rationale.[77] Historically, declarations have been terse, as Sidak himself admits.[78] Of course, declarations have been focused and have been given specific meaning by the president's request for them. "The President's recommendation for war serves a useful function"[79] and is an important part of the legislative history of a declaration. But a recommendation for less formal authorization can serve a similar function, as shown by President Bush's "recommendation" for authorization of military force against Iraq,[80] and more pertinently for our focus, by President Lyndon Johnson's request for the May 1965 supplemental appropriation for military activities in Vietnam.

Similarly, other procedures attending declarations—such as roll call votes, single-subject bills, and the assumed absence of logrolling and politics as usual—may lend visibility, and therefore accountability, to the war-making decision. But most of the key votes authorizing the Vietnam War were roll call votes, none of the initial authorizations were "bundled" with other legislation disguising their significance, and there is no evidence of legislative logrolling in their overwhelming approval. Less formal legislation *is* undeniably likely to be more ambiguous than a declaration in deciding upon war, but the joint resolution approving the use of force against Iraq, and the debate surrounding the approval of the May 1965 supplemental appropriation for the Vietnam War, show that it need not be.

Finally, any practical accounting of principles of constitutional governance must take into account the costs as well as the benefits of formality. Sidak argues for formal declaration partly on the grounds of its irreversibility, on the theory that war is a "discrete" rather than a "continuous variable."[81] This theory would have baffled Clausewitz, who taught that "war is nothing more than the continuation of politics by other means."[82] Congress avoided formally declaring war on France in 1798 precisely because it wanted to be able to halt or reverse its informal escalation of conflict in the hope of avoiding an all-out war for which it was ill-prepared and for which it had little domestic support.[83]

Sometimes, too, foreign relations may call for the fine calibration that Sidak disdains in informal authorizations for war. Congress may therefore rationally opt to avoid the domestic and international legal consequences of formal declaration in determining on war.[84] It was precisely this concern that Secretary of War McHenry (after being tutored by Hamilton) voiced to President Adams regarding the naval war with France:

> An express declaration of hostility . . . would . . . subject us to all the chances of evil which can accrue from the vengeance of a nation stimulated by . . . extraordinary success. . . . A mitigated hostility will [therefore] be

the most likely to fall in with the general feeling, while it leaves a door open for negotiation, and secures some chances to avoid some of the extremities of a formal war.[85]

More than 150 years later, during the Vietnam War, the court of appeals in *Orlando v. Laird*[86] made the same observation:

> If there can be nothing more than minor military operations conducted under any circumstances, short of an express and explicit declaration of war by Congress, then extended military operations could not be conducted even though both the Congress and the President were agreed that they were necessary and were also agreed that a formal declaration of war would place the nation in a posture in its international relations which would be against its best interests.

Whether in hindsight the political branches were right in the Vietnam War is surely debatable, but it hardly follows that the Declaration Clause forbids them from making the same judgment in any setting for which Sidak would require a formal declaration.

The Superclear Statement Objection

If the accountability rationale does not compel formal declaration, it still makes a strong claim for a requirement of clear statement for congressional authorization of military hostilities. In fact, as we noted in chapter 11, the courts have adopted a general rule of narrow construction of legitimating appropriations, which disfavors ratification by appropriation. But some scholars have suggested that the Constitution goes further, impliedly prohibiting acquiescence by appropriation altogether or imposing a "superclear" statement requirement so severe that not even the Vietnam War appropriations meet it.[87] Because some members of the Court have suggested that a clear statement rule of construction "relieves a court of the duty to give effect to all available indicia of the legislative will,"[88] adoption of a superclear statement rule for legitimating appropriations would substantially arrest their contribution to the development of customary national security law. In this section, however, we show that the chief authority for a superclear statement rule, *Greene v. McElroy*,[89] is distinguishable and does not require substituting such a rule for the general rule of narrow construction that was satisfied by the legitimating appropriations in the Vietnam War.

In *Greene*, the government argued that continued appropriations for a clearance program had impliedly delegated the authority to conduct security clearance proceedings without affording respondents the rights of confrontation or cross-examination. The Court responded:

> If acquiescence or implied ratification were enough to show delegation of authority to take actions within the area of questionable constitutionality, we might agree . . . that delegation has been shown here. . . . But . . . [b]efore we are asked to judge whether, in the context of security clearance cases, a person may be deprived of the right to follow his chosen profession without full hearings where accusers may be confronted, it must be made clear that the President or Congress, within their respective constitutional pow-

> ers, specifically has decided that the imposed procedures are necessary and warranted and has authorized their use. *Such decisions cannot be assumed by acquiescence or nonaction. . . . Ex parte Endo,* 323 U.S. 283, 301–302. They must be made explicitly not only to assure that individuals are not deprived of cherished rights under procedures not actually authorized, but also because explicit action, especially in areas of doubtful constitutionality, requires careful and purposeful consideration by those responsible for enacting and implementing our laws.[90]

There are several reasons, however, to believe that *Greene*'s seeming dismissal of acquiescence should be not taken literally or understood to impose a super-clear statement rule on all national security actions.

First, *Greene* itself cites *Ex parte Endo,*[91] another case in which the government unsuccessfully sought to infer authority for constitutionally suspect national security activities from lump-sum appropriations. But in *Endo,* the Court did not completely rule out acquiescence or ratification by appropriation. It only applied the general rule of narrow construction discussed in chapter 11 to hold that the appropriation should have shown more clearly the authority claimed, when its exercise involved the involuntary detention of loyal Americans.

Second, both *Greene* and *Endo* involved national security activities that impinged on individual rights in domestic settings. As noted above, the delegation doctrine arguably applies with greater force in domestic affairs than in foreign affairs, exacting greater specificity from Congress when it legislates domestically than when it authorizes military or diplomatic activity abroad. Many commentators are also agreed that it has more bite when the delegated authority directly impinges on constitutionally sensitive individual rights than when it does not.[92] Chief Justice Marshall drew just this distinction as early as *McCulloch v. Maryland,*[93] when he asserted that acquiescence in a practice of government may put to rest or at least help resolve "a doubtful question [of constitutional law], . . . in the decision of which the great principles of liberty are not concerned, but the respective powers of those who are equally the representatives of the people, are to be adjusted . . . ."[94]

The individual rights and domestic affairs distinctions should not be pressed too hard. The legal challenges to the Vietnam War ultimately involved the individual rights of the soldiers that were being sent to war, and it is no original insight to note that governmental powers are separated primarily in order to protect individual rights.[95] Similarly, national security activities with "domestic" effects are sometimes undertaken for foreign affairs purposes (e.g,. seizing steel plants to assure the flow of armaments for an overseas war, or suspending claims by U.S. nationals in U.S. courts in order to carry out a claims settlement with a foreign nation), seriously blurring the geographic distinction.[96] Nevertheless, in cases like *Greene* the effect of the activities on individual rights is arguably *more* direct and more domestic in locus than in cases like those deciding challenges to the legality of the Vietnam War. As David Schoenbrod puts it, "[t]o be sure, the conduct of a war or the terms of a treaty may affect domestic rights and duties but this will be incidental to their international aspects."[97]

Finally, the Court in *Greene* opined that the authority claimed by the government was "in conflict with our long-accepted notions of fair procedures."[98] Instead of evidencing acquiescence in a long-continued practice of the executive branch, the congressional appropriations were invoked to justify what in the Court's view was an extreme departure from tradition; the authority claimed from appropriations, if not flatly contrary to customary law as the Court saw it, at least drew no support from it. In fact, the effect of the appropriation came closer to an implied repeal of what the Court regarded as the tradition of fair procedure. By contrast, the authority claimed from the Vietnam appropriations was not a departure from customary law (although there was admittedly also no prior customary national security law concerning military engagements on the scale of Vietnam).

Greene is therefore no obstacle to the development of customary national security law by appropriations on appropriate facts. It should either be read simply as affirming the general rule of narrow construction of legitimating appropriations and the rule against implied repeal by appropriation, or distinguished as requiring a superclear statement of authorization for only those activities that infringe on constitutionally sensitive rights in domestic settings, or both.

The War Powers Resolution Objection

Even if the Constitution does not require a superclear statement in all legitimating appropriations, Congress has enacted its own such requirement in the War Powers Resolution.[99] Section 8(a)(1) of the resolution provides the following:

> Authority to introduce United States Armed Forces into hostilities or into situations wherein involvement in hostilities is clearly indicated by the circumstances shall not be inferred . . . from any provision of law (whether or not in effect before November 7, 1973), including any provision contained in any Appropriation Act, unless such provision specifically authorizes the introduction of United States Armed Forces into hostilities or into such situations and states that it is intended to constitute specific statutory authorization within the meaning of this chapter . . . .

The legislative history[100] indicates that this provision was intended to "counteract the opinion in *Orlando v. Laird*[[101]]." If this provision controls, it would prevent inferences of authorization, ratification or acquiescence from appropriations that do not specifically authorize the use of force *and* specifically refer to the War Powers Resolution. We conclude, however, that the resolution's clear statement requirement does not control the construction of subsequent appropriations or other legislation. Instead, absent ambiguities, it is their own plain words and their enactors' legislative intent that controls their construction. As a result, a legitimating appropriation may authorize or ratify a deployment of U.S. armed forces into hostilities even if it omits the resolution's magic passwords and thus violates its clear statement provision.

By enacting section 8, the 93d Congress was asserting what Michael Glennon calls a "first-in-time" rule of statutory construction.[102] All subsequent legislation, including legitimating appropriations, must be read *in pari materia* with and subordinate to section 8, he asserts. Its clear statement requirement for authorization of deployments of U.S. armed forces is effectively an implied rider to all subsequent acts from which the executive seeks to infer authorization.[103] John Hart Ely describes the section somewhat differently, but with identical effect. "What the War Powers Resolution gave us was a strong rule of construction," he asserts, "telling us how to read the intent of later Congresses."[104] Until it is repealed, therefore, "the conventions it establishes should control."[105]

Ely's characterization of the provision is correct, but his conclusion does not follow. Section 8 is no ordinary rule of statutory construction, like one of the much-maligned canons. It is a "*strong* rule," indeed, a "rule of constitutional construction" or "superstatute,"[106] because it does not just *advise* us how to construe subsequent legislation, it *compels* us and purports to regulate the content, not just the construction, of future enactments[107] by self-referentially insisting on a cross-reference to the War Powers Resolution before we may find authorization in a legitimating appropriation. Thus, even when the appropriation's plain words, or clear legislative history and customary law context, leave no doubt of the enacting Congress's intent to authorize a troop deployment, we must disregard that intent if the appropriation does not contain the magic passwords required by the resolution.

But this is not and cannot constitutionally be the law. In *Marcello v. Bonds*,[108] the Supreme Court pointedly refused to apply a similar rule of construction codified in the Administrative Procedure Act[109] to require a later Congress "to employ magical passwords in order to effectuate an exemption from the Administrative Procedure Act."[110] The usual rule of statutory construction is a "last-in-time" rule, by which the intent of the later Congress controls over the intent of the earlier.[111] Alexander Hamilton explained this rule in *The Federalist*. When two statutes clash, he said,

> [t]he rule which has obtained in the courts for determining their relative validity is that the last in order of time shall be preferred to the first . . . . It is a rule not enjoined upon the courts by legislative provision, but adopted by themselves, as consonant to truth and propriety . . . . They thought it reasonable that between the interfering acts of an *equal* authority that which was the last indication of its will should have the preference.[112]

Contrary to Michael Glennon,[113] moreover, there is a reason why this last-in-time rule controls even if Congress indicates otherwise in the War Powers Resolution, namely the Constitution's implied rule against "entrenched" legislation—legislation that purports to bind future legislatures.[114] The implication of the Constitution's carefully prescribed requirements for periodic reelection is that the voters—the principals—give a temporally limited mandate to their agents in a particular Congress.[115] Because the principals themselves change over time, and because the circumstances their agents face also change, the legislative mandate of any particular Congress is for a limited period, not perpetual. Julian Eule explains:

> Each election furnishes the electorate with an opportunity to provide new direction for its representatives. This process would be reduced to an exercise in futility were the newly elected representatives bound by the policy choice of a prior generation of voters. . . . In the end, therefore, it is the spirit of article I, § 2, cl. 1, and § 3, cl. 1, that prohibits entrenchment. The people's mandate has temporal limits. By enacting [entrenching legislation], the [nth] Congress exceed[s] those boundaries and the [n + 1 Congress] remains free to discard or simply ignore the enactment. An agent without authority can bind neither the principal nor the principal's future representatives.[116]

Thomas Jefferson made the same observation in 1786 in the Statute of Virginia for Religious Freedom when he declared that "we well know this Assembly, elected by the people for the ordinary purposes of legislation only, ha[s] no power to restrain the acts of succeeding Assemblies constituted with the powers equal to our own . . . ."[117]

It follows that the 93d Congress that enacted the War Powers Resolution cannot control the way in which the 103d Congress express their intent. Both Hamilton and Jefferson declared that the powers of these congresses are at least equal; in light of the temporal limits on their mandates, we would argue that the power of the latter is superior. What matters in construing an enactment of the 103d Congress under either view is what the enactment says and what that Congress intended, and not what the 93d Congress said or intended. Even if the enactment's plain language is not dispositive, the clearly expressed legislative intent of the 103d Congress, if one can be found, controls. Thus the Supreme Court in *Marcello* properly construed the later enactment by examining its "background" and legislative history, even though the statute did not meet the clear statement requirement of the Administrative Procedure Act.[118]

This is not to make a dead letter out of the whole of the War Powers Resolution's rule of construction. Its self-referential insistence on "passwords" is without effect. We never have occasion to need the rest of it, if we can ascertain the meaning and intent of a legitimating appropriation from its plain words or clear legislative history. If we cannot, then the resolution's clear statement requirement sounds a useful advisory caution against inferring authority from ambiguous appropriations measures, and thus operates like any canon of statutory construction, by supplying helpful, but not controlling guidance in statutory construction.[119] In doing this, it reinforces the rule of narrow construction of appropriations as ratification.

The Ratification Objection

We have defined appropriations from which the executive infers authority to take national security actions as "legitimating appropriations" in order to encompass both those appropriations that supply prior approval and those that ratify the actions after they have been initiated. Ratification by appropriation, however, is subject to the objection that the Constitution requires prior approval of military actions. An additional objection is that even if ratification is constitutionally permissible, it is impossible as a practical matter to construe national security appropriations as ratification because of the "rally-round-the-flag" pressures under which they are enacted. We conclude that there is no constitutional impediment to ratification of national security actions and that the practical difficulty of construing appropriations as ratification is overdrawn.

One form of the constitutional objection need not detain us long. Gregory Sidak speculates that ratification by appropriation "very possibly is unconstitutional," because "it is elemental that the rule of law requires that legislation exhibit prospectivity and generality" and the "granting of retroactive approval is obviously neither prospective nor general."[120] As a general proposition, this objection fails because its predicate fails. It is too late in the day to deny that a civil statute may constitutionally operate retroactively provided that such retroactivity is fair and intended.[121] The very existence of the general rule of statutory construction disfavoring ratification by appropriation is evidence of the legal possibility of such ratification, and the courts have indeed held it permissible for decades.[122] Finding that subsequent legislation ratified the acquisition of land for the Panama Canal, the Supreme Court declared in 1907 that "subsequent ratification is equivalent to original authority."[123] Thirty years later, the Court found ratification of an executive reorganization by the appropriation of funds for salaries and expenses of the reorganized function.[124] In a companion case, challenging the constitutionality of the executive action, the Court stressed that

> [i]t is well settled that Congress may, by enactment not otherwise inappropriate, "ratify . . . acts which it might have authorized," and give the force of law to official action unauthorized when taken. . . . The mere fact that the validation is retroactive in its operation is not enough, in the circumstances of this case, to render it ineffective.[125]

More recently, a majority of federal courts found that the executive transfer of certain enforcement responsibilities to an executive agency was ratified by appropriations of funds to the agency.[126]

Sharpening the general objection to putative ratifications of war making, however, gives it more color. If the Constitution requires antecedent congressional approval of war, partly to assure a sobering pause before we make it, then ratification comes too late, depriving us of the protection afforded by the pause. William van Alstyne makes this argument against inferences of authority from the legitimating appropriations in the Vietnam War:

> The necessity for . . . antecedent congressional action, not subject to correction or repair by anything that even Congress might do later on as war was to develop, is built into the declaration of war clause itself: a pause must occur following the first use of war power even in emergencies and *prior* to any further deterioration of relationships; inertial movement down the slippery face of war is momentarily arrested by the force of constitutional requirement and cannot be resumed save on deliberate choice affirmatively asserted by joint declaration of war by both Houses. For this reason it is not possible to conjure up suitable later substitutes for any congressional action which may have failed at the time as a requisite declaration of war.[127]

This narrowed objection to ratification, however, was apparently rejected by the Supreme Court in the *Prize Cases.*[128] There President Lincoln had ordered a naval blockade of the Confederacy while Congress was not in session. The Supreme Court upheld the legality of the order partly on the ground that Congress ratified it after they returned.

> Without admitting that such an act was necessary under the circumstances, it is plain that if the President had in any manner assumed powers which it was necessary should have the authority or sanction of Congress, that on the well known principle of law, "*omnis ratihabitio retrotrahitur et mandato equiparatur,*" this ratification has operated perfectly to cure the defect. . . . The objection made to this act of ratification, that it is *ex post facto,* and therefore unconstitutional and void, might possibly have some weight on the trial of an indictment in a criminal Court. But precedents from that source cannot be received as authoritative in a tribunal administering public and international law.[129]

Black's Law Dictionary renders the quoted Latin phrase as "Every ratification relates back and is equivalent to a prior authority."[130] Moreover, the Court subsequently gave retroactive legal effect even to the formal declaration of war against Spain.[131]

John Hart Ely implies that the *Prize Cases* dictum may simply reflect judicial abstention or cowardice in refusing to challenge the joint judgment of the political branches.[132] While this may account for the result, it does not account for the language or cabin the "well known principle of law" that the Court invoked.

A more promising distinction is that ratification was unnecessary to the result, as the Court itself implied ("without admitting that such an act was necessary under the circumstances"), because the president had inherent authority to order the blockade to defend against sudden attack and insurrection. The Court held that when war is made by invasion or insurrection, "the President is not only authorized but bound to resist force by force. He does not initiate the war, but is bound to accept the challenge without waiting for any special legislative authority."[133] Did the Court endorse application of the doctrine of ratification to executive war making only when ratification is constitutionally gratuitous?

This hardly seems logical and is hard to square with the Court's language. It clearly was positing an alternative legal basis for the president's action. Furthermore, even if an initial military response lies within the president's inherent constitutional power to repel sudden attacks, continuation of military action may require congressional approval after the emergency passes or is brought under control. The *Prize Cases* dictum is consistent with the application of ratification in these circumstances.

In short, if it is still good law, the *Prize Cases* decision appears to assert that Congress may, by ratification, make constitutional executive military action that would have been unconstitutional without ratification; Congress can "cure the defect" by supplying its authorization retroactively. Subsequently, in *Youngstown Sheet & Tube Co. v. Sawyer,*[134] Justices Douglas and Frankfurter both implied that this was still good law by approving the doctrine of congressional ratification of constitutionally unauthorized executive action.[135] So, arguably, does the War Powers Resolution, by providing that legislation enacted as late as ninety days *after* the introduction of troops into hostilities can supply the constitutionally required congressional authorization for such deployment.[136]

A last-ditch objection is that the doctrine of ratification is tantamount to a theory of executive power based on necessity (or "higher law").[137] "It is an invitation not only for Congress to usurp Executive power," argues Gregory Sidak, "but also for the President to become a tyrant—for he routinely would have to operate 'above the law' (which is to say, without regard for the law) and subsequently use political power to prevent his impeachment."[138]

This misconceives the doctrine as it evolved in the debates of the first congresses and presidents, described in chapter 4, and ignores the consequences of the alternative. Ratification by appropriation can render constitutional executive acts that would be unconstitutional without it. But until Congress ratifies, the acts remain unconstitutional. As Justice Douglas noted in *Youngstown*, the president might seize private property and Congress might subsequently ratify the seizure, "[b]ut until and unless Congress acted, no condemnation would be lawful."[139] Necessity compels or invites the executive to act, but it does not authorize the action; only Congress's subsequent legislation can supply the authority. Necessity gives the executive a reason, not a legal excuse to act; only ratification can supply the excuse. Recall Hamilton's statement of the consensus Republican-Federalist view: When unilateral executive action is "unavoidable," the executive must rely on "an *after* legislative sanction and provision."[140]

It is true that the prospect of ratification after the fact may encourage the usurping executive,[141] but the gravity of the necessity will always be the primary motive for action. And, if such encouragement is the price paid for the doctrine of ratification, one benefit is that the executive usurpation creates no legal precedent of "inherent" executive emergency authority that can be invoked the next time.[142] The alternative—rationalizing the executive action *ab initio* as an exercise of a nebulous inherent constitutional power—is far more damaging to the rule of law in the long run, because it creates a constitutional basis and legal precedent of executive authority for similar executive acts in the future.[143]

There remains the practical objection that it is impossible to construe national security appropriations as ratification because of the circumstances of their enactment. Thus, Chief Judge Bazelon and Judge Wyzanski observed, in refusing to find ratification of the Vietnam War in appropriations or other legislation, that

> in voting to appropriate money or to draft men a Congressman is not necessarily approving of the continuation of the war no matter how specifically the appropriation or draft act refers to that war. A Congressman wholly opposed to the war's commencement and continuation might vote for military appropriations and for draft measures because he was unwilling to abandon without support men already fighting. An honorable, decent, compassionate act of

> aiding those already in peril is no proof of consent to the actions that placed and continued them in that dangerous posture. We should not construe votes cast in pity and piety as though they were votes freely given to express consent.[144]

These observations echoed the complaints of congressmen themselves, as they voted appropriations for the war,[145] and were also adopted by antiwar scholars.[146] Michael Glennon generalizes the objection into a predicate for congressional acquiescence in the development of customary law: an "institutional capacity to object."[147] By swiftly deploying troops into combat situations, the president can present Congress with a fait accompli and no choice but to rally round the flag, according to this objection.

The objection is exaggerated and ahistorical. It seems to proceed on the assumption that Congress's choices are all or nothing; fund or deny all funding. But the Vietnam War itself showed that Congress has intermediate options,[148] including funding phaseouts, prospective cutoffs, and, subject to separation of powers limits,[149] area limitations. In fact, given the scope of the president's commander-in-chief powers, it is doubtful that Congress constitutionally *could* cut off the funds so abruptly that American lives would be placed at grave risk.[150] In any event, as John Hart Ely remarks, "the President is not going to be so callous (or so politically stupid) as to leave the troops on the battlefield defenseless, waiting to be slaughtered: Instead he will withdraw them (and protect them while doing so)."[151]

Furthermore, even with modern technology, substantial troop buildups take time. Soon after the initial U.S. troop deployments to Saudi Arabia in Operation Desert Storm, Congressman Bob Traxler (D., Mich.) asserted that he was against the operation, but that he would vote for a $1.9 billion appropriation for it anyway because he did not want to jeopardize lives of Americans already sent to the Gulf region, adding that he thought they should be brought home right away.[152] But at the time of the congressman's remarks, almost two months had already passed since the initial U.S. deployments, the buildup was far from complete (a large increase came two months later), and no troops had yet been committed to combat. In the circumstances, the congressman's agony was crocodilian; there was no reason why Congress could not have pulled the plug on the operation and the troops withdrawn under air cover without jeopardy.

Not only can Congress thus often calibrate its appropriations power and cooperate with the commander in chief to accomplish a safe exit from war, but under the historical understanding of the national security appropriations power, it *must* if it decides that the continuation of war is bad policy. "They are not *at liberty* to vest in the executive department permanent funds for the support of the army," Hamilton emphasized in *The Federalist;* the Constitution obliges them to "deliberate on the propriety of keeping a military force on foot" at least once every two years.[153] In fact, now that defense appropriations are annual, and supplemental or emergency appropriations for particular military engagements even more frequent, Congress has that obligation at every appropriation vote. The framers did not expect that it would be easy ("The provision for the support of a military force will always be a favorable topic for declamation."[154]), but they hardly thought that the political difficulty of the decision somehow excused Congress from responsibility for making it.

Especially in light of the fact that Congress did eventually pull the plug on the war in Indochina, this objection to ratification by appropriation smacks of hypocrisy. It is another instance of Congress "cheering with one hand and sitting on the other," in Senator Mark Hatfield's memorable phrase,[155] or perhaps more accurately, wringing the other. Like the superclear statement objections to legitimating appropriations, it is valid only to the extent that it reinforces the general rule of statutory construction disfavoring ratification by appropriation; it is not a reason to deny ratification when the rule is rebutted by appropriate legislative history and context, as we have argued it was during most of the Vietnam War.

13

Restrictive Appropriations

The paradigm of what we call restrictive appropriations—appropriations which restrict national security activities by the executive—are the Boland amendments from 1982 to 1986. We have already described the legislative process by which they were enacted. In this chapter, we use them as examples to discuss the substantive scope of restrictive appropriations. We begin by applying the analysis set out in chapter 11 to determine their force and effect as law. We then consider the general objection that restrictive national security appropriations violate the separation of powers by impermissibly intruding on the inherent constitutional authority of the president. Finally, we consider this objection to the most restrictive Boland amendment and to restrictive appropriations during the Vietnam War.

The General Force and Effect of the Boland Amendments

The purpose of this section is to examine how, if at all, the previously described legislative process that produced the Boland amendments, and the fact that they were appropriations measures, affect their proper statutory construction.[1] We conclude that nothing in the appropriations process necessarily or uniquely contributed to ambiguities in the Boland amendments, and that the presumption against implied repeal by appropriations is inapplicable to the strictest of them. What the Boland amendments mean does not turn on what they were—appropriations measures as opposed to "ordinary" legislation.

Brief Review of the Substance of the Boland Amendments

Most of the Boland amendments were amendments to defense appropriations acts (themselves parts of continuing resolutions) or to intelligence authorization acts.[2] The first published Boland amendment[3] was a floor amendment to the DOD Appropriations Act. It prohibited support of any group or individual for the purpose of overthrowing the Sandinistas.[4] It thus allowed continued military support of the Contras for the purpose of interdicting Sandinista arms shipments to neighboring states.

The distinction between overthrowing the Sandinistas and interdicting their arms shipments proved elusive in implementation, however. When the administration took the view that the objectives of the Contras were irrelevant to the legality of U.S. military support for them,[5] as long as the United States was not itself seeking the overthrow of the Sandinistas, the House Permanent Select Committee on Intelligence (chaired by Congressman Boland) voted to tighten the restriction.[6] After extensive debate, much procedural maneuvering, and no fewer than seven roll call votes, the House passed what was known as the Boland-Zablocki amendment, a forerunner of the later-enacted, most restrictive Boland amendment.[7] In contrast, the Senate voted unrestricted aid.[8] What emerged from the resulting conference was a compromise, capping the amount of Contra aid for fiscal 1984 at $24 million. This cap was enacted in the DOD Appropriation Act and the Intelligence Authorization Act for fiscal 1984, both providing in relevant part that

> not more than $24,000,000 of the funds available to the Central Intelligence Agency, the Department of Defense, or any other agency or entity of the United States involved in intelligence activities may be obligated or expended for the purpose or which would have the effect of supporting, directly or indirectly, military or paramilitary operations in Nicaragua by any nation, group, organization, movement, or individual.[9]

Although the House restriction thus did not prevail, the cap assured that the covert aid program could not long continue without further appropriations. In addition, the "funds available to" formula prevented the CIA from resorting to contingency funds after the cap was reached.[10] After the disclosure in April 1984 that the CIA had helped to mine Nicaraguan harbors[11] and had apparently tried to disguise the resulting overrun of the funding cap by charging the $1.2 million cost of a mine-laying vessel to its overall operating budget,[12] both houses voted to condemn the mining[13] and voted down the administration's request for a supplemental appropriation to support the Contras.[14] The House Permanent Committee on Intelligence subsequently reported the most severe restriction to date—essentially the old Boland-Zablocki amendment—as a provision of the intelligence authorization bill. The House voted to approve this restriction and eventually incorporated it into a continuing resolution as well.[15] The Senate rejected a comparably restrictive floor amendment to the continuing resolution.[16]

This time the House prevailed in conference, although the conferees agreed to revisit the issue in four months. The conferees reported and Congress approved amendments to the DOD Appropriation Act and the Intelligence Authorization Act for fiscal 1985 (hereinafter *the 1984 Boland amendment*) providing in pertinent part that

> [d]uring fiscal year 1985, no funds available to the Central Intelligence Agency, the Department of Defense, or any other agency or entity of the United States involved in intelligence activities may be obligated or expended for the purpose or with the effect of supporting, directly or indirectly, military or paramilitary operations in Nicaragua by any nation, group, organization, movement, or individual.[17]

During the House debate, Congressman Boland asserted that "this prohibition applies to all funds available in fiscal year 1985 regardless of any accounting procedure at the agency. It clearly prohibits any expenditure, including those from accounts for salaries and all support costs. . . . To repeat, the compromise provision clearly ends U.S. support for the war in Nicaragua."[18] President Reagan signed this restriction into law on October 12, 1984, without apparently publicly expressing any qualms about its constitutionality.[19] The 1984 Boland amendment prohibited support of the Contras from October 12, 1984, until at least August 8, 1985.[20]

On that date, Congress enacted the first of a series of measures gradually lifting the restrictions on aid to the Contras, by allowing $27 million in humanitarian aid.[21] Even as it loosened the restrictions, however, it showed distrust of the CIA and the Defense Department by providing that the aid was to be distributed by an agency designated by the president, "except the Central Intelligence Agency or the Department of Defense."[22] At the same time, it enacted separate legislation prohibiting the exchange of foreign aid or arms for a recipient nation's assistance to the Contras (the Pell amendment)[23] and prohibiting the use of any funds to support activities against the Sandinistas that had not been authorized pursuant to law and which would place the United States in violation of international law (the Kerry amendment).[24] A supplemental appropriation of funds for this humanitarian assistance incorporated by reference the restrictions of the 1984 Boland amendment but stated that nothing therein prevented the exchange of information with the Contras or the use of the funds for humanitarian assistance.[25] Not until December 4, 1985, did Congress expressly authorize resumption of limited military aid to the Contras.[26] More than a year later, Congress appropriated $100 million for the Contras, of which $70 million could be used for nonhumanitarian purposes.[27]

The Appropriations Process and the Statutory Construction of the Boland Amendments

The Minority Report of the Iran-Contra Committee begins its analysis of the proper construction of the 1984 Boland amendment by asserting that "it is important to bear in mind that [the amendment] w[as] a rider, or a limitation amendment, to an appropriation bill. . . . An appropriations rider, even if it reaches salaries, is nothing more than a limitation on the way Federal funds may be used. It does not reach a person's whole life and does not make activities criminal."[28]

The Minority Report thus from the outset fell into the same trap as the courts and commentators that disparage "mere appropriations." As we have shown in chapter 11, an appropriation rider is the constitutional equivalent of ordinary legislation. Of course, "it does not reach a person's whole life," whatever that means. But given the Appropriations Clause and the Anti-Deficiency Act, it reaches the government's "whole life." Moreover, violation of the Anti-Deficiency Act, and therefore spending in violation of an appropriation rider, *is* criminal.[29]

The Minority Report's assumptions reflect a second error that infected its statutory analysis. When the issue is foreign military assistance, "the way Federal funds may be used" is not incidental to or just a means for executing policy; it *is* policy. It was therefore inevitable that the appropriation process became the forum for policy debate, as we suggested previously.[30] Aid to the Contras was appropriately debated in the intelligence committees, which originated the intelligence authorization acts, in the appropriations committees, which originated the DOD appropriations acts, on the floor, and in conference when the houses disagreed. The Boland-Zablocki amendment, the forerunner of the 1984 Boland amendment, was also referred to and considered by the House Foreign Affairs Committee.[31] The running Boland amendments debate did not bypass the appropriate committees.

Did it, nevertheless, avoid full deliberation, thereby generating a truncated legislative history? A student commentator asserts that the Boland amendments were "floor amendments, . . . each . . . passed as part of an appropriation bill, without detailed debate and consideration of the individual merit of the provision as it would impact United States support for the Contras."[32] He concludes, therefore, that "[t]he legislation was not the product of a well-reasoned and thoughtful process," recommending that Congress send such legislation through its intelligence and foreign affairs committees.[33] He is thus describing what we have called the "indeterminate legislative history" often associated with appropriations measures, which may justify or require narrow construction.[34]

The flaw in this critique is that it does not describe the legislative history of the Boland amendments. Even though the first nonclassified Boland amendment was a floor amendment, the Boland-Zablocki amendment originated in the House Permanent Select Committee on Intelligence, which reported it out with a committee report. Most of the other Boland amendments did not originate as floor amendments and did go through the intelligence committees. Moreover, the running debate in both houses was extensive and focused precisely on how each amendment "would impact United States support for the Contras," filling more than four hundred pages of the *Congressional Record*.[35] One can question whether the end result was "well-reasoned" and good policy, but its defects cannot tenably be attributed to the process or an insufficient legislative history. Indeed, from the perspective of the legal scholar, if anything, the Boland amendments suffer from too much, not too little, legislative history.

A more telling criticism that may affect the statutory construction of the Boland amendments is their variability. The Congressional Research Service identified no fewer than thirteen amendments (counting the first classified restriction), changing from year to year and sometimes within a year. The Minority Report of the Iran-Contra Committee argues that this variability shows that "Congress has changed its collective mind virtually every year over policy toward Nicaragua."[36] Using the appropriation process to make policy required Congress to revisit the policy annually, or more often, when the administration sought supplemental appropriations. It also left puzzling gaps and ambiguities about the duration of the policy enacted. One restriction was in place only eight days, for example, because it was enacted as a rider to a stopgap continuing resolution,[37] and even the Congressional Research Service, with the benefit of hindsight, is unable to say precisely when the 1984 Boland amendment lapsed.[38]

Yet the variability of the Boland amendments was neither random nor incomprehensible. House Majority Leader Foley reminds us that

> Congress did not, and does not, act in a vacuum, and in the series of Boland Amendments was responding to a succession of policy changes by this administration. . . .
>
> The [1984] Boland Amendment was developed and approved by Congress because the administration kept changing its justification for the contra aid program.[39]

The initial restriction accommodated the first administration justification for Contra aid: that it was for interdicting Sandinista arms shipments. The second was a response to the administration's apparent departure from this justification. The third was partly in response to the CIA's alleged use of contingency funds to avoid the prior restriction.

Of course, as the extensive legislative history shows, Congress was never of a single mind about military assistance to the Contras, and its policy did change. But law is not made by acclamation or unanimity. In the heavily checked legislative process established by the Constitution, law is most commonly made by precisely the kinds of compromises that marked the evolution of the Boland amendments. While the resulting variability and compromise may reflect poorly on Congress's institutional capacity to make foreign policy[40] (or not—given the need for flexibility in foreign policy), it does not necessarily render the meaning or congressional intent behind any individual Boland amendment indeterminate.[41] Nor does it dilute a specific amendment's legal effect while the amendment is the law. Even the Minority Report of the Iran-Contra Committee concedes as much by admitting that a "clear statement would have to govern for as long as it stayed in effect."[42] More accurately stated, the principle is that *any* duly enacted law, including an appropriation rider, governs as long as it stays in effect, whether or not it is easy to construe.

The 1984 Boland amendment was indisputably in effect between October 12, 1984, and at least August 1985. The Iran-Contra Committee therefore properly focused primarily on it in assessing violations of law in the Iran-Contra affair. This assessment poses at least three questions of statutory construction of the 1984 Boland amendment.[43]

The first question concerns the reach of the "no funds available" formula carried forward from the prior Boland amendment. This formula clearly extended the restriction in the 1984 Boland amendment beyond the DOD appropriations to which it was attached.[44] On the other hand, the 1984 Boland amendment did not use the common formula "No part of any appropriation contained in this *or any other Act* shall be used."[45] The Minority Report of the Iran-Contra Committee argues that the failure to use this formula is evidence that Congress did not want to enact "an airtight prohibition" that would have covered the National Security Council (NSC).[46] But the Intelligence Committee's familiarity with black budgeting for the CIA,[47] the initial funding of Contra aid from CIA contingency funds, and the CIA's alleged accounting legerdemain to conceal its overrun of the first spending cap all explain the less common "all funds available" formula. They reinforce the common sense construction that it covers not just funds from any appropriation, but all funds however obtained[48] and however accounted.[49]

A second question of statutory construction is presented by the phrase "for the purpose or which would have the effect of supporting, directly or indirectly, military or paramilitary operations." On its face, this phrase extends the prohibition to any activity that would have the effect even indirectly of supporting military operations. It thus seemingly includes information exchanges and intelligence sharing that would have that effect, a point to which we later return.

The most hotly disputed question of construction, however, is whether "agency or entity of the United States involved in intelligence activities" included the National Security Council. On this question, the Minority Report of the Iran-Contra Committee, already led astray by its erroneous characterization of appropriation measures, compounded its error by misapplying customary national security law and the rule against implied repeal by appropriation. The fulcrum of its argument that this phrase is a term of art that does not include the NSC[50] is that Congress had acquiesced for forty years in the president's use of the NSC in intelligence matters without subjecting it to oversight by legislation targeting "the intelligence community."[51] "It is fanciful to maintain that Congress intended to break almost 40 years of complete deference to the President's use of the NSC without provoking some extended discussion or controversy," the Minority Report concludes, citing *TVA v. Hill*,[52] the leading case declaring the rule against implied repeal by appropriation.

Our analysis of customary national security law teaches, however, that the first predicate for such law is a systematic and long-pursued executive practice that permits one to identify a custom in the practice and to articulate and delimit the authority that it establishes.[53] Had the systematic and long-pursued executive practice prior to enactment of the 1984 Boland amendment been to use the NSC for covert *operations*, then Congress's failure explicitly to include the NSC in intelligence oversight legislation might be deemed an acquiescence in the practice. If Congress then intended to repeal the resulting customary national security law by an appropriation rider applicable to NSC operations, it would be fair to require it to say so expressly. But the systematic and long-standing executive practice prior to the Iran-Contra affair was *not* to use the NSC to conduct intelligence and covert operations. The CIA was the primary operational agent for covert activities, and the NSC chiefly a consumer and coordinator of intelligence by statute[54] and experience.[55] As former National Security Adviser Zbigniew Brzezinski has explained:

> Membership on the NSC staff by definition confers a staff role—to plan strategy, to coordinate, to supervise, and, for the national security adviser, to advise the president. Active and sustained involvement in bureaucratic operations or covert intelligence activity militates against fulfilling these roles. Fortunately, that danger has been recognized throughout most of the NSC's history, *and deviations from the rule have been few, the Iran-contra scandal notwithstanding.*[56]

This is not to say that the NSC did not, from time to time, assume a more operational role on special assignments,[57] but only to note that they were the exception. As Larry Eig of the Congressional Research Service concluded in 1987, "there may not appear to be a precedent for direct NSC staff operational involvement in covert intelligence activities of the type currently at issue [in the Iran-Contra affair]."[58]

Contrary to the Minority Report of the Iran-Contra Committee, there was therefore no customary law for the Boland amendment to repeal. There was no forty-year practice of congressional acquiescence to the president's *operational* use of the NSC for the simple reason that the president had not often or consistently used the NSC to conduct intelligence or covert operations. Even if the Iran-Contra affair introduced a new operational era for the council,[59] the administration not only gave Congress no notice of this change, but affirmatively denied that there was any change. Consequently, Congress could not have knowingly acquiesced in any new operational role for the NSC.

The amendment may therefore be given its plain meaning, without benefit of any narrowing construction required for implied repeals. It applies not to any "intelligence entity" or "entity of the intelligence community," but more broadly to "any . . . entity of the United States involved in intelligence activities." Whatever the prior executive practice, "the plain fact is that the NSC under North and company *was* 'involved in intelligence activities.'"[60] Congress did not identify the NSC by name because there was no reason from past practice to expect it to conduct covert operations. But after targeting the chief operational agencies by name, Congress included "any entity of the United States involved in intelligence activities" as a catchall to assure complete cessation of U.S. support for the military and paramilitary activities of the Contras. This was how the national security adviser, head of the NSC staff, and the Office of Legal Counsel in the Department of Justice contemporaneously interpreted the 1984 Boland amendment.[61] This part of the 1984 Boland amendment should be read to mean what it says; there is no reason to go behind it to legislative history or tortured tours of *pari materia* legislation.

But our purpose here is not to settle the questions of statutory construction surrounding the 1984 Boland amendment or the other Boland amendments. Even if they do present serious ambiguities in this or other respects, there is nothing about the process by which they were enacted or their typical form, as restrictive appropriation measures, that necessarily accounts for that ambiguity or that requires application of special, narrow rules of construction. Our tentative conclusion is that what the Boland amendments mean depends on what they said, not on what they were or how they were enacted.

The Separation-of-Powers Objection to Restrictive National Security Appropriations

The foregoing conclusion is tentative, however, because we have yet to account for a constitutional rule of statutory construction. The Supreme Court has repeatedly cautioned that "[w]hen the validity of an act of Congress is drawn in question, and even if a serious doubt of constitutionality is raised, it is a cardinal principle that this Court will first ascertain whether a construction of the statute is *fairly possible* by which the question may be avoided."[62] This principle is incorporated into the following syllogism by proponents of the narrow construction of restrictive national security appropriations. Congress may not use national security appropriations to accomplish what it may not constitutionally do directly. Restrictive national security appropriations may restrict the president's inherent constitutional national security authority in a way that Congress could not do constitutionally by direct legislation. If they are not unconstitutional outright on that account, therefore, they must at least be read narrowly to avoid infringing the president's inherent authority.[63]

In this section we consider this general objection to restrictive national security appropriations. We show that it frequently invokes the wrong mode or tier of separation-of-powers analysis and that national security appropriations carry special historical weight under the correct mode, by which they will usually be found constitutional.

Lovett and Two-Tiered Separation-of-Powers Analysis

To the frequent assertion that the appropriation power is "plenary,"[64] defenders of a presidential prerogative have a powerful, if obvious rejoinder. "Congress cannot use the appropriations power to control a Presidential power that is beyond its direct control," as Attorney General William Barr put it.[65] Asserting that Congress may not impose unconstitutional conditions on the president by way of earmarking or restriction is another way of making the same point.[66] Indeed, Attorney General Barr went so far as to assert that under these principles, Congress "ultimately only has the power to provide a lump sum" for the constitutional activities of the president.[67]

The leading authority cited for these propositions is *Lovett v. United States*.[68] There the House Committee on Un-American Activities, after secret hearings, had found three federal employees guilty of "subversive activity." As a result, the House voted a rider to a wartime appropriation forbidding the executive branch from disbursing salaries to them unless they were reappointed with the advice and consent of the Senate. Because the House would not approve any appropriation without the rider, the Senate agreed to it and the president reluctantly signed it into law, though he maintained that it was unconstitutional. The Supreme Court ultimately agreed, finding that the rider was an unconstitutional bill of attainder.[69] While the majority opinion focused principally on the proper definition of a bill of attainder, its conclusion is consistent with the statement of a concurring judge in the lower court that "the power of the purse may [not] be constitutionally exercised to produce an unconstitutional result such as a taking of a citizen's liberty or property without due process of law, a conviction and punishment of a citizen for wholly innocent conduct, *or a trespass upon the constitutional functions of another branch of the Government.*"[70] What could be called the *Lovett* principle has since been applied in the relatively few other cases striking down appropriations measures as unconstitutional.[71]

The first problem with application of the *Lovett* principle to national security appropriations is that it states a conclusion, not an analysis. No serious student of the power of the purse dissents from the *Lovett* principle.[72] But asserting it merely restates the question whether a particular appropriation measure *does* violate the Constitution.[73]

In *Lovett,* the answer to this question was easy. Once the Court characterized the rider as a bill of attainder, the constitutional text supplied a clear and unequivocal answer: Congress may not pass bills of attainder. By retroactively punishing specific federal employees without benefit of judicial trial, Congress attempted to exercise a "power which the Constitution unequivocally declares Congress may never exercise."[74] In *United States v. Will,*[75] the answer was easy, too. By using an appropriation measure to reduce effectively the compensation of sitting federal judges, Congress ran afoul of the express and unequivocal textual command of the Constitution that their "Compensation . . . shall not be diminished during their Continuance in Office."[76] In most of the remaining cases applying the *Lovett* principle to appropriations, the answers were also easy: Congress violated the express textual commands of the First or Fifth Amendments.[77]

What *Lovett* and these cases have in common is that each turns on the Constitution's explicit textual prohibition of the Congress's exercise of a particular power. They thus take the same approach that the Court has taken to separation of powers issues in cases in which "the Constitution by *explicit text* commits the power at issue to the exclusive control of [another branch]."[78] In such cases, explains Justice Kennedy, courts do not balance the interests of the branches: "[W]e have refused to tolerate *any* intrusion by the Legislative Branch. . . . Where a power has been committed to a particular Branch of Government in the text of the Constitution, the balance has already been struck by the Constitution itself."[79] Indeed, *Lovett* may itself be viewed as a separation-of-powers decision in this line, because the explicit text of the Bill of Attainder Clause withdraws the power of adjudication and punishment for past conduct from the legislative branch, reaffirming the textual commitment of "the judicial power of the United States" solely to the judicial branch.

On the other hand, when the explicit constitutional text does not either assign the power solely to any one branch or state a flat prohibition, and therefore does not already strike a balance between the branches, the Court, according to Justice Kennedy,

> [has] employed something of a balancing approach, asking whether the statute at issue prevents the President "'from accomplishing [his] constitutionally assigned functions,'" and whether the extent of the intrusion on the President's

> powers "is justified by an overriding need to promote objectives within the constitutional authority of Congress."[80]

Moreover, the Court has also suggested that in this balancing, general and undifferentiated claims by one branch must yield to the specific needs of another.[81]

Many scholars have also recognized that the Court has taken a hybrid approach to separation-of-powers cases, but they have labeled the approaches differently. Some have generally distinguished between *formal* and *functional* analysis,[82] others between *textual* and *historical* analysis,[83] and still others between *aggrandizement* (when one branch acquires powers assigned another, justifying formal and strict review by courts to guard against excessive concentration of power) and *diffusion* (when one branch restricts the power of a branch and thereby only indirectly increases the relative power of another branch, justifying more flexible and forgiving review because of the less direct threat to the separation of powers).[84] Some of these scholars have suggested that the analytic approaches are sequential (organized in tiers) rather than alternative.[85]

For our purposes, it matters not how the distinction is drawn, for under every hybrid approach the typical restrictive national security appropriation is distinguishable from the *Lovett* rider. The rider directly aggrandized the judicial power, threatening a concentration of adjudicative and legislative power in the Congress. The typical restrictive national security appropriation, by definition, seeks only to restrict the executive branch and thereby only indirectly increases the relative power of Congress.

Lovett and its progeny also involved textually explicit constitutional prohibitions, as noted previously. But the only relevant textually explicit prohibitions pertaining to national security appropriations (when neither individual nor state rights is involved)[86] are the Appropriations Clause and the two-year limit on appropriations for the army, the former directly and the latter indirectly restraining the *executive*. While the Constitution also makes numerous express assignments of affirmative national security powers, these are chiefly to Congress.[87] The grants to the president are, "by contrast, few and vague," as Abraham Sofaer observed in his landmark historical study of national security powers.[88] Presidents are given the status of commander in chief, but their textually explicit ambassadorial appointment and treaty powers are shared with the Senate, and all their other national security powers are implied or customary. Most important, these powers, too, are usually shared with the Congress in an indeterminate way.

While *Lovett*'s outcome was thus dictated by the Bill of Attainder Clause, with no call for weighing Congress's purposes or the degree of encroachment on the executive,[89] the appropriate mode of separation-of-powers analysis for most restrictive national security appropriations is balancing. To determine the constitutionality of a restrictive national security appropriation, we must ordinarily weigh the extent to which the restriction prevents the president from accomplishing constitutionally assigned functions against the need for the same restriction to promote objectives within the authority of Congress.[90]

The Historical Power of the Purse in the Balance

Using an inapposite separation-of-powers analysis is not the only problem with the application of the *Lovett* principle to restrictive national security appropriations. Even those who apply the appropriate balancing analysis often ignore or slight powerful historical and textual evidence that such appropriations are entitled to special weight in the balancing. Echoing the deprecatory characterization of "mere appropriations," which we have seen mars their statutory construction, such balancers find no independent significance in the fact that a particular restriction takes the form of a national security appropriation. The form is incidental to the substance of the restriction, in their view. The Appropriations Clause is not "an independent source of congressional power," but "is simply a procedural provision,"[91] or merely an "instrument of fiscal accountability," and, as such, in fact, more a "limitation on the legislative power" than on the executive![92] "[W]hen we hear discussions about Congress' weighty role in various areas of shared power, such as the foreign relations power, and Congress adverts to the 'power of the purse,'" Attorney General Barr complains, "it does not make sense. Congress still has to point to a substantive power. *The power of the purse under this approach is only procedural.*"[93]

If anything is clear from the history of the power of the purse in national security affairs, however, it is that this power is substantive, at least when it is used to control military activity. It is not just "the most complete and effectual weapon with which any constitution can arm the immediate representatives of the people," as James Madison said of the power of the purse in general,[94] but it was specially conceived as an antidote to executive abuse of military power and as a tool for congressional control of such power.[95] It was in these roles that the power of the purse carved a course in military affairs distinct from its course in civilian affairs in English and colonial history, as we have shown. Even if the civilian appropriation was merely "procedural," the military appropriation was anything but.

Furthermore, the constitutional text explicitly affirms the distinction between military and civilian appropriations. The only appropriation identified specifically in the text is the appropriation for raising and supporting armies, itself limited by a built-in, two-year "sunset" provision. Because this appropriation power is listed with Congress's enumerated substantive powers,[96] it makes no sense to denigrate the Appropriations Clause as just "procedural" when it enforces exercise of that substantive power.

Ironically, many defenders of presidential prerogatives effectively concede the special weight of the power of the purse in national security affairs when they cite Congress's power to withhold funding for military activities as a substitute for the necessity of prior congressional approval. Thus, former National Security Adviser Brent Scowcroft has testified that the president could alone initiate war in the Persian Gulf because Congress could stop it, if Congress disapproved:

> I was talking about the power of Congress to restrict the President's action in national security affairs. It seems to me that the power of the purse, whether it be the Persian Gulf or anywhere else—you could certainly prevent any moneys under any appropriations act from being used to outfit those forces in the Persian Gulf.[97]

President Reagan also acknowledged the weight of the power of the purse in national security affairs,[98] and President Bush's lawyers argued in court that "the ultimate check" on the president's deployment of force is "with the Congress itself which, under Article I, Section 8, has the power of the purse in raising and supporting Armies and providing and maintaining a Navy."[99]

Of course, they may contend, as Attorney General Barr has, that the appropriation power is all-or-nothing, a power either to appropriate a lump sum or to appropriate nothing.[100] But this view of the power runs counter to the practice of two hundred years of history before and after the Constitution was adopted.[101] It also makes no practical sense, because *every* appropriation and appropriation restriction is "all or nothing" insofar as its specific object is concerned, and "all appropriations . . . may be conceived of as lump-sum grants with 'strings' attached."[102]

In short, the *Lovett* objection to a restrictive national security appropriation usually requires a balancing analysis, in which Congress's power of the purse carries special historical weight.

Applying the Separation-of-Powers Analysis to the Boland Amendment and to Restrictive Appropriations in the Vietnam War

It remains to apply the proper separation-of-powers analysis illustratively to the 1984 Boland amendment and restrictive national security appropriations during the Vietnam War.[103]

The Constitutionality of the 1984 Boland Amendment

Concluding that the 1984 Boland amendment was unconstitutional, a student commentator explains that

> Congress' interest is in its *generalized* spending power while the President's power as the nation's intermediary with foreign governments is a *specific* grant of power. Absent a claim of an independent specific constitutional grant of power to formulate foreign policy and to function as the nation's intermediary with foreign governments, Congress cannot frustrate the President's foreign policy objectives by the use of its general appropriations power.[104]

This puts it exactly backward. The chief claims of authority for the president to assist the Contras were generalized, while the claims of congressional authority were anchored in textually explicit assignments of national security authority to the Congress.

The first presidential function cited by the student commentator and other critics of the constitutionality of the 1984 Boland amendment is variously described as "the President's power to conduct the nation's international affairs,"[105] the "President's foreign relations powers,"[106] the president's power to execute "*the president*'s policy objectives,"[107] and the president's role as "sole organ of the nation in international affairs."[108] This presidential function, however, is the paradigm of a generalized presidential function or authority, appearing nowhere in the constitutional text.

Claims of "sole organ" authority are usually supported by citation of *United States v. Curtiss-Wright Export Corp.*,[109] in which Justice Sutherland alluded in dictum to "the very delicate, plenary and exclusive power of the President as the sole organ of the federal government in the field of international relations."[110] But his "sole organ" reference was wrested from the context in which then Congressman, later Chief Justice, John Marshall placed it, a House debate on President John Adams's extradition of a British subject to England pursuant to the Jay Treaty of 1795. Defending Adams, Marshall added, "The treaty, which is a law, enjoins the performance of a particular object. . . . Congress, unquestionably, may prescribe the mode, and Congress may devolve on others the whole execution of the contract; but, *till this be done*, it seems the duty of the Executive department to execute the contract by any means it possesses."[111] President Adams was not executing his own foreign policy, but a treaty of the United States made with the consent of the Senate. Had Congress prescribed the mode of execution, the president would have been obliged to follow it. The president, Marshall was saying, is not the sole organ for making foreign policy, but rather the sole organ for communicating it.[112]

Of course, the president also inevitably, and often by congressional default, makes foreign policy, as well.[113] In this, however, the president is not the sole organ of foreign policy-making, but only one of the organs.[114] When the other organ has declared the policy, and the president has not vetoed it, as was the case in the 1984 Boland amendment, the president has "the duty to execute the contract," as Marshall put it. If the declared policy "intrudes" on the president's foreign policy objectives, they must give way, although he or she is free to try to persuade Congress to adopt them.

A second claim of authority for the president is the authority to execute international law. "The Boland Amendments were unconstitutional because they usurped the power of President Reagan to fashion a response to the multiple violations of international law perpetrated by the Sandinistas," writes Bruce Fein.[115] The president has the general duty to take care that the laws are executed, and those laws include customary international law "where there is no treaty, and no controlling executive or legislative act or judicial decision,"[116] according to the Court.

Just stating the proposition this boldly, however, is sufficient to refute this critique of the 1984 Boland amendment. The amendment was itself a "controlling . . . legislative act" and can hardly be said therefore to "hamstring the President's discretionary authority over international law enforcement."[117] His discretion was confined by law. Moreover, the amendment did not remove his discretion to enforce international law; it only "prescribe[d] the mode," as Marshall put it, by excluding the use of military or paramilitary force. The president was free and, indeed, encouraged to bring nonmilitary pressures to bear on the Sandinistas to obey international law.[118] Finally, this claim of authority will strike many as Orwellian in light of the International Court of Justice's finding

> that the United States of America, by training, arming, equipping, financing and supplying the *contra* forces or otherwise encouraging, supporting and aiding military and paramilitary activities in and against Nicaragua, has acted, against the Republic of Nicaragua, in breach of its obligation under customary international law not to intervene in the affairs of another state.[119]

Though the United States refused to recognize the court's jurisdiction, and though some may dispute its legal analysis,[120] it is untenable to argue that the president has constitutional discretion to enforce policies declared unlawful by *both* the Congress and the International Court of Justice.

A third claim of authority is that the president has implied authority as commander in chief to conduct covert war.[121] The commander-in-chief authority is, of course, explicitly assigned by the constitutional text, and there is a broad scholarly consensus that Congress may not interfere with the president's day-to-day command of an authorized war or defense against sudden attack.[122] Absent attack, however, it is Congress that must authorize the war, and the 1984 Boland amendment itself refutes any claim of congressional authorization for military hostilities. Moreover, though the president's power of command of the army and navy is plenary, "only Congress can provide him an army or navy to command."[123] As we argue below, this proposition applies as much to proxy armies as to public armies. By enacting the 1984 Boland amendment, Congress expressly refused to provide the president with a proxy army in Nicaragua.

"Absent attack" is an important qualification on these propositions. The 1984 Boland amendment literally seems to prohibit *any* use of funds "with the effect . . . of directly or indirectly" supporting the Contras' military or paramilitary operations. This restriction would literally prohibit the president from defending Americans in Nicaragua from attack, inasmuch as any defensive U.S. action would indirectly benefit the Contras. As Representative Daniel put it in floor debate, "The Boland Amendment makes clear that *no matter what happens*—even if the Sandinistas seize our Embassy or round up all Americans in Nicaragua—the President of the United States is not allowed to use the U.S. Armed Forces to protect American citizens."[124] If this reading of the amendment is correct, it intrudes deeply into the oft-claimed and generally recognized constitutional power of the president to defend and protect Americans against attack.[125]

Moreover, the president may also claim authority as commander in chief, as an organ of foreign affairs, and by customary national security law,[126] to conduct covert operations short of war. This is an authority that overlaps with the president's authority as sole organ of communications[127] to collect and exchange intelligence,[128] incident at least to the explicit textual power of the president to negotiate treaties. The president is not just the mouth, but the eyes and ears of the nation's foreign policy. Even if Justice Sutherland overstated the "sole organ" claim, few can dispute his assertion in *Curtiss-Wright* that the president,

> not Congress, has the better opportunity of knowing the conditions which prevail in foreign countries, and especially is this true in time of war. He has his confidential sources of information. He has his agents in the form of diplomatic, consular and other officials. Secrecy in respect of information gathered by them may be highly necessary . . . .[129]

The president's comparative advantage at intelligence gathering and the necessity for information in the exercise of the explicitly assigned treaty power thus also suggest an implied constitutional power of intelligence gathering, as well as a corollary power of intelligence exchange.[130] If the 1984 Boland amendment is given literal effect, it would seriously intrude on such intelligence gathering and exchange by prohibiting the exchange of intelligence with the Contras if such exchange could even indirectly lend support to their military or paramilitary activities.

On the other side of the balance, and by contrast, Congress can recite three textually express assignments of authority. First, the forgotten part of the War Clause, empowering Congress to grant letters of marque and reprisal,[131] may expressly grant it the power to support private armies such as the Contras. Charles Lofgren and Jules Lobel have shown that by the late eighteenth century, letters of marque and reprisal were granted to enable both public and private persons to conduct "imperfect," undeclared war on behalf of the state.[132] As Lobel summarizes his conclusions, the

> covert use of paramilitary force to conduct American foreign policy abroad is the modern day analogy to private wars for which letters of marque and reprisal were historically required. . . . The central difference between the two is that while the private wars of earlier times were fought by *American* private citizens authorized by the American government, modern-day covert warfare is fought primarily by non-American private citizens under the direction of American CIA officers. Furthermore, these private citizens are not necessarily acting intentionally on behalf of the United States, but instead are being aided by the United States in the achievement of their own ends. These distinctions are not problematic for two reasons. First, while covert operations often involve foreign citizens, letters of marque and reprisal were occasionally given to foreign nationals as well as Americans. Second, regardless of their personal or national aims, the actions taken by foreign nationals acting in concert with CIA officers and American military aid are often legally attributable to the United States.[133]

Although letters of marque and reprisal are long since obsolete, the structural allocation of power that they evidence is not. The framers frequently expressed the fear that "reprisals," or imperfect war conducted by private persons whose activities might be attributed to the United States, could escalate and embroil the sovereign itself in armed conflict. The marque and reprisal part of the War Clause was an assertion of congressional control over this risk, reinforcing the control vested by the declaration of war part itself.[134] The 1984 Boland amendment can be viewed as a comparable assertion of control, premised on the same structural allocation of power.

Second, it can also be premised on the textually explicit assignment of the power to "define and punish . . . Offences against the Law of Nations."[135] Even if one rejects the International Court of Justice's declaration of the relevant international law in *Nicaragua v. United States,* Congress is not confined to domesticating international law; it may "define" offenses against the law of nations, not just punish them.[136] In fact, it did just that as early as 1794 by enacting the Neutrality Act,[137] prohibiting a variety of supportive activities within the United States (including financial assistance) for any military enterprise carried on from the United States against a country with which we are at peace. The act's criminal prohibitions went well beyond the contemporaneous international law of neutrality[138] in order at least in part to protect congressional war powers.[139] Moreover, the act was directed at "any person" who assists a warlike expedition and thereby "usurp[s] . . . the public power, vested in Congress, to declare war and issue letters of Marque and Reprisal,"[140] including executive officers.[141] Justice Paterson, framer of the New Jersey Plan at the Convention, wrote in *United States v. Smith,*[142] a prosecution under the Neutrality Act, that

> the President of the United States cannot control the statute, nor dispense with its execution, and still less can he authorize a person to do what the law forbids. If he could, it would render the execution of the laws dependent on his will and pleasure; . . . . [T]he law is paramount. Who has dominion over it? None but the legislature . . . .[143]

The Congress has comparably explicit constitutional authority to prevent executive officers from providing support to paramilitary activities against the government of Nicaragua, with which we were at peace. The 1984 Boland amendment can be viewed as a companion to the Neutrality Act in defining international law as the Congress perceived it and/or as a necessary and proper reinforcement of such law and reaffirmation of congressional control over activities that risk war. Not surprisingly, therefore, the running debate about the Boland amendments was studded with references by their proponents to international law,[144] and Congress later incorporated its concern about violations of international law expressly into the Kerrey amendment.[145] That Congress both before and after the 1984 Boland amendment approved military aid is no rebuttal to this construction of the amendment. Even if the power to define offenses against international law does not include the power to redefine them, Congress always has the power to override international law by legislation.[146]

Finally, Congress may assert authority for the 1984 Boland amendment based on its power to raise and support armies. When this nation still fought imperfect wars by granting letters of marque and reprisal, the wars were partly self-financing because the "privatized" armies were entitled to prize money. Indeed, the case law growing out of the quasi-war with France discussed in chapter 12, chiefly involved prizes. Now such war is no longer self-financing, and the armies must be financed by the government. Appropriations for such armies, including all appropriations for assistance to the Contras, are therefore either based squarely on the authority to raise and support armies or less directly on the War Clause. In either case, so based, they directly invoke the power of the purse at its full historical weight. As noted above, even defenders of presidential war powers give lip service to the ultimate congressional appropriation control on war making. It applies with no less force to proxy wars financed on the authority of the Army and War Clauses than it does to American wars similarly financed. Ultimately, therefore, the 1984 Boland amendment is a classical exercise of the historical congressional power to deny appropriations for a war of which it disapproves.

To summarize so far, the 1984 amendment may be read as significantly intruding on the president's implied constitutional power of intelligence collection and exchange, and theoretically at least, on his implied commander-in-chief power to repel sudden attacks on Americans. On the other hand, it is also arguably justified by an overriding need to promote textually explicit constitutional grants to Congress of the war power (in the form of the power to grant letters of marque and reprisal), the power to define violations of international law, and the power to raise and support armies. Moreover, it carries all the weight of the historical congressional appropriation control on (proxy) war making by the president. We believe that the generalized and implied claims of authority by the president are outweighed by the specific and textually rooted claims of authority for Congress and that the balance thus favors the amendment.

But we do not have to decide this question, as we noted at the outset of this section, if "a construction of the statute is *fairly possible* by which the question may be avoided." We think there is such a construction that can be reached without "wholesale judicial dismemberment" of the statute.[147] The 1984 Boland amendment targets the expenditure of funds "for the purpose or with the effect of supporting, directly or indirectly, military or paramilitary operations." *Any* expenditure that would have the effect of undermining the Sandinista government, including trade embargoes, diplomatic efforts to isolate Nicaragua, and even official speeches critical of the Sandinista regime, would also at least indirectly support the Contra effort, yet no one has contended that the amendment reaches so far as to prevent these initiatives.

"Indirectly" therefore presents an ambiguity through which a fair saving construction is possible. "It is also axiomatic," the courts have said, "that Congress is not presumed to have usurped power constitutionally forbidden to it . . . ."[148] The amendment should not be read to prohibit intelligence collection activities or intelligence exchanges incidental thereto that are primarily for the purpose of gathering information.[149] This, in fact, was the retroactive construction placed on the amendment by a provision of the Supplemental Appropriations Act for fiscal year 1985, explaining that nothing in the 1984 Boland amendment or its immediate successor "shall be construed to prohibit the United States Government from exchanging information with the Nicaraguan democratic resistance."[150] Indeed, by 1984, it is arguable that Congress had acquiesced in a long-established executive practice of covert intelligence collection and exchange.[151] The rule against implied repeal thus reinforces the principle of avoidance in construing the 1984 Boland amendment to allow the practice to continue even in connection with Nicaragua. So construed, the statute is not a model of legislative clarity,[152] or necessarily good policy, but it is constitutional.

The same rule applies to the argument that the 1984 amendment would prohibit the United States from militarily defending its embassy or nationals in Nicaragua against attack. Even if the Commander-in-Chief Clause itself did not impliedly vest a defensive authority in the president to order military force for self-defense, rescue, and protection, long-standing executive practices, in which Congress has knowingly acquiesced, establish customary national security law to that effect.[153] There is no evidence that Congress intended to repeal this law in the 1984 Boland amendment, even if it could, despite the broad language of the amendment.

Moreover, this constitutional challenge is premised on an extreme and conjectural application of the amendment to a situation—attack on Americans—well beyond any envisioned by its sponsors. But the fact that a statute "might operate unconstitutionally under some conceivable set of circumstances is insufficient to render it wholly invalid," the Court has declared, "since we have not recognized an 'overbreadth' doctrine outside the limited context of the First Amendment."[154] If "some quite straightforward applications . . . [of a statute] would be constitutional . . . that is enough to defeat . . . [the] assertion that . . . [it] is facially unconstitutional," Justice O'Connor explains.[155] Quite straightforward applications of the 1984 Boland amendment to prohibit arms shipments to the Contras in the absence of any attack on Americans in Nicaragua are plainly constitutional according to the balancing we performed above, and the amendment is not rendered "wholly invalid" by the possibility that under an unlikely set of circumstances its application might violate the Constitution.

Restrictive National Security Appropriations in the Vietnam War

Concerned about the escalation of the ground war in Indochina, Congress enacted a rider to the Defense Appropriations Act of 1970 providing that "none of the funds appropriated by this Act shall be used to finance the introduction of American ground combat troops into Laos or Thailand."[156] After an allied land "incursion" into Cambodia in 1970, Congress also enacted an amendment to the Supplemental Foreign Assistance Authorization Act of 1971 providing that "none of the funds authorized or appropriated pursuant to this or any other Act may be used to finance the introduction of United States ground troops into Cambodia, or to provide United States advisers to or for Cambodian military forces in Cambodia."[157] Both measures were prefaced with the phrase, "[i]n line with the expressed intention of the President of the United States," suggesting that the president had publicly agreed to the restrictions.

As the war wore on, Congress became increasingly disenchanted with it. Its disenchantment was reflected in the Mansfield amendment, a rider to the Armed Forces Appropriations Authorization Act of 1971,[158] declaring it the "policy of the United States to terminate at the earliest practicable date all military operations of the United States in Indochina, and to provide for the prompt and orderly withdrawal of all United States military forces at a date certain," subject to release of and accounting for American prisoners of war. President Nixon signed the legislation, but commented that the amendment merely "expresses a judgment about the manner in which American involvement in the war should be ended. However, it is without binding force or effect, and its does not reflect my judgment about the way in which the war should be brought to a conclusion."[159] The war continued.

Finally, after President Nixon had successfully vetoed an earlier cutoff, Congress approved and the president signed an amendment to the Joint Resolution Continuing Appropriations for Fiscal 1974[160] providing:

> Notwithstanding any other provision of law, on or after August 15, 1973, no funds herein or heretofore appropriated may be obligated or expended to finance directly or indirectly combat activities by United States military forces in or over or from off the shores of North Vietnam, South Vietnam, Laos, or Cambodia.

American ground troops had been withdrawn prior to this cutoff date, and American bombing of Cambodia was halted on August 14, 1973.[161]

Were these exercises of Congress's power of the purse in national security constitutional? The president would assert a single, textually explicit constitutional authority implicated by these restrictions: the authority of the commander in chief to conduct a congressionally authorized war. This power of command necessarily includes tactical control of day-to-day combat operations in the theater of war and defense of the troops deployed in them. "He is authorized to direct the movements of the naval and military forces placed by law at his command, and to employ them in the manner he may deem most effectual to harass and conquer and subdue the enemy," the Court has declared.[162] Clearly, the 1971 amendment intruded on this power by placing both a use restriction (no United States ground combat troops, as opposed to air or naval forces) and an area restriction (Cambodia) on the president's command of troops during the Vietnam War.

Congress would rest its authority to enact the restriction on the War Clause and the Army Clause. The War Clause gives Congress authority to authorize limited war, as we have seen in chapter 12, and it used that authority early in our history to authorize the naval war with France. That authorizing legislation, in effect, placed both use restrictions (initially just public armed vessels, then armed U.S. merchantmen) and area restrictions (initially just engagements with vessels "found hovering" off the U.S. coast, then engagements on the high seas)[163] on the ensuing conflict. Not only does this precedent and the judicial opinions it generated establish that Congress may limit the scope of an authorized war from the outset,[164] it suggests that Congress may change the limits and therefore the scope of that war while it is being fought.

It does not necessarily follow, however, that Congress has the same authority in "real time"[165] as it has at the outset of a war. Once under way, war generates its own tactical necessities that fall within the command discretion of the commander in chief as long as the hostilities continue. The congressional war power, Chief Justice Chase observed, does not extend to such legislation "as interferes with the command of the forces and the conduct of campaigns. That power and duty belong to the President as commander-in-chief."[166]

Reliance on the Army Clause as the source of congressional authority to enact a "real time" area or use restriction is also problematical when it is not clearly used to deauthorize the war that the commander in chief is conducting. The 1970 ground troops restriction did not withdraw authorization for the war in Vietnam. At the time, Assistant Attorney General William Rehnquist argued in defense of the prerestriction Cambodian border "incursion" that President Nixon

> has an obligation as Commander-in-Chief to take what steps he deems necessary to assure the safety of American Armed Forces in the field. On the basis of information available to him, he concluded that the continuing build-up of North Vietnamese troops in sanctuaries across the Cambodian border posed an increasing threat both to the safety of American forces [in South Vietnam] and to the ultimate success of the Vietnamization program. He also determined that, from a tactical point of view, combined American-South Vietnamese strikes at these sanctuaries had a very substantial likelihood of success. He, therefore, ordered them to [strike].[167]

Weighing the intrusion on the command function against the congressional authority to control the scope of the war, there is a strong argument, given the geographic proximity of the alleged sanctuaries to American forces in the Saigon area, that President Nixon had constitutional authority as commander in chief to issue the same order *after* the restriction was enacted.[168]

On the other hand, if Congress enacted the 1970 restriction to deescalate the war, as the first step in a phased withdrawal of authorization for the Vietnam war itself, its authority would be reinforced by the historical role of appropriation measures to stop war of which Congress disapproves. The Cambodian restriction was, in fact, followed by successively broader restrictions until the 1973 restriction cut off all funding prospectively.

Moreover, Congress also must have the power to prohibit the president from starting a new war, so different in location, magnitude, or risk that it cannot fairly be encompassed with the initial authorization for war.[169] If so, this power would probably not support application of the 1970 restriction to prohibit the Cambodian border incursion, but it would arguably support application of the restriction to prevent U.S. occupation of Cambodia. Rehnquist impliedly acknowledged the validity of the distinction when, in justifying the prerestriction incursion, he insisted that "[b]y crossing the Cambodian border to attack sanctuaries used by the enemy, the United States has in no sense gone to 'war' with Cambodia."[170]

Given the arguable tactical necessity for the Cambodian border incursion, we believe that the balance here favors the president, and that insofar as it would have prohibited the incursion, the 1970 restriction would be unconstitutional.

In contrast, the later restrictions are classic exercises of the power of the purse to withdraw funds for the purpose of ending a war of which Congress no longer approves. While President Nixon was correct in his assertion that the Mansfield amendment was not binding, that was because it was merely hortatory by its own terms and not because Congress lacked the constitutional authority to cut off funds for the war. The 1973 cutoff was binding, unmistakable in its sweep, and the purest expression we have seen of giving "check to the Dog of War" by refusing to pay.[171] The only qualification on its effect is that it could not deny the president the discretion to conduct a safe and orderly withdrawal of U.S. troops, for the same reasons that we argued above that the 1984 Boland amendment cannot be applied (and should not be construed) to prohibit defense of U.S. nationals in Nicaragua.

14

National Security Spending Without Appropriation

The constitutional analysis proposed in chapter 13 suggests that few restrictive national security appropriations unconstitutionally intrude on the president's domain. But supposing that one does, what are a president's alternatives? We first consider the examples furnished by the executive's solicitation of unappropriated funds and use of diverted arms sales profits to support the Contras after the Boland amendment cut off appropriations in 1984 and Congress's attempts in 1989 to limit third-party funding. We next consider whether, if an appropriation restriction violated presidents' Article II national security powers, they could either ask a court to declare the restriction invalid and severable from the unrestricted appropriation or themselves "excise" the restriction and spend as if it were not there.

We also consider a president's recourse when the Congress, instead of restricting the use of appropriated funds, fails to appropriate for a national security activity desired by the president. Could presidents obtain a court order requiring Congress to appropriate funds to carry out core Article II activities? Could they solicit and spend third-party funds? Or do they have inherent constitutional authority to spend without specific appropriations in order to carry out core Article II activities?

We conclude that the doubtful constitutional status of the president's authority to spend without an appropriation has, practically, been unimportant to date, in light of the customary and statutory discretion presidents enjoy to spend appropriated funds for purposes not necessarily contemplated by the appropriators. Once again, the Vietnam War and Iran-Contra affair illustrate the wide-ranging options available to presidents to meet their national security objectives through strategic execution of spending discretion pursuant to general appropriation.

Funding the Contras Without an Appropriation

As described in chapter 13, Congress terminated United States assistance to the Contras during fiscal year 1985, and permitted only certain specified humanitarian assistance during fiscal year 1986. Months before the actual funding cutoff in 1984, however, administration officials knew that available funds were depleted,[1] that the harbor mining disclosure made additional appropriations unlikely,[2] and that outside funds would have to be found to continue the Contra program.[3]

As National Security Adviser McFarlane later testified, it was during spring and summer 1984 that President Reagan directed the NSC to keep the Contras together "body and soul."[4] McFarlane, Oliver North, and CIA Director Casey responded in part by organizing foreign country solicitations.[5] It was revealed during North's trial in 1989 that at least ten countries were solicited for contributions to the Contras.[6] Several were subsequently apparently rewarded with increased U.S. foreign aid.[7] Exhibits first made available during the North trial described in detail an explicit quid pro quo arrangement with Honduras,[8] including careful planning within the administration, approval by the president, and written transmission of the arrangement to Honduras.[9]

In March 1985, hearings suggested that third-party funding for the Contras was being sought, notwithstanding the Boland amendment prohibition.[10] Assistant Secretary of State Langhorne A. Motley, appearing for the administration, assured the Senate Foreign Relations Committee that the administration would not seek to circumvent the Boland amendment by soliciting third-party funds,[11] and the State Department, CIA, and NSC each officially took the position that the Boland amendment prevented any third party solicitation.[12]

In response to the reports of solicitations and notwithstanding administration denials, in August 1985 Congress enacted the Pell amendment prohibiting the United States from conditioning, "expressly or impliedly," aid to foreign governments on assistance to the Contras.[13] While the Pell amendment conferees were careful to point out that administration officials were permitted to discuss Central American policy with foreign leaders, and that those nations could "on their own volition" contribute to the Contras, the amendment proscribed any quid pro quo arrangements.[14] Soon thereafter, Congress also expressly permitted the secretary of state to solicit contributions from foreign governments for humanitarian assistance to the Contras.[15]

Between June 1984 and February 1986 the NSC/CIA network raised $34 million for the Contras from foreign countries.[16] In addition, United States citizens, some of whom received photo opportunities with President Reagan, briefings with Oliver North, and White House presentations, donated $10 million to the Contras in 1985 and 1986.[17] Finally, $16 million in profits from arms sales to Iran in 1985 and 1986 provided North's Contra resupply effort with another $3.8 million.[18]

After the new information about quid pro quo solicitations came to light in the North trial in 1989, Congress sought to enact legislation to control attempts to circumvent appropriation restrictions through third-party funding in the future. In July 1989 the Senate approved the Moynihan amendment to the State Department authorization bill, which would have criminalized quid pro quos, broadly defined as the provision of funds with the "purpose or direct effect" of inducing reciprocal assistance, and solicitations on behalf of foreign causes or governments prohibited from receiving United States aid directly.[19]

Although a conference committee narrowed the amendment's definition of quid pro quos by eliminating the words "or direct effect," criminalized quid pro quos and solicitations only when U.S. officials exercise direct control over donated funds, and merely required the president to report all other solicitations to Congress,[20] President Bush vetoed the bill because of its "serious constitutional problems" and "an unacceptable risk that it will chill the conduct of our Nation's foreign affairs."[21] After vetoing a similar measure originating in the House,[22] President Bush signed a weaker version, which prohibits only explicit quid pro quo agreements and includes no criminal sanctions.[23]

Excising or Severing the Unconstitutional Restriction

Chapter 13 assessed constitutional questions about restrictive appropriations. The easy cases are by now familiar. An appropriation may not deny certain executive officials their salaries,[24] create a national church,[25] interfere with the president's pardon power,[26] or diminish the salaries of federal judges or the president.[27] The hard cases concern appropriation restrictions in an area of shared powers, such as national security. As chapter 13 demonstrated, the constitutionality of a restrictive national security appropriation is determined by balancing the extent to which the restriction prevents presidents from accomplishing their constitutionally assigned functions against the need for the restriction to promote objectives within the authority of Congress.

Assume that the 1984 Boland amendment prohibited soliciting third-party funds for the Contras and thereby unconstitutionally limited the president's powers to conduct the nation's foreign affairs. The president's first option is really an obligation—to object to the bill in advance and to threaten to veto it if it is passed.[28] As exemplified by the 1989 congressional debate over third-party funding, the president is an influential player in the legislative process. Threats of a presidential veto are usually sufficient to change the shape of a bill, and such vetoes are rarely overridden.[29]

If the Boland amendment as construed had been enacted over President Reagan's veto, however, the president would have had to decide whether to seek relief from the courts or to act himself to "excise" the unconstitutional restriction and spend the appropriation without the offensive limitation. Kate Stith argues that the president must go to court to seek the removal of an unconstitutional appropriation restriction.[30] The president should not, Stith reminds us, "pay . . . heed only to his own vision of the Constitution."[31] If the president sought declaratory and injunctive relief to void an unconstitutional appropriation restriction, the court could decide whether the restriction is unconstitutional, and, if so, whether it is severable.[32] "Unless it is evident that the Legislature would not have enacted those provisions which are within its power [the unrestricted appropriation], independently of that which is not [the restriction]," the Court has said, "the invalid part may be dropped if what is left is fully operative as a law."[33] If a court finds an appropriation restriction severable, therefore, it would give full effect to the unrestricted appropriation.

The alternative view advanced by Gregory Sidak and Thomas Smith is that presidents may themselves "excise" appropriation restrictions they find offensive.[34] According to Sidak and Smith, a constitutional power of excision, although effectively an item veto, is inherent in a president's duty to faithfully execute the law and defend the Constitution.[35] The president would, under this theory, sign the legislation with the offensive provision and then issue a statement indicating that the executive branch would not enforce the offensive provision because it was unconstitutional and therefore void and severable from the act.[36]

There are at least three objections to the president's unilateral excision of unconstitutional restrictions on appropriations. The first is that it gives legal effect to a presidential signing statement, a proposition that remains in serious constitutional doubt.[37] One view is that because presidential signing statements occur after enactment, they cannot affect congressional intent or the resulting construction of the statute.[38] On the other hand, a bill may not become law without a presidential signature (or override of a veto). So viewed, the signing statement is part of the process that precedes the creation of law.[39]

A more serious objection is that excision serves to veto legislation without affording Congress its required opportunity to override the veto within ten days of presentment.[40] It therefore violates the "finely wrought" Article I legislative process to which the Supreme Court paid homage in *Chadha*.[41]

A third objection is that the "take care" clause does not imply the power *not* to enforce laws.[42] The Ninth Circuit has held that it was impermissible for President Reagan to order executive branch officials to disregard sections of the Competition in Contracting Act of 1984, which he signed.[43] According to the Ninth Circuit, construing "[the] duty to faithfully execute the laws as implying the power to forbid their execution perverts the clear language of the 'take care' clause."[44]

Whether presidents may ask the courts to sever an unconstitutional appropriation restriction or whether they may "excise" it themselves, however, is not important for our purposes. The practical difference between the theories boils down to who goes to court first: the president to invalidate the suspect restriction, or Congress to enforce it. Under either theory, no violence is done to the Appropriations Clause after the court severs the unconstitutional restriction because the president ultimately only spends appropriated funds.

Unconstitutional Failures to Appropriate

If a court finds an unconstitutional appropriation restriction nonseverable, however, the entire appropriation falls with the restriction. Thus, if a court declared the 1984 Boland amendment unconstitutional because it prohibited information-sharing for the Contras, and found it nonseverable from the DOD Appropriation Act and Intelligence Authorization Act to which it was appended, the president would have had no appropriated funds at his disposal to support the Contras and he would not have been able to use appropriated funds, even for the salaries of his staff, to try to raise unappropriated funds in their place. This reading of the Boland amendment permits a brief examination of three related theories of presidential spending power—that Congress *must* appropriate to fund actions taken pursuant to unarguable Article II powers; that, notwithstanding the Appropriations Clause, the president may solicit third-party funds to carry out such activities that Congress has refused to fund; and that the president has an inherent Article II power to "obligate" the treasury[45] by spending unappropriated funds or incurring debts to permit the performance of such activities.

Mandatory Appropriations

As we have shown in chapter 13, if the 1984 Boland amendment prohibited the president or his staff from communicating with foreign governments or heads of state regarding support for the Contras, the restriction may have unconstitutionally denied the president the funds to carry out the constitutionally assigned diplomatic task of communicating with foreign leaders.[46] Louis Henkin has concluded that "[w]here the President has independent constitutional authority to act, Congress is constitutionally bound to implement his actions, notably by appropriating the necessary funds."[47] Thomas McGarity disagrees, concluding that "[t]he President's duty to take care that the laws are faithfully executed does not imply an obligation on the part of Congress to appropriate any particular level of funding to aid the President."[48] In this conclusion he echoes Albert Gallatin, who responded to the same claim in 1798.

> [A]lthough there is no clause which directs that Congress shall be bound to appropriate money in order to carry into effect any of the Executive powers, some gentlemen, recurring to metaphysical subtleties, and abandoning the literal and plain sense of the Constitution, say that . . . we . . . are under a moral obligation in this instance to grant the money [to maintain the diplomatic establishment that the president thought necessary]. It is evident that where the Constitution has lodged the power, there exists the right of acting, and the right of discretion.[49]

While he thus rejected the doctrine of mandatory appropriation, however, Gallatin admitted that the president's requests "will ever operate as powerful motives upon our deliberations."[50]

Even assuming away for now the difficulties of defining and sorting out independent spheres of constitutional authority, the problem of enforcement of any putative constitutional duty to appropriate remains. Could the president sue to compel Congress to appropriate the required funds? While Kate Stith implies that he could and that the courts would be able to order appropriations,[51] the Supreme Court has only done so when affirming lower court orders for spending to remedy violations of individual rights provisions in the Constitution.[52] In *Reeside v. Walker*,[53] a claimant who sought payment of a debt owed by the United States was refused mandamus because there was no appropriation for the debt.[54] The Court stated:

> No officer, however high, not even the President . . . is empowered to pay debts of the United States generally . . . . The difficulty in the way is the want of any appropriation by Congress to pay this claim. . . . However much money may be in the Treasury at any one time, not a dollar of it can be used in the payment of any thing not thus previously sanctioned. Any other course would give to the fiscal officers a most dangerous discretion. . . . [W]ithout . . . an appropriation [the debt] cannot and should not be paid by the Treasury, whether the claim is by a verdict or judgment, or without either. . . .[55]

The lower courts that have ordered local governments to spend, for example, to desegregate schools,[56] have based their decisions on individual rights guarantees and the broad power of lower federal courts to remedy constitutional violations.[57]

It is unclear whether the courts would intervene similarly to protect one branch from the other.[58] Certainly the strength of the Appropriations Clause as an independent source of congressional power and the president's substantial power of self-defense (for example, to hold other congressionally favored programs hostage by vetoing appropriations for them until Congress votes appropriations for presidential functions, or to go to the voters) would counsel hesitation.

Third Party Spending

The 1984 Boland amendment provided that "no funds available to . . . any . . . agency or entity of the United States involved in intelligence activities may be obligated or expended for the purpose or which would have the effect of supporting [the Contras], directly or indirectly . . . ."[59] Thus, unless the "agency or entity involved in intelligence activities" qualifier failed to include the NSC, the restriction implicitly prohibited the solicitation by U.S.-salaried officials of third-party funds for the Contras, whether or not conditioned on some sort of quid pro quo arrangement. Notwithstanding the Boland amendment, however, Oliver North later asserted that the president "could authorize and conduct covert operations with nonappropriated funds."[60] Further, Attorney General Barr stated that "the appropriations clause does not say that the President cannot use other sources of funds."[61] In our view, North and Barr are wrong. The history of the Appropriations Clause and of the power of the purse generally in national security justifies at least the inference that Attorney General Barr was unwilling to draw.

The development of the power of the purse in sixteenth-century England was in direct response to the king's efforts to find "other sources of funds," and the clear thrust of parliamentary efforts was to control those efforts. The free availability of third-party funding outside the scope of the Appropriations Clause is inconsistent with this history and the subsequent colonial history of the power of the purse. Moreover, the framers clearly placed the power of the purse with Congress and carefully divided national security authority by making the president commander in chief and chief diplomat and making Congress the holder of the purse strings for military operations. The Appropriations Clause requires that all expenditures from the U.S. Treasury must be authorized, however generally or specifically, by Congress.[62] As the Court has put it, the president's power "cannot touch moneys in the treasury of the United States, except expressly authorized by act of Congress."[63] Thus, to the extent that third-party funding affords the president the means to fund a military operation explicitly opposed by Congress, it undermines at least the spirit, if not the letter of the Appropriations Clause.[64]

Congress has also buttressed the Appropriations Clause with legislation. The Miscellaneous Receipts Act of 1849[65] as amended, provides that any "official or agent of the Government receiving money for the Government from any source shall deposit the money into the Treasury."[66] The Anti-Deficiency Act[67] has, since 1870,[68] prohibited expenditures in excess of appropriations, and, since 1905, punished violations with criminal penalties.[69] Finally, until it was repealed in 1990,[70] a "gift act" authorized the secretary of the treasury to accept gifts made to aid the defense activities of the government.[71] Although the act gave the executive discretion to spend the gifts without additional appropriation, such gifts still had to be deposited first in the treasury.[72] They were therefore subject to the Appropriations Clause requirement for appropriation, as well as any appropriation restriction, such as the Boland amendment, applicable to all "available funds."[73] The Appropriations Clause and corollary legislation therefore control the expenditure of third-party funds paid to the United States.

What, however, of third-party funds that are not paid into the treasury first, but are instead solicited for direct expenditure by the third party on congressionally proscribed ends? To the extent that such funds are solicited within the United States, the Neutrality Act of 1794[74] may apply because it forbids persons within the United States from beginning, taking part in, or providing the means or money for military expeditions against a foreign government. Furthermore, when such direct third-party expenditures are a quid pro quo for U.S. financial or military assistance, funds from the U.S. Treasury are effectively "laundered" through the third party. Quid pro quo third-party spending can therefore be viewed as an indirect raid on the U.S. Treasury, and thus unlawful under the Appropriations Clause and related statutes. To that extent, quid pro quo arrangements should be regulable under the power of the purse.

On the other hand, presidents arguably have constitutional power, incident to their power of diplomatic communication, to encourage third parties to pursue the policies that they favor. Any congressional ban on third-party fundraising that transcends quid pro quo arrangements to inhibit ordinary diplomatic communication may violate the Constitution. The real constitutional difficulty in controlling third-party fundraising thus lies in distinguishing between a quid pro quo arrangement, which directly implicates the spending of U.S. funds and is therefore regulable under the power of the purse, and mere solicitation, which only incidentally implicates the fisc (through officials' salaries and related expenses) but also implicates the president's power of diplomatic communication.[75]

The latter power is strongest when regulation of third-party funding extends to solicitations of foreign leaders or governments, based not so much on constitutional text as on practice, congressional acquiescence, and a few judicial decisions. Textually, the treaty[76] and recognition[77] powers suggest cooperative treaty making with the Senate and some presidential authority to communicate with foreign governments.[78] Historically, however, Congress has not challenged the president's exclusive control over communications with foreign governments.[79] Decisions such as *United States v. Curtiss-Wright Export Corp.*[80] and *Dames & Moore v. Regan*[81] have, in dicta, contributed to the broad reading of executive diplomatic communication powers. As we noted in chapter 13, in *Curtiss-Wright* Justice Sutherland quoted then Congressman, later Chief Justice, John Marshall in declaring that the president "is the sole organ of the nation in its external relations,"[82] while forty-five years later in *Dames & Moore* Justice Rehnquist confirmed the president's authority over "normalizing United States' relations with a foreign state."[83]

On the other hand, that Congress has sometimes acquiesced in the president's conduct of the nation's foreign relations does not mean that it is constitutionally disabled from regulating in the foreign relations field.[84] As Justice Jackson observed in *Youngstown*, finding that the president may conduct foreign relations without congressional authority is not to say "that he might act contrary to an Act of Congress."[85] To the extent that U.S. funds are inevitably spent for at least the salaries and overhead of executive branch officials who solicit direct third-party spending, the regulation of such solicitation would enforce the Appropriations Clause and its goal of separating the purse and the sword. The restriction would be "an attempt to control the uses to which United States funds are put,"[86] namely the salaries of the officials who make the solicitations. According to Kate Stith, a denial of appropriated funds forecloses the executive from

> all means of engaging in the prohibited activity because employee salaries and other overhead costs are almost invariably paid out of appropriated funds . . . . In principle, a government employee acting in an official capacity—including the President—may not spend one minute to make one phone call to solicit private funds (for use of the government or directly for a third party) for an activity explicitly denied appropriated funds.[87]

Given the president's constitutional interest in unfettered diplomatic communication and the Congress's express constitutional interest in controlling expenditures from the treasury, we think that the constitutionality of congressional restrictions on third-party fund-raising depends upon the balancing analysis previously described in chapter 13.[88]

Congress tackled this issue in 1989. Compromises between President Bush and congressional leaders produced the 1989 Foreign Operations, Export Financing, and Related Programs Appropriations Act of 1990,[89] which in part regulates quid pro quo arrangements without forbidding solicitation of foreign leaders. The 1989 provision declares that any future Boland-like prohibition that is "express" may not be circumvented by third-party funding if the third party is acting "in exchange for" U.S. foreign aid funds.[90] The act does not purport to regulate solicitations, even though earlier bills had criminalized quid pro quos and solicitations alike. President Bush also persuaded sponsor Congressman Obey to record his view on the floor of the House that "the word 'exchange' should be understood to refer to a direct verbal or written agreement."[91] For the president, this version of the bill avoided the "serious constitutional problems" and "unacceptable risk . . . [of chilling] the conduct of our Nation's foreign affairs"[92] presented by earlier versions.

Although we believe that the president overstated his constitutional case, he accurately flagged the problem of drafting to avoid constitutional overbreadth. How should a statute define what constitutes the forbidden solicitation of contributions for the proscribed activity? If specific examples are codified, executive officials could find other ways to get the job done.[93] If drafters sought to legislate comprehensively, they would have to forbid such a broad range of discussions that constitutionally protected diplomatic communication would perhaps be impermissibly burdened.[94] It is obviously difficult, and it may simply be impossible, to frame a definition of "solicitation" that can survive the constitutional balancing test.

Alternately, as the Moynihan amendment would originally have provided, Congress could require that the executive merely report all efforts to solicit funds on behalf of any cause or government barred from receiving direct United States assistance. Such a requirement would alert Congress to the president's diplomatic initiatives and enable it to use its constitutional political powers to discourage them or alter them. Moreover, the disclosure of such third-party fund raising to Congress could well also discourage the third parties from spending in support of the president's policies, out of fear of congressional retaliation in foreign aid or trade legislation.[95] We believe that the reporting approach to regulating solicitations would pass constitutional muster under the appropriate balancing mode of separation-of-powers analysis.

Inherent Spending Authority

If Congress refuses to appropriate funds for constitutionally mandated functions of the president—such as diplomatic communication—does the president have inherent constitutional authority to obligate the treasury anyway to the extent necessary to fund the function? Although Kate Stith concedes that appropriation restrictions may unconstitutionally "prevent the President from fulfilling indispensable constitutional duties,"[96] she finds no inherent spending power and relegates the president to political remedies[97]—persuasion and bargaining, elections, and impeachment—or an unconstitutional though perhaps necessary act of spending in an emergency.[98]

Gregory Sidak would go much further. He asserts that "Article II is an authorization by law—law that has supremacy over any statute—by which the President may encumber the treasury for the minimum amount reasonably necessary for him to perform his constitutional duties and exercise his constitutional prerogatives."[99] Thus, he reasons, presidential spending power is a "necessary and proper" power of the president to carry out the duties and prerogatives of the office.[100]

There are numerous flaws in this theory. First, it proceeds from the assumption that "Appropriation by *Law*" as used in the Appropriation Clause includes "Appropriation by Constitution Article II."[101] Yet "law" is used elsewhere in Article I to refer strictly to the bills approved by the Congress and presented to the president, and even the Supremacy Clause juxtaposes "laws of the United States" with "the Constitution."[102] As noted in chapter 9, the president participates in the appropriation process, often wielding considerable influence, but a president's constitutional role in it is limited to signing or vetoing and returning to Congress a bill presented to him or her. Thus, although Sidak is correct to point out that the Supreme Court exaggerated when it asserted in *Lovett*[103] that "Congress under the Constitution has complete control over appropriations,"[104] the president's power to affect the outcome of appropriation decisions is explicit and limited to the veto power. Particularly in light of the hard-fought history of the power of the purse and origins of the Appropriations Clause, it is untenable to suggest that the clause refers to anything other than enactments of Congress.

Second, Sidak's reliance on the Necessary and Proper Clause[105] is misplaced because that clause expressly vests power "to make laws necessary and proper" only in the Congress, not in the president.

Third, just as the constitutional text will not bear the weight of Sidak's implied powers argument, neither will the practice and understanding of the first congresses and presidents. As we noted in chapter 4, when Jefferson ordered military stores in the *Chesapeake* incident without prior appropriation, he did not purport to act on inherent spending authority. Instead, he returned to Congress in a successful quest for *ex post* appropriation, necessary to ratify his unilateral action. Federalists and Republicans were agreed that although the executive branch had the *power* to spend without appropriation in cases of military necessity, it acted at its own risk and on the condition that it report to Congress at the earliest opportunity and obtain *ex post facto* appropriation.

Fourth, the courts have not supported Sidak's theory either, and recent dicta are inconsistent with it. According to the Supreme Court, the Appropriations Clause "means that no money can be paid out of the Treasury unless it has been appropriated by an act of Congress,"[106] and "[a]ny exercise of a power granted by the Constitution to one of the other Branches of Government is limited by a valid reservation of congressional control over funds in the Treasury."[107] Even with respect to the unilateral and unambiguous pardon power of the president, the Court has refused after a pardon to order repayment from the treasury of the proceeds derived from the sale of a convict's forfeited property:[108]

> [I]f the proceeds have been paid into the treasury, the right to them has so far become vested in the United States that they can only be secured to the former owner of the property through an act of Congress. Moneys once in the treasury can only be withdrawn by an appropriation by law. However large, therefore, may be the power of pardon possessed by the President, and however extended

> may be its application, there is this limit to it, as there is to all his power,—it cannot touch moneys in the treasury of the United States, except expressly authorized by act of Congress. The Constitution places this restriction on the pardoning power.[109]

Citing this holding, the Court as recently as 1990 reaffirmed that the president's express and otherwise plenary "pardon power cannot override the command of the Appropriation Clause."[110]

Finally, Sidak's theory has no practical limit. Like any inherent power, the president's discretion to obligate the treasury is not tethered by law, constitutional or otherwise. Recognizing this, Sidak asserts that the ballot—political controls—will suffice as a limit on inherent presidential spending. He thus conveniently ignores his own pointed attack on the efficacy of such controls as an answer to Congress's failure to appropriate.[111]

Congress may violate a command of the Constitution or encroach on the powers of the president through an appropriation restriction. The Appropriations Clause makes it just as clear, however, that the president has no inherent power to obligate the treasury in response. This is an instance in which two constitutional wrongs do not make a right.

The President's Discretion to Spend Appropriated Funds

It is admittedly difficult to accept a constitutional theory that may leave the president without a constitutional remedy for an infringement of Article II duties by Congress. Fortunately, there is a practical way out of the theoretical conundrum—inherent presidential spending authority has historically been unnecessary.

As we showed in chapter 8, the president has acquired substantial discretion to spend appropriated funds. Certainly in the national security context, history demonstrates that, far from being hamstrung by a Congress unwilling to fund presidential national security initiatives, the president has spent freely with Congress's acquiescence. Kate Stith objects that "[t]he appropriations requirement would be superfluous if the executive branch could avoid appropriation restrictions by transferring funds among appropriation accounts, by selling government assets and services, or by independently financing executive activities with private funds."[112]

This objection overlooks the fact that the president has consistently employed discretionary spending techniques conferred by statute without congressional restriction, and sometimes despite congressional restriction, aided by various relatively unaccountable spending methods. Both Attorney General Barr[113] and Gregory Sidak[114] assert that the president may have authority to spend from another fund or account if appropriated funds are not available in the fund prescribed for a given activity. Monroe Leigh, legal adviser to the State Department during the Vietnam War, too, drew a distinction in testimony to Congress

> between the condition subsequent in an appropriation not yet completely spent and new appropriations . . . . If [the] President has used up all the

money appropriated and then Congress refuses to provide any more, I think the Congress has effectively stopped the President from continuing the military action. I don't know how he can go on. If, on the other hand, he still had moneys that were unexpended, he could continue to spend those until such time as there was a court challenge and the court found he was acting illegally.[115]

As we showed in chapter 4, from the very start of the Republic the president has employed a pattern of presidential spending without or in advance of appropriations,[116] commingling or transferring funds for purposes other than those for which they were appropriated,[117] and spending all available funds early in the fiscal year and then seeking a deficiency appropriation to be able to continue to operate.[118] The custom originates with the defeat of Gallatin's proposal for line itemization in the debates with Hamilton and Wolcott around the turn of the eighteenth century. We noted in chapter 4 that the transfer custom was partly codified in an 1809 statute authorizing the president, "on the application of the secretary of the proper department . . . to direct . . . that a portion of the moneys appropriated for a particular branch . . . of that department, be applied to another branch of expenditure in the same department."[119]

But Congress soon took steps to curb what it perceived to be abuses of transfer authority, at first by ordering transfers reported to it. As early as 1820, an appropriation required the secretaries of war and navy to report annually to Congress balances under each specific heading of the preceding year's appropriation.[120] An 1834 statute required the navy to report any transfers of appropriated funds to another executive agency.[121] Similar measures intended to strengthen fiscal control were taken by Congress until the Civil War years.[122]

After Congress removed the restraints on spending discretion to better enable the president to wage the Civil War, the earlier abuses recurred without abeyance during and after the war.[123] Congress reacted expeditiously in 1868, however, to terminate the 1809 and all other transfer authority,[124] and in 1870 to end the practice of coercive deficiencies.[125] Deficiency spending continued after 1870 until 1906 amendments in what is now known as the Anti-Deficiency Act[126] broadened the 1870 act to cover all "obligations" (instead of just contracts), prohibited the acceptance of voluntary services, required apportionment of funds by monthly allotments, added criminal penalties, and forbade waiver of apportionment except in emergencies or unusual circumstances.

If Congress plugged the holes with respect to customary presidential transfer authority, there still remains significant statutory and customary spending authority on which the president may draw without specific appropriation. As we described in chapter 8, the executive branch took advantage of contingency accounts, emergency funds, reprogramming, massive lump-sum accounts, and transfer authorities to continue waging war in Southeast Asia. From 1962 to 1969, the United States supported a mostly secret war in Laos, funded principally from CIA funds, often channeled through AID accounts.[127] When President Nixon announced to the nation on April 30, 1970, that the United States had invaded Cambodia to attack North Vietnamese army strongholds, he also said that Cambodian territory had not been invaded before the announced attack.[128] Actually the administration had been directing secret bombings of

Cambodia for thirteen months in an operation run out of the basement of the White House by then national security adviser, Henry Kissinger, and his aide, Colonel Alexander Haig, Jr., apparently financed out of lump-sum operating accounts in the regular fiscal year appropriations for defense.[129] Although the chair of the Joint Chiefs and the defense secretary knew of and approved the bombings, the air force secretary, embassy personnel, and congressional committees did not.[130]

For the publicly announced intervention in Cambodia in 1970, President Nixon obligated more than $100 million by relying on Foreign Assistance Act transfer authority to siphon foreign aid funds budgeted for programs in Greece, Turkey, Taiwan, the Philippines, and Vietnam. Then he appealed to Congress for an appropriation, part of which would restore the transferred funds.[131]

As described in chapter 8, the Iran-Contra affair provides an even more complete picture of the possibilities for discretionary spending by the executive branch in the absence of a specific appropriation. The president obtained funds for the Contras from the CIA contingency fund; black budget programs that permit avoidance of congressional oversight of covert operations; drawdown, reprogramming, and transfer authority to circumvent appropriation limits; lump-sum appropriations for operation and maintenance to fund military operations not specifically approved by Congress; transfer under the Economy Act of Pentagon equipment to the CIA for its use in Contra resupply missions; and, perhaps most significant, third-party funding and directed profits from missile sales to Iran at inflated prices to carry on the Contra campaign after Congress cut off all appropriated funds in 1984.

Thus, although Congress has attempted to close the transfer authority loophole in the Appropriations Clause, it has by statute or by acquiescence left broad presidential discretion to finance activities for which it has not made specific appropriation. Of course, Congress can try to close the remaining holes in its control over spending. But until and unless it does, the president can usually avoid the constitutional crisis that invocation of inherent spending authority would otherwise precipitate.

15

Summing Up the Power of the Purse in National Security

Deep Throat, the anonymous source who helped *Washington Post* reporters Woodward and Bernstein expose the Watergate scandal, reportedly advised them that the best way to uncover an inside-the-Beltway scandal is to "follow the money."[1] And so we have, generically, by tracing the early history, mechanics, procedural constitutional limits, and substantive scope of the power of the purse in national security. It remains to summarize what we have uncovered.

The Early History of the Power of the Purse in National Security

The central lesson of the appropriations history we surveyed in part I is that the power of the purse is different in national security than in domestic affairs, evolving as an intended counterweight to the president's national security power.

We showed in chapter 1 that from the very start the bill of military supply evolved distinctly from the general power of the purse. English kings initially could finance their own households—or what we would loosely call the civilian side of government—without recourse to Parliament. But they were unable to finance foreign military adventures on their own. From the start, the fiscal requirements of national security drove the kings to Parliament for bills of extraordinary supply, and it was these bills with which the Parliament traded to enhance its own power and the rights of Englishmen. From the bills also evolved the first appropriations (typically specifying the military purposes for which funds could be expended), the restrictive spending formula[2] that was the forerunner of our own Appropriations Clause, and audit requirements.

In chapter 2, we described how the colonial legislatures applied the lessons of English parliamentary history with a vengeance in their conflicts with royal and proprietary governors. In colonial America, the power of the purse in national security stood out again from the general power of the purse, as the legislators took advantage of the Crown's insistence that the colonies finance their own defense. They wielded the power of the purse not just to secure political rights, but also to invade deeply the prerogative of military command by the executive. From colonial America we inherited not only a tradition of specific national security appropriations, but also the restrictive appropriation rider—a substantive legislative amendment or provision tacked onto a military appropriation, forcing the executive to take the bitter with the sweet.

The relatively spare record of how the war powers and appropriation provisions of the Constitution were framed and ratified, described in chapter 3, must be read and illuminated in the light of the lengthy prior history of a broad-scoped power of the purse. The brief and unhappy experience of the Continental Congress with committee conduct of military operations during the revolutionary war hardly convinced the framers to lay aside their primary historical weapon against executive abuse of national security power: the specific national security appropriation. Applying one lesson of the revolutionary war, they did vest a necessary tactical power in the president alone to conduct day-to-day military operations. But nothing in the framing and ratification of the Constitution suggests any retreat from this historically broad scope of the power of the purse in national security affairs.

To the contrary, the historical power was cited repeatedly as the chief bulwark against military dictatorship and the constitutional safeguard that permitted vesting of command authority in the president. There was no dissent to Madison's characterization of the appropriation power as "the most complete and effectual weapon with which any constitution can arm the immediate representatives of the people,"[3] and repeated affirmation during the ratification debates that this power had particular force in national security. Moreover, nothing in the debates supports contemporary claims that the power of the purse can only be exercised by an all-or-nothing decision to fund or not to fund, or that the framers and ratifiers intended to foreclose the kinds of specific appropriations and appropriation riders that had characterized the colonial period (except riders that tried to exercise tactical control over the conduct of war).

On the other hand, the practical problems of making government work shaped a somewhat different power of the purse during the early years of the Republic. In chapter 4, we showed how the First Congress made lump-sum appropriations for the military and how the first administrations mingled appropriated funds to meet the exigencies of military supply. Notwithstanding heated debate about this practice in Congress, the first congresses ultimately acquiesced in it, laying the groundwork for latter transfer and reprogramming discretion in the president.

Moreover, Federalists and Republicans alike conceded that necessity might compel the president to spend without appropriation in order to meet national security emergencies. They also agreed, however, that might did not make right; the president would have to meet such emergencies at his own constitutional risk, subject to subsequent reporting to Congress at the earliest possible opportunity and subsequent ratification by appropriation.

In short, the power of the purse in national security that emerges from the early history was unique in scope and specially crafted to control executive uses of national security power. Congress was given the power to specify the uses to which national security appropriations were put. In practice, however, Congress recognized the special need for flexibility in national security appropriation and was therefore generally content to apppropriate broadly. The Appropriations Clause was framed to restrict creative executive financing and thus prevent the evasion of appropriation controls that English kings had tried two centuries before. In practice, however, Congress acquiesced in executive mingling of accounts for national security purposes for the same reasons that it made lump-sum appropriations for the military. Finally, the Army Clause was written to force the executive back to Congress for prolonged military initiatives and, no less important, to force Congress openly and accountably to reappropriate for their continuation.

The Mechanics of National Security Appropriations

The story of the mechanics of the national security appropriation process that we traced in part II is really the story of two arguably related trends. The first is the collapse of the traditional bifurcated defense appropriation process into a chaotic combination characterized by legislative riders, omnibus continuing resolutions that tax the president's veto power, and a variety of nonstatutory appropriation controls. The other is the accretion of substantial customary and statutory national security spending discretion in the president.

In chapter 5, we examined the collapse of the traditional bifurcated authorization-followed-by-appropriation process. Already well under way in the nineteenth century, the collapse was not slowed by budget reforms, for they were overshadowed by the emergence of annual "appropriation authorizations" for defense. The reforms of 1974 and 1985, moreover, paradoxically hastened the collapse of the traditional process by encouraging continuing resolutions that both authorize and appropriate.

In chapter 6, we showed that the collapse of the traditional national security appropriation process has been accompanied by an expanded use of appropriation restrictions to make and influence national security policy. Even before continuing resolutions emerged, Congress began to attach to must-pass money bills restrictions that might otherwise fail for lack of a majority in Congress or a presidential veto. During the Vietnam War, appropriation restrictions became the preferred legislative device for controlling the president's use of military forces abroad.

Beginning in 1981, all of the anarchic tendencies of the national security appropriation process were aggravated by the emergence of the continuing resolution as the omnibus package for funding and making policy for much or all of the government in each fiscal year. Since the congressional rules against legislating in the appropriation process do not apply to continuing resolutions, members have freely appended their favorite legislative agendas to omnibus funding bills for two reasons. They may hope to catch their colleagues fatigued from the weight and size of the legislative package coming so late in the year, and they may hope to coerce a signature from the president who wants to preserve the balance of the resolution and to avoid the dislocation of shutting down government services and programs.

The Contra funding case study in chapter 6 shows dramatically how national security policy issues have been resolved in the appropriation process. On the one hand, it highlights the chaos and inefficiency of the new process and the resulting framing of the final legislative product by just a few House and Senate conferees working against an imminent shutdown of government services. On the other hand, it "worked" by producing a compromise, if not consensus, on a divisive policy issue, after substantial, albeit sometimes redundant and inefficient deliberation and debate. It also left doubt that any other legislative process would have worked better given the intense political conflict produced by the Contra funding question. As we noted in drawing the lessons of this case study in chapter 6, the new national security appropriation process may not produce disorder so much as reflect it.

Alongside the relative chaos of the new appropriation process, the tradition of lump-sum funding explains, in part, the emergence of nonstatutory legislative controls on national security spending, which we discussed in chapter 7. We showed that other reasons for their emergence, however, are the immunity of informal controls from congressional rules against appropriation restrictions and the executive's need for flexibility in national security spending. Congress gives the executive that flexibility in exchange for informal controls and nonstatutory understandings about informal committee approvals, such as the Bipartisan Accord on Central America (the Good Friday Accords).[4]

Critics of such controls, who characterize them as unconstitutional legislative vetoes, make a common but mistaken assumption about their legal effect. Precisely because informal controls and accords are not enacted as law, they have no *legal* effect. They are legally unenforceable, and the president and the executive branch may vindicate them without legal penalty, if not without political or moral effect. As Louis Fisher so neatly put it, they have no legal effect, but they are, in effect, legal.

The complexity of the modern national security appropriation process does not end with the enactment of appropriation law. Chapter 8 supplies an important, oft-neglected piece of the puzzle of the purse in national security by analyzing what happens next: how national security funds are spent. Notwithstanding the Appropriations Clause and its implementing legislation, such as the Anti-Deficiency Act, which purport to prohibit spending without appropriations, we showed that Congress has given the president substantial spending discretion.

Of course, the general use of lump-sum appropriations for national security itself confers a large measure of discretion. But Congress has expanded this discretion by permitting spending from contingency funds (especially under the Foreign Assistance Act and for the Central Intelligence Agency), emergency spending (notably under the feed and forage law), drawdowns from lump-sum funds, spending of donated funds and gifts, and dispositions of "surplus" property, all without further specific appropriation. It has also authorized the executive to reprogram funds from one account to another, to transfer funds between accounts, to transfer property between agencies under the Economy Act, and to impound funds.

At one time or another, the president has abused each of these sources of spending discretion, prompting congressional countermeasures. Although these countermeasures have narrowed or conditioned spending discretion, they have left presidents a substantial spending cushion for their own national security adventures. Congress has lacked the will, or—given the obscure nature of the customary and statutory authority for the discretion—the knowledge, to eliminate it.

Constitutional Limits on the Making of National Security Appropriations

The politicization of the appropriation process has inevitably deflected attacks on policy outcomes to the process itself. In part III, we considered and rejected the two principal constitutional challenges, based, respectively, on the Veto Clause and the Statement and Account Clause.

The first challenge asserts that the increasing use of omnibus continuing resolutions that often bundle multifarious legislative proposals, the attachment to such resolutions of restrictive riders, the narrowing of presidential impoundment authority, and the impact of "automatic" deficit reduction mechanisms have unconstitutionally diluted presidents' veto powers by confronting them with "must-pass" appropriation legislation. The fiscal year 1988 resolution furnishes a graphic example, as it bundled more than $600 billion of funding for government operations into a single 1,057-page bill presented to the Congress and the president two months into the fiscal year for which it was appropriating funds.

We concluded in chapter 8, however, that neither the constitutional text, nor its structure, nor its practice supports this constitutional challenge. Although, as we showed in chapter 2, colonial legislators knew and used nongermane riders and were familiar with executive abuses of impoundment authority equivalent to an item veto, the framers neither prohibited the former nor authorized the latter in the Constitution. The text is silent on the meaning of "bills" and does not in terms confer even the veto (which is merely implied), let alone an item veto. Furthermore, immediately after the Constitution was adopted, Congress adopted rules limiting nongermane riders. Had such riders been unconstitutional, this rule making would have been superfluous. So would the subsequent Republican-Federalist debate about the propriety of lump-sum appropriations for national security that were omnibus, if small-scale.

Of course, the later and modern practice is also utterly inconsistent with the constitutional challenge to bundled legislation. Long-continued practice cannot make constitutional what is clearly unconstitutional, but all the evidence suggests that the Ninth Circuit Court of Appeals was correct in concluding that the

Constitution "does not empower the President to employ a so-called 'line-item veto.'"[5]

What is more, the president does not need one. The very monster that serves to illustrate the omnibus appropriations—the fiscal year 1988 bill—also proves this point. President Reagan, in fact, threatened to veto the resolution unless it included assistance for the Contras and omitted a provision directed at the Federal Communications Commission. His veto threat carried the day, and the resolution was changed in conference to reflect these demands. President Bush subsequently vetoed six spending bills, one of which was an omnibus bill. Thus, omnibus appropriations are not veto-proof and the efficacy of the veto—whether it is brought to bear *in terrorem* before or exercised more visibly after presentment—turns on political factors that attend all legislation. Arguing that an item-veto power exists or should be granted, in view of the actual political powers of the contemporary president in the legislative process and in spending, is like arguing for moving the home run fence in for Babe Ruth.

The power of the purse is not just "between friends" but a protection for the people. The Statement and Account Clause of the Constitution helps ensure the political branches' accountability to the people by supplying vital information concerning how their money is spent. In chapter 10, we showed that this public accounting requirement is inconsistent with any permanently secret black-budgeting process for the intelligence community.

The framers expressly recognized the importance of public disclosure to democratic accountability, but they also acknowledged the necessity for secrecy in diplomatic and national security affairs. Their failure to exempt such affairs from the operation of the Statement and Account Clause, in contrast to their provision for secret journals, suggests that the need for secrecy was to be accommodated by delaying rather than permanently excusing the publication of black budgets.

Nevertheless, Congress had not only consistently appropriated in secret, but also consistently authorized secret spending on nothing more than executive officials' certifications. Recent reforms have increased executive accountability to Congress for secret spending, but have not improved accountability to the people by mandating any degree of public disclosure. Citing Congress's plenary authority over the appropriation process, the courts have also refused to enforce the Statement and Account Clause.

Yet their very reasoning reaffirms Congress's authority to require more. If "Congress has plenary power to exact any reporting and accounting requirement it considers appropriate," as the Supreme Court has said,[6] then it may require publication of the aggregate black budget, as well as more detailed accounting for how the budget is spent. Under threat of presidential veto, Congress recently pulled back from a disclosure requirement, but a fair reading of the constitutional history indicates that a veto cannot be justified on constitutional grounds. Congress unquestionably has the power, if not the duty, to insist on more disclosure of black budgets and greater accounting for black spending.

The Substantive Scope of the Power of the Purse in National Security Affairs

In part IV, we finally reached the legal question that lies at the heart of modern debate about the power of the purse in national security affairs: What is the substantive scope of that power? How *should* we and how constitutionally *must* we construe both legitimating appropriations (from which the executive infers national security authority) and restrictive appropriations (which restrict the exercise of national security authority)?

When national security issues are recast as fiscal issues, arguments about policy are recast as arguments about the substantive scope of appropriation measures in national security affairs. This displacement may account for the resilience and intensity of the often expressed view that "mere" appropriations do not carry the same force and effect as "ordinary" or "substantive" legislation. But we showed in chapter 11 that this displacement does not make that view correct. As Thomas Jefferson asked, "Where is the rule of legal construction to be found which ascribes less effect to the words of an appropriation law, than of any other law?"[7] The constitutional text makes no distinction between appropriation measures and other legislation. Bills that satisfy the requirements of bicameral approval and presentment have the force and effect of law, whether they affect legal rights, duties, or status directly, or only indirectly, by controlling appropriations.

The persistence of the deprecatory appellation "mere" ultimately reflects doubt not about the force and effect of appropriation measures, but about their intent. Bicameral approval may follow a truncated and time-pressured debate, or no debate at all, as we showed in part II, generating a truncated legislative history. Unless the plain language of the measure is clear, the manner of its making may thus leave at best confused, and at worst indeterminate, legislative history with which to construe its intent. The practical difficulty of statutory construction is often compounded by the durational limits of successive appropriation measures.

The courts have responded by adopting rules of narrow construction for appropriation measures. These rules cannot be applied to national security appropriation measures, however, without taking account of the special role of custom and congressional acquiescence in the evolution of customary national security law. National security appropriations may supply especially good evidence of acquiescence, or, when they restrict executive action, of disapproval, by Congress.

In light of this theory of customary national security law, the normal rule against ratification by appropriation should be relaxed in favor of a contextual analysis of a national security appropriation. That analysis must take into account the length and consistency of an executive national security practice, collateral evidence of congressional intent to approve or disapprove the practice, and the question whether the practice impinges directly on constitutionally sensitive rights. The normal rule against implied repeal by appropriation must also be relaxed when a restrictive national security appropriation repeals not prior statutory directives, but prior customary law dependent for its continued vitality on congressional acquiescence.

Applying the foregoing analysis to the legitimating appropriations for the Vietnam War, we concluded in chapter 12 that they satisfy the predicate for ratification by appropriation: Congress knew of and approved the military actions in Vietnam for which funds were earmarked. On the other hand, the secrecy of the bombing of Cambodia from 1969 to 1970—which was not justified by any military necessity—prevented Congress from *knowingly* acquiescing in the bombing when it voted appropriations for military activities in Southeast Asia during this time period. These appropriations therefore did not authorize the secret bombing.

None of the objections to this reliance on legitimating appropriations as authorization for war are sound. The formalist objection is inconsistent with the framers' contemporaneous understanding of the power to declare war, ignores the Marque and Reprisal Clause, and is refuted by practice and the resulting customary national security law, under which Congress has repeatedly authorized war without formal declaration. The clear statement objection merely reaffirms the rule of narrow construction of legitimating appropriations and the rule against implied repeal by appropriation. The War Powers Resolution did not appeal the Constitution's implied rule against "entrenched" legislation and therefore cannot constitutionally control the construction of subsequent legitimating appropriations. Finally, the Court has repeatedly ruled that Congress may ratify acts that were unconstitutional when taken, and that the "ratification . . . operate[s] perfectly to cure the defect."[8]

In chapter 13, we turn from legitimating appropriations to restrictive appropriations, and begin by applying force-and-effect analysis to classic examples: the Boland amendments. We show that nothing about the form or process of their enactment necessarily or uniquely contributed to any ambiguities in the amendments. What they mean does not turn on what they were—appropriation measures as opposed to "ordinary" legislation. Moreover, contrary to critics of the 1984 Boland amendment, the presumption against implied repeal is inapplicable to it. Because there was no prior practice of using the National Security Council for covert operations, construing the amendment's prohibition on spending by any "agency or entity of the United States involved in intelligence activities" to include the National Security Council does not repeal customary law.

Whether applying the 1984 Boland amendment to the National Security Council would violate the Constitution cannot be determined simply from the constitutional text. When explicit constitutional text does not assign national security powers solely to one branch or state a flat prohibition, we must determine the constitutionality of a restrictive appropriation by weighing the extent to which the restriction prevents presidents from accomplishing their constitutionally assigned functions against the need for the restriction to promote objectives within the authority of the Congress. In this balancing, restrictive national security appropriations carry special weight derived from their unique history as controls on executive abuse of military power, which we traced in part I.

Applying the proper balancing test to the 1984 Boland amendment, we conclude that it was constitutional as applied to the National Security Council. Against the limited intrusion on the president's generalized and implied claims of authority as "sole organ" of foreign affairs, executor of international law, and commander in chief, we would balance Congress's textually rooted and specific claims of authority to enlist private armies under the Marque and Reprisal Clause, to define and punish offenses against the law of nations, and to raise and support armies. To the extent that the amendment could be read to restrict, and therefore intrude upon, the president's implied constitutional authority to conduct intelligence collection and exchange and to defend Americans in Nicaragua against attack, the rule against implied repeal justifies a narrow reading that avoids the intrusion and preserves the amendment's constitutionality.

Applying the same balancing test to restrictive appropriations in the Vietnam War, we conclude that 1970 area restrictions on combat in Cambodia arguably intruded too far on the president's express constitutional authority as commander in chief to conduct military operations. On the other hand, other restrictive appropriations clearly enacted to end the war were classic exercises of Congress's power to withdraw funds for the purpose of ending a war of which it no longer approves and, as such, were squarely supported by our constitutional and preconstitutional history.

Assuming, arguendo, that the 1984 Boland amendment was unconstitutional, in chapter 14 we finally consider the president's constitutional alternatives. First, the President should object to the bill in advance and threaten to veto it. We showed in part III that the death of the veto threat is much exaggerated, notwithstanding the rise of continuing resolutions and appropriation riders.

Second, the president can ask the court to sever the unconstitutional restriction. Some scholars have also argued that the president may excise the unconstitutional restriction and spend the appropriation as if it were not so restricted. The practical difference between the presidential excision and judicial severance options is simply who goes to court first: the Congress, to force the president to abide the restriction, or the president, to have it severed. Either way, no violence is done the Appropriations Clause because, if the courts hold the appropriation restriction severable, the president ultimately only spends appropriated funds without the unconstitutional restriction.

Neither alternative is availing, however, if the problem arises from Congress's failure to appropriate any funds necessary for the president to execute a constitutionally assigned duty. The theoretical alternatives left the president then are mandatory appropriations, third-party funding, inherent presidential spending authority, or statutory/customary spending authority without specific appropriation.

Although theory suggests that Congress has a mandatory duty to appropriate such funds, it is unclear whether federal courts would order such appropriations (as they have ordered local governments to spend in order to remedy constitutional violations), or whether presidents would be left to their substantial powers of political self-defense.

We concluded that third-party funds are not a constitutional substitute for "mandatory" appropriations. The unique history of the power of the purse outlined in part I refutes claims by Oliver North and Attorney General William Barr that the president can use third-party funds for presidential ends. It was precisely the danger that the executive would solicit third-party funds to conduct military adventures that fueled the parliamentary evolution of the power of the purse and led to the framing of the Appropriations Clause.

We also concluded in chapter 14 that the president does not enjoy any inherent constitutional spending authority. The Appropriations Clause stands as an insurmountable barrier to any such claim, especially when construed in light of the hard-fought history of the power of the purse described in part I. The Supreme Court has declared that even the president's express and otherwise plenary "pardon power cannot override the command of the Appropriations Clause."[9] An inherent presidential spending authority knows no practical limit and is therefore constitutionally intolerable.

Of course, lack of authority does not mean lack of power. In a case of emergency, the president can encumber funds without appropriation. We showed in chapter 4 that the early leaders of the Republic agreed that he should do so. But they also agreed that he would then spend at his own constitutional risk, acting unconstitutionally until and unless Congress ratifies the spending by *ex post facto* appropriation. The exercise of executive spending *power* without appropriation is therefore as risky as the claim of inherent constitutional spending *authority* is intolerable.

Fortunately, it has also generally been unnecessary. In chapter 8, we showed that the president continues to enjoy a substantial cushion of national security spending discretion by statute and custom dating back to the early years of the Republic, as discussed in chapter 4. The Iran-Contra affair itself is testimony to the rich menu of discretionary spending authorities enjoyed by the president, from contingency funds, drawdown, reprogramming and transfer authorities, and lump-sum appropriations for operation and maintenance to Economy Act transfers. By picking from this menu presidents have successfully stretched the law instead of breaking it. Although critics of presidential national security initiatives assert that continuation of this discretionary spending authority makes the appropriation requirement "superfluous," it also gives the president intended and, in our view, often desirable flexibility and gives both branches constitutional breathing room for at least short-term national security spending.

Chief Justice Burger was not the first to notice the "hydraulic pressure inherent within each of the separate Branches to exceed the outer limits of its power."[10] As early as the seventeenth century, this hydraulic pressure caused monarchs to search for alternatives to Parliament-controlled bills of military supply for funding their foreign military adventures. The subsequent evolution of the power of the purse, first in England, then in colonial America, and finally in constitutional America was a sustained effort to regulate the hydraulic pressure for executive national security power.

At first, this use of the power of the purse was straightforward. Without a large standing army or military stockpiles, the president was unable to start any unilateral national security initiative without prior appropriation. But time eroded antecedent pursestring controls as the military establishment grew, fast-moving events became more unpredictable, and Congress itself conferred broad customary and statutory national security discretion on the president. The force of events has induced Congress increasingly to use its power of the purse contemporaneously or after the fact by discrete restrictive appropriations, annualized reauthorizations, and informal controls.

Some have traced this development to the legislature's own hydraulic pressure "to exceed the outer limits of its power" by micromanaging national security. Such pressure, of course, also must be resisted to preserve our separation of powers. But the Constitution places few procedural limits on the Congress's power of the purse, as we have seen. And in deciding the outer substantive limits of that power in national security, wooden references to the constitutional text or "inherent" powers of the commander in chief yield no answers. Those limits can only be found by weighing the extent to which an appropriation restriction prevents presidents from accomplishing their constitutionally assigned functions against the need for the restriction. When all is said and done, the power of the purse is not plenary, even in national security, but history—and often constitutional text—usually tips the scales in favor of its exercise.

Notes

Introduction

1. 15 *The Papers of Thomas Jefferson* 397 (J. Boyd ed., 1958).

2. U.S. Const., art. I, § 8, cl. 11 ("The Congress shall have the Power . . . [t]o Declare War, [and] grant Letters of Marque and Reprisal . . . .").

3. U.S. Const., art. I, § 8, cl. 1 ("The Congress shall have Power . . . to pay the Debts and provide for the common Defense . . . .").

4. U.S. Const., art. I, § 8, cl. 12 ("To raise and support Armies . . . .); cl. 13 ("To provide and maintain a Navy . . . .").

5. U.S. Const., art. I, § 8, cl. 18.

6. *Id.* § 9, cl. 7 ("No money shall be drawn from the Treasury, but in Consequence of Appropriations Made By Law . . . .").

7. *Id.* ("[A] regular Statement and Account of the Receipts and Expenditures of all public Money shall be published from time to time.").

8. When the appropriation power is used to authorize or control the conduct of overt and covert military action, intelligence collection and analysis, domestic security, or foreign affairs, we refer to it as the *national security appropriation power*. Defense appropriations are part of this power and have a unique historical origin in "bills of supply," as discussed later in chapter 1.

9. *See, e.g.*, Jason A. Rosenberg et al., Note, "Historical and Structural Limitations on Congressional Abilities to Make Foreign Policy," 50 *B.U. L. Rev.* 51 (Spec. Issue 1970).

10. *See, e.g.*, Kate Stith, "Congress' Power of the Purse, 97 *Yale L.J.* 1343, 1360–61 nn.83–86 (1988); Michael J. Glennon, "Strengthening the War Powers Resolution: The Case for Purse-Strings Restrictions," 60 *Minn. L. Rev.* 1 (1975); Eli E. Nobleman, "Financial Aspects of Congressional Participation in Foreign Relations," 289 *Annals* 145 (1953); Garry S. Wooters, Note, "The Appropriations Power as a Tool of Congressional Foreign Policy Making," 50 *B.U. L. Rev.* 34 (Spec. Issue 1970).

11. *See* Monroe Freedman, "Pale Horse, Pale Justice," *Legal Times*, March 23, 1992, at 21 (quoting Thomas Reed Powell).

12. *See, e.g.*, Massachusetts v. Laird, 451 F.2d 26 (1st Cir. 1971); Orlando v. Laird, 443 F.2d 1039, 1043 (2d Cir.), *cert. denied*, 404 U.S. 869 (1971).

13. Mitchell v. Laird, 488 F.2d 611, 615 (D.C. Cir. 1973) (Wyzanski, J., in an opinion in which C. J. Bazelon joined) ("An honorable, decent, compassionate act of aiding those already in peril is no proof of consent to the actions that placed and continued them in that dangerous position.").

14. Kent v. Dulles, 357 U.S. 116 (1958); Greene v. McElroy, 360 U.S. 474 (1959); *Ex parte* Endo, 323 U.S. 283, 303 n.24 (1944).

15. Haig v. Agee, 453 U.S. 280 (1981). *See also* Lichter v. United States, 334 U.S. 742, 754 (1948); *cf.* Department of the Navy v. Egan, 484 U.S. 518, 530 (1988).

16. 50 U.S.C. § 1541 et seq. (1988 & Supp. III 1991)

17. Pub. L. No. 91-652, § 7, 84 Stat. 1942, 1943 (1971).

18. Pub. L. No. 91-172, § 643, 83 Stat. 487 (1969).

19. *See, e.g.*, John N. Moore, *Law and the Indo-China War* 560–61, 563 (1972); John Hart Ely, "The American War in Indochina, Part II: The Unconstitutionality of the War They Didn't Tell Us About," 42 *Stan. L. Rev.* 1099, 1103 (1990); Terry Emerson, "War Powers, An Invasion of Presidential Prerogative," 58 *A.B.A.J.* 809, 813–14 (1972); William H. Rehnquist, "The Constitutional Issues—Administrative Position," 45 *N.Y.U. L. Rev.* 628, 638–39 (1970).

20. 41 U.S.C. § 11 (1988).

21. *See generally* Elias Huzar, *The Purse and the Sword* 321, 339–45, 345–54 (1950); Wooters, *supra* note 10, at 34–46.

22. *See, e.g.*, Joint Resolution Continuing Appropriations for Fiscal 1974 § 108, Pub. L. No. 93-52 (1973); the "Eagleton Amendment," 29 *Cong. Q. Almanac* 102 (1973); the "Mansfield Amendment" to the Armed Forces Appropriations Authorization Act of 1971 § 601, Pub. L. No. 92-156, 85 Stat. 430 (1971).

23. The nonclassified amendments are summarized in a chart in Congressional Research Service, *Legislative Histories of Statutory Restrictions on Funding for Covert Assistance for Military or Paramilitary Operations in Nicaragua, FY 1983–FY 1986* (1987).

24. *See also* Anti-Deficiency Act, 31 U.S.C. §§ 1341–1351 (1988 & Supp. III 1991).

25. *See also* Miscellaneous Receipts Act, 31 U.S.C. § 3302(b) (1988).

26. *See, e.g., Report of the Congressional Comm. Investigating the Iran-Contra Affair*, S. Rep. No. 100-216, H.R. Rep. No. 100-433, 100th Cong., 1st Sess. 492 (1987) [hereinafter *Iran-Contra Report*] (Minority Report). *Cf.* National Federation of Federal Employees v. United States, 688 F. Supp. 671, 684 n.17 (D.D.C.) (stating that congressional appropriation restricting presidential authority over national security information "is merely an appropriations measure by which no substantive rights or causes of action are created") [hereinafter *NFFE I*], *vacated and remanded sub nom.* American Foreign Service Assn. v. Garfinkel, 490 U.S. 153 (1989), *dismissed as moot,* 730 F. Supp. 13 (1990). *See also* Sierra Club v. Andrus, 581 F.2d 895, 910–11 (D.C. Cir. 1978) (MacKinnon, J., concurring and dissenting in part), *rev'd,* 442 U.S. 347 (1979).

27. *See, e.g.*, Frank G. Collela, Note, "Beyond Institutional Competence: Congressional Efforts to Legislate United States Foreign Policy Toward Nicaragua—The Boland Amendments," 54 *Brooklyn L. Rev.* 131 (1988); Eugene Rostow, *President, Prime Minister, or Constitutional Monarch?* 18 (Inst. for Natl. Strategic Studies 1989).

28. *Iran-Contra Report, supra* note 26, at 475–76 (Minority Report).

29. Lovett v. United States, 328 U.S. 303 (1946), is typically cited for this truism. *See, e.g., NFFE I, supra,* note 26 at 684 n.17; *Iran-Contra Report, supra* note 26, at 476 (Minority Report).

Chapter 1

1. *See* Abraham D. Sofaer, *War, Foreign Affairs and Constitutional Power: The Origins* 6 (1976) ("The hazards of interpolating from British history are formidable. Did

the Framers (or at least some of them), for example, form meaningfully detailed conceptions of the British experience? Were those conceptions accurate? Which British practices or events affected the Framers, and in what way?").

2. Judge Sofaer quotes the response of Representative William Findley of Pennsylvania in 1810 to another member's reliance on English parliamentary practice during a congressional debate: "It is well known that the powers of the House of Commons have been very different at different times. . . . At which of these periods does the gentleman apply the proceedings of the House of Commons as a model for this House?" *Id.* at 12, *quoting* 21 *Annals of Cong.* 1735–36 (1853).

3. The emigration from England to America began in earnest just as power swung away from the Crown to Parliament. John F. Burns, *Controversies Between Royal Governors and Their Assemblies in the Northern American Colonies* 12 (1923). Early emigrants are more likely to have understood English government in light of this trend than to have appreciated subsequent swings back in the other direction.

4. Even in the colonies, analogies to English government were sometimes expressly rejected as unsuited to American circumstances. *See, e.g.*, Gordon S. Wood, *The Creation of the American Republic, 1776–1787* 241 (1969) (quoting Virginia Senate's rejection of the English analogy in arguing for a right to amend money bills); Burns, *supra* note 3, at 259.

5. Forrest McDonald, *Novus Ordo Seclorum* 6 (1985).

6. *See, e.g.*, *infra* chap. 3 text accompanying note 35 (quoting Wilson Nicholas at the Virginia Convention).

7. *See, e.g.*, *infra* note 73 (quoting Albert Gallatin).

8. Paul Einzig, *The Control of the Purse* 30 (1959). *Cf.* John Brewer, *The Sinews of Power* 8–10 (1988). Einzig's analysis was anticipated as early as 1749 in the observation that "[t]he Army causes Taxes, the Taxes cause Discontents, and the discontents are alleged to make an Army necessary. Thus you go in a circle." *Id.* at 54 (quoting Bath).

9. *Id.* at 35.

10. 25 Edw. 1, c. 5, 6 (1297), quoted in Francis L. Coolidge, Jr. & Joel D. Sharrow, Note, "The War-Making Powers: The Intentions of the Framers in the Light of Parliamentary History," 50 *B.U. L. Rev.* 5, 6 (Special Issue 1970).

11. Einzig, *supra* note 8, at 39–40. The right of the Commons to be considered an integral part of Parliament was firmly established by the second quarter of the fourteenth century. *Id.* at 41.

12. David L. Keir, *The Constitutional History of Modern Britain* 12; Einzig, *supra* note 8, at 29; Gerhard Casper, "Appropriations of Power," 13 *U. Ark. Little Rock L.J.* 1, 3 (1990).

13. Keir, *supra* note 12, at 7. *See also* Einzig, *supra* note 8, at 29.

14. Keir, *supra* note 12, at 12, 14.

15. Statutes I. 290, *cited in* Einzig, *supra* note 8, at 79.

16. *Rot. Parl.*, ii 271, cited in Coolidge & Sharrow, *supra* note 10, at 6.

17. Einzig, *supra* note 8, at 79.

18. *Id.* at 42.

19. *Id.* at 43, 89.

20. *Id.* at 88.

21. *Id.* at 89.

22. Keir, *supra* note 12, at 13, *quoting* T. F. T. Plucknett, *Tudor Studies* 20, 23 (R. W. Seaton-Watson ed., 1969). *See also* F. W. Maitland, *The Constitutional History of England* 277 (1908) (noting that Edward III granted a petition providing that "no man be

compelled to go out of his shire [to bear arms], but where necessity requireth and sudden coming of strange enemies into the realm").

23. Keir, *supra* note 12, at 181; J. R. Tanner, *English Constitutional Conflicts of the Seventeenth Century 1603–1689,* at 8–9 (1971).

24. Keir, *supra* note 12, at 187.

25. Maurice Ashley, *England in the Seventeenth Century* 66 (1954).

26. 3 Car. 1, c. 1, § 1 (1628), from Coolidge & Sharrow, *supra* note 10, at 7.

27. Einzig, *supra* note 8, at 60.

28. Ashley, *supra* note 25, at 64.

29. *Id.* at 65.

30. Ashley, *supra* note 25, at 60.

31. Einzig, *supra* note 8, at 60, 65.

32. *Id.* at 100–06. *See also* Brewer, *supra* note 8, at 17–19.

33. 13 Car. 1 (1637).

34. *See generally* D. L. Keir, "The Case of Ship Money," 52 *L.Q.R.* 546; Keir, *supra* note 12, at 206.

35. Einzig, *supra* note 8, at 97; Ashley, *supra* note 25, at 58.

36. Keir, *supra* note 12, at 210, *quoting* Samuel R. Gardiner, 9 *History of England* 108 (1904).

37. Ashley, *supra* note 25, at 72.

38. *Id.* at 73.

39. Einzig, *supra* note 8, at 61–62; Ashley, *supra* note 25, at 62–63.

40. Governor Lewis Morris of New Jersey later complained that the representatives in the lower house of the legislature "are generally so fond of the example of the parliament of 1641 . . . that until some measures are taken in England to reduce them to Propper limits, I suspect they will not mend much." Burns, *supra* note 3, at 29 (citation omitted).

41. Keir, *supra* note 12, at 182.

42. *Id.* at 161.

43. *Id.* at 219–20; Einzig, *supra* note 8, at 62.

44. Einzig, *supra* note 8, at 62.

45. *Id.* at 62.

46. Maitland, *supra* note 22, at 326.

47. Einzig, *supra* note 8, at 142; Brewer, *supra* note 8, at 143.

48. Ashley, *supra* note 25, at 119. In 1680, Parliament declared that lending money to the king without parliamentary consent was a breach of privilege punishable by imprisonment. Einzig, *supra* note 8, at 99.

49. Keir, *supra* note 12, at 249; Ashley, *supra* note 25, at 127; Einzig, *supra* note 8, at 91; J. S. Omond, *Parliament and the Army* 30–31 (1933). *See* Casper, *supra* note 12, at 3–4 ("[T]he Moneys payable . . . are for the service of Your Majestie in the said Warr respectively.").

50. *See* C. Allen, *The Supreme Command in England, 1640–1748,* at 138 (1966). By 1757, Parliament was sufficiently secure in its control over the standing army to give the king another military force by the Militia Act, but provided that it should be employed only for insurrection, rebellion, or invasion, and could not be transported or compelled to march out of the kingdom "otherwise than by the laws of England ought to be done." Maitland, *supra* note 22, at 455–56.

51. Einzig, *supra* note 8, at 113–14.

52. Coolidge & Sharrow, *supra* note 10, at 8–9.

53. 1 W. & M., c. 5 (1689).

54. Maitland, *supra* note 22, at 328–29; Omond, *supra* note 49, at 28–29.

55. Maitland, *supra* note 22, at 373.

56. Keir, *supra* note 12, at 278.

57. *Id.* at 278; Ashley, *supra* note 25, at 187.

58. Quoted in Charles J. Cooper, "The Line-Item Veto: The Framers' Intentions," in *Pork Barrels and Principles: The Politics of the Presidential Veto* 37 (National Legal Center for the Public Interest 1988); *see also* R. Luce, *Legislative Problems* 422 (1935).

59. Cooper, *supra* note 58, at 37 (footnote omitted).

60. Einzig, *supra* note 8, at 118.

61. An Act for a Grant, 1688, 1 W. & M., Sess. 2, c. 1, §§ 35ff. *See* Casper, *supra* note 12, at 4; Einzig, *supra* note 8, at 159.

62. Keir, *supra* note 12, at 276. *See also* Brewer, *supra* note 8, at 139 ("The price that MPs exacted for supporting the [Nine Years] war was the opportunity to subject its operations to unparalleled surveillance."). By 1765, a typical bill of supply contained over thirty separate sections and items of appropriation, combining diverse national security items together. *See* 5 Geo. 3, c. 40, 12, 13, 15, 20, 22 (1765), *quoted in* Cooper, *supra* note 58, at 36.

63. Einzig, *supra* note 8, at 173; Brewer, *supra* note 8, at 151; Casper, *supra* note 12, at 4.

64. Brewer, *supra* note 8, at 151.

65. Einzig, *supra* note 8, at 143.

66. *Id.* at 144–45.

67. *Id.* at 129.

68. *Id.* at 165.

69. *Id.* at 165 (paraphrasing Pitt speech).

70. *Id.* at 120, 143, 147–48.

71. *Id.* at 146.

72. *Id.* at 123–24.

73. The corruption was so notorious that it was well known in the United States both before and after the Revolution. For example, in 1798 Albert Gallatin told the House of Representatives that "[i]t is during that period [i.e., after the Revolution of 1688] that a progressive patronage, and a systematic, corrupting influence have sunk Parliament to a nominal representation, a mere machine, the convenience used by Government for the purpose of raising supplies; the medium through which the Executive reaches with ease the purse of the people." 5 *Annals of Cong.* 1133 (1798).

74. Einzig, *supra* note 8, at 119 (emphasis added).

75. *See id.*

76. Omond, *supra* note 49, at 58.

77. 3 *Elliot's Debates* 393 (Jonathan Elliot ed., 1836). *See also Essays on the Constitution of the United States* 263–64 (P. Ford ed., 1970) (quoting New York governor, George Clinton, as observing that "though it may be asserted that the King of Great Britain has the express power of making peace or war, yet he never thinks it prudent to do so without the advice of the Parliament, from whom he is to derive support"); Brewer, *supra* note 8, at 43–44 ("though 'the Government, Command and Disposition of the Army' was one of the prerogatives of the crown, it could only be exercised effectively with parliamentary approval"), 137–38. This is not to say that parliamentary control was synonymous with a limited military establishment. On the contrary, the seventeenth century saw a phenomenal growth in that establishment, transforming England into an international military power in the succeeding century. *See generally* Brewer, *supra* note 8. Nor is this to say that parliamentary control of the military was operational. Sofaer

sums up this period of English history with the conclusion that it vested "ultimate but not necessarily operational authority in Parliament." Sofaer, *supra* note 1, at 14.

Chapter 2

1. The development and use of the power of the purse by colonial assemblies was similar from colony to colony because of their similar problems, shared intellectual analogies to English parliamentary history and practice, and shared family and commercial ties. Jack P. Greene, *The Quest for Power* 8 (1963). *See also* John F. Burns, *Controversies Between Royal Governors and Their Assemblies in the Northern American Colonies* 416, 420–21 (1923). It is therefore realistic to speak of a colonial model and to generalize from detailed case studies of some of the colonies.

2. Gerhard Casper, "Appropriations of Power," 13 *U. Ark. Little Rock L.J.* 1, 5 (1990) (citation omitted).

3. *See, e.g.*, Charles L. Raper, *North Carolina: A Study in English Colonial Government* 85–86 (1904).

4. Percy S. Flippin, *The Royal Government in Virginia* 198, 200–201 (1966); Raper, *supra* note 3, at 35–36, 87; Burns, *supra* note 1, at 53.

5. Burns, *supra* note 1, at 30.

6. J. Greene, *supra* note 1, at 15. *See also* Raper, *supra* note 3, at 223–24; Burns, *supra* note 1, at 13–14.

7. J. Greene, *supra* note 1, at 15 (quoting royal instructions) (citation omitted). *See also* Raper, *supra* note 3, at 86.

8. Evarts B. Greene, *The Provincial Governor* 92 (1898).

9. The colonists argued that long-standing imperial acquiescence in "local precedents, habits, traditions, and statutes . . . was tantamount to consent and that precedents thus established could not be undone without their approval." J. Greene, *supra* note 1, at 16.

10. *Cf.* Burns, *supra* note 1, at 26, 417.

11. Casper, *supra* note 2, at 5; Flippin, *supra* note 4, at 289–90.

12. *See generally* Raper, *supra* note 3, at 97–99, 185, 201.

13. J. Greene, *supra* note 1, at 62.

14. *Id.* at 62–63.

15. *Id.* at 64–65.

16. Flippin, *supra* note 4, at 118.

17. *Id.* at 119.

18. Burns, *supra* note 1, at 354–55.

19. Burns, *supra* note 1, at 45.

20. Burns, *supra* note 1, at 66 (quoting the journal of the house).

21. Burns, *supra* note 1, at 73.

22. Raper, *supra* note 3, at 97, 98–99, 185, 201.

23. E. Greene, *supra* note 8, at 180.

24. *See* Burns, *supra* note 1, at 68 (quoting 1721 Massachusetts bill).

25. E. Greene, *supra* note 8, at 188–89.

26. J. Greene, *supra* note 1, at 89 (footnotes omitted).

27. Flippin, *supra* note 4, at 211. Flippin reports that using specific military appropriations "the Assembly practically had charge of military affairs" during Governor Fauquier's administration. *Id.*

28. J. Greene, *supra* note 1, at 104, 304–05.

29. E. Greene, *supra* note 8, at 189.

30. *Id.* at 189–90. *See also* Burns, *supra* note 1, at 65, 144–45 (citing Massachusetts appropriations specifying period, place, and number of troops to be raised).

31. Burns, *supra* note 1, at 333. *See also id.* at 339 (citing New York supply bill specifying how and by whom military defenses were to be built).

32. E. Greene, *supra* note 8, at 164. *See also* Flippin, *supra* note 4, at 208 (describing defense appropriations riders as the "most effective" counter to the Crown's efforts to restrict legislative independence in Virginia).

33. J. Greene, *supra* note 1, at 67, 102. On this occasion, the council declined to pass the bill, sharply protesting the nongermane rider. *Id.* at 103.

34. *Id.* at 100; Raper, *supra* note 3, at 58, 206–07. *See also* Burns, *supra* note 1, at 264 (describing similar rider in general supply bill for New York).

35. Raper, *supra* note 3, at 207. Forrest McDonald has asserted that the colonial governors exercised an item veto, in support of his argument that the constitutional veto power includes the power to disapprove parts of a bill. Forrest McDonald, "Line-Item Veto: Older than Constitution," *Wall St. J.*, Mar. 7, 1988, at 16, col. 4 [hereinafter McDonald]. In fact, Evarts Greene, the only authority he cites for this proposition, concludes just the opposite, that the governor "had himself only a right of veto upon appropriation bills as a whole." E. Greene, *supra* note 8, at 122. *See generally* Charles J. Cooper, "The Line-Item Veto: The Framers' Intentions," in *Pork Barrels and Principles: The Politics of the Presidential Veto* 37–38 (National Legal Center for the Public Interest 1988) (systematically refuting McDonald's proposition). As Cooper concludes, "[h]ad the governor been authorized to veto parts of a bill, . . . the devices described [*supra* in the text] could not have coerced the governor." *Id.* at 38.

36. J. Greene, *supra* note 1, at 76.

37. *Id.* at 93. *See also* Raper, *supra* note 3, at 200.

38. Burns, *supra* note 1, at 334.

39. Wood, *supra* note 57, at 154.

40. J. Greene, *supra* note 1, at 358. The colonial assemblies did make comparably effective use of the power to appropriate the governors' salaries. *See, e.g.*, Burns, *supra* note 1, at 99–101.

41. J. Greene, *supra* note 1, at 297–98.

42. *Id.* at 303. Appropriations bills were the primary, but not the sole, lever for colonial legislative control of military affairs. The militia laws also controlled the organization, training, and mustering of the militia and often included limitations on their place of service outside the colony. *Id.* at 298–99. Recognizing the governors' dependency upon local militia for local defense, the assemblies also took care to make the militia acts temporary for terms of one, two, or three years at most. E. Greene, *supra* note 8, at 101.

43. J. Greene, *supra* note 1, at 97; E. Greene, *supra* note 8, at 103; Burns, *supra* note 1, at 151 (noting assemblies' acknowledgment, citing English parliamentary practice, of discretionary spending authority in the governor on "Occasions of evident Necessity" and "when the very Being of a Government is in imminent danger").

44. E. Greene, *supra* note 8, at 103.

45. Don Higginbotham, *The War of American Independence* 17 (1971).

46. George Chalmers, 2 *An Introduction to the History of the Revolt of the American Colonies* 300–01 (1845), *quoted by* E. Greene, *supra* note 8, at 192.

47. E. James Ferguson, *The Power of the Purse* xv (1961).

48. Burns, *supra* note 1, at 26.

49. Charles C. Thach, *Creation of the Presidency 1775–89*, at 28 (1923), *quoted in*

Abraham D. Sofaer, *War, Foreign Affairs and Constitutional Power: The Origins* 17 (1976).

50. *See* 1 Francis N. Thorpe, *The Federal and State Constitutions, Colonial Charters, and Other Organic Laws* 563 (Delaware) (allowing such amendments, however), 3 *id.* at 1692 (Maryland), 4 *id.* at 2452 (New Hampshire), 5 *id.* at 2596 (New Jersey), 5 *id.* at 2791 (North Carolina), 6 *id.* at 3252 (North Carolina), 7 *id.* at 3816 (Virginia). Massachusetts adopted similar money bill origination provisions in 1780, vesting its upper house with the power to concur with amendments. 3 *id.* at 1899.

51. 3 *id.* at 1902–03 (Massachusetts); 3 *id.* at 3252 (South Carolina).

52. Casper, *supra* note 2, at 8.

53. Robert Luce, *Legislative Problems* 423 (1935).

54. Casper, *supra* note 2, at 8.

55. *Id.*

56. Sofaer, *supra* note 49, at 18.

57. *Id.* at 18–19 (*quoting* Gordon S. Wood, *Creation of the American Republic, 1776–1787,* at 452 (1969)).

58. *Id.* at 19.

59. Jerrilyn G. Marston, *King and Congress* 304 (1987).

60. John N. Moore, "The Constitution, Nuclear Weapons, and Deterrence: An Analysis of the FAS Proposal," in *First Use of Nuclear Weapons* 28 (P. Raven-Hansen ed., 1989). *See also* Robert F. Turner, "Congressional Limits on the Commander in Chief: The FAS Proposal," *id.* at 45 ("[A] major reason for placing the control of foreign affairs and the direction of whatever military force Congress provided in the hands of an independent President was precisely because the earlier system had been such a disaster.").

61. Jennings B. Sanders, *Evolution of Executive Departments of the Continental Congress 1774–1789,* at 6–7 (1935).

62. Jack N. Rakove, *The Beginnings of National Politics* 196 (1979). Palmer distinguishes among grand strategy, strategy, and tactics by using the example of the invasion of Canada during the war. "The decision to invade Canada was grand strategy, sending Benedict Arnold up the Kennebec River and Richard Montgomery up the Lake Champlain Route was strategy, and the final assault on the fortress of Quebec was tactics." David R. Palmer, "American Strategy Reconsidered," in *Military History of the American Revolution* 52–53 (S. Underdal ed., 1974). Although it is sometimes charged that the Continental Congress attempted regularly to direct the tactics of the Continental army, *see, e.g.*, Willard M. Wallace, *Appeal to Arms* 172 (1951), there is little evidence that this was the case. Indeed, distances and communications would have made any degree of tactical control by Congress quite impossible.

63. Jonathan G. Rossie, *The Politics of Command in the American Revolution* 15–16 (1975); Sofaer, *supra* note 49, at 21 & n.77.

64. Rakove, *supra* note 62, at 197 (quoting Thomas Burke).

65. E. Wayne Carp, *To Starve the Army at Pleasure* 19, 29, 32 (1984).

66. Sanders, *supra* note 61, at 4; Rakove, *supra* note 62, at 196.

67. Carp, *supra* note 65, at 22; Ferguson, *supra* note 47, at 27.

68. Higginbotham, *supra* note 45, at 82.

69. Frances V. Greene, *The Revolutionary War and the Military Policy of the United States* 288–93 (1911); Higginbotham, *supra* note 45, at 390–93.

70. Carp, *supra* note 65, at 59–60.

71. Marston, *supra* note 59, at 305.

72. *Quoted in id.* at 307.

73. Sanders, *supra* note 61, at 5, 11.

74. Ferguson, *supra* note 47, at 116 (1961); Marston, *supra* note 59, at 307; Sanders, *supra* note 61, at 5.

75. Rakove, *supra* note 62, at 196–97; Higginbotham, *supra* note 45, at 93; Sofaer, *supra* note 49, at 21 & n.78, 23 & n.90. *Cf. generally,* Rossie, *supra* note 63. Higginbotham argues that Congress's increasing deference to its military commanders was also due in part to the emergence of a broad consensus about the essentially defensive strategy of the war. Higginbotham, *supra* note 45, at 92.

76. Sofaer, *supra* note 49, at 20.

77. Marston, *supra* note 59, at 307–08.

78. Ferguson, *supra* note 47, at 46.

79. Carp, *supra* note 65, at 175.

80. Rakove, *supra* note 62, at 122–23; Higginbotham, *supra* note 45, at 295–96.

81. Carp, *supra* note 65, at 184; Higginbotham, *supra* note 45, at 296.

82. Carp, *supra* note 65, at 220. 3 *Elliot's Debates* 228 (Jonathan Elliot ed., 1836) (quoting John Marshall in the Virginia Convention) ("The inability of Congress, and the failure of states to comply with the constitutional requisitions, rendered our resistance less efficient than it might have been. The weakness of that government caused troops to be against us which might have been on our side, and prevented all resources of the community from being called at once into action.").

83. Rakove, *supra* note 62, at 277; Ferguson, *supra* note 47, at 57 *et seq.*

84. Carp, *supra* note 65, at 211–12.

85. Carp, *supra* note 65, at 214.

86. *See* Max Farrand, *The Framing of the Constitution* 220–21 (1913).

87. *Id.* at 211, 216. When an opponent of the constitutional power of direct taxation cited the quota provision of the Articles of Confederation as an alternative, John Marshall responded rhetorically by asking, "Suppose the states should refuse?" 3 *Elliot's Debates, supra* note 82, at 229.

88. Ferguson, *supra* note 47, at 124, 128, 131, 138.

89. Higginbotham, *supra* note 45, at 438.

90. Sanders, *supra* note 61, at 96.

91. Letter from George Washington to Alexander Hamilton (March 31, 1783), in 26 *The Writings of George Washington, 1745–1799,* at 277 (John C. Fitzpatrick ed., 1938).

92. Ferguson, *supra* note 47, at 27.

93. Rakove, *supra* note 62, at 205.

94. Ferguson, *supra* note 47, at 27.

95. *Quoted in* Marston, *supra* note 59, at 297. *See also* Sofaer, *supra* note 49, at 22 (quoting Washington on the need for secrecy and dispatch in oversight of the military), 22–23 (quoting Hamilton to same effect).

Chapter 3

1. *See* Stephen Dycus, Arthur L. Berney, William C. Banks & Peter Raven-Hansen, *National Security Law* 17–23 (1990).

2. Don Higginbotham, *The War of American Independence* 453 (1971).

3. The evolution of the clause can be traced at 2 *Records of the Federal Convention of 1787,* at 142, 167, 326, 326–27, 366, 392, 414, 493 (Max Farrand ed., 1911) [hereinafter *Records*]; 3 *id.* at 99, 483–484, 487.

4. Charles J. Cooper, "The Line-Item Veto: The Framers' Intentions," in *Pork*

Barrels and Principles: The Politics of the Presidential Veto 34 (National Legal Center for the Public Interest 1988).

5. James Madison, *Notes of Debates in the Federal Convention of 1787*, at 443 (1966).

6. *Id.* at 444.

7. Cooper, *supra* note 4, at 35 & n.8 (quoting also James McHenry's notes arguing against "lodging in the house of representatives the sole right of raising and appropriating money, upon which the Senate had only a negative," on the ground "[t]hat without equal powers they were not an equal check upon each other").

8. 2 *Records, supra* note 3, at 274–75.

9. *Id.* at 279. *See generally* Abraham D. Sofaer, *War, Foreign Affairs and Constitutional Power: The Origins* 30 (1976).

10. 2 *Records, supra* note 3, at 548.

11. *Id.*

12. Cooper, *supra* note 4, at 34–35.

13. 2 *Records, supra* note 3, at 505.

14. "Explanation," Nov. 11, 1795, in 8 *Works of Alexander Hamilton* 122, 128 (H. C. Lodge ed., 1885) (emphasis in original).

15. 2 *Records, supra* note 3, at 143.

16. *Id.* at 168.

17. *Id.* at 329–30.

18. *Id.* at 330. Mr. Williamson "reminded him of Mr. Mason's motion for limiting appropriation of revenue as the best guard in this case." *Id.* at 327, 330.

19. 3 *Records, supra* note 3, at 207. *See also* Bernard Donahoe & Marshall Smelser, "The Congressional Power to Raise Armies: The Constitutional and Ratifying Conventions, 1787–1788," 33 *Rev. of Pol.* 202, 204 (1971).

20. *See, e.g.*, Sofaer, *supra* note 9, at 25–38; W. Taylor Reveley III, *War Powers of the President and Congress* 74–115 (1981).

21. The debates, in fact, supply at best circumstantial evidence of the scope of the Commander-in-Chief Clause. The New Jersey Plan gave a plural executive the power "to direct all military operations" without the power to assume personal command. Max Farrand, *The Framing of the Constitution* 231 (1913). The designation of the president as commander in chief in the Constitution presumably incorporated at least this power of direction. Subsequently, when "make" was changed to "declare," Rufus King spoke in favor of the change because "'make' war might be understood to 'conduct' it which was an Executive function." 2 *Records, supra* note 3, at 318–19. George Mason also warned that if the legislature were given the power "to make and direct war, I shall agree to a restraining power of the Legislature either in the Executive or council of revision." 1 *Records, supra* note 3, at 144.

22. Sofaer, *supra* note 9, at 38.

23. 2 *Records, supra* note 3, at 540 (N. Gorham).

24. Sofaer, *supra* note 9, at 38.

25. The importance of the ratification debates to an understanding of the Constitution has been long recognized. As early as 1796, James Madison opined, "If we were to look . . . for the meaning of that instrument beyond the face of the instrument, we must look for it, not in the General Convention which proposed, but in the State Conventions which accepted and ratified it." *Quoted in* Charles Warren, *The Making of the Constitution* 794 (1937). Among the most comprehensive set of commentaries that influenced the debates are *The Federalist* papers, though their influence is arguably greater now than it was then. *See generally* Reveley, *supra* note 20, at 100–101; Sofaer, *supra* note 9, at 39.

26. The Appropriations Clause, on the other hand, was apparently not much debated. Indeed, *The Federalist* papers fail to mention it at all.

27. Jackson Turner Main, *The Antifederalists: Critics of the Constitution, 1781–1788,* at 144 (1961) (quoting Melancthon Smith at New York ratifying convention).

28. 3 *Elliot's Debates* 393 (J. Madison) (John Elliot ed. 1836). *See also* Donahoe & Smelser, *supra* note 19, at 209.

29. 2 *Elliot's Debates, supra* note 28, at 348–49.

30. *The Federalist* No. 26, at 169 (A. Hamilton) (C. Rossiter ed., 1961) (emphasis in original); 2 *Elliot's Debates, supra* note 28, at 98 (T. Dawes).

31. *The Federalist* No. 24, at 158 (A. Hamilton) (C. Rossiter ed., 1961).

32. *The Federalist* No. 26, at 170 (A. Hamilton) (C. Rossiter ed., 1961).

33. *The Federalist* No. 8, at 68 (A. Hamilton) (C. Rossiter ed., 1961).

34. *The Federalist* No. 58, at 359 (J. Madison) (C. Rossiter ed., 1961).

35. 3 *Elliot's Debates, supra* note 28, at 16–17 (W. Nicholas).

36. 4 *Elliot's Debates, supra* note 28, at 114 (R. Spaight in the North Carolina Convention). *See also id.* at 107–08 (J. Iredell); IV *id.* at 258 (C. Pinckney in South Carolina Convention); *The Federalist* No. 69, at 417–18 (A. Hamilton) (C. Rossiter ed., 1961); Donahoe & Smelser, *supra* note 19, at 208.

37. *The Federalist* No. 69, at 418 (A. Hamilton) (C. Rossiter ed., 1961) (emphasis in original).

38. 3 *Elliot's Debates, supra* note 28, at 498.

39. The power to maintain a navy was not an issue, because the navy posed no domestic threat to individual liberties or state independence and because the need for it to guard against foreign invasion was self-evident. "The palpable necessity of the power to provide and maintain a navy has protected that part of the Constitution against a spirit of censure which has spared few other parts." *The Federalist* No. 41, at 260 (J. Madison) (C. Rossiter ed., 1961).

40. *The Federalist* No. 26, at 171–72 (A. Hamilton) (C. Rossiter ed., 1961) (emphasis in original). *See also The Federalist* No. 41, at 259–60 (J. Madison) (C. Rossiter ed., 1961); Donahoe & Smelser, *supra* note 19, at 210.

41. *The Federalist* No. 26, at 172 (A. Hamilton) (C. Rossiter ed., 1961) (emphasis in original).

42. *See* Higginbotham, *supra* note 2, at 459 (summarizing nine proposed amendments).

43. *See* Reveley, *supra* note 20, at 330–31 n.3.

44. *Id.* at 105–06.

Chapter 4

1. *See, e.g.,* Burrow-Giles Lithographic Co. v. Sarony, 111 U.S. 53, 57 (1884) ("The construction placed upon the Constitution by the first act of 1790 and the act of 1802, by the men who were contemporary with its formation, many of whom were members of the convention which framed it, is of itself entitled to very great weight . . . .").

2. *See, e.g.,* Lucius Wilmerding, Jr., *The Spending Power* (1943) (the classic study on which all others rely); Abraham D. Sofaer, *War, Foreign Affairs and Constitutional Power: The Origins* (1976) (relating the appropriation history to war and foreign affairs); Gerhard Casper, "Appropriations of Power," 13 *U. Ark. Little Rock L.J.* 1 (1990) (tracing the appropriation power more generally through to the Jefferson administration).

3. 1 *Annals of Cong.* 894 (J. Gales ed., 1789). *See generally* Casper, *supra* note 2, at 9; Sofaer, *supra* note 2, at 70.

4. Act of Sept. 29, 1789, ch. 23, 1 Stat. 95.

5. *See* Wilmerding, *supra* note 2, at 21.

6. Wilmerding, *supra* note 2, at 21. Maclay's critique was leveled almost two hundred years later at omnibus continuing resolutions. *See infra* chap. 6.

7. *Id.* at 21–22.

8. *See* Casper, *supra* note 2, at 13; Wilmerding, *supra* note 2, at 23.

9. 3 *Annals of Cong.* 889–90 (1793). *See generally* Wilmerding, *supra* note 2, at 24.

10. Act of Feb. 28, 1793, ch. 28, 1 Stat. 325, 328.

11. Act of Nov. 29, 1794, ch. 1, 1 Stat. 403.

12. *See, e.g.*, Wilmerding, *supra* note 2, at 28; Casper, *supra* note 2, at 16; Sofaer, *supra* note 2, at 72, 118–19.

13. *Quoted in* Wilmerding, *supra* note 2, at 31.

14. *Quoted in id.*, at 29.

15. 5 *Annals of Cong.* 1481 (1796) (statement of Speaker J. Dayton).

16. 6 *Annals of Cong.* 2040–41 (1797) (statement of Rep. W. Smith).

17. 8 *Works of Alexander Hamilton* 256 (H. C. Lodge ed., 1885). *See generally* Wilmerding, *supra* note 2, at 51–52. Hamilton's use of forage for the army as an example is particularly interesting in light of the subsequent enactment and use of the feed and forage law. *See infra* chap. 8.

18. *Quoted in* Wilmerding, *supra* note 2, at 39.

19. 5 *Annals of Cong.* 1477 (1796).

20. In fairness to Gallatin, it should be noted that even he did not intend excessive detail in appropriations. "The most proper way would perhaps be not to enter so many details . . . but to divide the general appropriation under a few general heads only, allowing thereby sufficient latitude to the executive officers of government, but confining them strictly, in the expenditure under each of the general heads, to the sum appropriated by law." 3 *The Writings of Albert Gallatin* 117 (H. Adams ed., 1879, & photo reprint 1960), *quoted in* Casper, *supra* note 2, at 17 n.77.

21. 3 *Annals of Cong.* 900 (1793).

22. 5 *Annals of Cong.* 1499 (1796).

23. Act of March 3, 1797, ch. 17, 1 Stat. 508–09. This formula echoes early parliamentary formulae. *See* Casper, *supra* note 2, at 17 & n.76; *supra* chap. 1.

24. *Quoted in* Wilmerding, *supra* note 2, at 47 (quoting 2 George Gibbs, *Memoirs of the Administrations of Washington and John Adams* 45 (New York, w. Van Norden, 1846).

25. Casper, *supra* note 2, at 17.

26. Sofaer, *supra* note 2, at 74; Wilmerding, *supra* note 2, at 44–46.

27. Act of June 12, 1798, ch. 52, 1 Stat. 563. *See* Wilmerding, *supra* note 2, at 47–48; Casper, *supra* note 2, at 17–18.

28. *See* Act of May 7, 1800, ch. 47, 2 Stat. 62 and Act of March 3, 1801, ch. 27, 2 Stat. 117.

29. Wilmerding, *supra* note 2, at 48.

30. *See* 1 *Compilation of the Messages and Papers of the Presidents* 317 (James D. Richardson ed., 1897).

31. Sofaer, *supra* note 2, at 170–71.

32. Letter from Thomas Jefferson to Albert Gallatin, Feb. 19, 1804, in 11 *Writings of Thomas Jefferson* 6 (Memorial ed., 1907).

33. 15 *Annals of Cong.* 1021 (1806) (statement of Rep. R. Nelson).

34. *Id.*

35. Act of March 3, 1809, ch. 25, 2 Stat. 535.

36. *Id.*

37. Wilmerding, *supra* note 2, at 13.

38. Act of Feb. 11, 1791, ch. 6, 1 Stat. 190.

39. 3 *Annals of Cong.* 901 (1793) (statement of Rep. W. Smith).

40. 3 *Annals of Cong.* 922 (1793).

41. 11 *Annals of Cong.* 324 (1801).

42. 8 *Annals of Cong.* 1317 (1798).

43. Wilmerding, *supra* note 2, at 6, 19 (emphasis added). Although Wilmerding alludes to the president's "right" in cases of necessity, he elsewhere makes it clear that the law of necessity creates only a *power* or contingent authority subject to legislative ratification. *Id.* at 12, 19.

44. Letter from Alexander Hamilton to (Secretary of War) McHenry (Nov. 12, 1799), 7 *Works of Alexander Hamilton* 172 (H. C. Lodge ed., 1885) (emphasis added).

45. 3 *Annals of Cong.* 922 (1793).

46. 11 *Annals of Cong.* 324 (1801).

47. 1 *The Works of Thomas Jefferson* 415 (Paul L. Ford ed., 1904).

48. 1 *Compilation of the Messages and Papers of the Presidents* 416 (James D. Richardson ed., 1897).

49. Act of Nov. 24, 1807, ch. 1, 2 Stat. 450.

50. 5 *Writings of Thomas Jefferson* 544 (H. A. Washington ed., 1853–54).

51. *Cf.* Wilmerding, *supra* note 2, at 15.

52. Even John Randolph, on the outs with Jefferson and opposed to his unauthorized spending in the *Chesapeake* case, grudgingly voted for the *ex post facto* appropriation in the end, likening his position to that of a husband with a spendthrift wife or a man paying a gambling debt to a swindler. 17 *Annals of Cong.* 825, 850, 852–53 (1807).

Part II

1. *See* Allen Schick, *Legislation, Appropriations, and Budgets: The Development of Spending Decision-Making in Congress* 6–26 (Cong. Res. Serv. No. 84-106) (1984).

Chapter 5

1. *See* U.S. General Accounting Office, *Principles of Federal Appropriations Law* 1-2 (2d ed. 1991) [hereinafter *Appropriations Principles*] (defining the "congressional power of the purse" as "the power of Congress to appropriate funds and to prescribe conditions governing the use of those funds").

2. U.S. General Accounting Office, *A Glossary of Terms Used in the Federal Budget Process* 39 (1981) [hereinafter *Glossary*].

3. *Appropriation Principles, supra* note 1, at 2-33.

4. 36 Comp. Gen. 240, 242 (1956). The absence of a constitutional distinction between authorization and appropriation has been found to permit appropriating without any authorizing legislation, although this practice is exceptional. Louis Fisher, "The Authorization-Appropriation Process in Congress: Formal Rules and Informal Practices," 29 *Cath. U. L. Rev.* 51, 63–64 (1979).

5. *Glossary, supra* note 2, at 42.

6. *Id.* at 39; *Appropriations Principles, supra* note 1, at 2-42 to 2-43.

7. *See Jefferson's Manual: Rules of the House of Representatives of the United States*, H.R. Doc. No. 256, 101st Cong., 2d Sess. § 843 (1991) [hereinafter *House Rules*]; *see also* Allen Schick, *Legislation, Appropriations, and Budgets. The Development of Spending Decision-Making in Congress* 14 (Cong. Res. Serv. No. 84-106) (1984).

8. *House Rules, supra* note 7, at Rule 21, cls. 2 & 5; S. Doc. No. 1, 101st Cong., 1st Sess. 15, Rule 16, cls. 1, 2 & 4 [hereinafter *Senate Rules*]. The applicability of the rules "is exclusively within the province" of the House and Senate. *Appropriations Principles, supra* note 1, at 1-18. The effect of the rules or any statute that provides that it shall not be in order to consider a bill containing a certain item is to subject the objectionable proposal to a "point of order."

A point of order is a procedural objection raised by a member alleging a departure from a rule or statute governing the conduct of business. It differs from an absolute prohibition in that (a) it is always possible that no one will raise it and (b) if raised, it may or may not be sustained. Also, some measure may be considered under special resolutions waiving points of order. If a point of order is raised and sustained, the offending provision is effectively killed, and may be revived only if it is amended to cure the noncompliance. *Id.* If a point of order is raised and not sustained, an enacted provision is "no less valid." *Id.*

9. *Appropriations Principles, supra* note 1, at 1-17.

10. *See id.* at 2-28; *cf.* Kate Stith, "Congress' Power of the Purse," 97 *Yale L.J.* 1343, 1362 (1988).

11. *See Appropriations Principles, supra* note 1, at 1-9 (suggesting that a rider is *any* substantive legislative provision attached to an appropriation bill).

12. *See* Neal E. Devins, "Regulation of Government Agencies Through Limitations Riders," 1987 *Duke L.J.* 456; Susan L. Bloch, "Orphaned Rules in the Administrative State: The Fairness Doctrine and Other Orphaned Progeny of Interactive Deregulation," 76 *Geo. L.J.* 59, 112 & n.112 (1987) (referring to a *limitation rider* as both an addition to and a provision of an appropriation bill); Fisher, *supra* note 4, at 78–81 (using *limitation rider* and *appropriation rider* interchangeably to refer to any amendment tacked to an appropriation bill).

13. The following description of the national security appropriations process is based primarily on Louis Fisher, *The Politics of Shared Power* 178–97 (3d ed. 1993); Fisher, *supra* note 4, at 52–53; *Appropriations Principles, supra* note 1, at 1-18 to -19; Walter Oleszek, *Congressional Procedures and the Policy Process* 47–80 (3d ed. 1989); Schick, *supra* note 7, at 1–5.

14. A statute defines "intelligence community" to include:

> (A) the Office of the Director of Central Intelligence, which shall include the Office of the Deputy Director of Central Intelligence, the National Intelligence Council (as provided for in section 105(b)(3)), and such other offices as the Director may designate;
> (B) the Central Intelligence Agency;
> (C) the National Security Agency;
> (D) the Defense Intelligence Agency;
> (E) the central imagery authority within the Department of Defense;
> (F) the National Reconnaissance Office;
> (G) other offices within the Department of Defense for the collection of specialized national intelligence through reconnaissance programs;
> (H) the intelligence elements of the Army, the Navy, the Air Force, the

Marine Corps, the Federal Bureau of Investigation, the Department of the Treasury, and the Department of Energy;

(I) the Bureau of Intelligence and Research of the Department of State; and

(J) such other elements of any other department or agency as may be designated by the President, or designated jointly by the Director of Central Intelligence and the head of the department or agency concerned, as an element of the intlligence community.

Intelligence Organization Act of 1992, Pub. L. No. 102–496, § 702, 106 Stat. 3188.

Funding for the intelligence function is not a product of the traditional authorization-appropriation process. It will be separately examined later in this chapter.

15. *See generally* Fisher, *supra* note 4; Schick, *supra* note 7.

16. U.S. Const. art. I, § 1. ("All legislative powers herein granted shall be vested in a Congress of the United States . . ."). *But see infra* chap. 11.

17. Schick, *supra* note 7, at 6.

18. *Id.*

19. Act of Sept. 29, 1789, ch. 23, 1 Stat. 95, *quoted supra* chap. 4 in text accompanying note 4.

20. Schick, *supra* note 7, at 7. Appropriations must be spent within the time period specified by Congress. 31 U.S.C. § 1502 (1988). In addition, the Constitution states that army appropriations must be limited to two years. U.S. Const., art. I, § 8, cl. 12. The object limitation has also been codified: "[a]ppropriations shall be applied only to the objects for which the appropriations were made except as otherwise provided by law." 31 U.S.C. § 1301(a) (1988).

21. Act of Aug. 17, 1789, 1 Stat. 49.

22. Gerhard Casper, "Appropriations of Power," 13 *U. Ark. Little Rock L.J.* 1, 8–9 (1990).

23. *Id.* at 7–10. Procedurally, appropriation bills were, also by custom, first considered by the House, where the Committee of the Whole considered the bills with the items to be funded specified, but with no funding levels set. The House then "filled in the blanks" for each line item. Later the Ways and Means Committee reported both appropriations and taxation bills, as did the Senate Finance Committee. In the Senate, appropriation bills were sometimes assigned to the authorizing committee, until the Finance Committee gained complete control over them in the 1830s. Schick, *supra* note 7, at 10; Fisher, *supra* note 4, at 54.

24. *See* Casper, *supra* note 22, at 11–18.

25. In 1790, when an attempt was made from the House floor to amend the appropriation bill to reimburse Charleston, South Carolina, for lighthouse expenses, the proposal was defeated with the admonition that the bill under consideration was "a bill of appropriations, and not of grants." 2 *Annals of Cong.* 1450 (1790) (statement of Rep. Bland).

26. Act of April 29, 1816, 3 Stat. 321; *see also* Act of May 8, 1792, 1 Stat. 284 (appropriating money to support an additional regiment).

27. Act of Feb. 21, 1825, 4 Stat. 83; *see also* 4 Stat. 84 (naval appropriation); 4 Stat. 91 (appropriation for support of the government).

28. *See* Schick, *supra* note 7, at 15.

29. The 1837 House rule stated: "No appropriation shall be reported in such general appropriation bills, or be in order as an amendment thereto, for any expenditure not previously authorized by law." "Rules & Orders of the House," Rule 59, *Cong. Globe,* 25th Cong., 1st Sess. 31 (1837). Congress continued to legislate in appropriation bills

throughout the 1840s, in part because the rule against riders applied only to the House. Because the Senate had no general germaneness rule, it could attach nongermane riders to appropriations. As senators increasingly exploited their advantage with private additions to spending bills, the Senate adopted a rule less restrictive than the House rule in 1850, then weakened it further in 1852 and 1854 to permit unauthorized appropriations "moved by direction of a standing (or select) committee of the Senate." While the Senate rule permitted it to retain an advantage over the House in reviewing House-passed appropriations, the combination of the Senate's unlimited debate tradition and the growing complexity of appropriations led to delays in passing needed appropriations. In 1877, the Senate adopted a rule expressly forbidding legislation in appropriation bills. *See* Schick, *supra* note 7, at 18. Its current text reads: "The Committee on Appropriations shall not report an appropriation bill containing amendments to such bill proposing new or general legislation or any restriction on the expenditure of funds appropriated which proposes a limitation not authorized by law if such restriction is to take effect or cease to be effective upon the happening of a contingency, and if an appropriation bill is reported to the Senate containing amendments to such bill proposing new or general legislation or any such restriction, a point of order may be made against the bill, and if the point is sustained, the bill shall be recommitted to the Committee on Appropriations." *See Senate Rules, supra* note 8, at Rule 16, cl. 3.

30. *See* Schick, *supra* note 7, at 18–19.

31. Fisher, *supra* note 4, at 55.

32. *Id.*

33. *Id.* at 57; Schick, *supra* note 7, at 19–20.

34. Schick, *supra* note 7, at 21; for the current version of the Holman rule, *see House Rules, supra* note 7, at Rule 21, cl. 2. Such a rider would have been a limitations rider in any event.

35. 20 Stat. 152 (1878); *see* Edward C. Mason, *The Veto Power: Its Origin, Development, and Function* 48 (1967).

36. Schick, *supra* note 7, at 23–26. By one count, there were 387 riders to appropriation bills between 1862 and 1875. Horace Davis, *American Constitutions* 30 (3d series 1885) *quoted in,* Mason, *supra* note 35, at 48 n.4. Among them was a rider curtailing President Andrew Johnson's commander-in-chief war powers. *Id.* at 48 n.1.

37. Schick, *supra* note 7, at 26; *see, e.g.*, naval contingency appropriation: "For all emergencies and extraordinary expenses, exclusive of personal services in the Navy Department, or any of its subordinate bureaus or offices at Washington, District of Columbia, arising at home or abroad, but impossible to be anticipated or classified, to be expended on the approval and the authority of the Secretary of the Navy, and for such purposes as he may deem proper . . . ." Act of Aug. 29, 1916, Pub. L. No. 64-241, 39 Stat. 556. *See also* army contingency appropriation: "For all contingent expenses of the Army not otherwise provided for and embracing all branches of the military service, including the office of the Chief of Staff; for all emergencies and extraordinary expenses, including the employment of translators and exclusive of all other personal services in the War Department, or any of its subordinate bureaus or offices in Washington, District of Columbia, or in the Army at large, but impossible to be anticipated or classified; to be expended on the approval and authority of the Secretary of War, and for such purposes as he may deem proper . . . ." Act of Aug. 29, 1916, Pub. L. No. 64-242, 39 Stat. 620.

38. Budget and Accounting Act of 1921, ch. 18, 42 Stat. 20.

39. Schick, *supra* note 7, at 27.

40. *Id.*; *Senate Rules, supra* note 8, at Rule 16, cl. 2. The rule provided that the

bill would be recommitted to committee if a point of order was sustained against the bill. *Id.*

41. *See* 31 U.S.C. §§ 1104, 1105 (1988 & Supp. III 1991). The authority of agencies to submit their own budget proposals was also restricted.

42. *Id.*, tit. 3, 31 U.S.C. §§ 3000 *et seq.* (1988 & Supp. II 1990).

43. Schick, *supra* note 7, at 30–32. Exceptions to the rule included construction projects and grant-in-aid programs, which usually were authorized for definite amounts for fixed periods of time. *Id.* at 30.

44. *Id.* at 38. Virtually all defense activities now have annual authorizations. *See* Louis Fisher, "Annual Authorizations: Durable Roadblocks to Biennial Budgeting," 3 *Pub. Budget & Fin.* Spring 1983, at 23, 26–30. The share of the defense budget requiring annual authorization grew from 2 percent in 1961, to 31 percent in 1971, to 100 percent in 1983. Center for Strategic & Int'l Studies, *Congressional Oversight of National Security* 13 (1992) [hereinafter *Congressional Oversight*].

45. Schick, *supra* note 7, at 38–39.

46. *Id.* at 38–40. The annual authorizations have sometimes been used to influence the appropriation process and the spending practices of agencies. Congress converted the State Department to an annual authorization after the Vietnam War, and did the same to the Justice Department and intelligence agencies after Watergate. *Id.* at 39. According to the Center for Strategic and International Studies, "the overall effect of annual authorizations and appropriations has been to intensify the rivalry among the Committees on Armed Services, the Budget, and Appropriations in each house over control of defense policy." *Congressional Oversight, supra* note 44, at 13.

47. Pub. L. No. 93-344, 88 Stat. 297 (codified as amended at 2 U.S.C. § 621 *et. seq.* (1988 & Supp. III 1991)). [hereinafter 1974 Act].

48. Pub. L. No. 99-177, 99 Stat. 1038, (codified as amended at 2 U.S.C. § 901 (1988 & Supp. III 1991)) [hereinafter Balanced Budget Act].

49. Pub. L. No. 101-508, § 13101, 104 Stat. 1388, 2 U.S.C. § 601 *et. seq.* (Supp. III 1991) [hereinafter BEA].

50. 1974 Act, *supra* note 47, §§ 101–102, 88 Stat. at 299–302.

51. *Id.*, §§ 201–203, 88 Stat. at 302–05.

52. Schick, *supra* note 7, at 41–43.

53. BEA, *supra* note 49, 2 U.S.C. § 631 (1988 & Supp. III 1991).

54. *Id.*, 2 U.S.C. § 602(f) (1988).

55. *Id.*, 2 U.S.C. § 632(a) (1988 & Supp III 1991).

56. *Id.*, 2 U.S.C. § 632(a)(1)–(4) (1988 & Supp. III 1991). "Reconciliation" legislation must then be passed if individual spending decisions do not match the totals in the second (September 15) binding budget resolution. The reconciliation measures instruct the relevant committees to find savings or additional revenues to meet the resolution. Schick, *supra* note 7, at 43.

The April budget resolution became the key document in the process after 1974, and its status was further elevated when the second resolution was scrapped. The second resolution was informally abandoned in the early 1980s when the first resolution was revealed as "the fundamental vehicle of congressional budgeting." Oleszek, *supra* note 13, at 62. The change was codified in 1985. *See* Balanced Budget Act, *supra* note 48, § 242(a), 2 U.S.C § 901 (1988 & Supp. III 1991).

57. *Id.*, § 301, 2 U.S.C. § 632 (1988 & Supp. III 1991).

58. There is a fifty-hour statutory limit on debate, and amendments are subject to a germaneness requirement. These rules are permitted by § 301(b)(4), 2 U.S.C. § 636

(1988 Supp. III 1991), which authorizes "any other procedure which is considered appropriate to carry out the purposes of this Act."

59. Balanced Budget Act, *supra* note 48, § 251(b), 2 U.S.C. § 901(a)(7) (1988 & Supp. III 1991).

60. 1974 Act, *supra* note 47, § 302, 2 U.S.C. § 633(a) (1988 & Supp. III 1991); *see also* Oleszek, *supra* note 13, at 61–63.

61. Schick, *supra* note 7, at 41–44. Fisher, *supra* note 4, at 103.

62. Oleszek, *supra* note 13, at 61–63.

63. *See* Balanced Budget Act, *supra* note 48.

64. Oleszek, *supra* note 13, at 66–67.

65. Pub. L. No. 100-119, 101 Stat. 784 (1987).

66. *See* BEA, *supra* note 49.

67. *Id.* at § 13101, 2 U.S.C. § 906(b) (1988 & Supp. III 1991).

68. *Id.*, 2 U.S.C. § 901(a) (1988 & Supp. III 1991).

69. *Id.*, 2 U.S.C. § 901(a)(3) (1988 & Supp. III 1991).

70. *See* 49 *Cong. Q. Weekly Rep.* 1110 (May 4, 1991). For example, in considering weapons programs, the subcommittees often recommend trimming or adding to the budget on various items, based on independent estimates of cost or production schedules. For 1992, after subcommittee review, the defense appropriations subcommittees trimmed the $560 million authorized for the F-117 stealth fighter. 44 *Cong. Q. Weekly Rep.* 53–54 (Dec. 7, 1991).

71. 49 *Cong. Q. Weekly Rep.* 1435 (June 1, 1991).

72. *See* Pub. L. No. 101-508, 104 Stat. 1388 (1991).

73. Both OMB and CBO must prepare and submit sequester reports by specified dates. CBO submits its report to Congress and the OMB. Five days after the transmission of the CBO reports, OMB submits its report to the president and Congress. OMB reports are then used to determine if a sequester is required, and if so, the OMB report serves as a basis for sequestration orders. Further, OMB reports must include an explanation of the differences between the OMB and CBO calculations. *See* BEA, *supra* note 49, 2 U.S.C. § 901(a)(7) (1988 & Supp. III. 1991).

74. *Wash. Post,* natl. weekly ed., July 22–28, 1991, at 13. The House passed the 1992 defense appropriations bill on June 7, 1991, H.R. 2521, 102d Cong., 1st Sess. (1991), while the Senate delayed final action until Sept. 26, 1991. S. Rep. No. 154, 102d Cong., 1st Sess. (1991); *see* Pub. L. No. 102-172, 105 Stat. 1150 (1991).

75. 49 *Cong. Q. Weekly Rep.* 3113 (Oct. 26, 1991).

76. Act of April 17, 1876, 19 Stat. 65.

77. Robert A. Keith, *An Overview of Continuing Resolutions* 5–8 (Cong. Res. Serv. 1980).

78. Neal E. Devins, "Appropriations Redux: A Critical Look at the Fiscal Year 1988 Continuing Resolution," 1988 *Duke L.J.* 389, 392–96; General Accounting Office, *Continuing Resolutions and an Assessment of Automatic Funding Approaches*, GAO/AFIND 86-16, Jan. 1986 [hereinafter GAO, *Continuing Resolutions*].

79. Devins, *supra* note 78, at 393; Schick, *supra* note 7, at 58–59; Oleszek, *supra* note 13, at 74.

80. *See House Rules, supra* note 7, at Rule 21; *see also* GAO, *Continuing Resolutions supra* note 77, at 11. Amendments to continuing resolutions must be germane. The House Rules Committee has also unevenly imposed special rules limiting the amendments that may be offered to continuing resolutions. While the Senate does consider continuing resolutions to be general appropriations bills, to which its rule against riders

(Rule 16, cl. 1) applies, the Senate has asserted an inherent right to amend the House version when the House has acted first to add a rider to an appropriation. *Id.*

81. Committee on the Budget, U.S. House of Representatives, *The Whole and the Parts: Piecemeal and Integrated Approaches to Congressional Budgeting* 37–39 (1987).

82. *Id.*

83. There are several officially secret federal programs that spend appropriated funds. While interest in the oversight and growth of black or special access programs has emerged in recent years, *see* Alice C. Maroni, *Special Access Programs and the Defense Budget: Understanding the "Black Budget,"* Cong. Res. Serv., IB87201, updated Oct. 24, 1989, and Congress has established reporting and justification requirements for some DOD black budget programs, Pub. L. No. 100-180, 101 Stat. 1150–53 (1987); Pub. L. No. 100-456, 102 Stat. 1918 (1988), an assessment of the full panoply of black budget programs is beyond the scope of this book. We focus on the National Foreign Intelligence Program.

84. Act of June 20, 1949, ch. 227, § 45, 63 Stat. 211, (codified as amended at 50 U.S.C. § 403(f) (1988 & Supp. III 1991)).

85. In recent years, the transfers have apparently been from the DOD budget. H.R. Rep. No. 1033, 99th Cong., 2d Sess. 2 (1986).

86. Maroni, *supra* note 83, at 3.

87. Other committees may review portions of the NFIP budget (e.g., Judiciary may review the FBI budget). *Id.* Former Director of the Central Intelligence Agency Robert Gates criticized the "conflicts between the authorizing committees and the appropriating committees . . . [because] the disparity in their respective legislation are imposing a great cost on the intelligence community." "Gates on Oversight," *ABA Natl. Sec. L. Rptr.* 1, 5 (Feb. 1993). Gates noted that, in contrast to the traditional willingness of the defense appropriations subcommittees to defer to the intelligence committees, recent years have produced statutes with different and sometimes inconsistent requirements: "when the appropriators tell us to do one thing and the intelligence committees have not acted or disagree we are paralyzed, caught in the middle." *Id.* at 4.

88. The appropriation detail is primarily contained in a classified annex to the defense appropriations bill. All members of Congress may see the annex. Pub. L. No. 102-172, § 8035, 105 Stat. 1150 (1991). The informal relationship between the congressional committees and black budget spending changed in 1990 when Congress stated that the classified annex of appropriations for secret programs, including spending instructions, "shall have the force and effect of law." Department of Defense Appropriations Act, Pub. L. No. 101-511, § 811(a), 104 Stat. 1856, 1904 (1991); *see also* Department of Defense Appropriations Act, Pub. L. No. 102-172, § 8124, 105 Stat. 1206 (1992) (stating that classified annex "is hereby incorporated into this Act").

89. *See* Intelligence Authorization Act for Fiscal Year 1991, H.R. Rep. No. 928, 101st Cong., 2d Sess., at 25–31 (1989).

90. Intelligence Authorization Act for Fiscal Year 1991, S2834, 101st Cong., 2d Sess. (1990).

91. Memorandum of Disapproval for the Intelligence Authorization Act, Fiscal Year 1991, 26 *Weekly Comp. Pres. Doc.* 1958–1959 (Nov. 30, 1990).

92. Pub. L. No. 99-169, § 401(a), 99 Stat. 1004, (codified as amended at 50 U.S.C. § 414 (1988 & Supp. III 1991)).

93. *Wash. Post,* Dec. 6, 1990, at A21.

94. H.R. 2038, 102d Cong., 1st Sess. (1991); H.R. Rep. No. 65, 102d Cong., 1st Sess. (1991); S. Rep. No. 172, 102d Cong., 1st Sess. 2 (1991).

95. Intelligence Authorization Act, Fiscal Year 1992, Pub. L. No. 102-183, § 701, 105 Stat. 1260, 1270 (1991); Intelligence Authorization Act for Fiscal Year 1993, Pub. L. No. 102-496, § 303, 106 Stat. 3180, 3183 (1992).

Chapter 6

1. *See* Edward C. Mason, *The Veto Power: Its Origin, Development, and Function* 47–49 (1967). In 1849 the Senate unsuccessfully sought to attach a rider to an appropriation bill that would have extended the Constitution and revenue laws to the newly acquired Mexican territory. In 1856 the House failed in an attempt to add a rider to an army appropriation that would have forbidden the use of federal troops for the enforcement of territorial law in Kansas. *Id.* at 48 n.1.

2. *Id.* at 48.

3. *See* discussion of the post–Civil War period in chap. 5.

4. Eli E. Nobleman, "Financial Aspects of Congressional Participation in Foreign Relations," 289 *Annals of Amer. Academy of Pol. & Soc. Sci.* 145, 150–55 (1953) (detailing attempts at prescribing defense restrictions in 1818, 1826, 1837, 1842 and 1867) [hereinafter *Annals*]. In 1912 Senator Bacon sought to amend the army appropriation bill to provide that, with certain exceptions, none of the funds appropriated by the bill should be used "for the pay of supplies or any part of the territory beyond the jurisdiction of the laws of the United States, or in going to or returning from points within the same." 48 *Cong. Rec.* 10921–30 (1912). When an objection was made that the amendments would encroach upon the president's commander-in-chief powers, the proposal was defeated without a record vote. 289 *Annals* at 154.

5. Albert Castel, *The Presidency of Andrew Johnson* 113 (1979); James E. Sefton, *Andrew Johnson and the Uses of Constitutional Power* 148–49 (1980). Johnson had earlier attempted to send Grant and the army to Mexico and he had "suggested" that Grant arm the Virginia militia. Grant ignored the suggestion. Castel, *supra,* at 113.

6. Act of Mar. 2, 1867, ch. 170, §§ 2, 6, 14 Stat. 485, 486–87.

7. Castel, *supra* note 5, at 113–14. Johnson did not know of Stanton's role in drafting the riders. Nor were the Republicans sure of Grant's political leanings, though they counted on him to check any hostile actions by Johnson. *Id. See also* Sefton, *supra* note 5, at 149.

8. Act of June 18, 1878, § 14, 20 Stat. 152.

9. Nobleman, *supra* note 4, 289 *Annals* at 155.

10. *Id.*

11. Act of Aug. 29, 1916, 39 Stat. 618.

12. Nobleman, *supra* note 4, 289 *Annals* at 155.

13. *Id.*

14. *Id.* at 155–56.

15. *Id.* at 158–63. The foreign aid limits are enacted pursuant to Congress's general spending power. *See generally,* Kate Stith, "Congress' Power of the Purse," 97 *Yale L.J.* 1343, 1360–61 nn.83–86 (1988).

16. Supplemental Foreign Assistance Authorization of 1971, Pub. L. No. 91-652, § 7, 85 Stat. 1942, 1943.

17. Pub. L. No. 93-189, § 30, 80 Stat. 714 (1973) ("[N]o funds authorized or appropriated under this or any other law may be expended to finance military or paramilitary operations by the United States in or over Vietnam, Laos, or Cambodia.").

18. Department of Defense Appropriations Authorization Act of 1975, Pub. L. No.

93-437, § 839, 88 Stat. 1212, 1231; Department of Defense Appropriations Act of 1974, Pub. L. No. 93-238, 87 Stat. 1026 (1973).

19. Department of State Appropriations Authorization Act of 1973, Pub. L. No. 93-126, § 13, 87 Stat. 454 (1973).

20. Continuing Appropriations Resolution of 1974, Pub. L. No. 93-52, § 107, 87 Stat. 130 (1973).

21. Fulbright Amendment to Second Supplemental Appropriations Act, 1973, Pub. L. No. 93-50, § 307, 87 Stat. 129 (1973).

22. Pub. L. No. 93-559, § 32, 88 Stat. 1795, 1804–1805 (1974).

23. President Ford ignored these funding restrictions when he deployed U.S. armed forces to evacuate American personnel from Cambodia and Vietnam and to rescue the crew of the *Mayaguez. See* Michael J. Glennon, "Strengthening the War Powers Resolution: The Case for Pursestrings Restrictions" 60 *Minn. L. Rev.* 1, 21–22 (1975).

24. *See* Clark Amendment to the Arms Export Control Act of 1976, Pub. L. No. 94-329, § 404, 90 Stat. 729, 757–58 (1976), *as amended by* Pub. L. No. 96-533, tit. 1. § 118(a)–(d), 94 Stat. 3141.

25. Pub. L. No. 99-83, 99 Stat. 279 (1985).

26. *See Jefferson's Manual: Rules of the House of Representatives of the United States,* H.R. Doc. No. 256, 101st Cong., 2d Sess. at Rule 21, cl. 3 (1991) [hereinafter *House Rules*]; S. Doc. No. 1, 101st. Cong., 1st Sess. at Rule 16 (1991) [hereinafter *Senate Rules*].

27. *See House Rules, supra* note 26, at Rule 21, cl. 5.

28. *See* Louis Fisher, "The Authorization-Appropriation Process in Congress: Formal Rules and Informal Practices," 29 *Cath. U. L. Rev.* 51, 61–65 (1979).

29. 36 Comp. Gen. 240, 242 (1956).

30. *House Rules, supra* note 26, at Rule 21, cl. 2.

31. *Id.* at cl. 5.

32. *Senate Rules, supra* note 26, at Rule 16.

33. *Id.* at cl. 4.

34. *Id.*

35. *Id.*

36. *See* Thomas Eagleton, *War and Presidential Power: A Chronicle of Congressional Surrender* 160–61 (1974).

37. 119 *Cong. Rec.* 17124–25 (1973).

38. 119 *Cong. Rec.* 17140 (1973). A point of order may still be heard after germaneness has been raised if a senator moves to lay the question of germaneness on the table. *See* Fisher, *supra* note 28, at 93.

39. Fisher, *supra* note 28, at 67.

40. Appropriations bills also pass through nonstatutory controls exercised informally by the committees. *Id.* at 87–88; *House Rules, supra* note 26, at Rule 21, cl. 3; *Senate Rules, supra* note 26, at Rule 16, cl. 8; *see* discussion of nonstatutory controls, *infra,* chap. 7.

41. *See* Fisher, *supra* note 28, at 70–71.

42. *Id.* at 67.

43. *Id.* at 70–71.

44. *Id.* at 93–94. The rules of the Senate may be suspended by a two-thirds vote to permit legislation in an appropriation bill, although the House rules do not permit suspension for this purpose. However, the House, unlike the Senate, may adopt a special rule waiving points of order that would otherwise lie against an appropriation bill. Such a special rule does not protect floor amendments. *Id.*

45. *See Senate Rules, supra* note 26, at Rule 16.

46. *See* Neal E. Devins, "Regulation of Government Agencies Through Limitations Riders," 1987 *Duke L.J.* 456, 469–71. *See also House Rules, supra* note 26, at Rule 21 (continuing resolution is not a "general appropriations bill").

47. Devins, *supra* note 46, at 469–71; *see also* Richard C. Sachs, *Limitation Amendments to Appropriation Bills: The Implementation of House Rules XXI(2)(d) in the Ninety-Eighth Congress* (Cong. Res. Serv. 1984); Stanley I. Bach, *The Status of Limitation Amendments Under the Rules of the House of Representatives for the 98th Congress* (Cong. Res. Serv. 1983).

48. *See generally* Devins, *supra* note 46.

49. Allen Schick, *Legislation, Appropriations, and Budgets: The Development of Spending Decision-Making in Congress* 70 (Cong. Res. Serv. No. 84-106) (1984).

50. Pub. L. No. 96-257, (*repealed by* Pub. L. No. 96-533, Title II, § 202, 94 Stat. 3142 (1980)).

51. *Report of the Congressional Comm. Investigating the Iran-Contra Affair*, S. Rep. No. 100-216, H.R. Rep. No. 100-433, 100th Cong., 1st Sess. 259 (1987) [hereinafter *Iran-Contra Report*].

52. Funding for the CIA is assessed *infra* chap. 10.

53. Intelligence Authorization Act for Fiscal Year 1983, Pub. L. No. 97-269, 96 Stat. 1142 (1982). The amendment was known by its sponsor, Edward P. Boland (D., Mass.).

54. Defense Appropriation Act for Fiscal Year 1983, Pub. L. No. 97-377, § 793, 96 Stat. 1833, 1865 (1982).

55. *Id.*

56. *Iran-Contra Report, supra* note 51, at 396–97.

57. *Id.* at 396.

58. Department of Defense Appropriations Act for Fiscal Year 1984, Pub. L. No. 98-212, 97 Stat. 1421 (1983).

59. Intelligence Authorization Act for Fiscal Year 1984, Pub. L. No. 98-213, § 108, 97 Stat. 1473, 1475 (1983).

60. *Id.*

61. *Id.* § 109, 97 Stat. 1476.

62. H.R.J. Res. 492, 98th Cong., 2d Sess., 130 *Cong. Rec.* S3472 (1984).

63. *Iran-Contra Report, supra* note 51, at 37.

64. For more detail on the enactment of this continuing resolution, *see* Edward M. Davis & Robert A. Keith, *Summary and Legislative History of Public Law 98-473: Continuing Appropriations for Fiscal Year 1985* (*H.R.J. Res. 648*) (Cong. Res. Serv. 1984).

65. Department of Defense Appropriations Act for Fiscal Year 1985, Pub. L. No. 98-473, § 8066, 98 Stat. 1837, 1935–36 (1984); Intelligence Authorization Act for Fiscal Year 1985, Pub. L. No. 98-618, § 801, 98 Stat. 3298, 3304 (1984).

66. *See* Davis & Keith, *supra* note 64, at 55.

67. *Iran-Contra Report, supra* note 51, at 406.

68. *Id.* at 395.

69. *Id.* at 395–410. For discussion of the contingency and discretionary funds, *see infra* chap. 8.

70. *See, e.g.*, Devins, *supra* note 46, at 464. During conference committee deliberations on the 1992 Defense Appropriation bill, Senator Ted Stevens sought to add a provision to the bill which would have gutted a post-Iran-Contra reform and deprived the intelligence committees of a significant portion of their oversight jurisdiction over intelligence activities conducted by the president. Stevens's proposal had not been

offered or considered in the House or Senate. Further, the conference session in question was attended by only the few conference committee members. In the end Stevens withdrew his proposal after several Intelligence Committee members objected to even considering such a significant and controversial proposal in the conference. "Secret Effort to Weaken Intelligence Oversight Rebuffed," 17 *First Principles* 10 (Jan./Feb. 1993).

71. Fisher, *supra* note 28, at 79.

72. Devins, *supra* note 46, at 464.

73. *Id.* at 464–65; Fisher, *supra* note 28, at 85–86; Walter Oleszek, *Congressional Procedures and the Policy Process* 74–76 (3d ed. 1989); Jeffrey A. Meyer, "Congressional Control of Foreign Assistance," 13 *Yale J. Int'l. L.* 69, 136–38 (1988).

74. Meyer, *supra* note 73, at 97 n.142.

75. *See* Oleszek, *supra* note 73, at 60 (assessing House and Senate differences regarding expertise on the Budget Committees).

76. *But see* Neal E. Devins, "Appropriations Redux: A Critical Look at the Fiscal Year 1988 Continuing Resolution," 1988 *Duke L.J.* 389, 421 (concluding that the "necessary compromise" made possible by continuing resolutions comes at "too high a price" to democracy).

Chapter 7

1. We consider reprogramming, a modern incarnation of nonstatutory controls on spending discretion, *infra* chap. 8.

2. Elias E. Huzar, *The Purse and the Sword* 354 (1950).

3. *See* Michael W. Kirst, *Government Without Passing Laws: Congress' Nonstatutory Techniques for Appropriations Control* 6 (1969).

4. *Id.* at 58–61.

5. Huzar, *supra* note 2, at 354. Huzar quotes a response by a senator to a DOD official who suggested statutory language to resolve a funding question: "Well, I do not think it is necessary to put in those words. If we just increased the amount and earmarked it in the [committee] report, I think it would be all right." *Id.*

6. *See* Louis Fisher, *Presidential Spending Power* 75–77 (1975); Huzar, *supra* note 2, at 354–59.

7. Huzar, *supra* note 2, at 18–20.

8. S. Rep. No. 303, 85th Cong., 1st Sess., at 9–10; *see also* H.R. Rep. No. 439, 88th Cong., 1st Sess., at 55 (urging committee caution in Defense Department development of a communications satellite).

9. Kirst, *supra* note 3, at 83.

10. H.R. Rep. No. 1607, 87th Cong., 2d Sess. 38 (1962).

11. *See* Kirst, *supra* note 3, at 91–92.

12. This case study is developed further later in this chapter.

13. David Hoffman, "Is There a Deal-Maker in the White House?," *Wash. Post*, Mar. 26, 1989, at A10.

14. *Id.*

15. "Bipartisan Accords on Central America," 25 *Weekly Comp. Pres. Doc.* 424, March 24, 1989; H.R. Rep. No. 23, 101st Cong., 1st Sess. 2 (1989).

16. The deal permitted the president to reprogram appropriated funds to support the Contras. Beginning in 1977, the Foreign Assistance Act conditioned the president's authority to reprogram appropriated funds (shift funds within an appropriations account

to different purposes) (*see infra* chap. 8) on his first notifying the foreign relations and appropriations committees. Foreign Assistance Act of 1961, § 634A, (codified as amended at 22 U.S.C. § 2394-1 (1988 & Supp. II 1990)). Only if none of the committees disapproved could the reprogramming occur. *Id.*

17. *See* Don Oberdorfer, "Contra Talks Were Intense, Personal and Secret," *Wash. Post,* Mar. 26, 1989, at A1. The statute itself renewed the Contra aid without mention of committee review.

18. *See, e.g.,* Gregory A. Sidak, "The President's Power of the Purse," 1989 *Duke L.J.* 1162, 1192, 1216 (describing instances in the Wilson, Franklin Roosevelt, and Eisenhower administrations where attorneys general or the presidents objected to congressional committee vetoes as violative of separation of powers).

19. Immigration & Naturalization Service v. Chadha, 462 U.S. 919 (1983).

20. Louis Fisher, *Constitutional Dialogues: Interpretation as Political Process* 228 (1988).

21. *See* Martin Tolchin, "The Legislative Veto, An Accommodation That Goes On and On," *N.Y. Times,* Mar. 31, 1989, at A11.

22. David Rapp, "OMB's Miller Backs Away from Report-Language Battle," 46 *Cong. Q. Weekly Rep.* 1928 (1988).

23. James A. Miller, "A Presidential Veto for Pork Spending," *Wall St. J.*, Jan. 30, 1990, at A18.

24. "Statement on Signing the Department of Defense Appropriations Act, 1990," 25 *Weekly Comp. Pres. Doc.* 1809, 1810 (Nov. 21, 1989); *see also* "Statement on Signing the Treasury, Post Service and General Government Appropriations Act, 1990," 25 *Weekly Comp. Pres. Doc.*, 1669, 1670 (Nov. 3, 1989); "Statement on Signing the Treasury, Post Service and General Government Appropriations Act, 1992," 27 *Weekly Comp. Pres. Doc.* 1517, 1525 (Oct. 28, 1991).

25. Pub. L. No. 101-511, 104 Stat. 1856 (1990).

26. Pub. L. No. 101-511, § 8111(a), 104 Stat. 1904 (1990); *see* Robert Pear, "Congress Changes Spending Rules on Secret Programs for Pentagon," *N.Y. Times,* Oct. 31, 1990, at A1.

27. Pub. L. No. 102-172, § 8124, 105 Stat. 1206 (1991). A similar provision in the 1993 act was apparently violated when the DOD National Reconnaisance Office ignored specific congressional instructions to obtain committee approval before contracting for a classified espionage program for a spy satellite. John H. Cushman Jr., "Pentagon Found to Have Ignored Congress in Buying Spy Satellite," *N.Y. Times,* Sept. 24, 1993, at A14.

28. Robert Pear, "Unease Is Voiced on Contra Accord," *N.Y. Times,* Mar. 26, 1989, at A1; *see also Wash. Post,* Mar. 26, 1989, at A5.

29. 462 U.S. at 952.

30. J. Gregory Sidak, "To Declare War," 41 *Duke L.J.* 27, 105 (1991).

31. "New Contra Plan: A Break from Past Approach," *N.Y. Times,* Mar. 25, 1989, at A5.

32. Judge Bork also found the side agreements "more objectionable" than the legislative veto in *Chadha* because one subcommittee's inaction could create "legislation." Letter to Sen. Jesse Helms, 135 *Cong. Rec.* S3885 (daily ed. April 13, 1989).

33. Sidak, *supra* note 18, at 1217.

34. *See* J. Gregory Sidak & Thomas A. Smith, "Four Faces of the Line Item Veto: A Reply to Tribe and Kurland," 84 *Nw. U. L. Rev.* 437, 448 (1990). *See also* LTV Aerospace Corp., 55 Comp. Gen. 307, 319 (1975) (finding that committee reports or other instructions contained in legislative history "do not establish any legal requirements on" the spending agency).

35. *See* Burton v. Baker, 723 F. Supp. 1550 (D.D.C. 1990). The district court dismissed a challenge to the accords by four members of Congress as nonjusticiable, noting that the plaintiffs "have a collegial remedy: they can persuade a majority of their fellows to change the law or abandon the 'side agreement.'" *Id.* at 1554.

36. 732 F.2d 1022 (F. Cir. 1984).

37. *Id.* at 1026.

38. *Id.* at 1026–27. *See also* Lincoln v. Vigil, 113 S. Ct. 2024, 2032 (1993) (noting that "an agency's decision to ignore congressional expectations may expose it to grave political consequences").

39. Louis Fisher, "Legislative Vetoes, Phoenix Style," *Extensions* 2 (Spring 1984).

40. *See supra* this chap., describing change in the way Congress controls black budget spending from committee report guidelines to codified restrictions.

41. A draft of the still-secret letter from Secretary of State Baker to the congressional leaders states that the accord "represents a unique agreement . . . [which] in no way establishes any precedent." *Implementation of the Bipartisan Accord on Central America of March 24, 1989,* H.R. Rep. No. 23, 101st Cong., 1st Sess. 4 (1989). *See also* Sidak & Smith, *supra* note 34, at 448 (observing that spending instructions in appropriations committee reports "do not have the force of the law").

Chapter 8

1. Our focus is not on what the agencies do at this stage, or whether they stay within the budget or make unauthorized commitments. For a general description of the techniques that allow executive branch officials to commit the government prior to an appropriation, *see* Louis Fisher, *Presidential Spending Power* 229–56 (1975).

2. *See* Kate Stith, "Congress' Power of the Purse," 97 *Yale L.J.* 1343, 1345–46 (1988).

3. 31 U.S.C. § 1341(a)(1)(a) (1988 & Supp. III 1991).

4. *See* U.S. General Accounting Office, *Principles of Federal Appropriations Law* 5–94 (1st ed. 1982) [hereinafter *Principles 1st*].

5. *See* Lincoln v. Vigil, 113 S. Ct. 2024, 2031 (1993) ("The allocation of funds from a lump-sum appropriation is . . . committed to agency discretion. . . . [T]he . . . point of a lump-sum appropriations is to give an agency the capacity to adapt to changing circumstances and meet its statutory responsibilities in what it sees as the most effective or desirable way.").

6. Act of Feb. 22, 1862, 12 Stat. 344 (Civil War).

7. Act of Mar. 9, 1898, 30 Stat. 274 (Spanish American War).

8. *See* Fisher, *supra* note 1, at 71–73 (describing wartime delegations).

9. 40 *Cong. Rec.* 1283 (1906) (statement of Rep. Leonidas Livingston).

10. Foreign Assistance Act of 1961, Pub. L. No. 87-195, § 451, 75 Stat. 434.

11. Fisher, *supra* note 1, at 67–68.

12. *Id.* at 68–69.

13. Foreign Assistance Act of 1973, Pub. L. No. 93-189, § 10, 87 Stat. 714, 719.

14. Pub. L. No. 93-559, § 28(c), 88 Stat. 1803 (1974); *see* Fisher, *supra* note 1, at 69–70.

15. President Reagan did report to the intelligence committees when he directed that the CIA contingency fund be used in support of the Contras. *See Report of the Congressional Comm. Investigating the Iran-Contra Affair,* S. Rep. No. 100-216, H.R. Rep. No 100-433, 100th Cong., 1st Sess. 395 (1987) [hereinafter *Iran-Contra Report*].

16. *Id.* at 395–410 (describing the administration's program of support and accompanying relations with Congress).

17. *Id.*

18. Bills in 1991 and 1992 that would have required disclosure of aggregate CIA spending were defeated after presidential opposition. *See infra* chap. 10.

19. *See* Bernard T. Pitsvada, "Flexibility in Federal Budget Execution," 3 *Pub. Budgeting & Fin.* 83, 91 (Summer 1983).

20. The act makes it unlawful for a federal agency to "make or authorize an expenditure or obligation exceeding an amount available in an appropriation." 31 U.S.C. §§ 1341-51 (1988 & Supp. III 1991).

21. *See* Fisher, *supra* note 1, at 235–38.

22. *See, e.g.*, 10 U.S.C. § 2201(a) (1988).

23. *Id.*, 10 U.S.C. §§ 2201(b), (c).

24. *Id.*, 10 U.S.C. § 2201(d).

25. Act of Mar. 3, 1799, § 24, 1 Stat. 754. The contemporary version of the feed and forage law is Pub. L. No. 98-557, 98 Stat. 2868, 41 U.S.C. § 11 (1988 & Supp. III 1991); *see generally* Fisher, *supra* note 1, at 238–47.

26. *Id.*

27. *Id.*

28. Act of Mar. 3, 1799, § 24, 1 Stat. 754.

29. Act of May 1, 1820, § 6, 3 Stat. 568; Act of Mar. 2, 1862, § 10, 12 Stat. 220.

30. *See* Fisher, *supra* note 1, at 245–47.

31. *Id.* at 245. The expansion and ongoing congressional acquiescence may have placed a gloss on the feed and forage law. *See infra* chap. 11.

32. *Foreign Assistance and Related Programs Appropriations for Fiscal Year 1973: Hearings Before the Senate Comm. on Appropriations*, 92d Cong., 2d Sess. 837 (1972); Fisher, *supra* note 1, at 325–26 n.27.

33. *Second Supplemental Appropriations for Fiscal Year 1973 (Part 2): Hearings Before the Senate Comm. on Appropriations*, 93d Cong., 1st Sess. 2025 (1973). Eventually, a funding cutoff was negotiated, *see supra* chap. 5.

34. Pub. L. No. 101-403, 104 Stat. 867 (1990); *see* GAO, *Operation Desert Shield/ Storm, Costs and Funding Requirements* 3, GAO/NSIAD-91-3-4 (Sept. 1991).

35. Pub. L. No. 102-28, 105 Stat. 161 (1991).

36. Defense Production Act, Act of Sept. 8, 1950, 50 U.S.C. §§ 2061 *et. seq.* (1988 & Supp. II 1990), *as amended by* Pub. L. No. 102-558, 106 Stat. 4198 (1992).

37. Note, "The Defense Production Act: Choice as to Allocations," 51 *Colum. L. Rev.* 350 (1951).

38. 49 *Cong. Q. Weekly Rep.* 3569 (Dec. 7, 1991).

39. H.R. 991, H.R. 3919, Pub. L. No. 102-99, 105 Stat. 487 (1991); Pub. L. No. 102-558, § 162, 106 Stat. at 4219 (1992) (extending authority through Sept. 30, 1995).

40. Pub. L. No. 102-558, § 2(a), 106 Stat. at 4199–4200 (1992).

41. 50 U.S.C. § 2071 (1988 & Supp. II 1990).

42. Pub. L. No. 102-558, § 107(b)(2), 106 Stat. at 4101-02 (1992).

43. 50 U.S.C. §§ 2091-92 (1988 & Supp. II 1990), *as amended by* Pub.L. No. 102-558, § 121, 106 Stat. at 4203–06 (1992).

44. *See* Exec. Order No. 12, 742, 3 C.F.R. 309 (1991) (relying in part on Defense Production Act to gain priority for government orders during the 1991 Gulf War).

45. Immigration & Naturalization Service v. Chadha, 462 U.S. 919 (1983).

46. *See* Allen v. Grand Central Aircraft Co., 347 U.S. 535, 553 (1954) (requiring manufacturer to exhaust administrative remedies before bringing nondelegation doc-

trine challenge); Eastern Airlines v. McDonnell Douglas Corp., 532 F.2d 957 (5th Cir. 1976) (no liability for nonperformance of contract because priority given to military orders pursuant to DPA); *In re.* Agent Orange Product Liability Litigation, 597 F. Supp. 740, 844 (E.D.N.Y. 1984) (DPA immunizes defense contractors from breach-of-contract damages).

47. Foreign Assistance Act of 1961, Pub. L. No. 87-195, § 614(a), 75 Stat. at 444.

48. *Id.* § 634(d), 75 Stat. at 455.

49. *Id.*, § 614(c), 75 Stat. at 444.

50. *Id.*, § 510(a), 75 Stat. at 437, (codified as amended at 22 U.S.C. § 2318(a) (1988 & Supp. II 1990)) (now limited to $75 million).

51. Jeffrey A. Meyer, "Congressional Control of Foreign Assistance," 13 *Yale J. Int'l L.* 69, 76 n.29 (1988).

52. Foreign Assistance Act of 1971, Pub. L. No. 92-226, 86 Stat. 20 (1972). In 1972, the Senate Foreign Relations Committee noted that President Nixon had used his special funds and transfer authorities to effect seventeen waivers of congressional restrictions in order to allot $110 million to Cambodia. S. Rep. No. 431, 92d Cong., 2d Sess. (1972).

53. Kenneth E. Sharpe, "The Post-Vietnam Formula under Siege: The Imperial Presidency and Central America," 102 *Pol. Sci. Q.* 549, 557 (1987).

54. The administration claimed that guerrilla destruction of aircraft at a Salvadoran air base created an emergency. *Id.*

55. *Id.* at 557–58.

56. *Id.* at 561–62.

57. *Iran-Contra Report, supra* note 15, at 51.

58. 41 U.S.C. § 11 (1988 & Supp. III 1991). The Economy Act is assessed *infra* in this chapter.

59. *Id.* at 35.

60. Act of Mar. 3, 1849, ch. 110, 9 Stat. 398 (codified as amended at 31 U.S.C. § 3302(b) (1988 & Supp. II 1990).

61. Statutes have created trust funds to receive private, 31 U.S.C. § 1321 (1988 & Supp. II 1990), and foreign government gifts, 5 U.S.C. § 7342 (1988 & Supp. II 1990). Gifts must be placed in the treasury and now spent only for objects defined by Congress, 31 U.S.C. § 3302 (1988), to "ensure that the executive branch remains dependent upon the congressional appropriations process." *Principles 1st, supra* note 4, at 5–65.

62. *See* Story v. Snyder, 184 F.2d 454, 461–63 (D.C. Cir. 1950), *cert. denied,* 340 U.S. 866 (1950) (appendix listing gift authority for agencies).

63. Second War Powers Act of 1942, ch. 199, § 1101, 56 Stat. 176, 183–84.

64. Act of July 27, 1954, Pub. L. No. 83-537, 68 Stat. 566, (codified as amended at 50 U.S.C. § 1151(a), *et seq.* (1988 & Supp. II 1990)).

65. *Id.*, 50 U.S.C. § 1154.

66. *See* Stith, *supra* note 2, at 1384–85.

67. *See Iran-Contra Report, supra* note 15, at 37–38.

68. *Id.* at 38–39. Israel, South Africa, Saudi Arabia, China, South Korea, and Taiwan were also solicited for contributions. *Id.* at 42, 44–45, 63.

69. *See* Alex Whiting, "Controlling Tin Cup Diplomacy," 99 *Yale L.J.* 2043, 2045 (1990).

70. Bowsher, *Cost and Financing of Operation Desert Shield,* Statement of the Comptroller General Before the Committee on Budget, U.S. House of Representatives 1, GAO/T-NSAID-91-03 (Jan. 4, 1991).

71. *Wash. Post,* Sept. 21, 1990, at A16. The administration had proposed a $1.9 billion

spending bill that would permit Pentagon spending of contributed funds upon approval by the OMB. *Id.*

72. Continuing Appropriations, Fiscal Year 1991, Pub. L. No. 101-403, § 2608(b), 104 Stat. 874.

73. *Id.*, § 2608(a), 104 Stat. at 873.

74. *Id.*, § 2608(f), 104 Stat. at 873. The secretary must file a quarterly report describing all property received valued at more than $1 million. *Id.*, § 2608(e), 104 Stat. at 873.

75. *Id.*, § 2608(a), 104 Stat. at 873.

76. U.S. General Accounting Office, *A Glossary of Terms Used in the Federal Budget Process* 74 (1991) [hereinafter *Glossary*].

77. *See* Pitsvada, *supra* note 19, at 97–98 (describing informal practices).

78. Unobligated funds are "[t]he portion of budget authority that has not yet been obligated." *Glossary, supra* note 76, at 40. "Obligations incurred" includes "[a]mounts of orders placed, contracts awarded, services received, and similar transactions during a given period that will require payments during the same or a future period." *Id.* at 68. The unobligated balance expires at the end of the fiscal year or for the period specified in multiple year accounts. *Id.* at 40–41.

79. *See* U.S. General Accounting Office, *Principles of Federal Appropriations Law* 2-25 to 2-27 (2d ed. 1991) [hereinafter *Appropriations Principles*]; *see also supra* chap. 7 for discussion of the legal effect of nonstatutory controls. A 1977 amendment to the Foreign Assistance Act denied the president reprogramming authority unless he first notified the foreign relations and appropriations committees in each house and none disapproved. Foreign Assistance Act of 1961, § 634A, 22 U.S.C. § 2394-1 (1988).

80. *See* Fisher, *supra* note 1, at 88–89. At times DOD has sought to pay for an unforseen but high priority activity by reprogramming funds that had been appropriated for programs it considered of low priority, only to have its efforts thwarted by a Congress reluctant to forego spending on favored projects. In 1993, the DOD announced plans to pay for $750 million in costs for operations in Somalia through reprogramming funds appropriated for other items. Rather than permit the reprogramming, Congress enacted a new appropriation for Somalia. Adam Clymer, "Without Request, House Adds Billion for Military," *N.Y. Times*, May 28, 1993, at A13.

81. *Id.* at 77. Reprogramming appears to trace its lineage to "virement" in England. *See supra* chap. 1.

82. *Id.* at 77–78.

83. For example, of the nearly $4.9 billion reprogrammed in fiscal 1990, $3.2 billion was reprogrammed in thirty-two transfers that required prior approval by the armed services and appropriations committees. In more than six hundred other instances, the funding shifts required only that notice be given to the four committees, or, in shifts of the smallest amounts, that they be described in an after-the-fact semiannual report. H.R. Rep. No. 95, 102d Cong., 1st Sess. 19 (1991).

Under current procedures, a reprogramming requires approval by the four committees if it increases the number of units of a major weapon to be purchased; affects a program that any of the four committees has designated an item of "congressional interest"; or shifts funds between the legally defined accounts in the defense appropriations bill (for example, from army aircraft to air force missiles).

For shifts that do not require prior committee approval, the committees require prior notification if they exceed certain dollar thresholds, such as increasing or decreasing any research and development project by $4 million or more. *See* H.R. Rep. No. 95 at 172; S. Rep. No. 154 at 228-29, 102d Cong., 1st Sess. (1991).

84. *Id.*

85. Kenneth E. Sharpe, "The Real Cause of Irangate," 68 *Foreign Policy* 19, 33 (1987–88); Sharpe, *supra* note 53, at 559–60. In 1984 the House Committee on Appropriations reported a finding of the comptroller general that funds appropriated for operation and maintenance of the armed forces were spent in Central America on military construction projects, security assistance activities, and civic action and humanitarian assistance. The committee protested that the diversion of funds from appropriated purposes was unwarranted and directed the Department of Defense to prevent such improprieties from occurring in the future. H.R. Rep. No. 1086, 98th Cong., 2d Sess. 40–41 (1984).

86. Department of Defense Appropriations Act of 1992, Pub. L. No. 102-172, § 8010, 105 Stat. 1173 (1991).

87. *Id.*, § 8014, 105 Stat. at 1174. Reprogramming of funds by agencies within the intelligence community may occur only with the DCI's prior approval, or pursuant to procedures approved by the DCI. Intelligence Organization Act of 1992, Pub. L. No. 102-496, § 104(c), 106 Stat. 3192.

88. *See generally Reprogramming of Appropriated Funds,* Department of Defense Directive No. 7250.5 (1980); Department of Defense, *Budget Guidance Manual* 431–2, DOD 7110-1-M (May 1990).

89. *See Appropriations Principles, supra* note 79, at 2–20; Fisher, *supra* note 1, at 104. The prohibition is codified at 31 U.S.C. § 1532(1988): "An amount available under any law may be withdrawn from one appropriation account and credited to another . . . only when authorized by law."

90. *See* Pitsvada, *supra* note 19, at 94.

91. Department of Defense Appropriations, Fiscal Year 1993, Pub. L. No. 102-396, § 9006, 106 Stat. 1876, 1901 (1992).

92. 31 U.S.C. § 1301(1) (1988): "Appropriations shall be applied only to the objects for which the appropriations were made except as otherwise provided by law."

93. Lucius Wilmerding, Jr., *The Spending Power* 78 (1943).

94. *Id.* at 73, 213.

95. Gary L. Hopkins & Robert M. Nutt, "The Anti-Deficiency Act and Funding Federal Contracts: An Analysis," 80 *Mil. L. Rev.* 51, 57 (1978).

96. Act of Feb. 12, 1868, ch. 8, § 2, 15 Stat. 35, 36.

97. 29 *Cong. Q. Almanac* 102 (1973).

98. Continuing Appropriations Act for Fiscal Year 1974, Pub. L. No. 93-52, § 108, 87 Stat. 134 (1973).

99. *See* Fisher, *supra* note 1, at 107–108.

100. Pub. L. No. 93-238, § 735, 87 Stat. 1044 (1974).

101. Sharpe, *supra* note 53, at 561–62; *see also* Theodore Draper, *A Very Thin Line: The Iran-Contra Affairs* 19–23 (1991).

102. *See* 31 U.S.C. § 1301(a) (1988); *Appropriations Principles, supra* note 79, at 2–21.

103. Act of June 30, 1932, § 317, 47 Stat. 411; *see generally* Wilmerding, *supra* note 93, at 180–84.

104. Economy Act of 1932, § 317, 47 Stat. 411; *see also* Fisher, *supra* note 1, at 105.

105. Economy Act of 1932, § 317, 47 Stat. 411.

106. *Quoted in* Wilmerding, *supra* note 93, at 183.

107. A statute in place in 1984 prohibited covert operations by the CIA "other than activities intended solely for obtaining necessary intelligence, unless and until the President *finds* that each such operation is important to the national security of the United States." Pub. L. No. 96-450, Title IV, § 407(a), 94 Stat. 1981, (codified as amended at 22 U.S.C. § 2422 (1988)) (emphasis added). The finding was then to be reported to various

members of Congress. *See* Stephen Dycus, Arthur L. Berney, William C. Banks, and Peter Raven-Hansen, *National Security Law* 315–17 (1990).

108. *Iran-Contra Report, supra* note 15, at 380. Another statute permits the Director of Central Intelligence, with the approval of the Director of OMB, to transfer funds from one agency to another within the intelligence community for "a higher priority intelligence activity." The need for the funds must be "based on unforeseen requirements," and the funds may not be transferred from the Federal Bureau of Investigation or to the contingency fund of the CIA. Intelligence Organization Act of 1992, Pub. L. No. 102-496, § 104(d), 106 Stat. 3192–93.

109. Louis Fisher, "Funds Impounded by the President: The Constitutional Issue," 38 *Geo. Wash. L. Rev.* 124 (1969). According to the GAO, "an impoundment is an action or inaction by an officer or employee of the United States that precludes the obligation or expenditure of budget authority provided by Congress." *Glossary, supra* note 76, at 63.

110. *See Appropriations Principles, supra* note 79, at 1, 21, 22.

111. Pub. L. No. 93-344, §§ 1001–1017, 88 Stat. 297, 332–337 (1974).

112. 8 *Annals of Cong.* 11, 14 (1803) (statement of President Jefferson).

113. *See* Fisher, *supra* note 1, at 150.

114. *See id.* at 148–49; *cf.*, Missouri Highway Commission v. Volpe, 479 F.2d 1099 (8th Cir. 1973) (deciding that the secretary of transportation could not lawfully refuse to obligate highway funds that had been obligated for the state of Missouri on the ground that the expenditures would aggravate inflation).

115. General Appropriations Act of 1951, ch. 896, § 1211(c)(2), 64 Stat. 595, 765.

116. *Id.* § 1214, 64 Stat. at 768.

117. Fisher, *supra* note 1, at 152–53.

118. *Id.* at 153–54.

119. *Id.* at 160.

120. *Id.* at 147.

121. *See* L. Harold Levinson & Jon. L. Mills, "Impoundment: A Search for Legal Principles," 26 *U. Fla. L. Rev.* 191, 199 (1974).

122. Supplemental National Defense Appropriations Act of 1948, ch. 333, § 2, 62 Stat. 259.

123. Fisher, *supra* note 1, at 162–63.

124. H.R. Rep. No. 1797, 81st Cong., 2d Sess., at 309–312 (1950).

125. *Quoted in* Fisher, *supra* note 1, at 164; *see* H.R. Rep. No. 1406, 87th Cong., 2d Sess. 1, 9 (1962). In 1958, and for a few years thereafter, Congress attached riders to defense appropriations and prescribed limits in authorization bills setting minimum personnel levels for military forces. The effect of these measures was to forestall Eisenhower administration plans to reduce the reserve components of the armed forces by impounding funds. Fisher, *supra* note 1, at 161.

126. 108 *Cong. Rec.* 4694 (1962).

127. Fisher, *supra* note 1, at 163–65.

128. *Id.*

129. H.R. Rep. No. 1679, 89th Cong., 2d Sess. 2 (1966).

130. John H. Stassen, "Separation of Powers and the Uncommon Defense: The Case Against Impounding of Weapons System Appropriations," 67 *Geo. L.J.* 1159, 1168–76 (1969).

131. General Appropriations Act of 1951, ch. 896, § 1211(c)(2), 64 Stat. 595, 765.

132. Fisher, *supra* note 1, at 156–57.

133. H.R. Rep. No. 1798, 81st Cong., 2d Sess. 31 (1950).

134. Fisher, *supra* note 1, at 175–77.

135. Pub. L. No. 93-344, § 1002, 88 Stat. 332 (1974).

136. Fisher, *supra* note 1, at 184–92.

137. Train v. City of New York, 420 U.S. 35 (1975).

138. *Id.* at 38, 39.

139. Pub. L. No. 93-344, 88 Stat. 298, (codified as amended at 2 U.S.C. § 621 *et seq.* (1988 & Supp. III 1991)).

140. *Id.*, 2 U.S.C. § 683(a) (1988):

> Whenever the President determines that all or part of any budget authority will not be required to carry out the full objectives or scope of programs for which it is provided or that such budget authority should be rescinded for fiscal policy or other reasons . . . the President shall transmit to both Houses of Congress a special message specifying: the amount to be rescinded, the departments involved, the reasons for the rescission and any other relevant facts pertaining to the rescission . . . Any amount of budget authority to be rescinded or that is to be reserved as set forth in such special message shall be made available for obligation unless, within the prescribed 45-day period, the Congress has completed action on a rescission bill rescinding all or part of the amount proposed to be rescinded or that is to be reserved. . . .

141. *Id.*, 2 U.S.C. § 684 (1988).

142. *Id.*, 2 U.S.C. § 686(a) (1988).

143. *Id.*, 2 U.S.C. § 686(b) (1988).

144. *Id.*, 2 U.S.C. § 687 (1988).

145. *See* Note, "Addressing the Resurgence of Presidential Budgetmaking Initiative: A Proposal to Reform the Impoundment Control Act of 1974," 63 *Tex. L. Rev.* 693, 705–708 (1984).

146. Immigration & Naturalization Service v. Chadha, 462 U.S. 919 (1983).

147. City of New Haven v. United States, 809 F.2d 900 (D.C. Cir. 1987).

148. *Id.* at 909.

149. *See, e.g.*, U.A.W. v. Donovan, 746 F.2d 855 (D.C. Cir. 1984) (no judicial review of Labor Department decision not to fund a training program where lump sum was appropriated "for expenses necessary to carry into effect" a range of training programs), *cert. denied*, 474 U.S. 825 (1985); Pennsylvania v. Lynn, 501 F.2d 848 (D.C. Cir. 1974) (termination by Housing and Urban Development (HUD) of housing projects where the projects were not achieving their congressionally intended purposes was permissible); Mid-Ohio Food Bank v. Lyons, 670 F.Supp. 403, 410 (D.D.C. 1987) (dismissing on procedural grounds suit against policy deferrals).

150. Instead of amending the 1974 act to cure its constitutional defect, Congress acted only to codify the *City of New Haven* decision by replacing the legislative veto with this language:

> (b) Consistency with Legislative Policy—Deferrals shall be permissible only—
> (1) to provide for contingencies
> (2) to achieve savings made possible by or through changes in requirements or greater efficiency of operations; or
> (3) as specifically provided by law.
> No officer or employee of the United States may defer any budget authority for any other purpose.

2 U.S.C. § 684(b)(1988). The new law is thus equivalent to the Anti-Deficiency Act as amended in 1974, described earlier in this chapter.

151. Pub. L. No. 100-119, 101 Stat. 786 (1987).

152. Staats v. Lynn, No. 75-0551 (D.D.C. Apr. 15, 1975); *see also* Note, "Who Decides? The Struggle for Control Over the Federal Government's Spending Power," 38 *Case W. Res. L. Rev.* 66 (1987).

153. *See, e.g.*, H.R. 5234, 99th Cong., 2d Sess. § 315 (1986).

154. *See* Irwin W. Kramer, "The Impoundment Control Act of 1974: An Unconstitutional Solution to a Constitutional Problem," 58 *UMKC L. Rev.* 157, 177 n.33 (1990).

155. *See* GAO, *Letter to the President of the Senate and the Speaker of the House of Representatives*, GOA/OGC-91-2 (May 7, 1991) [hereinafter *Letter to the President*].

156. *Id; see also* GAO, *Navy Budget: Potential Budget Reductions in Aircraft Procurement Budget*, GAO/NSIAD-91-65 (Jan. 1991).

157. GAO/OGC-90-4, B-237297.3 (Mar. 6, 1990).

158. Pub. L. No. 101-510, § 152, 104 Stat. 1485, 1505 (1990).

159. *Id.* § 211, 104 Stat. at 1519.

160. Pub. L. No. 101-511, 104 Stat. 1856, 1864 (Procurement), 1868 (Research and Development) (1990).

161. Pub. L. No. 102-27, 105 Stat. 130 (1991).

162. Apportionment is a "distribution made by the Office of Management and Budget of amounts available for obligation. The amounts so apportioned limit the amount of obligations that may be incurred." *Glossary, supra* note 76, at 34. Apportionment permits OMB to help agencies avoid deficiency spending. *Id.*

163. *Letter to the President, supra* note 155, at 3.

164. *Id.* at 3–6.

165. H.R. Rep. No. 923, 101st Cong., 2d Sess. 487, 488 (1990).

166. *Letter to the President, supra* note 155, at 6. The V-22 Osprey program suffered a setback when a prototype of the aircraft crashed into the Potomac River as it was preparing to land. All seven people aboard were killed. Stephen C. Fehr & Bill Miller, "Military Aircraft Crashes at Quantico," *Wash. Post*, July 21, 1992, at A1, A9.

167. B-224882 (April 1, 1987), *reprinted in* H.R. Doc. No. 61, 100th Cong., 1st Sess. 11 (1987).

168. The first OMB report on impoundments for fiscal year 1992 details seven deferrals totaling $806.8 million and no rescissions. 56 *Fed. Reg.* 65402 (Dec. 16, 1991). In March 1992 President Bush sought $3.6 billion in rescissions from sixty-eight fiscal 1992 spending projects, including sixty-six alleged pork barrel projects representing less than 10 percent of the dollar value of the rescissions. The two remaining proposals were to cancel two funded Seawolf nuclear submarines (saving $2.8 billion) and more than $500 million in approved public housing. By forcing congressional votes on scores of rescission proposals, the president sought to gain political advantage in an election year and to gain fiscal leverage by exposing small but symbolic congressional pork. *Wash. Post*, Mar. 23, 1992, at A13. The Seawolf and HUD proposals obviously represent policy differences between the branches, not attempts at programmatic savings.

Part III

1. *See* Hans A. Linde, "Due Process of Lawmaking," 55 *Neb. L. Rev.* 197 (1976).
2. U.S. Const., art. I., § 9, cl. 7.

Chapter 9

1. *See, e.g.*, Russell M. Ross & Fred Schwengel, "An Item Veto for the President?," 12 *Pres. Stud. Q.* 66, 69–72 (1982).

2. *See* Edward C. Mason, *The Veto Power: Its Origin, Development, and Function* 48 (1967); *see also supra* chap. 5.

3. Mason, *supra* note 2, at 48; *see also* Albert Castel, *The Presidency of Andrew Johnson* 113–14 (1979) (noting objectionable orders enacted after a reluctant Andrew Johnson signed an 1867 army appropriation bill).

4. *See, e.g.*, Veto Message of Rutherford B. Hayes (Apr. 29, 1879), *reprinted in* 7 *Compilation of the Messages and Papers of the Presidents* 523, 528 (J. Richardson ed., 1897).

5. *See* Robert J. Spitzer, *The Presidential Veto: Touchstone of the American Presidency* 126 (1988).

6. *Id.* at 134–35. Forty-three states provide an item veto for the governor. *See generally* Louis Fisher & Neal A. Devins, "How Successfully Can the States' Item Veto Be Transferred to the President?," 75 *Geo. L. J.* 159 (1986).

7. *See* Ross & Schwengel, *supra* note 1, at 69.

8. Spitzer, *supra* note 5, at 60 (1988) (quoting 4 *Messages and Papers of the Presidents* 4483 (1913)). *See also* Ross & Schwengel, *supra* note 1, at 70; Mason, *supra* note 2, at 48.

9. *See* Ross & Schwengel, *supra* note 1, at 72.

10. *See generally Pork Barrels and Principles: The Politics of the Presidential Veto* (1988) (published by the National Legal Center for the Public Interest) [hereinafter *Pork Barrels*]. Presidents also complain about pork barrel spending—projects approved by Congress that, for example, favor the district of an influential member of Congress, but which may constitute wasteful spending from the broader perspective of the public interest. President Bush criticized pork barrel spending in approved fiscal year 1992 appropriations. The president asked Congress to terminate spending projects totaling $5.7 billion in a speech in which he also asked Congress to give him the line-item veto. *Wash. Post*, Mar. 26, 1992, at A19; *see also Wash. Post*, Apr. 24, 1992, at A6.

11. For a description of the fiscal year 1985 continuing resolutions, *see* Edward M. Davis & Robert A. Keith, *Summary and Legislative History of Public Law 98-473: Continuing Appropriations for Fiscal Year 1985* (H.J.R. Res. 648) (Cong. Res. Serv. Dec. 1984).

12. "Statement on Signing the Intelligence Authorization Act for Fiscal Year 1985," 20 *Weekly. Comp. Pres. Doc.* 1817, Nov. 9, 1984.

13. *See* Neal E. Devins, "Appropriations Redux: A Critical Look at the Fiscal Year 1988 Continuing Resolution," 1988 *Duke L.J.* 389, 396–99.

14. *See* Fisher & Devins, *supra* note 6, at 159 nn.3–8; J. Gregory Sidak & Thomas A. Smith, "Four Faces of the Item Veto: A Reply to Tribe and Kurland," 84 *Nw. U. L. Rev.* 437, 459–60, (1990). At least twenty-two bills granting the president some form of the item veto were introduced during the first nine months of the 102d Congress. General Accounting Office, *Line Item Veto: Estimating Potential Savings* 16, GAO/AFMD-92-7 (Jan. 1992).

15. "Line-item veto" is a misnomer. The items in legislation are sections or provisions, and legislation is not itemized by line.

16. *See* Devins, *supra* note 13, at 396–99.

17. *See* Stephen Glazier, "Reagan Already Has Line-Item Veto," *Wall St. J.*, Dec. 4, 1987, at A14.

18. *See, e.g.*, Bruce Fein & William Bradford Reynolds, "Wishful Thinking on a Line-Item Veto," *Legal Times,* Nov. 13, 1989, at 30 (reporting that all arguments in favor of the constitutionality of the line-item veto "have been wholly discredited").

19. *See Wall St. J.*, Oct. 30, 1989, at A12.

20. 25 *Weekly Comp. Pres. Doc.* 1809, 1810 (Nov. 21, 1989). The constitutionality of nonstatutory controls is considered *supra* chap. 7. Similar examples of the president's purporting to excise objectionable provisions from defense and defense-related appropriations have since occurred, along with renewed efforts among some in the Congress to legislate a line-item veto. In February 1992, the Senate defeated by a vote of 54–44 a proposal to permit the president to strike individual items out of an appropriation bill after signing it. The rescissions would take effect unless Congress passed a resolution of disapproval within twenty days of the president's action. The resolution of disapproval would also have been subject to a presidential veto. "Senate Rejects Line-Item Veto," *Wash. Post,* Feb. 28, 1992, at A14.

21. U.S. Const., art. I, § 7, cl. 2:

> Every Bill which shall have passed the House of Representatives and the Senate, shall, before it become a Law, be presented to the President of the United States; If he approve he shall sign it, but if not he shall return it, with his Objections to the House in which it shall have originated, who shall enter the Objections at large on their Journal, and proceed to reconsider it.

Id., art. I, § 7, cl. 3:

> Every Order, Resolution, or Vote, to Which the Concurrence of the Senate and House of Representatives may be necessary . . . shall be presented to the President . . . and before the same shall take effect, shall be approved by him, or being disapproved by him, shall be repassed by two thirds of the Senate and House of Representatives, according to the rules and limitations prescribed in the case of a bill.

22. *See* Sidak & Smith, *supra* note 14, at 447.

23. *Id.* at 449. Sidak and Smith recognize the practical problems that could arise in attempting to sort out whether a veto is a subject or line-item veto when an appropriation bill has nongermane riders. *Id.*

24. *See* Stephen Glazier, "The Line-Item Veto: Provided in the Constitution and Traditionally Applied," in *Pork Barrels, supra* note 10, at 12–15.

25. *See* Sidak & Smith, *supra* note 14, at 452–60. The excision of unconstitutional national security appropriations restrictions is separately considered *infra,* chap. 13.

26. Sidak and Smith, *supra* note 14, at 473.

27. U.S. Const., art. I, § 4, cl. 2.

28. *Id.*, § 5, cl. 3.

29. *Id.*, § 9, cl. 7.

30. Sidak & Smith, *supra* note 14, at 473.

31. *See* Diane-Michele Krasnow, "The Imbalance of Power and the Presidential Veto: A Case for the Item Veto," 14 *Harv. J.L. & Pub. Pol'y* 583, 592–95 (1990).

32. *See* Sidak & Smith, *supra* note 14, at 475–76.

33. *Id.* at 445.

34. James Madison, *Notes of Debates in the Federal Convention of 1787*, at 66, 80–81, 629 (1966 ed.) (1840).

35. *See, e.g.*, Forrest McDonald, "The Framers' Conception of the Veto Power," in *Pork Barrels, supra* note 10, at 3–4.

36. *See* Sidak & Smith, *supra* note 14, at 441–46.

37. Madison, *supra* note 34, at 629; *The Federalist* No. 73, at 492, 495 (Alexander Hamilton) (C. Rossiter ed., 1961).

38. Sidak & Smith, *supra* note 14, at 469.

39. *See* Paul R. Q. Wolfson, "Is a Presidential Line-Item Veto Constitutional?," 96 *Yale L.J.* 838, 842–44 (1987).

40. Youngstown Sheet & Tube Co. v. Sawyer, 343 U.S. 579, 587 (1952) (Black, J.) ("The Constitution limits his functions in the lawmaking process to the recommending of laws he thinks wise and the vetoing of laws he thinks bad.").

41. U.S. Const., art. I, § 5, cl.2.

42. *See* Sidak & Smith, *supra* note 14, at 454, 460–61.

43. 462 U.S. 919 (1983).

44. *See* U.S. Const. art. I., § 2, cl. 5; § 3, cl. 6; art. II, § 2, cl. 2; art. V.

45. *Chadha*, 462 U.S. at 952.

46. *See* U.S. Const., art. I, §§ 1, 7. *See also Chadha*, 462 U.S. at 947 ("It is beyond doubt that lawmaking was a power to be shared by both Houses and the President."); *id.* at 952 (establishing that what is "legislative" depends on what is "legislative in its character and effect").

47. *See* Sidak & Smith, *supra* note 14, at 460-61.

48. U.S. Const., art. I, § 7, cl.2.

49. *Id.*

50. Charles A. Black, "Some Thoughts on the Veto," 40 *Law & Contemp. Probs.* 87, 92 (1976) (reporting that about 5 percent of vetoes are overridden).

51. *Cf.* Hans A. Linde, "Due Process of Lawmaking," 55 *Neb. L. Rev.* 197 (1976).

52. 143 U.S. 649 (1892).

53. *Id.* at 669.

54. *Id.* at 672.

55. The Pocket Veto Case, 279 U.S. 655, 679 (1929).

56. 286 U.S. 482 (1932).

57. *Id.* at 493.

58. Judith A. Best, "The Item Veto: Would the Founders Approve?," 14 *Pres. Stud. Q.* 183, 187 (1984).

59. *Id.; see also* Richard A. Givens, "The Validity of a Separate Veto of Nongermane Riders to Legislation," 39 *Temp. L.Q.* 60, 62 (1965); *Line Item Veto: Hearings on S.43 Before the Senate Committee on Rules and Administration,* 99th Cong., 1st Sess. 19 (1985).

60. *See* Evarts B. Greene, *The Provincial Governor* 164 (1898) (describing colonial practice). *See also supra* chap. 2.

61. *See* Krasnow, *supra* note 31, at 586–88. The item veto extended to appropriations. Walter Shepherd, *History of Proprietary Government in Pennsylvania* 41–42 (1967).

62. Jack P. Greene, *The Quest for Power* 51–71 (1963).

63. *See* E. Greene, *supra* note 60, at 164.

64. *See* Thomas Stefan Schroeder, "Original Understanding and the Veto Power: Are the Framers Safe While Congress Is in Session?," 7 *J.L. & Pol'y* 1, 18–26 (1991).

65. *See* e.g., Charles L. Raper, *North Carolina: A Study in English Colonial Government* 97, 98–99, 185, 201 (1904).

66. *See* Gordon S. Wood, *The Creation of the American Republic, 1776–1787,* at 134–41 (1969).

67. New York's 1777 Constitution provided for a council of revision, consisting of the governor, the chancellor, and the judges of the supreme court. *Id.* at 134–41. The council had an implicit item veto: if a majority objected to a bill, it was returned to the originating house of the legislature with comments. The legislature would incorporate the comments in a new version and again submit it to the council. *Id.* Although no explicit power to selectively veto parts of bills is otherwise found in the 1777 Constitution, the equivalent power was successfully exercised by the council of revision in 1778, and the legislation was later passed without the objectionable provisions. Forrest McDonald, "Line-Item Veto: Older Than Constitution," *Wall St. J.*, Mar. 7, 1988, at 16. This episode hardly suggests that the framers, who rejected a council of revision, contemplated an item veto. Quite the contrary, it is further evidence of their familiarity with a precedent that they did not adopt.

68. *See* Forrest McDonald, "The Framers' Conception of the Veto Power," in *Pork Barrels, supra* note 10, at 2.

69. Act of Sept. 29, 1789, 1 Stat. 95. As we noted at the start of chap. 4, practices of the early sessions of Congress are especially weighty in construing vague constitutional language because many of their members participated in the framing of the Constitution. *See* Marsh v. Chambers, 463 U.S. 783, 790 (1983).

70. *See* Gerhard Casper, "Appropriations of Power," 13 *U. Ark. Little Rock L.J.* 1, 10 (1990).

71. *See* Louis Fisher, "The Presidential Veto: Constitutional Development," in *Pork Barrels, supra* note 10, at 221.

72. The act is set out in its entirety *supra* in text accompanying note 4 in chap. 4.

73. *See* Act of Mar. 3, 1791, 1 Stat. 214; Act of Feb. 11, 1791, 1 Stat. 190; Act of Aug. 12, 1790, 1 Stat. 185; Act of Mar. 26, 1790, 1 Stat. 104; *see also* Casper, *supra* note 70, at 11–14, 17–21.

74. *Jefferson's Manual: Rules of the House of Representatives of the United States,* H.R. Doc. No. 256, 101st Cong., 2d Sess. § 843, Rule XVI (1991).

75. 1 Stat. 325–328 (1793).

76. 1 Stat. 563 (1798); *see also* Casper, *supra* note 70, at 17–21.

77. *See* Glazier, *supra* note 10, at 12–15.

78. As Justice Frankfurter put it in *Youngstown Sheet & Tube Co. v. Sawyer,* 343 U.S. 579, 610–11 (1952), "[A] systematic, unbroken, executive practice, long pursued to the knowledge of the Congress and never before questioned, engaged in by Presidents who have also sworn to uphold the Constitution, making as it were such an exercise of power part of the structure of government, may be treated as a gloss on 'executive power' vested in the President by § 1 of Art. II." *Id.* This theory of constitutional gloss has an important limitation, according to Justice Frankfurter: "Deeply embedded traditional ways of conducting the government cannot supplant the Constitution or legislation, but they give meaning to the words of a text or supply them." *Id.* at 610. *See generally infra* chap. 11.

79. *See supra* chap. 5. It is also unlikely that any customary or inherent power of presidential impoundment exists, in light of Kendall v. United States *ex rel.* Stokes, 37 U.S. (12 Pet.) 524 (1838), which found no authority for the executive to refuse to disburse appropriated funds. *Id.* at 527.

80. *See* Sidak & Smith, *supra* note 14, at 447–48.

81. Pub. L. No. 98-369, 98 Stat. 1199, 31 U.S.C. §§ 3551-56 (1988 & Supp. II 1990).

82. Lear Siegler, Inc., Energy Products Division v. Lehman, 842 F.2d 1102 (9th Cir.), *rehearing granted,* 863 F.2d 683, *decision withdrawn on other grounds,* No. 87-5670 (9th Cir. July 17, 1989).

83. *Lear Siegler,* 842 F.2d at 1124; *see also* Thirteenth Guam Legislature v. Bordallo, 430 F. Supp. 405, 410 (D. Guam App. Div. 1977), *aff'd per curiam,* 588 F.2d 265 (9th Cir. 1978); Doe v. Mathews, 420 F. Supp. 865, 886 (D.N.J. 1976) ("[The Constitution . . . does not require the Congress to limit each Bill to one object, or to state that object in its title.").

84. *See* Devins, *supra* note 13, at 389, 396–400.

85. "Address Before a Joint Session of the Congress on the State of the Union," 24 *Weekly Comp. Pres. Doc.* 85, 87 (Jan. 25, 1988).

86. Devins, *supra* note 13, at 397.

87. *Id.* at 398.

88. *Id.* The president also threatened to veto the resolution if antiabortion counseling and foreign assistance funds were removed. Again, the threat worked. *Id.* at 399. In addition to agreeing to $23 billion in tax increases, the president signed the bill that included a smoking ban on some domestic fights, provisions to permit the states to raise the rural highway speed limit to 65 m.p.h., an extension of the Clean Air Act, and a rider, introduced in conference, prohibiting the Federal Communications Commission (FCC) from modifying its cross-ownership restrictions. *Id.*

89. President Bush's veto threat caused the House and Senate to drop from the fiscal 1993 DOD Appropriation bill a provision that would have repealed a ban on virtually all abortions at military hospitals overseas. Eric Schmitt, "Congressional Panel Trims '93 Military Budget by 9%," *N.Y. Times,* Oct. 2, 1992, at A14.

90. Devins, *supra* note 13, at 399–400.

91. *See* Adam Clymer, "The Gridlock Congress: The 102d Will Be Remembered as Much For Its Embarrassments as Its Legislation," *N.Y. Times,* Oct. 11, 1992, at A1.

92. "Line Item Veto: Small Change, Big Politics," *Wash. Post,* Mar. 26, 1992, at A19.

93. *See* Fisher & Devins, *supra* note 6, at 186, 190.

94. *Id.*

95. *See* Sidak & Smith, *supra* note 14, at 467.

96. A longstanding custom of presidential acquiescence may weaken even this separation-of-powers argument. *See infra* chap. 11.

97. Nixon v. Administrator of General Services, 433 U.S. 425, 443 (1977). *See infra* chap. 13 for a discussion of the appropriate mode of separation-of-powers analysis.

Chapter 10

1. U.S. Const., art. I., § 9, cl. 7.

2. U.S. Const., art. I, § 8, cl. 11.

3. U.S. Const., art. I., § 9.

4. Miscellaneous Receipts, Act of Mar. 3, 1849, ch. 110, 9 Stat. 1214 (codified as amended at 31 U.S.C. § 3302(b) (1988)) (stating that all funds of the government must be claimed as public revenues, subject to constitutional controls); Anti-Deficiency Act, Act of Mar. 3, 1905, ch. 1484, § 4, 33 Stat. 1214 (codified as amended at 31 U.S.C. §§ 1341–1351 (1988 & Supp. III 1991)) (stating that no public funds may be spent except pursuant to an appropriation); General Accounting Office Act of 1980, Pub. L. No. 96-226, 94 Stat. 311, 31 U.S.C. § 3524 (1988).

5. Richardson v. United States, 465 F.2d 844, 853 (3d Cir. 1972), *rev'd,* 418 U.S. 166 (1974).

6. 19 *Annals of Cong.* 1330–31 (1809).

7. *See* Daniel Hoffman, *Governmental Secrecy and the Founding Fathers* 11–20 (1981).

8. *See id.* at 20–24.

9. U.S. Const., art. I., § 5.

10. U.S. Const., art. II, § 3.

11. 2 *Records of the Federal Convention of 1787,* at 618–19 (Max Farrand ed., 1911) [hereinafter *Records*].

12. *Id.* at 619.

13. *Id.* at 618–19. Wilson, who seconded Madison's motion, opined that "[m]any operations of finance cannot be properly published at certain times." *Id.* Madison stated that the publication "from time to time" would leave enough to the discretion of the Legislature "but . . . would be more full and satisfactory to the public." *Id.* at 618–19; 3 *Records, supra* note 11, at 326. Gouverneur Morris objected that publication would be "impossible in many cases." 2 *Records, supra* note 11, at 618–19.

14. 3 *Elliot's Debates* 459 (John Elliott ed., 1936).

15. *See* Hoffman, *supra* note 7, at 18–20.

16. *The Federalist* No. 64, at 12–13 (J. Jay) (C. Rossiter ed., 1961).

17. 2 *Records, supra* note 11, at 618. Morris may have been alluding to the need for secrecy in military affairs and diplomacy. *See* Louis Fisher, "Confidential Spending and Governmental Accountability," 47 *Geo. Wash. L. Rev.* 347, 350 (1979).

18. 31 U.S.C. § 3524 (1988).

19. The Combined Statement is published in compliance with 31 U.S.C. § 331 (1988) to implement the Statement and Account Clause.

20. 50 U.S.C. § 403j(b) (1988).

21. A limited audit of some unvouchered expenses is carried out, 31 U.S.C. § 3524 (1988), although the act specifically exempts the CIA from any audit and permits the president to exempt sensitive foreign intelligence and law enforcement activities. *Id.*

22. *See* Louis Fisher, *Presidential Spending Power* 205–13 (1975).

23. *Id.* at 213.

24. Act of July 1, 1790, 1 Stat. 128–29.

25. Act of Feb. 9, 1793, 1 Stat. 300; 31 U.S.C. § 3526(e) (1988).

26. Act of Aug. 29, 1916, 39 Stat. 557.

27. Fisher, *supra* note 22, at 207.

28. Fisher, *supra* note 17, at 361.

29. *Id.*; *see* Act of July 12, 1943, ch. 218, 57 Stat. 432; Act of June 28, 1944, ch. 304, 58 Stat. 599 (proscribing spending on a "function or project" earlier rejected by Congress or the appropriations committees).

30. Fisher, *supra* note 17, at 361–62.

31. Louis Fisher, *Constitutional Conflicts Between the President and Congress* 206–07 (3d ed. 1991).

32. Pub. L. No. 89–367, § 401, 80 Stat. 37 (1966); Pub. L. No. 89-375, § 102, 80 Stat. 82 (1966); Pub. L. No. 90-22, § 301, 81 Stat. 53 (1967); Pub. L. No. 90-96, § 639, 81 Stat. 248 (1967).

33. *Id.*

34. *See* Louis Fisher, "Presidential Spending Discretion and Congressional Controls," 37 *Law & Contem. Probs.* 135, 139–42 (1972).

35. Fisher, *supra* note 22, at 226–27.

36. Fisher, *supra* note 17, at 363–65. Most earlier confidential funds were in authori-

zation appropriations. Fisher, *supra* note 22, at 207–13. Authorization appropriations are defined in chap. 5.

37. Pub. L. No. 102-172, tit. 2, 105 Stat. 1150, 1152 (1991).

38. The fiscal 1993 budget for the intelligence community is estimated at $28 billion. 51 *Cong. Q. Weekly Rep.* 2167 (Aug. 7, 1993).

39. 50 U.S.C. § 403j (1988).

40. *Id.*

41. *See* John Ranelagh, *The Agency: The Rise and Decline of the CIA* 281–85 (1986).

42. Pub. L. No. 92-226 § 655, 86 Stat. 20 (1972). *See* Fisher, *supra* note 22, at 217–19.

43.

> No funds appropriated under the authority of this chapter or any other Act may be expended by or on behalf of the Central Intelligence Agency for operations in foreign countries, other than activities intended solely for obtaining necessary intelligence, unless and until the President finds that each such operation is important to the national security of the United States. Each such operation shall be considered a significant anticipated intelligence activity for the purpose of section 413 of Title 50.

Pub. L. No. 87-195, Pt. III, § 662, 88 Stat. 1804, repealed by Pub. L. No. 102-88, § 601 (1991).

44. *Id.*

45. *See* Scott Breckenridge, *The CIA and the U.S. Intelligence System* 266 (1986).

46. Intelligence Authorization Act, Fiscal Year 1991, Pub. L. No. 102-88, § 405, 105 Stat. 429.

47. *See* discussion of the black budget, *supra* chap. 5. The earlier proposals are described in Fisher, *supra* note 22, at 249–51. *See also* Senate Select Committee on Intelligence, Rep. No. 102-117, 102d Cong., 1st Sess. 9–14 (1991).

48. Intelligence Authorization Act, Fiscal Year 1991, Pub. L. No. 102-88, § 102(b), 105 Stat. 429.

49. 31 U.S.C. § 3524 (1988).

50. *Id.*

51. *Report of the Congressional Comm. Investigating the Iran-Contra Affair*, S. Rep. No. 100-216, H.R. Rep. No. 100-433, 100th Cong., 1st Sess. 31–32 (1987) [hereinafter *Iran-Contra Report*].

52. *Id.* at 397.

53. *Id.* at 399–401.

54. "Special forces" is a generic term to describe military operations budget lines that are black or unvouchered. *See* Alice C. Maroni, *Special Access Programs and the Defense Budget: Understanding the "Black Budget"* 4, Cong. Res. Serv. IB89201, updated Oct. 24, 1989.

55. Kenneth Sharpe, "The Post-Vietnam Formula Under Siege: The Imperial Presidency and Central America," 102 *Pol. Sci. Q.* 549, 561-62 (1987). *See supra* chap. 8 for details.

56. *Iran-Contra Report, supra* note 51, at 380.

57. *See* United States v. Richardson, 418 U.S. 166 (1974); Harrington v. Bush, 553 F.2d 190 (D.C. Cir. 1977); Halperin v. Central Intelligence Agency, 629 F.2d 144 (D.C. Cir. 1980).

58. *See* Kate Stith, "Congress' Power of the Purse," 97 *Yale L.J.* 1343, 1383–84 (1988).

59. The No-Transfer Act, 3 Stat. 471–2, enacted in 1811, permitted the president to seize land south of Georgia and delayed publication so that local Spanish authorities

would not know what was coming. The act was finally published in 1818. Fisher, *supra* note 22, at 214.

Ironically, there have been times when CIA directors themselves have voiced no objection to publication of an aggregate budget figure for the intelligence community. Fisher, *supra* note 22, at 249–50. After the Church Committee found the 1949 act "inconsistent" with the Statement and Account Clause, S. Rep. No. 755, 94th Cong., 2d Sess. 367 (1976), President Carter agreed that it would be appropriate to publish an aggregate figure. Fisher, *supra* note 22, at 250–51. However, the post-Watergate reform movement was not up to the task in this instance, and no statutory reforms of the appropriation process for the intelligence community have been enacted. More recently, CIA Director Robert Gates endorsed making the aggregate budget of the intelligence community public during his confirmation hearings. 49 *Cong. Q. Weekly Rep.* 3397 (Nov. 16, 1991.) Opposition from President Bush prompted Congress to recommend rather than require disclosure of the aggregate figure, beginning in 1993, in the 1992 Intelligence Authorization Act. *Id.*, *see* Pub. L. No. 102-183, § 701, 105 Stat. 1260 (1991). In light of continuing opposition by the Clinton administration, efforts in the Congress to mandate release of the aggregate intelligence budget have failed. 51 *Cong. Q. Weekly Rep.* 2168 (Aug. 7, 1993).

60. Stith, *supra* note 58, at 1384 n.201.

61. 418 U.S. at 166, 178 n.11

62. Stith, *supra* note 58, at 1392–93 (discussing justiciability barriers).

63. 49 *Cong: Q. Weekly Rep.* 3397 (Nov. 16, 1991).

Part IV

1. Of course, by specifying the object for which funds can be expended, every legitimating appropriation also operates as an implied restriction on the executive to spend the money on the specified object and no other. *See generally* Kate Stith, "Congress' Power of the Purse," 97 *Yale L.J.* 1343, 1353 (1988) ("All appropriations . . . may be conceived of as lump-sum grants with 'strings' attached. These strings, or conditions of expenditure, constitute legislative prescriptions that bind the operating arm of the government."). *Cf.* Spaulding v. Douglas Aircraft, 60 F. Supp. 985, 988 (S.D. Cal. 1945) ("Congress in making appropriations has the power and authority not only to designate the purpose of the appropriation, but also the terms and conditions under which the executive department . . . may expend such appropriations."). For this reason, some commentators have argued that the distinction between legitimating and what we call restrictive appropriations is only semantic. *See* Michael J. Glennon, *Constitutional Diplomacy* 291 (1990). We argue in chapter 11 that the difference is more than semantic in the development of customary national security law.

2. In light of the Appropriations Clause, U.S. Const. art. I, § 9, cl. 7, Congress's failure to appropriate money at all for a particular national security activity operates as a restriction on executive expenditure of public funds for that activity.

Chapter 11

1. National Federation of Federal Employees v. United States, 688 F. Supp. 671, 684 n.17 (D.D.C. 1988), *vacated and remanded sub nom.* American Foreign Service Ass'n v. Garfinkel, 490 U.S. 153 (1989).

2. *See, e.g.*, Lovett v. United States, 328 U.S. 303, 313 (1946) (observing that no "mere appropriation measure" was there at issue); Philip Minis v. United States, 40 U.S. 423, 445 (1841) (narrowly construing "mere appropriations law"); Kansas v. Adams, 608 F.2d 861, 867 (10th Cir. 1979) (contrasting intent behind substantive legislation with that of a "mere appropriations measure"); Rosebud Sioux Tribe v. Kneip, 375 F. Supp. 1065, 1070 (D.S.D. 1974) (act was "merely a change in an appropriations matter"). A computer search found over ninety federal cases using the deprecatory "mere" to describe appropriation measures.

3. *Cf.* TVA v. Hill, 437 U.S. 153, 190 (1978) (contrasting "substantive enactments" with appropriations, which "have the limited and specific purpose of providing funds for authorized programs").

4. U.S. General Accounting Office, *A Glossary of Terms Used in the Federal Budget Process* (1981).

5. *Id.* at 40.

6. Andrus v. Sierra Club, 442 U.S. 347, 361 (1979) (quoting House Budget Comm., *Congressional Control of Expenditures* 19 (Comm. Print 1977)).

7. *See, e.g., Andrus*, 442 U.S. at 359–61; Preterm, Inc. v. Dukakis, 591 F.2d 121, 125 (1st Cir. 1979); Sierra Club v. Andrus, 581 F.2d 895, 910–12 (D.C. Cir. 1978) (MacKinnon, J., dissenting), *rev'd*, 442 U.S. 347 (1979); Environmental Defense Fund v. Froehlke, 473 F.2d 346, 355 (D.C. Cir. 1972); Committee for Nuclear Responsibility, Inc. v. Seaborg, 463 F.2d 783, 785 (D.C. Cir. 1971).

8. *See, e.g., Andrus*, 442 U.S. at 359–61.

9. *Jefferson's Manual: Rules of the House of Representatives of the United States*, H.R. Doc. No. 256, 101st. Cong., 2d Sess. 573–74 (1991) [hereinafter *House Rules*].

10. S. Doc. No. 1, 101st Cong., 1st Sess. 15 (1991) [hereinafter *Senate Rules*].

11. *See Preterm, Inc.*, 591 F.2d at 138 (Bownes, J., dissenting).

12. Archie Parnell, "Congressional Interference in Agency Enforcement: The IRS Experience," 89 *Yale L.J.* 1360, 1378 (1980). *See* Jacques LeBoeuf, "Limitations on the Use of Appropriations Riders by Congress to Effectuate Substantive Policy Changes," 19 *Hastings Const. L.Q.* 457, 473 (1992) (commenting on Parnell).

13. U.S. Const. art. I, § 7.

14. *Id.*, § 8, cl. 12.

15. *Id.*, § 9, cl. 7.

16. 462 U.S. 919 (1983).

17. *Id.* at 951.

18. Sable Communications v. FCC, 492 U.S. 115, 133 (1989) (Scalia, J., concurring) (emphasis added). *See also* Fullilove v. Klutznick, 448 U.S. 448, 478 (1980) ("Congress, of course, may legislate without compiling the kind of 'record' appropriate with respect to judicial or administrative proceedings.").

19. National Treasury Employees Union v. Devine, 733 F.2d 114, 117 n.8 (D.C. Cir. 1984) (emphasis in original). Indeed, John Hart Ely wryly notes that "most legislation would be at risk were inattention a nullifying factor." John Hart Ely, "The American War in Indochina, Part I: The (Troubled) Constitutionality of the War They Told Us About," 42 *Stan. L. Rev.* 877, 888 (1990).

20. *See* Shurberg Broadcasting of Hartford, Inc. v. FCC, 876 F.2d 902, 940 (D.C. Cir. 1989) (Wald, C. J., dissenting) ("[D]eliberativeness must be presumed as long as Congress had before it sufficient information for the formation of a considered opinion.").

21. *See supra* chaps. 5 & 6.

22. *See generally supra* chap. 6; Louis Fisher, "Budget Concepts and Terminology: The Appropriations Phase," in 1 *Studies in Taxation, Public Finance and Related*

Subjects—A Compendium 437 (Fund for Public Policy Research ed., 1977); Stanley Bach, "The Senate's Compliance with Its Legislative Rules: The Appeal of Order," 18 *Cong. & Pres.* 77 (1991).

23. Neal E. Devins, "Regulations of Government Agencies through Limitations Riders," 1987 *Duke L.J.* 456, 470–71; Bach, *supra* note 22, at 83.

24. Bach, *supra* note 22, at 91 nn.14–15 (referring to Senate votes on the objection of nongermaneness).

25. *Id.*

26. *House Rules, supra* note 9, at 594; *Senate Rules, supra* note 10, at 16.

27. Devins, *supra* note 23, at 471.

28. Berk v. Laird, 317 F. Supp. 715, 728 (E.D.N.Y. 1970).

29. *See Preterm, Inc.*, 591 F.2d at 138 (Bownes, J., dissenting).

30. Louis Fisher, "The Authorization-Appropriations Process in Congress: Formal Rules and Informal Practices," 29 *Cath. U. L. Rev.* 51, 53 (1979). *See also* U.S. General Accounting Office, *Principles of Federal Appropriations Law* 2-34, 2-43 to 2-44, 2-48 to 2-49 (2d ed. 1991) [hereinafter *Appropriations Principles*].

31. *See, e.g.*, United States v. Dickerson, 310 U.S. 554, 555 (1940) ("There can be no doubt that Congress could suspend or repeal the authorization . . . ; and it could accomplish its purpose by an amendment to an appropriation bill"); City of Los Angeles v. Adams, 556 F.2d 40, 49 (D.C. Cir. 1977) ("Where Congress chooses to do so, . . . we are bound to follow Congress's last word on the matter even in appropriations law."); Friends of the Earth v. Armstrong, 485 F.2d 1, 9 (10th Cir. 1973) ("Appropriations acts are just as effective a way to legislate as are ordinary bills relating to a particular subject. An appropriation act may be used to suspend or to modify prior Acts of Congress."). *See also Appropriations Principles, supra* note 30, at 2-37 to 2-38.

32. Robertson v. Seattle Audubon Society, 112 S. Ct. 1407, 1414 (1992).

33. Devins, *supra* note 23, at 480.

34. *See* United States v. Will, 449 U.S. 200, 222 (1980) (stating that there is no doubt that appropriations can change existing law, but "'[t]he whole question depends on the intention of Congress . . . .'") (quoting *United States v. Mitchell*, 109 U.S. 146, 150 (1883)).

35. See *supra* chaps. 5 & 6. *See generally* Devins, *supra* note 23, at 458, 464–65 (summarizing procedural defects of appropriation-based policy-making); LeBoeuf, *supra* note 12, at 474.

36. *See supra* chap. 6. *See also* TVA v. Hill, 437 U.S. 153, 191 (1978) (construing appropriation measure narrowly in part because the appropriations committee had no jurisdiction over subject of measure and held no "extensive hearings"). Appropriation limitations that are written into an authorization, however, usually originate in the authorizing committee with subject-matter jurisdiction.

37. *See Preterm, Inc.*, 591 F.2d at 121, 129 (reporting that Hyde amendment was introduced as an appropriation rider to bypass subcommittees and committees in which comparable legislation was "languishing," according to Rep. Hyde); Parnell, *supra* note 12, at 1374 & n.99; Devins, *supra* note 23, at 464 (noting tendency of conservatives to use appropriations as vehicle for substantive legislation when committees are controlled by Democrats).

38. *See, e.g.*, Shurberg Broadcasting v. FCC, 876 F.2d 902, 926 (D.C. Cir. 1989) (finding no guidance for construing appropriation rider in "terse" appropriations committee report or conference report); *Preterm, Inc.*, 591 F.2d at 128 (noting absence of any conference or committee reports with which to construe the Hyde amendment, an appropriation rider).

39. *See supra* chap. 5; *cf. TVA v. Hill*, 437 U.S. at 192 (noting that the appropriations committee did not represent the views of the full Congress).

40. *See Preterm, Inc.*, 591 F.2d at 121, 135 (Bownes, J., dissenting).

41. *See generally* Devins, *supra* note 23, at 498–99; *Appropriations Principles, supra* note 30, at 2-29 (noting rebuttable presumption that an appropriation is for the fiscal year).

42. *See supra* chap. 6.

43. *See Appropriations Principles, supra* note 30, at 2-29 to 2-31, 2-44 to 2-45 (noting factors that rebut presumption of fiscal year duration); Devins, *supra* note 23, at 492–93, 496.

44. *See, e.g.*, Winter Park Communications, Inc. v. FCC, 873 F.2d 347, 364 (D.C. Cir. 1989); Connecticut v. Schweiker, 684 F.2d 979, 995 (D.C. Cir. 1982).

45. LeBoeuf, *supra* note 12, at 474.

46. *See, e.g.*, Rincon Band of Mission Indians v. Harris, 618 F.2d 569, 573 (9th Cir. 1980) (requiring showing of congressional awareness of action and purpose to approve it); City of Santa Clara v. Andrus, 572 F.2d 660, 672 (9th Cir. 1978) (noting that proponent of ratification by appropriations bears a heavy burden of demonstrating congressional knowledge), *cert. denied*, 439 U.S. 859 (1978); *see generally Sutherland's Statutory Construction* § 49.10 at 77 (5th ed. 1992) ("'Ratification by appropriation is not favored and will not be accepted where prior knowledge of the specific disputed action cannot be demonstrated clearly.'") (quoting D.C. Federation of Civic Associations, Inc. v. Airis, 391 F.2d 478, 482 (D.C. Cir. 1968); *Appropriations Principles, supra* note 30, at 2-52 to 2-54.

47. *Ex parte* Endo, 323 U.S. 283, 303 n.24 (1944).

48. *See, e.g.*, Fleming v. Mohawk Co., 331 U.S. 111, 116 (1947); Brooks v. Dewar, 313 U.S. 354, 361 (1941) (noting that repeated appropriations of funds raised by administrative practice with congressional knowledge of that practice constituted ratification of practice); United States v. Gerlach Live Stock Co., 339 U.S. 725, 735-36 (1950) (finding that nine appropriations over twelve years evidence approval of administrative practice); Alaska Steamship Co. v. United States, 290 U.S. 256, 262 (1933) (finding that annual appropriations for more than thirty-five years indicate congressional approval of practice for which they were spent).

49. *See, e.g.*, Sierra Club v. Andrus, 610 F.2d 581, 601–602 and cases cited at 602 n.30 (9th Cir. 1979), *vacated sub nom.* Sierra Club v. Watt, 451 U.S. 965 (1981).

50. *Appropriations Principles, supra* note 30, at 2-54.

51. *See* United States v. Will, 449 U.S. 200, 221–22 (1980); TVA v. Hill, 437 U.S. 153, 189–90 (1978). *See generally Sutherland's Statutory Construction* § 23.16.50 at 377 (4th ed. 1986); *Appropriations Principles, supra* note 30, at 2-37.

52. *See, e.g.*, Morton v. Mancari, 417 U.S. 535, 549–50 (1974); United States v. Borden Co., 308 U.S. 188, 198 (1939).

53. TVA v. Hill, 437 U.S. at 190 (emphasis added).

54. Minis v. United States, 40 U.S. 423, 445 (1841). *Cf.* Posadas v. National City Bank, 296 U.S. 497, 503 (1936) (treating the burden needed to overcome the general presumption against implied repeal).

55. *See, e.g.*, United States v. Dickerson, 310 U.S. 554, 561 (1940) (finding requisite intent in reported floor debates, over objection that plain language was clear); United States v. Will, 449 U.S. 200, 222 (1980); Preterm, Inc. v. Dukakis, 591 F.2d 121, 133 (1st Cir. 1979) (finding requisite intent in "the heated and lengthy debates that led to passage of the numerous versions of the Hyde Amendment . . . on the floor of each house, and the views expressed . . . [by] a wide spectrum of its members"); City of Los Angeles v.

Adams, 556 F.2d 40, 48–49 (10th Cir. 1977) (finding requisite intent in committee reports); Friends of the Earth v. Armstrong, 485 F.2d 1, 8–9 (10th Cir. 1973) (finding requisite intent in "formal" appropriations committee reports and hearings).

56. *Friends of the Earth,* 485 F.2d at 9.

57. *Preterm, Inc.*, 591 F.2d at 131.

58. TVA v. Hill, 437 U.S. 153, 192–93 (1978).

59. *See* Rincon Band of Mission Indians v. Harris, 618 F.2d 569, 574 n.7 (9th Cir. 1980) (finding the rule of ratification by appropriation applies with special force to cases involving land condemnation).

60. Dames & Moore v. Regan, 453 U.S. 654, 678 (1981). *See generally* J. Gregory Sidak, The President's Power of the Purse, 1989 *Duke L.J.* 1162, 1238 ("An exhaustive definition of Executive action is inherently difficult to produce in the abstract, for the Executive is the branch called upon to act in the face of greatest uncertainty. . . . Executive action, like jazz, is structured improvisation."); James F. Basile, "Congressional Assertiveness, Executive Authority and the Intelligence Oversight Act: A New Threat to the Separation of Powers," 64 *Notre Dame L. Rev.* 571, 580 (1989) ("[T]hose who conduct foreign policy cannot be subject to the regularity of legal norms. Quick action in response to fluid situations cannot be slowed by the legal restraints normally imposed on other policy areas.") (footnote omitted).

61. United States v. Curtiss-Wright Export Corp., 299 U.S. 304, 320 (1936). *Accord,* Zemel v. Rusk, 381 U.S. 1, 17–18 (1965).

62. Lichter v. United States, 334 U.S. 742, 778–79 (1948). *See generally* 3A Norman J. Singer, *Statutes and Statutory Construction* § 71.09 (5th ed. 1992) ("It is imperative that legislation providing for national defense and the conduct of war should be interpreted in ways that are most conducive to the achievement of its important objectives.").

63. Youngstown Sheet & Tube Co. v. Sawyer, 343 U.S. 579, 637 (1952).

64. Michael J. Glennon, *Constitutional Diplomacy* (1990) at 15–16 ("The President's initiatives here are contingently constitutional; their invalidity depends on congressional *inaction.*") (emphasis in original), *id.* at 30 ("Congress, especially in foreign affairs, has been primarily a reactive institution"); Phillip R. Trimble, "The Constitutional Common Law of Treaty Interpretation: A Reply to the Formalists," 137 *U. Pa. L. Rev.* 1461, 1480 (1989) ("The President initiates. The Congress oversees, and reverses if necessary."); Charles Tiefer, "The FAS Proposal: Valid Check or Unconstitutional Veto?," in *First Use of Nuclear Weapons: Under the Constitution, Who Decides?* 152 (P. Raven-Hansen ed., 1987) ("Authorization consists of the balance between the claimed inherent presidential powers and any congressional powers of limitation, looking at various shades of acquiescence and challenge by each branch in the respective claims and limits. . . . Many steps in foreign affairs and wartime occur on a level of responsive interaction and cue-following by the executive and Congress, not strict delegation.").

65. Harold H. Koh, *The National Security Constitution* 70 (1990); *cf.* Trimble, *supra* note 64, at 1475 (constitutional "common law").

66. *Youngstown,* 343 U.S. at 610–11. *See also* United States v. Midwest Oil Co., 236 U.S. 459, 469–75 (1915).

67. *See, e.g.*, Haig v. Agee, 453 U.S. 280, 300 (1981) (inferring statutory authority to restrict the right to travel on national security grounds from congressional acquiescence in executive practice and declared policy).

68. *See, e.g.*, Zemel v. Rusk, 381 U.S. 1, 17–18 (1965) (foreign affairs delegation takes "its content from history"). *See generally* Robert J. Gregory, "The Clearly Expressed Intent and the Doctrine of Congressional Acquiescence," 60 *UMKC L. Rev.* 27, 30 (1991); William N. Eskridge, Jr., "Interpreting Legislative Inaction," 87 *Mich. L. Rev.* 67, 69

(1988); John C. Grabow, "Congressional Silence and the Search for Legislative Intent: A Venture into 'Speculative Unrealities,'" 64 *B.U.L. Rev.* 737 (1985).

69. 453 U.S. 654 (1981).

70. 50 U.S.C. §§ 1701–06 (1992).

71. 22 U.S.C. § 1732 (1992).

72. 453 U.S. at 678–79.

73. *Id.* at 679–80 & n.8. *But see* Lee R. Marks & John G. Grabow, "The President's Foreign Economic Powers after Dames & Moore v. Regan: Legislation by Acquiescence," 68 *Cornell L. Rev.* 68, 87 (1982) (disputing length and consistency of prior practice).

74. 453 U.S. at 680–82 & n.10.

75. Glennon, *supra* note 64, at 59. *See also* Edwin Corwin, "The President's Power," *New Republic,* Jan. 29, 1951, at 15, 16 ("The Constitution does not consist primarily of precedents, but of principles with which precedents to be valid, must be squared."); Alan Watson, "An Approach to Customary Law," 1984 *U. Ill. L. Rev.* 561 ("[T]he nature of any source of law requires theoretical underpinnings regardless of whether these underpinnings are always implicit and never expressed. Accordingly, for custom to be regarded as law . . ., more than simple usage must be and is required, even if the usage is general and has long flourished. The principal issue is that one cannot derive an *ought* from an *is.*") (emphasis added).

76. *See* Glennon, *supra* note 64, at 55–58 (relevant factors include consistency, numerosity, duration (period of time over which repeated), density (number of times over period), regularity, and normalcy of executive practice); Michael J. Glennon, "The Use of Custom in Resolving Separation of Powers Disputes," 64 *B.U. L. Rev.* 109, 129–34 (1984) (noting that consistency is always required to create custom); *cf.* Anthony A. D'Amato, *The Concept of Custom in International Law* 56 (1971) (noting that relevant factors in the making of customary international law include duration, repetition, continuity, and generality).

77. *See* Glennon, *supra* note 64, at 63; Glennon, *supra* note 76, at 134; *cf.* D'Amato, *supra* note 76, at 76–86 (noting that factors in the making of customary international law include knowledge or reason to know and the practical possibility of action).

78. John Hart Ely would add the requirement that the American people have notice of the practice, as a control on congressional acquiescence. He argues that

> one consequence of the fact that [members of Congress] . . . aren't really expected to find out what's going on (before public and media outrage forces them to), and then aren't expected to come clean about how much they knew at the time, is to render any constitutional test geared to the knowledge of either Congress or its leadership unadministrable. . . . The test . . . must therefore be what the theory of our government suggested that it should have been all along, whether *the American people* knew what was going on.

John Hart Ely, "The American War in Indochina, Part II: The Unconstitutionality of the War They Didn't Tell Us About," 42 *Stan. L. Rev.* 1099, 1123 (1990) (emphasis in original). He fails, however, to supply any administrable test for measuring whether "the people" are on notice. Is it the existence of media reports about the practice? If so, what media? Will an exposé in *I.F. Stone Weekly* suffice? Or must the practice be unveiled on national television? Ely's requirement *is* arguably rooted in "the theory of our government," but it is operationalized through notice to the people's representatives in Congress. In any event, it is unclear that his requirement adds much to the requirement of notice to Congress because it is highly improbable that a controversial executive national security practice of which Congress is on notice will not eventually be leaked to the press, if not denounced publicly by some members of Congress. *But see id.*, at 1131 (observing that sporadic leaks about the secret war in Laos, consistently denied by the administration, did not put the American people on notice).

79. *See* Powell v. McCormack, 395 U.S. 486, 546–47 (1969) ("That an unconstitutional action has been taken before surely does not render that same action any less unconstitutional at a later date."). In *Chadha,* for example, the Supreme Court overturned more than fifty years of legislative practice on the ground that it violated the lawmaking provisions of the Constitution. Immigration & Naturalization Service v. Chadha, 462 U.S. 919 (1983). *See generally* Thomas A. Curtis, Note, "Recess Appointments to Article III Courts: The Use of Historical Practice in Constitutional Interpretation," 84 *Colum. L. Rev.* 1758, 1783-84 (1984).

80. *See, e.g.*, Zuber v. Allen, 396 U.S. 168, 185–86 n.21 (1969) ("The verdict of quiescent years cannot be invoked to baptize a statutory gloss that is otherwise impermissible.").

81. Glennon, *supra* note 64, at 62.

82. *See* Gregory, *supra* note 68, at 30–31 ("Acquiescence by silence is presumably the weakest of the acquiescence theories;" acquiescence by rejection "is no more constitutionally significant than mere silence"); Eskridge, *supra* note 68, at 67, 98–103; Grabow, *supra* note 68, at 749–50; Edwin Chemerinsky, "Controlling Inherent Presidential Power: Providing a Framework for Judicial Review," 56 *S. Cal. L. Rev.* 863, 888 (1983); Paul Gewirtz, "The Courts, Congress and Executive Policy-Making: Notes on Three Doctrines," 40 *Law & Contemp. Probs.* 46, 79 (Summer 1976) (footnotes omitted) ("Congress often acquiesces in the executive's action for reasons having nothing to do with the majority's preferences on the policy issues involved.").

83. Johnson v. Transportation Agency, 480 U.S. 616, 672 (1987) (Scalia, J., dissenting). *See generally* Henry Hart & Albert Sachs, *The Legal Process* 1395–96 (tentative ed. 1958) (listing additional factors creating interpretative ambiguity).

84. *See* Gregory, *supra* note 68, at 33; Eskridge, *supra* note 68, at 95–98; Laurence H. Tribe, "Toward a Syntax of the Unsaid: Construing the Sounds of Congressional and Constitutional Silence," 57 *Ind. L.J.* 515, 530 (1982).

85. *See* Gregory, *supra* note 68, at 31.

86. Glennon, *supra* note 76, at 143.

87. Zuber v. Allen, 396 U.S. 168, 186 n.21 (1969).

88. *See* Gregory, *supra* note 68, at 31 ("Armed with the shield of a congressional enactment, the reenactment doctrine stands the best chance of withstanding the formalist purge of extra-constitutional lawmaking.").

89. *See, e.g.*, Grabow, *supra* note 68, at 764 n.152.

90. Panel Discussion, "The Appropriations Power and the Necessary and Proper Clause," 68 *Wash. U. L.Q.* 623, 651 (1990) (remarks of Kate Stith).

91. Dames & Moore v. Regan, 453 U.S. 654, 688 (1981).

92. Glennon, *supra* note 76, at 139.

93. Senate Comm. on Governmental Affairs, *Study on Federal Regulation: Congressional Oversight of Regulatory Agencies* 31 (Comm. Print 1977).

Chapter 12

1. *See generally* Stephen Dycus, Arthur L. Berney, William C. Banks, and Peter Raven-Hansen, *National Security Law* 178–85 (1990) (and sources there listed); John

Hart Ely, "The American War in Indochina, Part I: The (Troubled) Constitutionality of the War They Told Us About," 42 *Stan. L. Rev.* 877 (1990) [hereinafter *Ely Part I*]; John Hart Ely, "The American War in Indochina, Part II; The Unconstitutionality of the War They Didn't Tell Us About," 42 *Stan. L. Rev.* 1093 (1990) [hereinafter *Ely Part II*]; J. Terry Emerson, "Congress and the Commitment to Vietnam," in American B. Ass'n, Standing Comm. on Law and Nat'l Security, *Congress, the President and Foreign Policy* 57, 65–67 (1984). Our debt in the following pages to John Hart Ely's exhaustive reconstruction and powerful analysis of the legal basis for the war in Indochina will be obvious.

2. Pub. L. No. 88-408, 78 Stat. 384 (1964).

3. Dycus *et al.*, *supra* note 1, at 184.

4. 111 *Cong. Rec.* 9282 (1965).

5. *Id.*

6. *Id.* at 9283.

7. *Id.*

8. 111 *Cong. Rec.* 9540-41, 9772 (1965).

9. Pub. L. No. 89-18, 79 Stat. 109 (1965).

10. Pub. L. No. 89-213, 79 Stat. 863, 872 (1965).

11. 2 *Weekly Comp. Pres. Doc.* 33 (Jan. 17, 1966). The bulk of the address was devoted to the war, which the president described as having escalated substantially during the past year. *Id.* at 34–37.

12. *Ely Part I, supra* note 1, at 899.

13. 112 *Cong. Rec.* 4474–75 (1966).

14. 112 *Cong. Rec.* 4366 (1966) (remarks of Sen. W. Morse). *See also id.* at 4375 (remarks of Sen. J. Javits announcing his vote for the appropriation but protesting "against future Presidential actions in Vietnam through the authorization and appropriations process, that is, through the back door"); *id.* at 4393 (remarks of Sen. W. Morse urging Congress to use its power of the purse to "check" the presidential escalation of the war: "I am merely asking that we check the President *and not give him that authorization*") (emphasis added).

15. 112 *Cong. Rec.* 4411 (1966). *See* Pub. L. No. 89-367, 1966 U.S.C.C.A.N. (80 Stat.) 42.

16. 112 *Cong. Rec.* 4406 (1966). The rider would have required specific congressional authorization for deployments of draftees to Vietnam. It was defeated in part on the strength of the argument that it would "set up an entirely new standard *in the middle of the fighting in Vietnam.*" *Id.* at 4405 (statement of Sen. Russell) (emphasis added).

17. *Id.* at 4404.

18. Pub. L. No. 90-5, 81 Stat. 5–6 (1967).

19. Pub. L. No. 90-40, 81 Stat. 100 (1967).

20. Pub. L. No. 91-672, § 12, 84 Stat. 2053 (1971).

21. *See Ely Part I, supra* note 1, at 907.

22. Stanley Karnow, *Vietnam* 491 (1983).

23. *Id.* at 491, *as corrected in Ely Part I, supra* note 1, at 899 n.98.

24. Congress's knowledge and therefore authorization of military activities in Laos and Cambodia was never as clear. John Hart Ely argues that appropriations did not authorize "the Cambodian ground incursion in 1970 because there had been no prior notice to Congress that the funds might be thus used." *Ely Part I, supra* note 1, at 911. He finds that the incursion was nonetheless authorized because the Gulf of Tonkin Resolution impliedly permitted activities outside Vietnam that were necessary to protect American forces and their South Vietnamese allies in Vietnam. *Id.* at 902–05, 908–911. It is not clear to us why, by the same logic, appropriations to support fighting in South

Vietnam did not also constitute authorization for military activities in Cambodia that were necessary to support the fighting; the congressional knowledge necessary to find ratification is knowledge of the fighting in Vietnam, not (at least at first) of every activity the president might have ordered to protect troops engaged in that fighting. In any event, after repeal of the Gulf of Tonkin Resolution, Congress continued appropriations with full knowledge of the bombing of Cambodia and therefore approved it until 1973. *Id.* at 911. Ely convincingly shows why restrictive appropriations enacted between 1970 and 1973 did not deauthorize the bombing. *Id.* at 911–19.

The secret bombing of Cambodia from 1969 to 1970 and the secret war in Laos from 1962 to 1969, on the other hand, were not authorized by appropriation for the reasons stated in the text, *infra*.

25. The legality and effect of the Gulf of Tonkin Resolution is beyond the scope of this article. For one view, see *Ely Part I, supra* note 1, at 884–97.

26. Orlando v. Laird, 443 F.2d 1039, 1042 (2d Cir. 1971) (footnotes omitted), *cert. denied*, 404 U.S. 869 (1971).

27. *Id.* at 1043.

28. DaCosta v. Laird (DaCosta I), 448 F.2d 1368, 1369 (2d Cir. 1971).

29. DaCosta v. Laird (DaCosta III), 471 F.2d 1146, 1157 (2d Cir. 1973).

30. The secret special forces missions to knock out Iraqi air defenses immediately prior to the air attack on Iraq in Operation Desert Storm are recent examples.

31. Symposium, "The President's Power as Commander-in-Chief Versus Congress' War Power and Appropriations Power," 43 *U. Miami L. Rev.* 17, 33 (1988) (remarks of Geoffrey P. Miller).

32. 3 *Annals of Cong.* 922 (1793) (statement of Rep. William Findley). *See generally supra* chap. 4.

33. *See Ely Part II, supra* note 1, at 1142–46.

34. *Id.* at 1143–44.

35. *Id.* at 1137–46.

36. *Id.* at 1094–1132.

37. *See, e.g.*, Lawyers Committee on American Policy toward Vietnam, "American Policy vis-à-vis Vietnam, in Light of Our Constitution, the United Nations Charter, the 1954 Geneva Accords, and the Southeast Asia Collective Defense Treaty," *reprinted in* 112 *Cong. Rec.* 4397–4403 (1966).

38. 50 U.S.C. § 1541 (Supp. III 1991).

39. J. Gregory Sidak, "To Declare War," 41 *Duke L.J.* 27 (1991).

40. *Id.* at 33.

41. *Id.* at 71.

42. *Id.* at 79–81.

43. *Id.* at 90.

44. *Id.* at 91. The declaration of war against Mexico in 1846, however, was bundled with other legislation. *Id.* at 92.

45. *Id.* at 102.

46. *Id.* at 68–69, 81, 89, 100.

47. *Id.* at 102.

48. *Id.* at 95.

49. *See, e.g.*, Charles A. Lofgren, "War-Making Under the Constitution: The Original Understanding," 81 *Yale L.J.* 672 (1972); Abraham D. Sofaer, *War, Foreign Affairs and Constitutional Power: The Origins* 56 (1976).

50. Lofgren, *supra* note 49, at 680–81 & n.31.

51. *Id.* at 685. *See The Federalist* No. 41, at 256 (J. Madison) (C. Rossiter ed., 1961) (explaining that it would be superfluous to discuss the necessity for the power to declare war because "[t]he existing confederation establishes this power in the most ample form").

52. Sofaer, *supra* note 49, at 56 (footnote omitted).

53. U.S. Const., art. I, § 8, cl. 11.

54. Jules Lobel, "Covert War and Congressional Authority: Hidden War and Forgotten Power," 134 *U. Pa. L. Rev.* 1035, 1090 (1986) (footnote omitted); Lofgren, *supra* note 49, at 689–93.

55. Miller v. The Resolution, 2 U.S. (2 Dall.) 1, 21 (Ct. App. in Cases of Capture 1781).

56. *The Federalist* No. 25, at 165 (C. Rossiter ed., 1961) ("[T]he ceremony of a formal denunciation of war has of late fallen into disuse"). *See generally* J. F. Maurice, *Hostilities Without Declaration of War 1700–1870*, at 4 (1883).

57. *See* Dycus *et al.*, *supra* note 1, at 88 (citing statutes).

58. Francis D. Wormuth & Edwin B. Firmage, *To Chain the Dog of War* 155–56 (2d ed. 1989).

59. *Id.* at 126–33. As we noted in chap. 4, Congress appropriated money after the fact for the hostilities against the Wabash Indians.

60. Sofaer, *supra* note 49, at 208–27; Dycus et al., *supra* note 1, at 253–55. In fact, hostilities against the Barbary pirates were impliedly approved by appropriations and defense authorization acts. *Id.* at 253–54 & 255 n.4 (citing statutes and executive invocation of same as authority for orders to naval commander).

61. Sofaer, *supra* note 49, at 336–65.

62. Pub. L. No. 4, ch. 4, 69 Stat. 7 (1955) ("[T]he President . . . hereby is authorized to employ the Armed Forces of the United States.").

63. Pub. L. No. 85-7, § 2, 71 Stat. 5 (1957) ("[I]f the President determines the necessity thereof, the United States is prepared to use armed forces.").

64. 4 U.S. (4 Dall.) 37 (1800).

65. *Id.* at 40–41.

66. *Id.* at 41.

67. *Id.* at 43.

68. *Id.* at 45–46.

69. Burrow-Giles Lithographic Co. v. Sarony, 111 U.S. 53, 57 (1884). *Accord,* Prigg v. Pennsylvania, 41 U.S. (16 Pet.) 539, 621 (1842). American courts followed the reasoning of *Bas* in 1841 and 1886. *See People v. McLeod,* 1 N.Y. (Hill) 377 (1841); Gray v. United States, 21 Ct. Cl. 340 (1886).

70. Sidak, *supra* note 39, at 61.

71. He explains that "[s]aying that Congress has the power to authorize limited war does not necessarily imply that it holds that power exclusively." Sidak, *supra* note 39, at 60.

72. Talbot v. Seeman, 5 U.S. (1 Cranch) 1, 28 (1801) (emphasis added). Of course, nothing in this assertion, or in the conclusions reached in *Bas,* is inconsistent with a presidential role in deciding upon war, because Congress's "acts" are, like all legislation, subject to presentment.

73. *See, e.g.,* Orlando v. Laird, 443 F.2d 1039 (2d Cir. 1971); Mitchell v. Laird, 488 F.2d 611, 615 (D.C. Cir. 1973).

74. Sidak, *supra* note 39, at 69–70.

75. *Id.* at 34, 90, 99.

76. *See, e.g.*, Harold H. Koh, "Comment: The Coase Theorem and the War Power: A Response," 41 *Duke L.J.* 122, 128 (1991); *Ely Part I*, *supra* note 1, at 888. Congress debated the declaration of war against Great Britain in 1812 for eighteen days. *See* Sofaer, *supra* note 49, at 287.

77. Sidak, *supra* note 39, at 102.

78. *Id.* at 80. Ironically, he adopts the conclusion that only "[the] declaration of imperfect war against France in the Quasi-War of 1798–1800 . . . explained the nature of the warlike provocation . . . ," *id.*, even though the Quasi-War was authorized by a series of ordinary statutes and was never formally declared.

79. Sidak, *supra* note 39, at 80.

80. *Pub. Papers of George Bush* 13 (Jan. 8, 1991).

81. Sidak, *supra* note 39, at 95, 100–101, 103.

82. Carl von Clausewitz, *On War* 87 (M. Howard & P. Paret eds., 1976).

83. *See* Bas v. Tingy, 4 U.S. (4 Dall.) 37, 45 (1800) (Chase, J.) (noting that "the popular feeling may not have been ripe for a solemn declaration of war").

84. *See, e.g.*, Ann Thomas & A. J. Thomas, Jr., *The War-Making Powers of the President* 87 (1982) (footnote omitted); Symposium, *supra* note 31, at 31–32 (stating that the declaration "heightens conflict, challenges the other side, deters compromise, complicates relations with allies, and may even benefit the enemy by dignifying the very behavior that we are opposing") (remarks of Geoffrey P. Miller); Clyde Eagleton, "The Form and Function of the Declaration of War," 32 *Amer. J. Int'l L.* 19, 24 (1938).

85. *The Life and Correspondence of James McHenry* 291–95 (B. Steiner ed., 1907). *See generally* Sofaer, *supra* note 49, at 139–47.

86. 443 F.2d 1032, 1043, *cert. denied,* 404 U.S. 869 (1971). *See also* Mitchell v. Laird, 488 F.2d 611, 615 (D.C. Cir. 1973).

87. *See, e.g.*, Lawrence R. Velvel, *Undeclared War and Civil Disobedience* 60–61 (1970); *cf.* Paul Gewirtz, "The Courts, Congress and Executive Policy-Making: Notes on Three Doctrines," 40 *Law & Contemp. Probs.* 46, 66–67 (Summer 1976) (urging judge-made clear statement rule for when the executive claims statutory authority to make major policy). John Hart Ely also asserts very tentatively that "some such [clear statement] doctrine might properly be inferred from the requirements of the Constitution," *Ely Part I*, *supra* note 1, at 926 n.217, but he does not elaborate or explain how this assertion can be squared with his finding of implied authority from appropriations for the American war in Indochina. *See id.*, at 897–902. Presumably he means that no such doctrine has *yet* been inferred, and therefore none was applicable to the Vietnam-era appropriations.

88. EEOC v. Arabian American Oil Co., 499 U.S. 244, 26 (1991) (Marshall, Blackmun, & Stevens, JJ., dissenting). *See* William Luneberg, "Justice Rehnquist, Statutory Interpretation, the Policies of Clear Statement, and Federal Jurisdiction, 58 *Ind. L.J.* 211, 217 (1982) ("So-called clear-statement techniques of statutory interpretation function in part to free a court from its duty to abide by the results of its investigation into the meaning of a statute.").

89. 360 U.S. 474 (1959).

90. *Id.* at 506–07 (other citations omitted) (emphasis added). *See also* Kent v. Dulles, 357 U.S. 116, 129 (1958) (deciding that authority will not be inferred from general statute to restrict the right to travel) (1958); *cf.* Peters v. Hobby, 349 U.S. 331, 345–47 (1955) (finding that where "substantial rights affecting the lives and property of citizens are at stake," presidential silence does not constitute acquiescence in administrative assertion of power).

91. *Ex parte* Endo, 323 U.S. 283 (1944).

92. *See* Peter H. Aranson et al., "A Theory of Legislative Delegation," 68 *Cornell L. Rev.* 1, 12 (1982); Michael J. Glennon, *Constitutional Diplomacy* 65 (1990) (arguing a "noninterference-with-protected-freedoms" limitation on congressional acquiescence).

93. 17 U.S. (4 Wheat.) 316 (1819).

94. *Id.* at 401 (emphasis added).

95. *See, e.g.*, Edward Susolik, Note, "Separation of Powers and Liberty: The Appointments Clause, Morrison v. Olson, and the Rule of Law," 63 *S. Cal. L. Rev.* 1515 (1990).

96. *See, e.g.*, Andrew W. Hayes, Note, "The Boland Amendments and Foreign Affairs Deference," 88 *Colum. L. Rev.* 1534, 1558–59 (1988); Harold Edgar & Benno C. Schmidt, Jr., "Curtiss-Wright Comes Home: Executive Power and National Security Secrecy, 21 *Harv. C.R.-C.L. L. Rev.* 349, 352 n.7 (1986).

97. David Schoenbrod, "The Delegation Doctrine: Could the Court Give It Substance?," 83 *Mich. L. Rev.* 1223, 1261 (1985).

98. 360 U.S. at 506–07 (footnote omitted).

99. 50 U.S.C. § 1547(a)(1) (1988).

100. S. Rep. No. 220, 93d Cong., 1st Sess. 25 (1973).

101. 443 F.2d 1039, *cert. denied*, 404 U.S. 869 (1971). The case is discussed *supra*, at beginning of this chapter.

102. Michael J. Glennon, "Mr. Sofaer's War Powers 'Partnership,'" 80 *Amer. J. Int'l L.* 584, 586 (1986).

103. *Id. Cf.* Paul W. Kahn, "Gramm-Rudman and the Capacity of Congress to Control the Future," 13 *Hastings Const. L.Q.* 185, 194 (1986); Earl Crawford, *The Construction of Statutes* § 232 (1904).

104. John Hart Ely, "Suppose Congress Wanted a War Powers Act That Worked?," 88 *Colum. L. Rev.* 1379, 1418 (1988).

105. *Id.* at 1419.

106. Sidak, *supra* note 39, at 110, 111.

107. *Cf.* Kahn, *supra* note 103, at 203.

108. 349 U.S. 302 (1955).

109. 5 U.S.C. § 559 (1988) ("[A] subsequent statute may not be held to supersede or modify this subchapter . . . except to the extent that it does so expressly.").

110. 349 U.S. at 310.

111. *See, e.g.*, Julian N. Eule, "Temporal Limits on the Legislative Mandate: Entrenchment and Retroactivity," 1987 *Am. B. Found. Res. J.* 379, 397, 425 n.213; Crawford, *supra* note 103, § 137; U.S. General Accounting Office, *Principles of Federal Appropriations Law* at 2-37 (2d ed. 1991) [hereinafter *Appropriations Principles*].

112. *The Federalist* No. 78, at 468 (A. Hamilton) (C. Rossiter ed., 1961) (emphasis in original).

113. Glennon, *supra* note 102, at 586.

114. *See generally* Eule, *supra* note 111, at 379; Kahn, *supra* note 103; Testimony of Abraham Sofaer, Legal Adviser to the Department of State, before the Subcommittee on Arms Control, International Security and Science of the House Committee on Foreign Affairs (April 29, 1986), *reprinted in* 80 *Amer. J. Int'l L.* 636, 638 (1986) (asserting that the effort of War Powers Resolution section 8 to limit the "constitutional options" of later Congresses poses "serious constitutional problems"); *cf.* Sidak, *supra* note 39, at 111 (asserting that section 8 is "profoundly undemocratic"). The English principle is similar: "Acts of Parliament derogatory from the power of subsequent parliaments bind not." William Blackstone, 1 *Commentaries* 90 (Thomas Wait & Co. 1807).

Paul Kahn has also raised doubt whether a statutory rule of construction like the War

Powers Resolution's is constitutional, but does not reach a conclusion on this issue. *See* Kahn, *supra* note 103, at 203 & n.65.

115. *See* Eule, *supra* note 111, at 403–05; Kahn, *supra* note 103, at 199, 208.

116. Eule, *supra* note 110, at 404–05 (footnotes omitted).

117. "An Act for Establishing Religious Freedom [1779], passed in the Assembly of Virginia in the Beginning of the Year 1786," *reprinted in The Life and Selected Writings of Thomas Jefferson* 311, 313 (Adrienne Koch & William Peden eds., 1944), *quoted by* Sidak, *supra* note 39, at 112 n.415.

118. 349 U.S. at 307–10.

119. *Cf.* Crawford, *supra* note 103, § 223.

120. Sidak, *supra* note 39, at 1251–52.

121. *See generally* Charles B. Hochman, "The Supreme Court and the Constitutionality of Retroactive Legislation," 73 *Harv. L. Rev.* 692 (1960). In a recent decision declining to give retroactive effect to a statute, the Court noted that "congressional enactments . . . will not be construed to have retroactive effect unless their language requires this result." Bowen v. Georgetown University Hospital, 488 U.S. 204, 208 (1988).

122. Although the principal cases treating ratification of executive actions came later, ratification was recognized as early as 1814 in an opinion by Justice Story.

> I am perfectly satisfied . . . that no subject can legally commit hostilities, or capture property of an enemy, when, either expressly or constructively, the sovereign has prohibited it. But suppose he does, I would ask if the sovereign may not ratify his proceedings; and thus, by a retroactive operation, give validity to them? Of this there seems to me no legal doubt.

Brown v. United States, 12 U.S. (8 Cranch) 110, 133 (1814) (Story, J., dissenting).

123. Wilson v. Shaw, 204 U.S. 24, 32 (1907).

124. Isbrandtsen-Moller Co. v. United States, 300 U.S. 139, 147 (1937).

125. Swayne & Hoyt, Ltd. v. United States, 300 U.S. 297, 301–02 (1937) (citations omitted). *Accord,* Fleming v. Mohawk Co., 331 U.S. 111, 116 (1947); Brooks v. Dewar, 313 U.S. 354, 360–61 (1941).

126. *See* cases cited in *Appropriations Principles, supra* note 111, at 2-53.

127. William van Alstyne, "Congress, the President, and the Power to Declare War: A Requiem for Vietnam," 121 *U. Pa. L. Rev.* 1, 20 (1972). *See also Ely Part II, supra* note 1, at 1105 n.61; Lawyers Committee on American Policy, *supra* note 37, at 4403; *cf.* Memorandum *Amicus Curiae* of Law Professors at 6–7, Dellums v. Bush, 752 F. Supp. 1141 (D.D.C. 1990) (No. 90-2866), *reprinted in* 27 *Stan. J. Int'l L.* 257 (1991).

128. 67 U.S. (2 Black) 635 (1862).

129. *Id.* at 671 (emphasis in original). The Court quoted the 1814 opinion of Justice Story in Brown v. United States, 12 U.S. (8 Cranch) 110, 131–33 (1814) (dissenting) as correctly stating the doctrine of ratification. *See supra* note 122.

130. *Black's Law Dictionary* 1239 (4th ed. 1951).

131. *See* The Pedro, 175 U.S. 354 (1899). *See generally* Eagleton, *supra* note 84, at 30.

132. *Ely Part II, supra* note 1, at 1105 n.61 ("[I]t may . . . be doubtful that a *court* should ever hold post facto ratification of a war of which Congress had become aware to have been insufficient.") (emphasis in original).

133. 67 U.S. (2 Black) at 668. In addition, prior legislation did authorize the president "to called [*sic*] out the militia and use the military and naval forces of the United

States . . . to suppress insurrection." *Id.* (citing Acts of Feb. 28, 1795, and March 3, 1807).

134. 343 U.S. 579 (1952).

135. *See* 343 U.S. at 631 & n.1 (Douglas, J., concurring) ("The President might seize and the Congress by subsequent action could ratify the measure."); 343 U.S. at 611 (Frankfurter, J., concurring) (noting that Lincoln seized railroads during the Civil War "and his order was ratified by the Congress").

136. 50 U.S.C. § 1544(b) (1988).

137. J. Gregory Sidak, "The President's Power of the Purse," 1989 *Duke L.J.* 1162, 1250–51.

138. *Id.* at 1251.

139. 343 U.S. at 631 (Douglas, J., concurring).

140. *Quoted supra* chap. 4 in text accompanying n.44 (emphasis added). *See generally supra* chap. 4.

141. *See, e.g.*, letter from Thomas Jefferson to John B. Colvin (Sept. 20, 1810), *reprinted in* 11 *The Works of Thomas Jefferson* 147 (P. Ford ed., 1908) (rationalizing the unauthorized acquisition of the Louisiana territory by the prospect that Congress will subsequently ratify it by appropriation).

142. *See generally* Jules Lobel, "Emergency Power and the Decline of Liberalism," 98 *Yale L.J.* 1385 (1989); Kate Stith, "Congress' Power of the Purse," 97 *Yale L.J.* 1343, 1351 & n.35 (1988).

143. Lobel, *supra* note 142, at 1396 (footnote omitted):

> Most early leaders of the Republic . . . generally believed that the problems associated with creating a constitutional basis for the exercise of emergency power outweighed the dangers of allowing the President to act extra-constitutionally and unlawfully in extreme crisis situations. A requirement that the President act unconstitutionally ensures that Congress will have to decide whether or not to ratify his actions.

Lobel's characterization of the beliefs of the early leaders is completely consistent with their debate about emergency executive spending authority, discussed *supra* chap. 4.

144. Mitchell v. Laird, 488 F.2d 611, 615 (D.C. Cir. 1973).

145. *See, e.g., Ely Part I, supra* note 1, at 900–01.

146. *See, e.g.*, Lawrence R. Velvel, *Undeclared War and Civil Disobedience* 56 (1970) ("As long as American soldiers were fighting in Vietnam, even if they were fighting there as a direct result of the usurpation of Congress' power to declare war, Congressmen felt morally and politically and patriotically forced to provide the money which was necessary for their survival."); Note, "Congress, the President, and the Power to Commit Forces to Combat," 81 *Harv. L. Rev.* 1771, 1801 (1968) (noting that after hostilities have already begun, "the effective choice remaining to Congress is likely to be severely limited").

147. Michael J. Glennon, *Constitutional Diplomacy* 64 (1990).

148. *See Ely Part I, supra* note 1, at 899–900.

149. *See infra* chap. 13.

150. *Id.*

151. *Ely Part I, supra* note 1, at 901 (footnote omitted).

152. Dan Morgan, "'Team Player' Breaks Ranks on Support of U.S. Troop Deployments," *Wash. Post*, Sept. 27, 1990, at A37.

153. *The Federalist* No. 26, at 171–72 (A. Hamilton) (C. Rossiter ed., 1961) (emphasis in original), *quoted more fully supra* chap. 3.

154. *Id.* at 171–72.

155. *Quoted by* Michael J. Glennon, "The Gulf War and the Constitution," 70 *Foreign Affairs* 88, 96 (1991).

Chapter 13

1. Thus, we do not attempt to conduct a complete statutory construction of the amendments, let alone to decide whether they were violated, matters debated at length elsewhere. *Compare, e.g., Report of the Congressional Comm. Investigating the Iran-Contra Affair,* S. Rep. No. 100-216, H.R. Rep. No. 100-433, at 395–411 (1987) [hereinafter *Iran-Contra Report*] *with id.* at 489–500 (Minority Report).

2. The nonclassified amendments are summarized in a chart in Congressional Research Service, *Legislative Histories of Statutory Restrictions on Funding for Covert Assistance for Military or Paramilitary Operations in Nicaragua, FY 1883–FY 1986,* 133 Cong. Rec. 16075–80 (1987) [hereinafter *CRS Legislative Histories*].

3. A prior restriction was enacted as a classified annex to the Intelligence Authorization Act for Fiscal Year 1983, Pub. L. No. 97-269, 96 Stat. 1142 (1982). *CRS Legislative Histories, supra* note 2, at 15665.

4. The Defense Appropriation Act for Fiscal Year 1983, Pub. L. No. 97-377, § 793, 96 Stat. 1833, 1865 (1982), provided that:

> [n]one of the funds provided in this Act may be used by the Central Intelligence Agency or the Department of Defense to furnish military equipment, military training or advice, or other support for military activities, to any group or individual, not part of a country's armed forces, for the purpose of overthrowing the Government of Nicaragua or provoking a military exchange between Nicaragua and Honduras.

5. *See Iran-Contra Report, supra* note 1, at 396 (quoting legal opinions for the administration).

6. *CRS Legislative Histories, supra* note 2, at 15685 *et seq.*

7. *Id.* at 15811. The House approved the same restriction as a provision to the intelligence authorization bill for fiscal 1984. *Id.* at 15858.

8. *Iran-Contra Report, supra* note 1, at 396–97 & n.23.

9. *See* Department of Defense Appropriations Act for Fiscal Year 1984, Pub. L. No. 98-212, § 775, 97 Stat. 1452 (1983); Intelligence Authorization Act for Fiscal 1984, Pub. L. No. 98-215, § 108, 97 Stat. 1475 (1983).

10. *See Iran-Contra Report, supra* note 1, at 397. The Department of Defense Appropriation Act also expressly prohibited transfers and reprogramming of funds for intelligence or "special activities" (covert operations) without prior express notice by the director of central intelligence or the secretary of defense to the appropriations committees. Pub. L. No. 98-212, § 766, 97 Stat. at 1451 (1983).

11. *See Wall St. J.*, Apr. 6, 1984, at A6.

12. *Iran Contra Report, supra* note 1, at 401 n.75. Katrina J. Church, Note, "The Briar Patch of Reality: A Legal Analysis of the Mining of Nicaragua's Harbors," 18 *N.Y.U. J. Int'l L. & Pol.* 169, 196 (1985). The clarity and completeness of the CIA's reporting to Congress is a subject of dispute, however.

13. *Iran-Contra Report, supra* note 1, at 397 n.32.

14. *Id.* at 397.

15. *Id.* at 398.

16. *CRS Legislative Histories, supra* note 2, at 15917.

17. Department of Defense Appropriations Act for Fiscal Year 1985, Pub. L. No. 98-473, § 8066, 98 Stat. 1837, 1935 (1984). *See also* Intelligence Authorization Act for Fiscal Year 1985, Pub. L. No. 98-618, § 801, 98 Stat. 3298, 3304 (1984).

18. *CRS Legislative Histories, supra* note 2, at 15918 (statement of Rep. Boland).

19. *Compare* Statement on Signing the Intelligence Authorization Act, Fiscal Year 1989, at 1988 *Pub. Papers* 1249–50 (Sept. 29, 1988) (remark of President Reagan on signing a Boland-like restriction, noting that he "signed the Act with the understanding that the extension of the restriction to all entities of the United States Government is not intended to, and does not, apply in a manner or to an extent that would conflict with my constitutional authority and duty to conduct the foreign relations of the United States").

20. In fact, both of these dates are somewhat misleading. Because the $24 million cap was exhausted sometime in June, 1984, no funds were available until Congress voted humanitarian aid on August 8, 1985, as described *infra*. Even after that vote, however, Boland's restrictions on covert military aid continued until at least September 30, 1985. *See CRS Legislative Histories, supra* note 2, at 16076 (discussing termination date of most restrictive Boland amendment).

21. International Security and Development Cooperation Act of 1985, Pub. L. No. 99-83, § 722(g), 99 Stat. 254 (1985).

22. *Id.*

23. *Id.* § 722(d), 99 Stat. 254.

24. *Id.* § 722(e), 99 Stat. 254.

25. Supplemental Appropriations Act, Pub. L. No. 99-88, § 102(b), 99 Stat. 325 (1985).

26. *Iran-Contra Report, supra* note 1, at 404 (citing acts).

27. Military Construction Appropriation, enacted as Continuing Appropriations for Fiscal Year 1987, Pub. L. No. 99-500, §§ 206– 208, 100 Stat. 1783-299 to 1783-300 (1986).

28. *Iran-Contra Report, supra* note 1, at 492 (Minority Report).

29. *See* 31 U.S.C. § 1350 (1988) (making violation of the Anti-Deficiency Act a crime punishable by fine of not more than $5,000 and imprisonment for no more than two years, or both).

30. *See supra* chap. 6.

31. *CRS Legislative Histories, supra* note 2, at 15691–93.

32. Frank G. Collela, Note, "Beyond Institutional Competence: Congressional Efforts to Legislate United States Foreign Policy Toward Nicaragua—The Boland Amendments," 54 *Brook. L. Rev.* 131, 167 (1988) (footnote omitted).

33. *Id.* at 164.

34. *See supra* chap. 11.

35. Of course, Congress did not debate each Boland amendment to the same degree. The earlier debates, especially those attending Boland-Zablocki and comparable restrictions that were ultimately defeated in the Senate, were the most extensive. By the time this restriction came back, Congress had already been through most of the issues.

36. *Iran-Contra Report, supra* note 1, at 489 (Minority Report). *See also* Collela, *supra* note 32, at 168 (noting that congressional policy was "fluctuat[ing]" and "inconsistent").

37. Continuing Appropriations, Pub. L. No. 98-441, § 106(c), 98 Stat. 1700 (1984).

38. *See supra* note 20.

39. Thomas S. Foley, "We Made Ourselves Quite Clear," *Wash. Post*, July 7, 1987, at A15.

40. *See* Collela, *supra* note 32, at 165 (so arguing); Thomas M. Franck & Edward

Weisbrod, *Foreign Policy by Congress* 22 (1979) ("[T]he 'let's split the difference down the middle' type of legislative compromise, so much a part of the way Congress and the President traditionally interact on domestic issues, can produce the worst of all possible worlds when applied to foreign policymaking.").

41. Andrew W. Hayes, Note, "The Boland Amendments and Foreign Affairs Deference," 88 *Colum. L. Rev.* 1534, 1571 n.271 (1988). ("Congress may have frequently changed its mind, but that does not make the individual statutes vague: Congress knew exactly what it wanted each time."). We would probably not go so far. Congress probably did not think through what it wanted, or what it had accomplished, each time. But whether it did or did not involves an individualized amendment-by-amendment inquiry that cannot be avoided by disparaging generalizations about changing policy.

42. *Iran-Contra Report, supra* note 1, at 490 (Minority Report).

43. *See* Stephen Dycus, Arthur L. Berney, William C. Banks, and Peter Raven-Hansen, *National Security Law* 349–56 (1990).

44. In contrast, the common formula for an appropriations limitation proper—one applying only to use of the appropriation in which it appears—is "[n]o part of any appropriation *contained in this act* shall be used . . . ." U.S. General Accounting Office, *Principles of Federal Appropriations Law* 2-28 (2d ed. 1991) (emphasis added) [hereinafter *Appropriations Principles*].

45. *Id.* (emphasis added).

46. *Iran-Contra Report, supra* note 1, at 492–93 (Minority Report).

47. *See supra* chap. 5.

48. *See* Larry M. Eig (Congressional Research Service), *Contra Aid: Analysis of Whether the National Security Council (NSC) and the NSC Staff Are an "Agency or Entity Involved in Intelligence Activities" Covered by Section 8066(A) of the Department of Defense Appropriations Act, FY 1985 (Boland Amendment)* 9 (May 11, 1987) ("The secret nature of CIA funding and the possible existence of funds in the CIA contingency reserve, whose original source may be highly uncertain, may explain in part why section 8066(a) is phrased in terms of 'no funds available,' instead of 'no appropriations contained in this Act or any other Act.'").

49. *See also supra* text accompanying note 18 (remarks of Rep. Boland).

50. *Iran-Contra Report, supra* note 1, at 496 (Minority Report) ("[T]here is no evidence of an intention to change a well-known term of art that excluded the NSC into one that included it.") (footnote omitted).

51. *Id.* at 493–97.

52. 437 U.S. 153, 189–90 (1978). *See supra* chap. 11.

53. *See supra* chap. 11.

54. 50 U.S.C. § 402 (1988 & Supp. III 1991).

55. *See, e.g.*, Eig, *supra* note 48, at 3–5; Congressional Quarterly, "National Security Council," 1 *Editorial Research Reports* 18–27 (1987); Roy M. Melbourne, "Odyssey of the NSC," 11 *Strategic Rev.* No. 3, 51–64 (Summer 1983); *Final Report of the Select Committee to Study Governmental Operations With Respect to Intelligence Activities*, S. Rep. No. 94–755, 94th Cong., 2d Sess., Book 1 at 44 (1976) [hereinafter *Church Committee Report*].

56. Zbigniew Brzezinski, "The NSC's Midlife Crisis," *Foreign Policy*, Winter 1987–88, at 97–98 (emphasis added).

57. *Id.* at 99 (citing national security adviser's secret mission to China); *Church Committee Report, supra* note 55, at 44–60.

58. Eig, *supra* note 48, at 5.

59. *Cf.* American Enterprise Inst., *National Security Policy Organization in Per-*

spective 32 (L. Korb & L. Hahn eds., 1981) ("[W]e are moving in the direction of a national security adviser and a National Security Council staff that *will become* more operational.") (remarks of David Aaron) (emphasis added).

60. Louis Fisher, "How Tightly Can Congress Draw the Purse Strings?," 83 *Amer. J. Int'l L.* 758, 761 (1989) (emphasis added). Moreover, the National Security Act provided until recently that there "is established *under the National Security Council* a Central Intelligence Agency," 50 U.S.C. § 403(a) (1989) (emphasis added) (repealed by Pub. L. No. 102-496, § 704, 106 Stat. 3189 (1992)), and Executive Order 12,333, issued December 4, 1981, before the Iran-Contra affair, charges the NSC with the "review of, guidance for and direction to the conduct of *all* national foreign intelligence, counterintelligence, and special activities [covert operations], and attendant policies and programs." Exec. Order 12,333, § 1.2, 49 *Fed. Reg.* 59,941 (1981), *reprinted in* 50 U.S.C. § 401 (1988).

61. *See Iran-Contra Report, supra* note 1, at 399–400 (quoting these officials, as well as other contemporary analyses).

62. Crowell v. Benson, 285 U.S. 22, 62 (1932) (emphasis added). One court has declared that this principle "is particularly important regarding legislative appropriations, since the Constitution vests Congress with plenary power to disperse or withhold federal money." Walker v. U.S. Dept. of Hous. and Urban Dev., 912 F.2d 819, 829 (5th Cir. 1990). For an application of the principle to an appropriation measure, *see* Brown v. Califano, 627 F.2d 1221, 1233–34 (D.C. Cir. 1980) (narrowly construing appropriation prohibition of agency support for mandatory busing to avoid finding it an unconstitutional prohibition of agency enforcement of the constitutional right to equal protection).

63. *Cf.* Christopher R. J. Pace, "The Art of War Under the Constitution," 95 *Dick. L. Rev.* 557, 567 (1991) ("A narrow construction of Congress's wartime military power secures the President in his ability to manage a war without undue and constitutionally-unwarranted interference from Congress.") (footnote omitted).

64. Ann Thomas & A. J. Thomas, Jr., *The War Making of the President* 140–41 (1982); Michael J. Glennon, *Constitutional Diplomacy* 100 (1990). *See also Iran-Contra Report, supra* note 1, at 412 (claiming that the Appropriations Clause gives Congress "an absolute check on Executive action requiring expenditure of funds").

65. Panel Discussion, "The Appropriations Power and the Necessary and Proper Clause," 68 *Wash. U. L.Q.* 623, 628 (1990) (remarks of William Barr) [hereinafter *Panel Discussion*]. *See also* Jacques LeBoeuf, "Limitations on the Use of Appropriations Riders by Congress to Effectuate Substantive Changes," 19 *Hastings Const. L.Q.* 457, 480 (1992); *Iran-Contra Report, supra* note 1, at 476 (Minority Report); J. Gregory Sidak, "The President's Power of the Purse," 1989 *Duke L.J.* 1162, 1207.

66. *See, e.g.*, Louis Henkin, *Foreign Affairs and the Constitution* 113–15 (1972) ("Even when Congress is free not to appropriate, it ought not to be able to regulate Presidential action by conditions on the appropriation of funds to carry it out, if it could not regulate the action directly. . . . Congress cannot impose conditions which invade Presidential prerogatives to which the spending is at most incidental, or which violate individual rights . . . ."); *Constitutionality of Proposed Legislation Affecting Tax Refunds*, 37 Op. Att'y Gen. 56, 61 (1933) ("Congress holds the purse strings, and it may grant or withhold appropriations as it chooses, and when making an appropriation may direct the purposes to which the appropriation shall be devoted and impose conditions in respect to its use, provided always that the conditions do not require operation of the Government in a way forbidden by the Constitution."); Sidak, *supra* note 65, at 1217–22; John N. Moore, "Do We Have an Imperial Congress?," 43 *U. Miami L. Rev.* 139, 145–46 & n.25 (1988).

67. *Panel Discussion, supra* note 65, at 631.

68. 328 U.S. 303 (1946).

69. *Id.* at 315.

70. 66 F. Supp. 142, 152 (1945) (Madden, J., concurring) (emphasis added), *aff'd on other grounds*, 328 U.S. 303 (1946).

71. *See, e.g.*, United States v. Will, 449 U.S. 200, 225–226 (1980); Clarke v. United States, 886 F.2d 404, 414 (D.C. Cir. 1989); News Am. Publishing Inc. v. FCC, 844 F.2d 800, 815 (D.C. Cir. 1988); Blitz v. Donovan, 538 F. Supp. 1119, 1128 (D.D.C. 1982); National Fed'n of Fed. Employees v. United States, 688 F. Supp. 671, 684 n.17 (D.D.C. 1988), *vacated and remanded sub nom.* American Foreign Service Ass'n v. Garfinkel, 490 U.S. 153 (1989); *cf.* Brown v. Califano, 627 F.2d 1221, 1233–34 (D.C. Cir. 1980).

72. *See, e.g., Panel Discussion, supra* note 65, at 635 (remarks of Louis Fisher; citing *Lovett*); *id.* at 646 (remarks of Kate Stith) ("[I]t is *not* a *plenary* power—Congress' exclusive power of appropriation does not trump the rest of Constitution"; citing *Lovett*) (emphasis in original).

73. Fisher, *supra* note 60, at 762.

74. *Lovett*, 328 U.S. at 307. Article I, section 9, clause 3 of the Constitution provides that "[n]o Bill of Attainder or ex post facto law shall be passed."

75. 449 U.S. 200, 225–26 (1980).

76. U.S. Const. art. III, § 1.

77. *See, e.g.*, Clarke v. United States, 886 F.2d 404, 414 (D.C. Cir. 1989) (finding that legislation that makes expenditure of appropriation contingent on D.C. City Council's enactment of specific law violates First Amendment); News Am. Publishing Inc. v. FCC, 844 F.2d 800, 815 (D.C. Cir. 1988) (appropriation measure that precludes use of funds to extend time period of existing waivers of newspaper-broadcast cross-ownership rules violates First and Fifth Amendments); Blitz v. Donovan, 538 F. Supp. 1119, 1128 (D.D.C. 1982) (finding that appropriation measure that denies funds to persons who advocate overthrow of the government violates the First Amendment); *cf.* Brown v. Califano, 627 F.2d 1221, 1233–34 (D.C. Cir. 1980) (construing appropriation prohibition of agency support for mandatory busing narrowly to avoid finding it an unconstitutional prohibition of agency enforcement of constitutional right to equal protection).

78. Public Citizen v. United States Dept. of Justice, 491 U.S. 440, 485 (1989) (Kennedy, J., concurring in an opinion in which Rehnquist, C. J., and O'Connor, J., join) (emphasis added).

79. *Id.* at 484–85.

80. *Id.* at 2581 (quoting, respectively, Morrison v. Olson, 487 U.S. 654, 695 (1988) (itself quoting Nixon v. Administrator of General Services, 433 U.S. 425, 443 (1977)), and *id.* at 443). *See generally* Michael L. Yoder, Note, "Separation of Powers: No Longer Simply Hanging in the Balance," 79 *Geo. L.J.* 173 (1990) (endorsing J. Kennedy's hybrid separation-of-powers analysis).

81. *See* United States v. Nixon, 418 U.S. 683, 705–06 (1974).

82. *See, e.g.*, Peter Strauss, "Formal and Functional Approaches to Separations-of-Powers Questions—A Foolish Inconsistency?," 72 *Cornell L. Rev.* 488 (1987).

83. *Cf., e.g.*, Glennon, *supra* note 64, at 44–49; Michael J. Glennon, "The Use of Custom in Resolving Separation of Powers Disputes," 64 *B.U. L. Rev.* 109, 146 (1984).

84. *See, e.g.*, Todd Peterson, "Prosecuting Executive Branch Officials for Contempt of Congress," 66 *N.Y.U. L. Rev.* 563, 589–92 (1991); Harold J. Krent, "Separating the Strands in Separation of Powers Controversies," 74 *Va. L. Rev.* 1253 (1988).

85. Krent, *supra* note 84, at 1257.

86. *See* U.S. Const. art I, § 9 (providing for suspension of writ of habeas corpus),

cl. 2; art. I, § 10 (stating sundry prohibitions on state national security authority); art. III, § 3 (providing limitations on treason prosecutions).

87. *E.g.*, U.S. Const., art. I, § 8, cls. 3, 10–16.

88. Abraham D. Sofaer, *War, Foreign Affairs and Constitutional Power: The Origins* 3 (1976).

89. The Court expressly reserved this question in *Lovett*, 328 U.S. at 307.

90. *See* Connie F. Bryan, Note, "Limiting the Use of Funds Appropriated for Executive Functions: Is the 1984 Boland Amendment Constitutional?," 13 *Okla. City U. L. Rev.* 569, 595–96 (1988); *see also* LeBoeuf, *supra* note 65, at 480–81 (asserting that hybrid approaches merge in foreign affairs because executive discretion is general and implied rather than express). Sidak denies the application of any balancing analysis to the appropriation power, Sidak, *supra* note 65, at 1184, but then concludes that the president has an inherent power to spend in support of only his "textually demonstrable" duties or prerogatives. *Id.* at 1201. This sounds a lot like first-tier separation-of-powers analysis. Since the text is sparse, he is then forced to argue that lack of textual specificity does not evidence the dispensability or unimportance of an executive duty. *Id.* at 1235.

91. *Panel Discussion*, *supra* note 65, at 629 (remarks of William Barr).

92. Sidak, *supra* note 65, at 1166. In fairness to Sidak, we should note that he does admit that "[b]ecause of the textual difference between military and nonmilitary appropriations, some of my conclusions regarding the impropriety of limiting presidential action through the Appropriations Clause in section 9 of Article I, . . . might not apply to military appropriations." J. Gregory Sidak, "To Declare War," 41 *Duke L.J.* 27, 99 n.362 (1991). We agree.

93. *Panel Discussion*, *supra* note 65, at 630 (remarks of William Barr) (emphasis added).

94. *The Federalist* No. 58, at 359 (J. Madison) (C. Rossiter ed., 1961).

95. *See supra* chap. 3; J. Terry Emerson, "Making War Without a Declaration," 17 *J. Legis.* 23, 29 (1990) (arguing that historically, "[b]y comparison [to the declaration of war], the power of the purse and the ability of limiting the supplies and size of the land and naval forces were by far the major means of controlling involvement in hostilities").

96. *See Panel Discussion*, *supra* note 65, at 629 (remarks of William Barr) (grudgingly acknowledging that congressional power to impose conditions in army appropriations "probably" stems from its "substantive" powers to raise and support and make rules for armies). *Cf.* Velvel v. Nixon, 415 F.2d 236, 239 (1969) (finding that "congressional appropriations for the [Vietnam War] are made under authority of the powers 'to raise and support Armies' and 'to provide and maintain a Navy' . . . [and] are not exercises of the power to spend for the general welfare") (footnotes omitted), *cert. denied*, 396 U.S. 1042 (1970).

97. *The War Power After 200 Years: Congress and the President at a Constitutional Impasse*, Hearings Before the Special Subcommittee on War Powers of the Senate Committee on Foreign Relations, 100th Cong., 1st Sess. 120 (testimony of Brent Scowcroft).

98. Glennon, *supra* note 64, at 291, 293–95.

99. United States Department of Justice, Memorandum of Points and Authorities in Opposition to Plaintiffs' Motion for Preliminary Relief and in Support of Defendant's Motion to Dismiss at 20, Dellums v. Bush, 752 F. Supp. 1141 (D.D.C. 1990) (No. 90–2866). *See also* Glennon, *supra* note 64, at 288 nn.35 & 36; Emerson, *supra* note 95, at 29; 135 *Cong. Rec.* S8033 (July 17, 1989) (remarks of Sen. Jesse Helms) ("Congress has the power to withhold the appropriations necessary to provide the means to execute a policy

if it disagrees with that policy. But please observe carefully, Mr. President, that Congress has only the power of the purse, period.").

100. *See, e.g.*, Don Wallace, Jr., "The President's Exclusive Foreign Affairs Powers over Foreign Aid: Part I," 1970 *Duke L.J.* 293, 320–21 (arguing that the Constitution confers upon the president exclusive powers over the making of foreign policy and "*all* diplomatic and Commander-in-Chief foreign affairs decisions, except for the following particular classes: . . . the withholding of appropriations altogether") (emphasis in original).

101. *See supra* chaps. 1–4.

102. *See* Kate Stith, "Congress' Power of the Purse," 97 *Yale L.J.* 1343, 1353 (1988).

103. Before doing so, however, we should reiterate the disclaimer in our introduction. Our purpose in this book is to explore the power of the purse in national security affairs, not the whole of national security law. The following discussion of the presidential and congressional powers implicated in the examples is therefore intended to be illustrative, not exhaustive.

104. Bryan, *supra* note 90, at 602 (emphasis in original).

105. *Id.* at 600.

106. *Id.* at 601.

107. Collela, *supra* note 32, at 164 (emphasis added). *See also id.* at 161–62.

108. Bryan, *supra* note 90, at 599. *See generally* Orrin Hatch, "Symposium: Foreign Affairs and the Constitution: The Roles of Congress, the President, and the Courts—What the Constitution Means by Executive Power," 43 *U. Miami L. Rev.* 165, 201 (1988):

> Congress oversteps its role when it undertakes to dictate the specific terms of international relations. This is a power granted specifically to the executive branch, which is equipped to acquire the information necessary for foreign policy creation. Thus, when the Congress enters into the process of creating new policies by, for example, permitting a certain form of humanitarian aid, but not others, it is venturing beyond its own constitutional mission and, in fact, attempting to formulate foreign policy.

109. 299 U.S. 304 (1936).

110. *Id.* at 320.

111. 10 *Annals of Cong.* 613–14 (1800) (remarks of Rep. J. Marshall) (emphasis added).

112. *See* Edward S. Corwin, *The President: Office and Powers 1787–1984*, at 177–80 (1984); Glennon, *supra* note 64, at 292.

113. *See* Louis Henkin, "Foreign Affairs and the Constitution," 66 *Foreign Aff.* 284, 294 (Winter 1987/88) ("[T]he distinction between making foreign policy and conducting foreign relations is essentially empty: the President makes foreign policy by conducting foreign relations, by the way he conducts them and the content and tone he gives them.").

114. This was how Alexander Hamilton characterized the president in the *Pacificus Papers*, from which Marshall mis-paraphrased. *See* 15 *The Papers of Alexander Hamilton* 38 (H. Syrett ed., 1969) ("the organ of intercourse between the Nation and foreign Nations"). The Minority Report tellingly misquotes Hamilton, too. *Iran-Contra Report*, *supra* note 1, at 470 n.1. *See* Theodore Draper, "The Constitution in Danger," *New York Rev. of Books*, March 1, 1990, at 41, 42 n.17.

115. Bruce E. Fein, "The Constitution and Covert Action," 11 *Hous. J. Int'l L.* 53, 67 (1988).

116. *The Paquete Habana*, 175 U.S. 677, 700 (1900). *See generally* Edwin D. Dickin-

son, "The Law of Nations as Part of the National Law of the United States," 101 *U. Pa. L. Rev.* 26 (1952).

117. Fein, *supra* note 115, at 67.

118. *See, e.g., CRS Legislative Histories, supra* note 2, at 15885 (remarks of Rep. Boland urging "an effective alternative to war," including arms interdiction assistance to El Salvador and support of Contadora peace efforts), 15891 (remarks of Rep. Panetta urging "the option of diplomacy"), 15892 (remarks of Rep. Hamilton urging "political negotiations").

119. Nicaragua v. United States, 1986 I.C.J. 14, 25 I.L.M. 1023, 1089 (1986). *See also* Declaration on Principles of International Law Concerning Friendly Relations and Co-operation Among States in Accordance With the Charter of the United Nations, art. I, ¶ 9, G.A. Res. 2625, 25 U.N. GAOR, Supp. No. 28, at 121, U.N. Doc. A/8028 (1970) ("Every State has a duty to refrain from organizing, instigating, assisting or participating in acts of civil strife or terrorist acts in another State or acquiescing in organized activities within its territory directed towards the commission of such acts, when the acts referred to in the present paragraph involve a threat or use of force.").

120. *Compare* John N. Moore, "The Secret War in Central America and the Future of World Order," 80 *Amer. J. Int'l L.* 43 (1986) *with* James P. Rowles, "'Secret Wars,' Self-Defense and the Charter—A Reply to Professor Moore," 80 *Amer. J. Int'l L.* 568 (1986).

121. *See* Letter from Eugene R. Rostow to William G. Miller and Frederick A. O. Schwartz, Jr., of Sept. 23, 1975, *reprinted in* 133 Cong. Rec. 15862 (1987).

122. *See, e.g.,* Robert F. Turner, "Congressional Limits on the Commander in Chief: The FAS Proposal," in *First Use of Nuclear Weapons: Under the Constitution, Who Decides?* 37, 39–45 (P. Raven-Hansen ed. 1987) [hereinafter *First Use*]; Peter Raven-Hansen, "Breeding Contempt: An Essay on the Too Familiar History of the War Clause," in *The U.S. Constitution and the Power to Go to War* 29, 35 (M. Halperin & G. Stern eds., 1994).

123. Youngstown Sheet & Tube Co. v. Sawyer, 343 U.S. 579, 644 (1952) (Jackson, J., concurring).

124. 133 *Cong. Rec.* 16004 (1987) (remarks of Rep. Daniel).

125. *See* Durand v. Hollins, 8 F. Cas. 111 (No. 4186) (C.C.S.D.N.Y. 1860). *See generally* Dycus *et al., supra* note 43, at 453–74; *Iran-Contra Report, supra* note 1, at 474–75.

126. *See* Dycus *et al., supra* note 43, at 295–97.

127. *See, e.g.,* Glennon, *supra* note 64, at 293 n.55; Henkin, *supra* note 66, at 45–47, 93.

128. *See* Louis Henkin, *Constitutionalism, Democracy, and Foreign Affairs* 32 (1990).

129. 299 U.S. at 320.

130. *Iran-Contra Report, supra* note 1, at 476 (Minority Report).

131. U.S. Const., art. I, § 8, cl. 11. *See generally* Raven-Hansen, *supra* note 122.

132. *See* Jules Lobel, "Covert War and Congressional Authority: Hidden War and Forgotten Power," 134 *U. Pa. L. Rev.* 1035, 1040, 1045 (1986); Charles A. Lofgren, "War-Making Under the Constitution: The Original Understanding," 81 *Yale L.J.* 672, 692–94, 695–97, 700 (1972).

133. Lobel, *supra* note 132, at 1051–52 (footnote omitted) (emphasis added).

134. *Id.* at 1059–69, 1089–94.

135. U.S. Const., art. I, § 8, cl. 10.

136. Indeed, the Constitutional Convention changed the wording of the Law of

Nations Clause from "to declare" to "to define." Howard S. Freedman, Comment, "The Offenses Clause: Congress' International Penal Power," 8 *Colum. J. Transnat'l L.* 279, 288–89 (1969). Lobel suggests that this change was more likely intended to make it clear that Congress could domesticate international law with sufficient precision to make it adequate for criminal prosecution than to give Congress the power to make new international law. Jules Lobel, "The Rise and Decline of the Neutrality Act: Sovereignty and Congressional War Powers in United States Foreign Policy," 24 *Harv. J. Int'l L.* 1, 15–16 n.86 (1983).

137. In its present form, it provides in relevant part that:

> Whoever, within the United States, knowingly begins or sets on foot or provides or prepares a means for or furnishes the money for, or takes part in, any military or naval expedition or enterprise to be carried on from thence against the territory or dominion of any foreign prince or state, or of any colony, district, or people with whom the United States is at peace, shall be fined not more than $3,000 or imprisoned not more than three years, or both.

18 U.S.C. § 960 (1988).

138. Lobel, *supra* note 136, at 16.

139. *Id.* at 27; Note, "Nonenforcement of the Neutrality Act: International Law and Foreign Policy Powers Under the Constitution," 95 *Harv. L. Rev.* 1955, 1966 (1982) [hereinafter *Nonenforcement*] (explaining that by the act "Congress' exclusive power to declare war is protected from usurpation by private parties *and from impairment by administrations that might choose to condone such activities*") (emphasis added) (footnote omitted). Lobel therefore concludes that authority for the Neutrality Act rests at least in part on congressional war powers. Lobel, *supra* note 136, at 28.

140. *Nonenforcement, supra* note 139, at 1965.

141. Lobel, *supra* note 136, at 31–33 (contrasting the Logan Act, 1 Stat. 613 (1799), which makes certain conduct unlawful only when undertaken "without the permission or authority of the government"). *See also Nonenforcement, supra* note 139, at 1966.

142. 27 F. Cas. 1192 (C.C.D.N.Y. 1806) (No. 16,342).

143. *Id.* at 1230. *See also* Dellums v. Smith, 577 F. Supp. 1449, 1452–53 (N.D. Cal. 1984) (construing the act to apply even to presidentially authorized actions), *rev'd on other grounds,* 797 F.2d 817 (9th Cir. 1986). *See generally* Peter J. Spiro, Note, "The Iran-Contra Affair, the Neutrality Act, and the Statutory Definition of 'At Peace,'" 27 *Va. J. Int'l L.* 343, 350 (1987).

144. *See, e.g.,* Lobel, *supra* note 136, at 61 n.318.

145. *See supra* note 21.

146. *See, e.g.,* Whitney v. Robertson, 124 U.S. 190, 194 (1888); L. Littlejohn & Co. v. United States, 270 U.S. 215, 226–27 (1926). *See generally* Henkin, *supra* note 66, at 163–64.

147. NLRB v. Catholic Bishop of Chicago, 440 U.S. 490, 511 (1979) (Brennan, J., dissenting).

148. Walker v. United States Dep't of Hous. and Urban Dev., 912 F.2d 819, 829 (5th Cir. 1990) (footnote omitted).

149. The report of the House Permanent Select Committee on Intelligence that accompanied the 1984 Boland amendment's forerunner, Boland-Zablocki, stated that the amendment did not

> prohibit the collection, production, or analysis of intelligence by U.S. intelligence elements, nor the provision of such intelligence to friendly foreign

> countries, as long as such activity does not support military or paramilitary operations in Nicaragua by any foreign nations or other entity.

H.R. Rep. No. 122, 98th Cong., 1st Sess. 14 (1983). This suggests that intelligence collection and exchange activities that are primarily for the purpose of information collection and not for the purpose of supporting military or paramilitary activities were permitted under the language of the amendments.

150. Pub. L. No. 99-88, § 102(b), 99 Stat. 325 (1985).

151. Intelligence oversight legislation before 1984 routinely excluded routine intelligence collection activities from its purview. *See, e.g.*, Hughes-Ryan Amendment to Foreign Assistance Act, 22 U.S.C. § 2422 (1988) (excluding "activities intended solely for obtaining necessary intelligence"); Intelligence Oversight Act of 1980, 50 U.S.C. § 413 (1982), adding § 501 to National Security Act of 1947, Pub. L. No. 96-450, § 407(b), 94 Stat. 1981 (1980) (same exclusion). This legislation cuts both ways, of course, for one can argue that Congress knew how to make the distinction explicit, and that its failure to do so in the 1984 Boland amendment is therefore intentional. In light of the principle of avoidance, however, this legislation is most convincingly read as acquiescence in customary and constitutional national security law that was left intact by the 1984 Boland amendment.

152. *See* Collela, *supra* note 32, at 153–56 (discussing interpretative difficulties and CIA implementation).

153. *See supra* note 122.

154. United States v. Salerno, 481 U.S. 739, 745 (1987).

155. Webster v. Reproductive Health Services, 492 U.S. 490, 524 (1989) (O'Connor, J., concurring in part and concurring in judgment).

156. Pub. L. No. 91-172, § 643, 83 Stat. 487 (1969).

157. Pub. L. No. 91-652, § 7(a), 84 Stat., 1943 (1971).

158. Pub. L. No. 92-156, § 601, 85 Stat. 430 (1971).

159. 3 *Pub. Papers* 1114 (Nov. 17, 1971).

160. Pub. L. No. 93-52, 87 Stat. 130 (1973).

161. *See* Dycus *et al.*, *supra* note 43, at 225.

162. Fleming v. Page, 50 U.S. (9 How.) 602, 615 (1851). *See generally* Clarence A. Berdahl, *War Powers of the Executive in the United States* 121–22, 125 (1921).

163. *See* Dycus *et al.*, *supra* note 43, at 88 (citing statutes).

164. *Accord* John N. Moore, *Law and the Indo-China War* 560 (1972).

165. The phrase is from John N. Moore, "The Constitution, Nuclear Weapons, and Deterrence: An Analysis of the FAS Proposal," in *First Use*, *supra* note 122, at 23, 31.

166. *Ex parte* Milligan, 71 U.S. (4 Wall.) 2, 139 (1865) (dictum) (Chase, C. J., concurring).

167. William H. Rehnquist, "The Constitutional Issues—Administrative Position," 45 *N.Y.U.L. Rev.* 628, 638 (1970). *See also* William D. Rogers, "The Constitutionality of the Cambodian Invasion," 65 *Am. J. Int'l L.* 26, 28–29 (1971) (summarizing the administration's domestic legal rationale).

168. *See* Rehnquist, *supra* note 167, at 639; Moore, *supra* note 164, at 566 (remarking that restriction bears "a heavy burden of constitutional justification" and "would seem highly doubtful"); Letter from Eugene V. Rostow, *et al.*, to Senator Gordon Allott, May 26, 1970, at 1 ("The constitutional validity of congressional action limiting the President's discretion with respect to attack upon the Cambodian sanctuaries seems highly dubious . . . ."); Robert H. Bork, "Comments on the Articles on the Legality of the United States Action in Cambodia," 65 *Am. J. Int'l L.* 79–80 (1971) ("Any detailed

intervention by Congress in the conduct of the Vietnamese conflict constitutes a trespass upon powers the Constitution reposes exclusively in the President. . . . It is completely clear that the President has complete and exclusive power to order tactical moves in an existing conflict, and it seems to me equally clear that the Cambodian incursion was a tactical maneuver and nothing more."). *But see* Rogers, *supra* note 167, at 31–34 (arguing that Cambodian incursion lacked support in customary law and violated rule of strict necessity underlying commander in chief's power of "preclusive self-defense").

169. Moore, *supra* note 164, at 564:

> [T]he President's authority to take command decisions incident to an ongoing conflict should not be absolute. One obvious example is that he should not have the authority to bomb Peking incident to the Indo-China War. Such a response runs a high risk of triggering a greatly enlarged war or even World War III. . . . Criteria for permissible presidential command decisions might include consistency with initial objectives in authorizing the use of force, whether the response is confined to actions against forces already committed as active belligerents, and whether the action runs a high risk of major escalation.

See also Bork, *supra* note 168, at 80 (noting that "the decision to bomb Chinese depots . . . would involve the decision to initiate a major war," which is "confined to the Congress"). *But see* Rogers, *supra* note 167, at 34–35 (denying that any line can be drawn that would make Cambodian incursion constitutional).

170. Rehnquist, *supra* note 167, at 639.

171. *See* Bork, *supra* note 168, at 81 (apparently agreeing with us; stating that Congress "can end our armed involvement in Southeast Asia and it can forbid entry into new wars to defend governments there.").

Chapter 14

1. National Security Adviser McFarlane wrote to President Reagan that, failing an additional appropriation, the Contra aid program "will have to be drastically curtailed by May or June" of 1984. *Report of the Congressional Comm. Investigating the Iran-Contra Affair*, S. Rep. No. 100-216, H.R. Rep. No. 100-433, 100th Cong., 1st Sess. 37 (1987) [hereinafter *Iran-Contra Report*].

2. In light of the harbor mining disclosures, the administration's proposal for a supplemental $21 million appropriation died. *Id.*

3. *Id.* at 37–39.

4. *Id.* at 37. These may have been McFarlane's words, rather than the president's, although Oliver North testified that the now-famous phrase was uttered by the president. *Id.*, at 37 n.110a.

5. *Id.* at 37–58. At a June 25, 1984, National Security Planning Group meeting, Secretary of State George Shultz advised that in the opinion of Chief of Staff James Baker it would be an impeachable offense if the United States served as a conduit for third-country funding to the Contras. *Id.* at 39. President Reagan, Vice President Bush, Secretary of State Shultz, Secretary of Defense Weinberger, CIA Director Casey, Counselor to the President Meese, and McFarlane were present at the meeting. Casey stated that third-country funding would be permissible if the United States were not involved as an intermediary, and Meese suggested that Attorney General Smith may have prepared an opinion to that effect. Although McFarlane recommended a Justice Department opinion on the matter before engaging in any further solicitation, the meeting

ended without any explicit decision and the solicitations and transfers to the Contras continued. *Id.*

6. Israel, South Africa, Saudi Arabia, China, South Korea, Taiwan, Honduras, Costa Rica, China, El Salvador, Guatemala, and Panama were solicited. *See* Stipulation of Facts, United States v. North (D.D.C. Apr. 6, 1989) (No. 88-0080-02).

7. *Iran-Contra Report, supra* note 1, at 16, 19–27. *See also Wash. Post,* Apr. 7, 1989, at A1 (reporting that Honduras, Costa Rica, Guatemala, and possibly El Salvador received enhanced assistance as a result of their contributions to the Contras).

8. There is apparently no commonly accepted definition of "quid pro quo" in the context of soliciting third-country funds. One interpretation requires an explicit agreement with the other government to contribute to the solicited cause in return for some form of U.S. assistance. *See* Foreign Operations, Export Financing, and Related Programs Appropriation Act of 1990, Pub. L. No. 101-167, § 582(a), 103 Stat. 1195, 1251 (1989), described *infra* in this chapter.

At the other extreme, a quid pro quo could occur whenever aid is provided to another government as a reward for a contribution to a cause favored by the solicitor. Under this interpretation, a purpose to induce the reciprocal arrangement is not required; a quid pro quo existed if the prospect of the U.S. aid induced the contribution. This view of quid pro quo was adopted in the failed Moynihan amendment to the 1989 State Department authorization bill. *See* 135 *Cong. Rec.* S8110 (daily ed. July 18, 1989), described *infra* in this chapter.

Additional murkiness attends the legal definition of "solicitations." However, any effort by U.S. employees to gain contributions from another government for an activity or cause restricted in an appropriation is forbidden where the U.S. exercises control over the receipt and expenditure of the funds. *See* U.S. Const., art. I, § 9, cl. 7; George Van Cleve, "The Constitutionality of the Solicitation or Control of Third-Country Funds for Foreign Policy Purposes by United States Officials Without Congressional Approval," 11 *Hous. J. Int'l L.* 69, 80 (1988). For example, the use of the nominally private companies in the North-Secord-Hakim "Enterprise" to accept and spend donated funds on behalf of the Contras was a constitutionally forbidden ruse because the "private" entity was in fact an arm of the government. *See Iran-Contra Report, supra* note 1, at 16, 413–14; *see also* Kate Stith, "Congress' Power of the Purse," 97 *Yale L.J.* 1343, 1361 (1988). Such a restriction on executive branch solicitation could nonetheless violate Article II foreign relations powers of the president. The effect of an unconstitutional failure to appropriate for proper Article II tasks is considered *infra.* The line between regulable solicitation and constitutionally protected executive branch diplomacy may be stated in the abstract, but it is practically difficult if not impossible to draw in legislation, as we discuss *infra* in the text.

9. *See* Alex Whiting, "Controlling Tin Cup Diplomacy," 99 *Yale L.J.* 2043, 2045–46 (1990).

10. *Security and Development Assistance: Hearings Before the Senate Comm. on Foreign Relations,* 99th Cong., 1st Sess. 908 (1985).

11. Motley testified that "[n]obody is trying to play games with . . . any Member of Congress." *Id.* at 910.

12. *Iran-Contra Report, supra* note 1, at 403.

13. International Security and Development Cooperation Act of 1985, Pub. L. No. 99-83, § 722(d), 99 Stat. 190, 254 (1985).

14. *Id.*; H.R. Conf. Rep. No. 237, 99th Cong., 1st Sess. 143 (1985).

15. Intelligence Authorization Act for Fiscal Year 1986, Pub. L. No. 99-169, § 105(b)(2), 99 Stat. 1002, 1003 (1985). Pursuant to the statute, Assistant Secretary of State

Elliott Abrams solicited $10 million from Brunei. The money was placed in the wrong bank account in Switzerland and never reached the Contras. *Iran-Contra Report, supra* note 1, at 148–49, 352–53.

16. *Iran-Contra Report, supra* note 1, at 4–5, 37–58, 85–103.

17. *Id.* at 85. Of the $10 million, only $4.5 million were received by the Contras. National Endowment for the Preservation of Liberty leaders Carl "Spitz" Channell and Richard Miller took the rest in salaries, fees, and expenses, including expenses incurred lobbying members of Congress opposed to Contra aid. *Id.* at 85–98.

18. *Id.* at 9, 274, 277–81.

19. 135 *Cong. Rec.* S8110 (daily ed. July 18, 1989).

20. 135 *Cong. Rec.* H8713 (daily ed. Nov. 9, 1989).

21. 25 *Weekly Comp. Pres. Doc.* 1806 (Nov. 21, 1989).

22. *Id.* at 1783 (Nov. 19, 1989).

23. Pub. L. No. 101–167, § 582, 103 Stat. 1251 (1989). Part of the Foreign Operations Appropriations Bill, the compromise provision states:

> None of the funds appropriated by this Act may be provided any foreign government (including any instrumentality or agency thereof), foreign person, or United States person in exchange for that foreign government or person undertaking any action which is, if carried out by the United States Government, a United States official or employee, expressly prohibited by a provision of United States law.

Id.

24. *Lovett v. United States,* 328 U.S. 303 (1946).

25. Flast v. Cohen, 392 U.S. 83, 103–04 (1968).

26. Hart v. United States, 118 U.S. 62 (1886); United States v. Klein, 80 U.S. (13 Wall.) 128 (1871).

27. United States v. Will, 449 U.S. 200 (1980).

28. *See* "The Appropriations Power and the Necessary and Proper Clause," 68 *Wash. U. L.Q.* 623, 635 (1990) (remarks of Fisher) [hereinafter *Panel Discussion*]; *id.*, at 649 (remarks of Stith).

29. *See, e.g.*, Neal E. Devins, "Appropriations Redux: A Critical Look at the Fiscal Year 1988 Continuing Resolution," 1988 *Duke L.J.* 389, 398, 413 (demonstrating that President Reagan prevailed by veto threats to shape much of the fiscal 1988 continuing resolution). *See also* Charles Black, "Some Thoughts on the Veto," 40 *Law & Contemp. Probs.* 87, 92–94 (1976).

30. *See Panel Discussion, supra* note 28, at 649 (remarks of Stith).

31. *Id.* at 650.

32. *See, e.g.*, Alaska Airlines v. Brock, 480 U.S. 678, 685 (1987).

33. Buckley v. Valeo, 424 U.S. 1, 108 (1976) (*per curiam*), *quoting* Champlin Refining Co. v. Corporation Comm'n of Oklahoma, 286 U.S. 210, 234 (1932).

34. *See* J. Gregory Sidak & Thomas A. Smith, "Four Faces of the Item Veto: A Reply to Tribe and Kurkland," 84 *Nw. U. L. Rev.* 437, 452–57 (1990).

35. *Id.* at 452.

36. *Id.* For example, in signing the 1990 defense appropriation, President Bush pointed to language in the statute instructing DOD to follow procedures for spending outlined in a committee report. The president stated that "such language has no legal force or effect," 25 *Wkly. Comp. Pres. Doc.* 1809, 1810 (Nov. 21, 1989).

37. *Id.* at 452–53; *see also* Marc N. Garber & Kurt A. Wimmer, "Presidential Sign-

ing Statements as Interpretations of Legislative Intent: An Executive Aggrandizement of Power," 24 *Harv. J. Legis.* 363 (1987).

38. *See* Laurence Tribe, *American Constitutional Law* 265 (1978). Presidential recommendations for appropriation arguably are distinguishable because they precede the congressional vote on legislation.

39. *See* Frank B. Cross, "The Constitutional Legitimacy and Significance of Presidential 'Signing Statements,'" 40 *Admin. L. Rev.* 209 (1988).

40. *See* Sidak & Smith, *supra* note 34, at 454, citing Lear Siegler, Inc. v. Lehman, 842 F.2d 1102, 1124 (9th Cir. 1987) ("Presumably, any extension of the veto power of the President would stop short of doing away with the power of Congress to override the veto.").

41. Immigration & Naturalization Service v. Chadha, 462 U.S. 919 (1983).

42. *See* Kendall v. United States ex rel. Stokes, 37 U.S. (12 Pet.) 524, 613 (1938); *see also* Jesse Choper, *Judicial Review and the National Political Process* 368–71 (1980); Charles Tiefer, The Constitutionality of Independent Officers as Checks on Abuses of Executive Power, 63 *B.U. L. Rev.* 59, 90 (1983).

43. *Lear Siegler,* 842 F.2d at 1102; *see also supra* chap. 9. The Third Circuit has stated *in dicta* that the president might have the power or duty to refuse to execute "a patently unconstitutional law or one infringing liberty interests or other fundamental rights of individuals ." Ameron Inc. v. United States Army Corps Eng'rs, 787 F.2d 875, 889 n.11 (3d Cir. 1986). As Sidak and Smith point out, the distinction between permitting excision of *patently* unconstitutional laws or those that infringe individual rights but not laws that infringe on powers of the president is difficult to defend, if not to describe. Sidak & Smith, *supra* note 34, at 455.

44. *Lear Siegler,* 842 F.2d at 1124. *See also* Arthur S. Miller, "The President and the Faithful Execution of the Laws," 40 *Vand. L. Rev.* 389, 398 (1987) ("To 'execute' a statute . . . emphatically does not mean to kill it.").

45. *See* U.S. General Accounting Office, *A Glossary of Terms Used in the Federal Budget Process* 68 (2d ed. 1981). The GAO defines "obligations" as "amounts of offers placed, contracts awarded, services received and similar transactions during a given period that will require payments during the same or a future period." *Id. See* 31 U.S.C. § 1501 (1988). OMB apportions budgeted amounts to executive branch agencies, thereby making appropriated funds available for obligation. 31 U.S.C. §§ 1511–16 (1988). *See* U.S. General Accounting Office, *Principles of Federal Appropriations Law* 1–19 (2d ed. 1991) [hereinafter *Appropriations Principles*].

46. *See Appropriations Principles, supra* note 45, at 1–19. However, as Glennon argues, "[w]ith narrow exceptions . . . this presidential power does not embrace the power to formulate policy, but rather to communicate policy made by others." Michael J. Glennon, *Constitutional Diplomacy* 18–34, 292 (1990).

47. Letter from Louis Henkin to Hon. Louis Stokes, *reprinted in H.R. 1013, H.R. 1371, and Other Proposals Which Address the Issue of Affording Prior Notice of Covert Actions to the Congress: Hearings Before the Subcomm. on Legislation, H. Perm. Select Comm. on Intelligence,* 100th Cong., 1st Sess. 220 (1987), *quoted in* Glennon, *supra* note 46, at 293 n.55.

48. Thomas McGarity, "Presidential Control of Regulatory Agency Decisionmaking," 36 *Am. U. L. Rev.* 443, 474 (1987).

49. E. Burrows, *Albert Gallatin and the Political Economy of Republicans, 1761–1800,* at 486 (1986).

50. 7 *Annals of Cong.* 1121–22 (1798).

51. *Panel Discussion, supra* note 28, at 649–50 (remarks of Stith).

52. *See, e.g.*, Califano v. Wescott, 443 U.S. 76, 89–91 (1979) (affirming order extending welfare benefits to unconstitutionally excluded class).

53. 52 U.S. (11 How.) 272 (1850).

54. *Id.* at 290–91.

55. *Id. See also* Rochester Pure Water District v. Environmental Protection Agency, 960 F.2d 180, 185–86 (D.C. Cir. 1992).

56. *See* Milliken v. Bradley (II), 433 U.S. 267 (1977) (affirming that state officials may be sued to compel them to share future costs of compliance with a school desegregation decree remedying violations for which they shared responsibility).

57. *See id.* at 287 (discussing remedial powers of lower court in ordering comprehensive desegregation program). *See also* Gerald Frug, "The Judicial Power of the Purse," 126 *U. Pa. L. Rev.* 715 (1978).

58. *See* Frug, *supra* note 57, at 750 (suggesting that the federal judicial power does not extend to an order to Congress to appropriate funds).

59. Department of Defense Appropriations Act for Fiscal Year 1985, Pub. L. No. 98-473, § 8066, 98 Stat. 1837, 1935 (1984). *See also* Intelligence Authorization Act for Fiscal Year 1985, Pub. L. No. 98-618, § 801, 98 Stat. 3298, 3304 (1984).

60. *Testimony of Lt. Col. Oliver North: Joint Hearings Before the H. Select Comm. to Investigate Covert Arms Transactions with Iran and the S. Select Comm. on Secret Military Assistance to Iran and the Nicaraguan Opposition*, 100th Cong., 1st Sess., pt. II, at 37 (1987).

61. *Panel Discussion, supra* note 28, at 655 (remarks of Barr).

62. Stith, *supra* note 8, at 1351–53.

63. Knote v. United States, 95 U.S. 149, 154 (1877). *See also* Republic National Bank of Miami v. United States, 113 S. Ct. 554, 562 (1992) (opinion of the Court regarding the Appropriations Clause Issue) (deciding that all money deposited into treasury is subject to the Appropriations Clause).

64. *But see* Van Cleve, *supra* note 8, at 76 ("[I]t is not possible to determine whether the Framers intended the direct language of [the Appropriations Clause] to cover third party funds.").

65. Act of March, 3, 1849, 9 Stat. 398 (*codified as amended* at 31 U.S.C. § 3302(b) (1988 & Supp. III 1991)).

66. *Id.*

67. 31 U.S.C. § 1341 (1988 & Supp. III 1991).

68. Act of July 12, 1870, ch. 251, § 7, 16 Stat. 251.

69. Act of Mar. 3, 1905, ch. 1484, § 4, 33 Stat. 1257.

70. *See* Continuing Appropriations, Fiscal Year 1991, Pub. L. No. 101-403, § 2608(b), 104 Stat. 874.

71. *See* Second War Powers Act of 1942, ch. 199, § 1101, 56 Stat. 176, 183–84; 50 U.S.C. § 1151 (1982). Gift authority is discussed *supra* chap. 8.

72. 50 U.S.C. §§ 1151, 1154 (1988 & Supp. III 1991).

73. *See* Stith, *supra* note 8, at 1362.

74. 18 U.S.C. §§ 960–62 (1988).

75. *See* Whiting, *supra* note 9, at 2057.

76. U.S. Const., art. II, § 2, cl. 2.

77. *Id.*, art. II, § 3, cl. 1; § 2, cl. 2.

78. *See* Edward Corwin, *The President: Office and Powers, 1787–1984*, at 208 (5th ed. 1984) (stating that the president is the "sole instrument of communication" in foreign

affairs); *see also* Glennon, *supra* note 46, at 164 ("The core presidential power . . . [in diplomacy] is negotiation").

79. *See* Harold H. Koh, "Why the President (Almost) Always Wins in Foreign Affairs: Lessons of the Iran-Contra Affair," 97 *Yale L.J.* 1255, 1306 (1988).

80. 299 U.S. 304 (1936).

81. 454 U.S. 654 (1981).

82. 299 U.S. at 319.

83. Dames & Moore v. Regan, 454 U.S. at 682–83.

84. *See supra* chap. 13 (discussion of Marshall's "sole organ" speech).

85. Youngstown Sheet & Tube Co. v. Sawyer, 343 U.S. 579, 635–36 (1952) (Jackson, J., concurring). *See also*, Stephen Dycus, Arthur L. Berney, William C. Banks, & Peter Raven-Hansen, *National Security Law* 59–61 (1990); Van Cleve, *supra* note 8, at 81 ("[I]f Congress makes its will to prevent executive action in [providing] tactical military advice unmistakably clear . . . Congress should prevail.").

86. Whiting, *supra* note 9, at 1057 n.76.

87. *See* Stith, *supra* note 8, at 1361–62. Stith notes statutes that forbid the augmentation of employee salaries with outside funding, e.g., 18 U.S.C. § 209 (1988 & Supp. III 1991), and a provision of the Anti-Deficiency Act that prohibits uncompensated service by government employees, 31 U.S.C. § 1342 (1988 & Supp. III 1991). Stith, *supra* note 8, at 1361 n.88. The Boland amendment proscribed third-party funding in declaring that "no funds" should be spent on the Contras. *Id.* at 1363; *see also* Laurence Tribe, "Reagan Ignites a Constitutional Crisis," *N.Y. Times*, May 20, 1987, A31 (reporting that the Boland amendment applies to "government revenues devoted to paying their salaries and expenses of intelligence operatives whenever their actions—such as the solicitation of contributions—[would aid the Contras]."). *See also* Congressional Research Service, "Legislative Histories of Statutory Restrictions on Funding for Covert Assistance for Military or Paramilitary Operations in Nicaragua, FY1983–FY1986," 133 *Cong. Rec.* at 15918 (1987) (statement of Rep. Boland that the restriction includes "accounts for salaries and all support cost").

88. *See generally* Nixon v. Administrator of General Services, 433 U.S. 425, 443 (1977). *But see* Van Cleve, *supra* note 8, at 77, 81 (arguing that solicitation of other countries is permissible "even against [the] will of Congress"); *Iran-Contra Report*, *supra* note 1, at 473 (Minority Report) (judging it "beyond question that Congress did not have the constitutional power to prohibit the President from . . . asking other governments to contribute to the Nicaraguan resistance"). George Van Cleve, one of the drafters of the Iran-Contra Investigation Minority Report, correctly asserts that solicitation may be part of the president's constitutional power of diplomatic communication. But he fails to acknowledge that solicitation implicates the Appropriations Clause, apart from how the donated funds are controlled. Van Cleve, *supra* note 8, at 77.

Alex Whiting recognizes that the Appropriations Clause power is implicated by the expenditure of public funds for executive salaries, but argues that this would be "a trivial exercise of that power." Whiting, *supra* note 9, at 1057 n.76. We have shown in part I, however, that the Appropriations Clause was intended in part to provide Congress with a means of sharing in national security decision making. If an appropriation restriction regulating solicitation furthers that end, then it is hardly "trivial." The real issue is whether it interferes impermissibly with the president's constitutional power of diplomatic communication.

89. Pub. L. No. 101-167, 103 Stat. 1195 (1989).

90. *Id.*, § 582(a), 103 Stat. 1251.

91. 135 *Cong. Rec.* H9231 (daily ed. Nov. 21, 1989).

92. 25 *Weekly Comp. Pres. Doc.* 1806 (Nov. 21, 1989). When he signed the compromise bill, the president said: "Diplomacy by its nature involves give-and-take. Many routine and unobjectionable diplomatic activities could be misconstrued as somehow involving a forbidden 'exchange.' Given the ease with which such activities would be so misconstrued, this type of provision can chill U.S. diplomats in the proper discharge of their duties." *Id.* at 1810.

93. *See Iran-Contra Report, supra* note 1, at 45. Robert McFarlane testified that, notwithstanding the Boland ban on solicitations, he thought it permissible to tell an ambassador "of the plight of the Contras and hope . . . for a contribution."

94. *See* Whiting, *supra* note 9, at 2058.

95. Apparently El Salvador declined to contribute because its government feared that Congress would learn and disapprove of its actions. Frances FitzGerald, "Annals of Justice: Iran-Contra," *New Yorker*, Oct. 16, 1989, at 72.

96. Stith, *supra* note 8, at 1352.

97. *Id.* at 1352 n.36, 1362 n.89. *See also* Tribe, *supra* note 38, at 248 n.7 ("[T]he President surely may not spend unappropriated funds in order to 'execute the laws.' In large part, then, it is up to Congress to provide the means whereby the President can discharge his duty; the President may not arrogate congressional powers by reference to this clause.").

98. *See* Stith, *supra* note 8, at 1351–52 ("Spending in the absence of appropriations is ultra vires."). For an analysis of presidential emergency power, *see* Jules Lobel, "Emergency Power and the Decline of Liberalism," 98 *Yale L.J.* 1385, 1392–97, 1401–04 (1989); *see also supra* chap. 12.

99. J. Gregory Sidak, "The President's Power of the Purse," 1989 *Duke L.J.* 1162, 1242–43.

100. *Id.* at 1187.

101. *See id.* at 1167–68, 1170–71 (emphasis added).

102. In addition to the Appropriations Clause, *see* U.S. Const., art. I, § 2, cl. 3; § 3, cl. 7; § 4, cl. 1, 2; § 6, cl. 1; § 7, cl. 2; § 8, cl. 4, 15, 18; § 9, cl. 3. The only exception is art. I, § 8, cl. 10, which empowers Congress "[t]o define and punish piracies and felonies committed on the high seas and offenses against the law of nations."

103. *Lovett v. United States*, 328 U.S. 303 (1946).

104. *Id.* at 313.

105. *See* Sidak, *supra* note 99, at 1187.

106. Cincinnati Soap Co. v. United States, 301 U.S. 308 (1937) (*citing* Reeside v. Walker, 11 How. 272, 291 (1851)).

107. Office of Personnel Management v. Richmond, 496 U.S. 414, 426 (1990).

108. Knote v. United States, 95 U.S. 149 (1877).

109. *Id.* at 154.

110. *Richmond*, 496 U.S. at 426. *But see id.* at 431 (White & Blackmun, JJ., concurring) ("Although *Knote* . . . held that the President's pardon power did not extend to the appropriation of moneys in the treasury without authorization by law for the benefit of pardoned criminals, it did not hold that Congress could impair the President's pardon power by denying him appropriations for pen and paper.").

111. *Compare* Sidak, *supra* note 99, at 1195–96 ("[T]he political process imposes a limiting principle on the President's unappropriated spending . . . . [T]here would be a political cost to the President in terms of Congress's ability to use its own prerogatives in a retributive manner.") *with id.* at 1232–33 (claiming that the argument that the political process is an adequate remedy for a failure to appropriate "is unrealistic as a

matter of politics, and probably also as a matter of constitutional law . . . . [The argument] presumes that an election would serve as a plebiscite on a single, relatively abstruse issue . . . .") (footnote omitted).

112. *See Panel Discussion, supra* note 28, at 646 (remarks of Stith). *See also* Laurence Tribe, *supra* note 87.

113. *See Panel Discussion, supra* note 28, at 654 (remarks of Barr) ("[T]here may be an argument that if the President finds no appropriated funds within a given category to conduct activity, but there is a lot of money sitting somewhere else in another category—and both categories are within his constitutional purview—he may be able to use those funds.").

114. *See* Sidak, *supra* note 99, at 1199 (asserting that President could "respect the total budget constraint established by Congress, simply by diverting funds from one . . . line item to the account necessary.").

115. *War Powers: A Test of Compliance: Hearings Before Subcomm. on Int'l Security and Scientific Affairs,* House Comm. on Int'l Relations, 94th Cong., 1st Sess. 92 (1975). Michael Glennon rejects Leigh's testimony that the president can use funds for one purpose that were designated for another as "nonsense" that could deprive Congress of its power to specify how money shall be spent. *See* Michael J. Glennon, "Strengthening the War Powers Resolution: The Case for Purse-Strings Restrictions," 60 *Minn. L. Rev.* 1, 31 (1975). But both Leigh and Glennon fail to distinguish among spending restrictions. As we will show *infra,* if the restriction takes the form of a limitations rider ("none of the funds provided in this act"), restricting only the use of a particular appropriation, the president may still have customary and statutory spending authority to transfer from or draw on another account. If, however, the restriction is general ("no funds available"), he or she probably does not. Leigh, in fact, was testifying in the context of a general restriction, suggesting that Professor Glennon was closer to the truth in that instance. *Id.* at 13 n.30 (identifying seven restrictions).

116. In 1870 Congress enacted deficiency appropriations to pay workers hired by the Navy Department. Act of Apr. 13, 1870, ch. 55, 16 Stat. 83. *See* Gary L. Hopkins & Robert M. Nutt, "The Anti-Deficiency Act and Funding Federal Contracts: An Analysis," 80 *Mil. L. Rev.* 51, 56 n.6 (1978).

117. *See* Lucius Wilmerding, Jr., *The Spending Power* 78, 80 (1943) (reporting John C. Calhoun speech on the evils "particularly in the War Department" of transfers).

118. *Id.* at 90. This is the so-called coercive deficiency, the "executive habit of creating obligations without appropriations." Hopkins & Nutt, *supra* note 116, at 58.

119. Act of Mar. 3, 1809, ch. 28, 2 Stat. 535–36.

120. *See* Act of May 1, 1820, ch. 52, §§ 1, 2, 3 Stat. 567–68; *see also* Wilmerding, *supra* note 117, at 73, 213.

121. Act of June 30, 1834, ch. 171, 4 Stat. 742.

122. *See* Hopkins & Nutt, *supra* note 116, at 57.

123. *Id.*

124. Act of Feb. 12, 1868, ch. 8, § 2, 15 Stat. 35, 36 (repealing all prior transfer authority and declaring that "no money appropriated for one purpose shall hereafter be used for any other purpose than that for which it is appropriated").

125. Act of July 12, 1870, ch. 252, § 7, 16 Stat. 251.

126. Act of Mar. 3, 1905, ch. 1484, § 4, 33 Stat. 1257; Act of Feb. 27, 1906, ch. 510, § 3, 34 Stat. 49.

127. *See* John Hart Ely, "The American War in Indochina, Part II: The Unconstitutionality of the War They Didn't Tell Us About," 42 *Stan. L. Rev.* 1093, 1094–99, 1096

n.18 (1990) [hereinafter *Ely Part II*]; *see also* John Ranelagh, *The Agency: The Rise and Decline of the CIA* 425, 543–44, 610 (1986).

128. *See* Kenneth E. Sharpe, "The Real Cause of Irangate," 68 *For. Pol'y* 19 (1987).

129. *See* John Prados, *Presidents' Secret Wars* 300 (1986) ("Nixon ordered unprecedented levels of secrecy. The regular Pentagon records . . . were falsified to indicate that the bombing missions were hitting South Vietnam. Pilots were briefed for flights over Vietnam and diverted at the last moment.").

Although the pre-1972 Foreign Assistance Act permitted the president to draw down up to $300 million from the DOD budget if he determined that it was "vital to the security of the United States," Foreign Assistance Act of 1961, § 510(a), 75 Stat. at 437, he was required to report his use of the funds, after the fact, to Congress. *Id.* § 634(d), 75 Stat. at 455. Up to $50 million in foreign aid funds could be spent when the president certified that "it is unadvisable to specify" how the funds were used. *Id.* § 614(c), 75 Stat. at 444.

130. *See* Sharpe, *supra* note 128, at 23–24. For a Senate Foreign Relations Committee report on the president's secret war in Cambodia, *see* S. Rep. No. 431, 92d Cong., 2d Sess. 13, *reprinted in* 1972 U.S.C.C.A.N. 1883, 1894–95; *see also Ely Part II*, *supra* note 127, at 1137–46.

131. *See* Louis Fisher, "The Authorization-Appropriation Process in Congress: Formal Rules and Informal Practices" 29 *Cath. U. L. Rev.* 51, 107–08 (1979); Jeffrey A. Meyer, "Congressional Control of Foreign Assistance," 13 *Yale J. Int'l. L.* 69, 76 n.29 (1988). *See generally supra* chap. 8.

Chapter 15

1. Philip A. Lacovara, "'Follow the Money:' Should Lawyers and Accountants Pay for the Sins of Their Clients?," *Wash. Post*, July 21, 1992, at A19.

2. *See* an Act for a Grant, 1688, 1 W. & M., Sess. 2, ch. 1, §§ 35ff.

3. *The Federalist* No. 58, at 359 (J. Madison) (C. Rossiter ed., 1961).

4. 25 *Weekly Comp. Pres. Doc.* 424, March 24, 1989; H.R. Rep. No. 23, 101st Cong., 1st Sess. 2 (1989).

5. Lear Siegler, Inc. v. Lehman, 842 F.2d 1102, 1124 (9th Cir.), *rehearing granted*, 863 F.2d 693 (1988), *decision withdrawn on other grounds*, No. 87-5670 (9th Cir. July 17, 1989).

6. United States v. Richardson, 418 U.S. 166, 178 n.11 (1974) (dictum).

7. Letter from Thomas Jefferson to Albert Gallatin (Feb. 19, 1804), *reprinted in* 11 *The Writings of Thomas Jefferson* 13 (A. Lipscomb ed., 1905).

8. The Prize Cases, 67 U.S. (2 Black) 635, 671 (1862).

9. Office of Personnel Management v. Richmond, 496 U.S. 414, 426 (1990). *See also* Knote v. United States, 95 U.S. 149 (1877).

10. Immigration and Naturalization Service v. Chadha, 462 U.S. 919, 951 (1983).

Index